D0164586

ABOUT ISLAND PRESS

ISLAND PRESS is the only nonprofit organization in the United States whose principal purpose is the publication of books on environmental issues and natural resource management. We provide solutions-oriented information to professionals, public officials, business and community leaders, and concerned citizens who are shaping responses to environmental problems.

In 2004, Island Press celebrates its twentieth anniversary as the leading provider of timely and practical books that take a multidisciplinary approach to critical environmental concerns. Our growing list of titles reflects our commitment to bringing the best of an expanding body of literature to the environmental community throughout North·America and the world.

Support for Island Press is provided by the Agua Fund, Brainerd Foundation, Geraldine R. Dodge Foundation, Doris Duke Charitable Foundation, Educational Foundation of America, The Ford Foundation, The George Gund Foundation, The William and Flora Hewlett Foundation, Henry Luce Foundation, The John D. and Catherine T. MacArthur Foundation, The Andrew W. Mellon Foundation, The Curtis and Edith Munson Foundation, National Environmental Trust, The New-Land Foundation, Oak Foundation, The Overbrook Foundation, The David and Lucile Packard Foundation, The Pew Charitable Trusts, The Rockefeller Foundation, The Winslow Foundation, and other generous donors.

The opinions expressed in this book are those of the author(s) and do not necessarily reflect the views of these foundations.

LAND USE AND SOCIETY

Land Use

RUTHERFORD H. PLATT

and Society

GEOGRAPHY, LAW, AND PUBLIC POLICY

Revised Edition

ISLAND PRESS *Washington ~ Covelo ~ London*

Library of Congress Cataloging-in-Publication data.

Platt, Rutherford H.
   Land use and society : geography, law, and public policy / Rutherford H. Platt.—Rev. ed.
      p. cm.
Includes bibliographical references and index.
   ISBN 1-55963-684-x (cloth : alk. paper) — ISBN 1-55963-685-8 (paper : alk. paper)
      1. Land use—Law and legislation—United States. 2. Land use—United States. 3. Physical geography—United States. I. Title.
      KF5698.P588 2004
      346.7304'5—dc22   2003024791

British Cataloguing-in-Publication data available.

Printed on recycled, acid-free paper ⊛

Design and composition by Wilsted & Taylor Publishing Services

Manufactured in the United States of America

10 9 8 7 6 5 4 3 2 1

TO JACK AND ELIZABETH ...

Grandchildren who are above average!

CONTENTS

INTRODUCTION

Geography, Law, and Landscape: Reflections on a Cross-Country Flight

To geographers and their fellow travelers, there are few greater treats than to fly a considerable distance over land on a clear day with a view unobstructed by the airplane wing. I recently enjoyed such a flight nonstop from San Francisco to Boston. Between the sourdough vendors and live lobster purveyors of those two airports stretch about 2,700 miles of air distance. Along this trajectory, the route traverses a succession of geographic regions marked by vivid contrasts in both physical and human characteristics. Even the casual observer can scarcely fail to notice and perhaps to wonder about the diversity of the perceived landscape: its physical landforms, land cover, and patterns of rural and urban land use. If the movie is really boring, the window-gazer may attempt to annotate the passing scene by assigning causative factors and implications—some definite, others hypothetical—to what is seen or imagined in the landscape below. *This is thinking geographically.*

The aircraft ascends over the crowded East Bay cities of Oakland and Berkeley, where world-class scholarship and abject poverty coexist. The hills and flatlands are riddled with seismic faults that caused the Nimitz Freeway to collapse in the October 17, 1989, earthquake and where 3,300 homes burned in the hills two years later (Figures I-1 and I-2). Homes yield to cattle and windmill "farms" (dating back to Carter administration sustainable energy policies). Now at high altitude, we roar eastward over the geometric patterns of irrigated fields of the Central Valley (handsomely subsidized by the federal taxpayer). Next we hurtle over the snowy peaks and steep declivities of the Sierra Nevada (where John Muir battled Gifford Pinchot over damming the Hetch Hetchy Valley to provide water supply for San Francisco after its 1906 fire).

We streak across the rocky wastes and hills of the Great Basin, where early nuclear weapons were tested and eternal debate today prevents use of the Yucca Mountain facility for high-level radioactive waste storage. Cities and irrigated agriculture briefly reappear in the Mormon settlement region east of Great Salt Lake. The Wasatch Range, crisscrossed by ski slopes and clear-cutting, gives way to the upper Colorado River Plateau, another sparsely inhabited region of high

FIGURE I-1 The Imperial Valley of California from high altitude, with intensively irrigated lowlands bordered by barren uplands. *(Photo by author.)*

desert, sage brush, and spectacular landforms. Downstream on the Colorado River, the one-armed geologist and geographer John Wesley Powell made his epic journey through the Grand Canyon in 1869 that stimulated his proposals for large-scale irrigation projects in the arid West. We pass near Dinosaur National Park, where Echo Park Dam, one of Powell's proposed irrigation projects, was defeated by David Brower in the 1950s at the dawn of the modern environmental movement.

We cross the cloud-shrouded Rocky Mountains whose dwindling snow cover (due to global warming) is a critical water source for cities and farms all the way to Los Angeles, San Diego, and northern Mexico. East of the Rockies lies the Front Range urban corridor, a chain of cities extending from Greeley to Pueblo, Colorado, anchored by smog-bound Denver. We glimpse the glistening white "tent" of the new Denver International Airport terminal surrounded by runways and brown nothingness. (Today, thousands of condos are gradually filling the nothingness between the airport and the rest of Denver.)

For the next hour, we traverse the vast checkerboard of the High Plains dominated by green *circles* of fields irrigated from groundwater distributed by rotating sprayers within the 160-acre *squares* ("quarter-sections") drawn by the Federal Land Survey over a century ago, a perfect illustration of geography, law, and tech-

FIGURE I-2
The High Plains
"checkerboard": circles of crops
irrigated from center pivot wells,
inside quarter-section squares
laid out by the Federal Land
Survey. *(Photo by author.)*

nology interacting to create a human landscape (Figure I-3). (On successive flights, it appears that the green circles are increasingly turning brown as irrigation is suspended due to high costs of pumping from the declining Ogallala Aquifer and, perhaps, from the effect of federal land retirement payments.)

We cross the Missouri River in the vicinity of the fabled "100th Meridian" (which roughly corresponds to the 20-inch average annual rainfall contour) where irrigation yields to rain-dependent agriculture. Towns begin to reappear as "beads on a string" along mainline railroad lines and old section-line highways. The rectangular farmscape increasingly gives way to rectangular cities, all interlaced by interstate highways leading to the really big midwestern cities: Kansas City, Minneapolis–St. Paul, St. Louis, Chicago. The alternation of town and farm across the nation's heartland is a totally human-dominated landscape. Few natural or unused areas of land are observed until the Appalachian Upland is reached in Pennsylvania and New York State.

Flight attendants collect headsets as the aircraft descends in humid summer twilight over the northeastern urban corridor for which geographer Jean Gottmann coined the name *Megalopolis*. This "stupendous monument erected by titanic efforts" (in Gottmann's laconic words) is still replete with forests and farms, from the air at least. The failing daylight permits a glimpse of Quabbin Reservoir,

FIGURE I-3 The Connecticut River Valley in west-central Massachusetts blends farms, forests, old industrial towns, vibrant college communities, and serious poverty and social distress. *(Photo by author.)*

Boston's primary water supply, surrounded by an "accidental wilderness" resulting from the forced abandonment of farms and villages when the state purchased the watershed in the 1930s. The plane swings over "the Nation's Technology Highway" (Massachusetts' Route 128) where the arms race fostered the illusion of prosperity during the 1980s. It banks over the built-up coastal barriers south of Boston (where hundreds of homes were damaged in 1978 and again in 1991) and lands at Logan International Airport, which, like our departure point at San Francisco, is constructed on a filled wetland.

The cross section of the North American landscape just described is viewed by thousands of travelers on any clear day, albeit without the running commentary. To many observers, the scene below is a pleasant but seemingly random series of abstract images, like the geometric patterns produced by a kaleidoscope. Yet patterns of human land use are by no means random. To one with geographic training or interests, the variation in the landscape offers not only aesthetic but intellectual stimulation. The geographer seeks to discern order, process, and coherency in the seemingly haphazard sequence of images.

The perennial question of geography is, *Why* is this place the way it is, and like or unlike other places? This question leads to additional ones: *What* benefits or costs arise from specific practices or ways of using land, air, and water and to whom do they accrue? *How* can we better manage the use of land and other resources to promote the public welfare, however defined, and reduce social costs and *Who* should make the necessary decisions? These questions ultimately lead to the central question of our time: *How may global resources be managed to sustain a world population that has more than doubled since 1950?*

Global resource crisis is at hand according to the Worldwatch Institute, World Resources Institute, the Smithsonian Institution, the National Academy of Sciences, and a host of international organizations. Global resource problems include widespread deforestation, atmospheric warming and ozone depletion, loss of biodiversity, land degradation, food shortages, energy shocks, accumulating wastes, and surface and groundwater pollution.

Geographers of course do not claim any special monopoly on wisdom, nor do they offer ready solutions to these travails, but they do offer the perspective of the *why* question. They seek lessons from the experience of the past and present, which may profitably be applied to the exigencies of the future. If we can better understand how we got to where we are in our inhabitation of Earth, or portions of it that we label *regions*, *nations*, or *communities*, we may gain some valuable insights into how to deal with the challenges ahead.

Unlike more narrowly focused disciplines, geographers view the land and its regions holistically and seek explanations (or solutions) through synthesis of diverse phenomena and the formulation of theories regarding the interaction of these variables. From time to time, certain classes of spatially distributed phenomena have been vested with greater importance than others as explanations of human settlement patterns and uses of resources. In the 1920s, the theory of *environmental determinism* sought to explain human actions in terms of the influence of climate and physical characteristics of regions. In the 1960s, *central place theory* and gravity models attributed human spatial behavior to economic forces operating through the private land market. In the 1980s and 1990s, the *political economy* provided a focus for postmodern interpretations of cities and land use.

Land Use and Society takes a different tack. Although not discounting physical, economic, and other spatial variables, the primary focus of this book is the role of *law* as a major factor in the way humans use their resources and design their patterns of settlement. The connection between geography and law regarding land use is logical although, to some people, unexpected. Whereas geography addresses the *what* and the *why* questions, law responds to the *how* and the *who*. Observing rural and especially urban landscapes, the role of law is omnipresent and complex. This book seeks to promote better understanding of the role of law, broadly construed, as it interacts with geography, technology, economy, and culture in the making of human landscapes and cityscapes.

Of course, law is not entirely an independent variable; laws are products of institutions reacting to their perceptions of exogenous circumstances such as desire for capitalist profit, for a habitable environment, or fear of disease, fire, flood, drought, famine, pollution, or crime. The rules for human activities established by law differ according to the rule maker's perception of external circumstances, (see the discussion of the *land use and society model* in Chapter 2). The rules often make up an imperfect, partial, or even counterproductive response to the actual problem. Furthermore, laws established to address one problem may compound others. In addition, laws have a habit of remaining in effect long after changes in circumstances have rendered them moot or even pernicious.

This book, then, is offered as an exploration of the influence of law over human use of land from the perspective of a geographer. The specific rules, doctrines, and practices discussed are drawn from the U.S. context, including its common-law roots in England. The role of law as a factor in the shaping of urban and rural land use, however, for better or worse, is a phenomenon of global applicability.

Organization of the Book

This book is a completely revised, expanded, and updated edition of the first Island Press edition of *Land Use and Society* published in 1996. Portions of that edition (and this one) first appeared in an earlier book, *Land Use Control: Geography, Law, and Public Policy* (Prentice Hall, 1991). This edition retains the historical flavor and approach of the earlier versions while improving its flow and updating it to reflect the 2000 U.S. Census and my own evolving interests and learning process. As before, Part 1, "Preliminaries: Land, Geography, and Law," considers the meanings of land and types of land uses in the United States (Chapter 1), followed by reflections on the disciplines of geography and law and their interaction with respect to land use (Chapter 2). The latter concludes with a general model, now grandly called "the land use and society model," which represents graphically the process of societal adaptation to perceived deficiencies of land use practices through law and related institutions.

In a significant change from the 1996 edition, Part 2, "From Feudalism to Federalism: The Social Organization of Land Use," traces the evolution of land use institutions in England and the United States in four consecutive chapters. Chapter 3 on the medieval origins of land use institutions is retained. Chapter 4 (formerly Chapter 6) continues the history of urban evolution in Europe and the United States through the nineteenth century. Two new chapters (5 and 6) summarize twentieth-century urban experience in the United States, respectively, before and since World War II, with new emphasis on the influence of racism and social injustice in national policies that have driven urban sprawl and neglect of central cities. Part 2 thus unifies the historical narrative as a continuous sequence of topics from the fourteenth century to the present. These chapters are connected by the thread of geography-law interaction, as represented by the land use and society model introduced in Chapter 2.

Part 3, "Discordant Voices: Property Ownership, Local Government, and the Courts," turns to the "nuts and bolts" of land use decision making in the United States. Chapter 7 (formerly Chapter 4 of the 1996 edition) summarizes the legal and geographical elements of real property ownership. Chapter 8, "The Tapestry of Local Governments" (formerly Chapter 5, as revised), reviews the geographic and legal nature of municipal governments, counties, and special districts in relation to land use. Chapter 9, "Local Zoning and Growth Management" (formerly Chapters 7 and 9), examines the principal land use tools of local government, including planning and zoning, subdivision regulation, land acquisition, and growth management, now including "smart growth." Chapter 10, "Land Use and the Courts" (formerly Chapter 8, as revised), reviews principles of constitutional law in relation to land use, particularly the perplexing "Takings Issue." (Chapter 10 is relatively freestanding and may be omitted by users of the book who do not wish to delve into the legal aspects of topics discussed elsewhere in the book.)

Part 4, "Beyond Localism: The Search for Broader Land Use Policies," reviews land use management at higher levels of government in the United States. Chapter 11, "Regional, State, and Federal Land Programs" (including portions of former Chapters 10 and 11), addresses public land acquisition and management, as well as efforts to protect and restore areas of regional significance such as Lake Calumet in Chicago and the New Jersey Pinelands. This chapter retains an abbreviated history of the federal public lands and their management. Chapter 12, "Congress and the Metropolitan Environment," reviews and updates selected federal environmental initiatives since 1970, including environmental impact assessment, coastal zone management, floodplain and wetlands programs, open space funding, and hazardous wastes. A case study of the Sears Island saga (Box 12-1) describes how the legal process may be confounded by failure of relevant decision makers to accurately assess the physical and economic geography of a land use controversy. Another case study (Box 12-2) examines the efforts of New York City and Boston to protect their water supplies through watershed management in response to the federal Safe Drinking Water Act.

Finally, the updated conclusion summarizes some positive and negative outcomes of urban land policies to date. The book ends on a note of cautious optimism inspired by the number of spontaneous local efforts to integrate nature and humans in urban settings across the United States, as documented by our Ecological Cities Project based at the University of Massachusetts, Amherst (www. ecologicalcities.org).

The book thus spans a broad spectrum of urban history, geography, and law. The 1996 preface ended with a warning about the possible repeal of land use and environmental laws at the hands of "property rights advocates." Although the U.S. Supreme Court has not changed in personnel, or presumably in its political view on land use restrictions since the 1992 *Lucas* decision, the predicted wave of "takings" suits against public land use measures has not materialized. On the other hand, one senses that "command and control" land use regulation is downplayed today in favor of partnerships and incentives to achieve regional and local land use objectives. In particular, the smart growth movement has breathed new energy into the century-old quest to improve community land use and development practices through public legal and financial guidance of private market decisions. Legal challenges to smart growth approaches so far are hard to find.

Today the nation and world are threatened on many fronts: political, economic, environmental, and public health. The great social upheavals of U.S. history, including abolition of slavery, labor reform, women's rights, civil rights, gay rights, and environmentalism, suggest that, despite setbacks, it is virtually impossible to set the clock back entirely to some earlier period of social evolution. Social change is incremental and often painful, but as viewed over time, it moves inexorably in a positive direction. That, at least, is my belief as informed by progressives and environmentalists whose contributions are mentioned somewhere in this book such as Frederick Law Olmsted, George Perkins Marsh, Ebenezer Howard, John Wesley Powell, John Muir, Gifford Pinchot, Theodore Roosevelt, Franklin D. Roosevelt, Lyndon Johnson, Garrett Hardin, Barry Commoner, Rachel Carson, Jane Jacobs, and Gilbert White. (Additions to this list are welcome!)

Social change does not happen easily. Reform in social policies and laws concerning land use is especially acrimonious: public interests clash with private rights, local governments rail against state and federal constraints, and "not in my backyard" interests oppose anything new in their "backyards." This book will inform those debates with an appreciation of past experience and the importance of understanding geographic and legal context of any land use dispute. Public intervention to control harmful externalities, protect the public health and welfare, remedy social injustice, and achieve a physically and emotionally healthy environment is not ideological. It is the purpose of an organized and mature society.

PART I

Preliminaries: Land,
Geography, and Law

CHAPTER 1

The Meanings and Uses of Land

> *For the Lord thy God bringeth thee into a good land. A land of wheat, and barley, and vines, and fig trees, and pomegranates; a land of oil olive, and honey; a land wherein thou shalt eat bread without scarceness, thou shalt not lack any thing in it; a land whose stones are iron, and out of whose hills thou mayest dig brass.*
>
> —DEUTERONOMY 8:7–9

> *The Earth is given as a common stock for man to labor and live on.... It is not too soon to provide by every possible means that as few as possible shall be without a little portion of land.*
>
> —THOMAS JEFFERSON, LETTER TO REV. JAMES MADISON, 1785, 390

> *It is a comfortable feeling to know that you stand on your own ground. Land is about the only thing that can't fly away.*
>
> —ANTHONY TROLLOPE, THE LAST CHRONICLE OF BARSET, 1867

What Is Land?

From the Old Testament to today, the subject of *land* arouses emotions: a vision of hope and faith, a source of wealth and social status, a subject of indignant political reform, and so on. It is therefore appropriate at the outset of a book on land use and society to ask, what really is "land"?

Land is one of the key constituents of life on Earth, along with water, oxygen, carbon, nitrogen, and sunlight. Lacking any of these components would make it unnecessary and in fact impossible for life to exist as we know it. Daniel Hillel (1994, 20) observes that since three-quarters of our planet is covered by oceans, it should be called "Water" rather than "Earth." True, but those who did the naming happened to stand on dry land (*terra firma*). Water, especially freshwater, is indispensable to the use of land and therefore to terrestrial life. Yet without land capable of benefiting from the application of water, either through natural precipitation or irrigation, life on the planet would be all wet, so to speak.

Unlike water, land cannot be summarized by a convenient chemical formula like H_2O. In fact, it is not easily summarized at all; it is many things simultaneously. First, land is the *physical material* of Earth's crust that supports all life. In this sense, "land" includes soils, vegetation, minerals, groundwater and surface water, oil and gas, sand and gravel, diamonds, coal, gold, silver, lead, and uranium. The concept of land as physical material was reflected in the medieval English practice of representing change of land ownership by a clod of earth handed by the seller to the buyer (known quaintly as *livery of seisin*). Nowadays, legal documents perform that role. (See Chapter 7.)

Land in the physical sense also includes the produce of the soil. The "pomegranates, oil olive, and honey" were part of the biblical Promised Land. Both natural and cultivated plants physically define the landscape and thus the nature of land, as do, for instance, the giant sequoia of the California coast, the spruce-fir forest of coastal Maine, the yellow pine of Texas and the Southeast, the corn and soybeans of the Midwest, the wheat of the Great Plains, and the grassy sand dunes of coastal shorelines. Vegetation native to or grown on land is part of the land, perceptually, functionally, and often legally. Wildlife, however, is not considered part of "the land," although domesticated livestock raised on land is subject to ownership independently of the land on which it grazes.

Second, land in Anglo-America is legally referred to as *real property* or *real estate*. For purposes of ownership and use, land is divided into units known as *parcels*. Each parcel represents a defined area of land surface set off by boundaries and owned by a particular individual, group, corporation, or government agency. In the rural context, parcels may extend to hundreds or thousands of acres. In urban areas, parcels typically range from a few acres to small fractions of an acre. (One acre equals 43,650 square feet, approximately a square of 200 feet on each side.) Parcels of "land" also extend upward and downward from the land surface (*grade level*). Portions of the volume above or below the surface may be enclosed with structures that become part of the real property in a legal sense. The conversion of land from essentially resource-based uses, such as agriculture, forestry, or outdoor recreation, to space-enclosing uses, such as homes, offices, shopping centers, and parking garages, is a critical and essentially irreversible step in the process of urbanization. (See Figure 7-1 and further discussion of these concepts in Chapter 7.)

The third concept of land is as an *object of capital value* capable of being owned

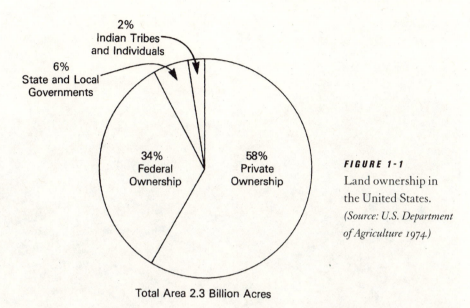

FIGURE 1-1
Land ownership in
the United States.
*(Source: U.S. Department
of Agriculture 1974.)*

and used by its owner to maximize economic return. Land in this sense is a
"bundle of rights and obligations" that are defined (often vaguely) and protected
(sometimes uncertainly) by the legal system of the country or society in which the
land is located. In its most abstract form, land is purely an investment to be bought
and sold like government bonds, corn futures, or pork bellies. Billions of dollars
are spent on land or structures attached to it with the investors never visiting the
site, never getting their shoes muddy, never watching the sunset from its highest
point, or never forming any personal attachment to the land whatsoever. In the
1990s, a financial instrument known as a *real estate investment trust* (REIT) allowed
tens of thousands of investors to participate in the building of anonymous shopping malls, office parks, and housing developments, without the slightest idea of
how or where their money was changing the landscape of America.

Nearly 60 percent of land in the United States is in private ownership (Figure
1-1). About one-third of the nation's land is held by the federal government under
various agencies such as the U.S. Forest Service (USFS), the Bureau of Land Management (BLM), and the National Park Service (NPS) (Figure 1-2). States and
local governments hold about 6 percent and Indian tribes about 2 percent of the
nation's land. Even on public lands, private uses are common under leases for such
activities as mining, timber cutting, water development, power generation, grazing, farming, and recreation. (See Chapter 11.) In addition, public lands are like
Swiss cheese, with many pockets of private ownership (*inholdings*) in the form of
villages, roadside businesses, tourist attractions, and private homes (Figure 1-3).

FIGURE 1-2 Public land writ large: a pinnacle in Rocky Mountain National Park. *(Photo by author.)*

Construction of spacious new homes on private tracts within forested public lands in the West is an increasing source of "urban-wildland" fire disasters (Platt 1999, Chapter 8), such as those in southern California in October 2003.

Not all land is "owned." Around the world, and in more traditional societies within the United States, land and the resources associated with it are held in some form of *common tenure*, that is, held by a cluster of families, a tribe, a village, or some other social group, The ways of using such common land—its arable soils, water, forests, wetlands, minerals, and living space—depend more on traditional or customary practices than on formal written laws (Jacobs 1998). This book is largely concerned with land that is owned—privately or publicly—in the capitalist sense, but further reference to common property is found in Chapter 3.

Fourth, land may also have noneconomic value, a *sense of place* defined by collective or individual experience and values. Ceremonial grounds of native peoples, a New England common, battlefields, burial grounds, England's Stonehenge, and Woodstock, New York, all exemplify places whose cultural meaning or overlay transcends their physical, legal, or locational characteristics. Sense of place was perhaps best expressed by Scarlett O'Hara in the movie *Gone with the Wind*: After the

FIGURE 1-3 Private land use in Estes Park, Colorado, the gateway to Rocky Mountain National Park. *(Photo by author.)*

Union armies have ravaged everything in sight, she gestures to the scorched land of her family's plantation and, as the theme music swells in the background, sighs, "There will always be Tara."

Sense of place is often rooted in the physical form and ecology of a site or region, as overlain by culture, as in the Florida Everglades, Vermont hill towns, the Indiana Dunes, and old mining towns of the Sierra Nevada. Art and literature have often helped define and interpret sense of place. The work of artists such as Thomas Cole and Frederick Church of the nineteenth-century Hudson River School, John James Audubon's bird paintings, Georgia O'Keeffe's images of the Southwest desert, and the writings of Henry David Thoreau (*Cape Cod*, *The Maine Woods*), John Steinbeck (*The Grapes of Wrath*, *Tortilla Flat*), Marjory Stoneman Douglas (*The Everglades: River of Grass*), James Michener (*Hawaii*, *Chesapeake*, *Centennial*), and John McPhee (*Coming into the Country*, *The Pine Barrens*) all illustrate a sense of place.

Many places with distinct natural and cultural significance have been the object of lengthy, sometimes bitter, efforts to protect them from change or loss of their sense of place. Beginning with John Muir's campaign to save the Hetch Hetchy

Valley from a reservoir in the early 1900s, campaigns to protect natural areas of scenic, geologic, or biotic significance have been rife in the United States and throughout the world. And, as Muir proved, passion can be aroused on behalf of a sense of place even among people who have not the slightest prospect ever to visit the site.

These efforts have in turn spread from truly extraordinary sites, such as the Grand Canyon, the Rocky Mountains, and the California redwoods, to less famous regional landscapes that harbor endangered species, offer scenic and recreational amenities, or contribute to the biological integrity of a larger ecosystem. The Indiana Dunes National Lakeshore with its distinctive sand dunes, forests, and wetlands near Chicago resulted from passionate efforts to "Save the Dunes" during the 1950s and 1960s. Local and regional conservation battles have sought to protect desert ecosystems in southern California, the old-growth forests of the Pacific Northwest, and the Pine Barrens in southern New Jersey and eastern Long Island (see Chapter 11). All these areas are ultimately related to the character, function, and value of land. A collective sense of *stewardship* of the planet's remaining natural areas confronts the more traditional resource-based and investment meanings of land. Who really "owns" the land is the question resounding in the legislatures, the courts, and the news media (Jacobs 1998). The debate is as fundamental as land itself.

How Much Land Do We Have?

> In the United States there is more land where nobody is than
> where anybody is. This is what makes America what it is.
> GERTRUDE STEIN, *The Geographical History of America,* 1936

In the early 1960s, resource economist Marion Clawson (1963, 1) noted that the total land area of the United States, about 2.1 billion acres, theoretically amounted to a "share" of 12.5 acres for every living American at that time. In 1920, this figure stood at 20 acres per capita; it would further decline, in Clawson's estimate, to 7.5 acres in the year 2000. His prediction was stunning: In 2000, the actual ratio of land to population was 7.42 acres per capita! This ratio was still considerably higher than most other industrialized nations and many times higher than most of the rest of the world.

Acreage per capita, however, is not a very useful statistic. In the first place, it masks regional variation and is a poor measure of social well-being. At a state level, the citizens of Connecticut have 1 acre per capita (dividing its land area by its population) and New Jerseyites have only two-thirds of an acre each, whereas the 642,000 residents of North Dakota "claim" almost 70 acres apiece. Does that mean that the people of North Dakota are better off than those of Connecticut? In economic terms, they clearly are not: in 2000, Connecticut ranked first in income per capita, whereas North Dakota was thirty-eighth among the fifty states. In terms of quality of life, that is a matter of personal judgment: windy grasslands and solitude of the Great Plains versus the crowding and culture of megalopolis.

Second, a large proportion of the nation's wealth of land resources is distant from the everyday habitat of most of us. Four-fifths of the U.S. population (225 million in 2000) lives in the nation's 331 metropolitan statistical areas (MSAs) designated by the U.S. Bureau of the Census. Those metropolitan areas occupy about 19 percent of the nation's land area and have an average density of 2.1 acres per capita. Yet even within MSAs, most of the population that does not live at the urban-rural fringe feels (and is) remote from "the country."

Most metropolitan-area residents live, work, and seek nearby recreation in crowded conditions, particularly on highways and in popular public open spaces like New York's Jones Beach on a warm summer weekend. Around holiday weekends, traffic backs up for miles to and from once-bucolic destinations such as Cape Cod, Maryland's Eastern Shore, the Outer Banks, northern Michigan, and the Colorado Rockies. Much of the urban population is too poor, elderly, ill, or busy to travel to places of natural or cultural beauty outside their immediate surroundings.

Furthermore, two-thirds of land in the United States is owned privately by a relatively small fraction of the total population and is not publicly accessible. A study by the U.S. Department of Agriculture (USDA) in the late 1970s found that 75 percent of the U.S. private land base was owned by the top 5 percent of the nation's 34 million landowners (Jacobs 1998, 247). Public acquisition at all levels of government has helped promote public access to scenic or cultural sites, but even in parks such as the Cape Cod National Seashore, much of the land is still privately owned and off-limits to the public.

A final limitation of the acres-per-capita measure of land wealth is the diversity of physical capabilities and use categories into which land resources may be classified. Overall totals of land area reveal little about the sufficiency of land for particular purposes such as production of food and fiber, forest products, watershed functions, recreation, natural habitat, and urban uses. Also, the growing importance of the global economy, the North American Free Trade Agreement (NAFTA), trade deficits, currency exchange rates, and multinational corporate ownership of land vastly complicates the task of appraising the adequacy of land resources in the United States or elsewhere.

With these qualifications in mind, the rest of this chapter briefly reviews the status of land usage in the United States and related issues. Some of these issues are treated in more detail in later chapters.

Classes of Land Use

About three-quarters of the total U.S. land area, including federal lands, is devoted to three primary categories of rural land usage: (1) cropland, (2) grazing land (including pasture and range), and (3) forestland. Each of these categories represents a productive and economically beneficial class of land resource, although the more remote forests and more arid grazing lands may seldom be exploited and are left relatively untouched by human activities. About 40 million acres of federal forestland, desert, and mountainous lands are designated as *wilderness areas* under the 1964 Wilderness Act. Other portions of undeveloped land resources are managed for specialized purposes, including endangered species habitat, water resource protection, recreation, and scenery. At the opposite end of the development spectrum, about 10 percent of land in the contiguous states is devoted to urban uses such as housing, shopping malls, factories, educational and religious institutions, and transportation. Most of this book is concerned with the last group of land uses, urban and metropolitan areas. First, though, let's look at the big picture with a summary of the rural as well as urban forms of land use.

Cropland

Cropland is the most sensitive and valuable of the nation's rural land resources. The protection of the cropland base, especially those portions of it deemed *prime land*, has been the subject of lively discussion and debate since the early 1980s, both among scholars and in the public media (Platt 1985). Both total cropland and harvested cropland fluctuate considerably from year to year (Table 1-1). Observing that total cropland in 2000 was nearly the same as in 1970 and that harvested cropland *increased* between those years, it cannot be concluded from such data that cropland has been significantly "lost" to urbanization or other conversions. The ups and downs in harvested cropland in particular are functions of weather, market prices, and government subsidies; they are not necessarily related to conversion of cropland to other uses.

Moreover, the average productivity of U.S. agriculture rose by 55 percent from a farm output index of 72 in 1970 to 112 in 1990, according to the USDA (U.S. Bureau of Statistics 1996). This increase, achieved partly through the massive use of fertilizers, pesticides, irrigation water, and genetic research (the "green revolution"), has expanded U.S. agricultural production by more than the equivalent of an additional 186 million acres of cropland. Indeed, the rising productivity of U.S. agriculture has had the ironic result of achieving such an abundance of farm commodities that low prices prevailed during part of the 1980s and 1990s, causing farmers to suffer widespread economic distress and eliciting huge federal price supports and other agricultural subsidies.

Despite the apparent sufficiency of cropland, the need for careful stewardship of this resource remains a public policy concern. In the first place, annual estimates of harvested cropland are not totally reliable. Such estimates are obtained from individual agricultural extension agents in most of the nation's 3,041 counties. There is thus a considerable margin of error due to variability in the accuracy of individual cropland estimates. Also, the inventories for different years are not strictly comparable due to changes in definitions, sampling techniques, and data management.

A second important qualification is that totals of harvested cropland give no indication of the *average quality* of land under cultivation. Much land is converted from one rural category to another as well as into urban and built-up status over time. The 1982 National Resources Inventory indicated that about 900,000 acres per year were being converted to urban and built-up purposes, essentially an irreversible process (U.S. Council on Environmental Quality 1984, 283). Because harvested cropland has remained relatively constant for since the 1970s, it is apparent

TABLE 1-1 *U.S. CROPLAND RESOURCES: 1959–2000 (IN MILLIONS OF ACRES)*

YEAR	TOTAL CROPLAND	HARVESTED ACREAGE	IRRIGATED ACREAGE
1959	392	N.A.	31
1970	332	289	
1980	382	342	49 (1982)
1985	372	334	46 (1987)
1990	341	310	
2000	343	323	N.A.

SOURCES: *Statistical Abstract of the U.S.—1994*, Tables 1120 and 1154; and *Statistical Abstract of the U.S.—2001*, Table 824.

that replacement land for cultivation has been drawn from other rural categories, principally forest, range, pasture, and wetlands.

Replacement land, however, is not necessarily equivalent in quality to the cropland converted to nonagricultural purposes. Heavier application of irrigation water, chemical fertilizers and pesticides, and labor is required to render such marginal lands productive. Furthermore, the continued drainage of wetlands for agriculture in Florida, the South Central states, and California—once consistent with national policy—now is viewed as threatening to the ecological values and functions of wetlands in their natural state.

The increased use of *fertilizer* had reached a point of diminishing returns by the 1980s:

> Per-acre applications of fertilizer grew much more slowly after 1972 as farmers moved toward more land-using technologies after that date.... The slower increase in per-acre applications of fertilizer after 1972 was consistent with the post-1973 slowdown in yield growth. Correspondingly, our belief that the trend of yields to 2010 will more nearly resemble the post- than the pre-1972 experience is based in good part on our belief that per-acre applications of fertilizer will grow more slowly. (Crosson and Brubaker 1982, 68)

Similarly, the use of *irrigation* to reclaim arid lands for cultivation may also have peaked. Between 1959 and 1982, irrigated land in seventeen arid western states plus Louisiana increased by 35 percent, from 31 million to 42 million acres. In 1982, the national total of irrigated land was 49.4 million acres, which represented 15 percent of total cropland. Continued expansion of the area under irrigation is doubtful as new groundwater and surface water supplies are increasingly scarce and are expensive to develop (Gleick 2001; Postel 2001; Jehl 2002).

Unless irrigated land is properly drained, salts in irrigation water will contaminate the soil zone ("salinization"), leading to destruction of the land's fertility (Hillel 1994). Environmental objections and economic costs have deterred the further expansion of irrigation facilities in recent years. Furthermore, the mining of groundwater in the Ogallala aquifer of the High Plains and the salinization of groundwater supplies in the Colorado Basin threaten to reduce the acreage currently receiving irrigation water.

Soil erosion is another source of concern about the future adequacy of the nation's cropland base. The USDA estimates that 44 percent of all cropland nationally is eroding at rates exceeding the normal rate of replacement through natural processes (which differ from one location to another). Especially high levels of soil erosion, ranging from 5 to 14 tons of soil per acre per year, have been identified in most of the North Central region—the corn belt—as well as in dissected uplands of the Southeast and the Southwest, including Texas (U.S. Council on Environmental Quality 1984, Fig. 5-10). The precise effects of soil erosion are difficult to quantify but represent a long-term loss of natural soil productive capacity.

The United States has experienced two periods of severe soil erosion that have prompted very different public policy responses. During the "dust bowl" of the 1930s, millions of acres were scoured by hot, dry winds driving Great Plains farmers to migrate to the California Central Valley, as immortalized by John Steinbeck's novel *The Grapes of Wrath*. With dusty winds literally reaching into the nation's capital, Congress in 1935 created the Soil Conservation Service (SCS), which launched a crusade to promote such conservation practices as contour plowing, windbreaks, and strip-cropping on erosion-prone farmland. (The SCS is now named the Natural Resources Conservation Services.) In the 1970s, high farm prices throughout the world stimulated farmers to plant "fencerow to fencerow," which started a new bout of soil erosion, estimated to reach 3 billion tons of lost topsoil in 1982. This time Congress established the Conservation Reserve Program, under which farmers are paid by the USDA to convert marginal cropland to grass or forest. Within five years, this program caused over 30 million acres of erodible land to be retired from production (Brown 2001, 64).

Globally, soil degradation is a worsening crisis, especially in the face of widespread droughts due in part to global warming. The causes of soil degradation are both physical and social, with cultural practices such as deforestation, farming on steep slopes, overuse of irrigation, and intensive cultivation of marginal soils all contributing to the problem (Blaikie and Brookfield 1987).

The available supply of cropland appears sufficient to support current domestic and export needs of the nation, even as reduced by the Conservation Reserve Program. Export needs, however, may expand in response to droughts and famine around the world and to world population growth and urbanization. Furthermore, reliance on technological inputs and the use of marginal land for cultivation may be nearing the point of diminishing returns. Environmental objections to the use of certain chemicals, shortage of water for irrigation, and declining soil quality due to erosion all suggest the need for wise management of land naturally suited to cultivation of crops.

Forestland

Total forestland, according to the U.S. Forest Service, appeared to increase from 664 million acres in 1952 to 737 million acres in 1992 (Table 1-2). "Timberland," however, has remained relatively constant, with a 1992 total only 19 million acres less than in 1952. Most of the increase in total forestland is actual, due to reforestation of abandoned farmlands, as in New England and the upper Midwest. Conversely, some forestlands have been cleared for cropland, as is happening on a small scale in rural New England. Still other forestland was converted to water bodies, highways, and urban development. The exact extent of these conversions is unknown.

About three-fourths of forested land is classified by the USFS as "commercial timberland," which is defined as being capable of yielding at least 20 cubic feet per acre per year of commercial wood products and is not closed to cutting by governmental prohibition (e.g., wilderness status). Contrary to popular impression, 76 percent of New England is forested and all but 5 percent of this land is designated as commercial timberland, although much of it is unmanaged. The preponderance of noncommercial forestlands is in the West and Alaska.

During the nineteenth century, most of the major forestlands accessible to loggers were cleared without consideration of adverse effects such as soil erosion, forest fires, and loss of regeneration capability. Out of concern for maintaining adequate forests for the nation's future needs, the National Forest System was ini-

TABLE 1-2 U.S. FOREST AND TIMBERLAND RESOURCES: 1952–1992 (IN MILLIONS OF ACRES)

YEAR	TOTAL FORESTLAND	TOTAL TIMBERLAND[a]	PRIVATE TIMBERLAND	PRIVATE TIMBERLAND (%)
1952	664	509	356	70.0
1962	759	515	363	70.4
1970	754	504	354	70.2
1977	737	491	347	70.6
1987	731	483	347	71.8
1992	737	490	358	73.0
1996	746	518	357	68.9

SOURCE: *Statistical Abstract of the U.S.—2001*, Table 850.

[a] Timberland is forestland that is producing or is capable of producing crops of industrial wood and not withdrawn from timber utilization by statute or administrative regulation.

tiated in 1891 at the urging of Gifford Pinchot, who was appointed by President Theodore Roosevelt as the first director of the U.S. Forest Service in 1905 (Miller 2001). The national forests now comprise a total land area of 230 million acres, which has barely changed since the 1960s. (About 190 million acres are actually forested.) National forests are managed to ensure a sustained yield of forest products while serving other public needs such as water supply, natural habitat, recreation, and mining. (See a further discussion of the federal lands in Chapter 11.)

Forestry practices on federal and private lands alike encounter controversy regarding cutting of old-growth stands, protection of endangered species, and construction of access roads in previously inaccessible areas such as the North Woods of Maine. In Oregon and northern California, cutting of old-growth timber has been adamantly opposed by wildlife activists, who have invoked the federal Endangered Species Act to protect natural habitat for the northern spotted owl and other species. The U.S. Department of the Interior has sought to broker a compromise plan to satisfy both logging and environmental interests with respect to these forests, with mixed success.

Grasslands

Grasslands comprise the prevalent land cover of the semiarid plains between the Missouri River and the Rocky Mountains, covering some 600 million acres. Grasslands include two very different subclasses: (1) cropland used for pasture and (2) rangeland. Although the former comprises only 10 percent of total grazing lands, it is generally located in the more humid regions of the United States and yields a very large share of total forage production (U.S. Department of Agriculture 1974, 8). Rangeland is substantially located in the Mountain and High Plains states and receives rainfall of only 10–20 inches annually. Such lands produce very little forage and must be grazed on a very land-extensive basis.

Ownership of western range lands is split among the federal government, states, and private owners. Federal grasslands total about 160 million acres, of which 130 million acres are administered by the Bureau of Land Management. The remainder is under the jurisdiction of the USFS. Grazing in the West has always involved joint usage of both private and public lands by ranchers. Before 1934, private use of federal range was generally unregulated, illegal, and the source of disputes among competing stakeholders. For instance, a rousing chorus in the musical *Oklahoma!* proclaimed, "The farmer and the cowboy should be friends!" which historically they were not. Nor were cattlemen and sheep raisers. The Taylor

Grazing Act of 1934 authorized the establishment of federal grazing districts and required permits from the General Land Office for private grazing rights on such lands, bringing a semblance of order to the prior chaos. Since the 1950s, both the BLM and the USFS have sought to reduce grazing pressure on federal rangelands to protect their productive capacity over the long term (Clawson 1983, 67).

Recreation Land

It is difficult to estimate the total amounts and trends in the supply of recreation land. In 1998, the National Park System comprised about 77.4 million acres (of which 30.5 million acres are in Alaska and virtually inaccessible). Additional federal lands administered by the BLM and the USFS are managed for multiple use, including recreation. (See Chapter 11.) Similarly, water resource projects of the Army Corps of Engineers, the Tennessee Valley Authority, and the Bureau of Reclamation usually incorporate recreation facilities, in part to bolster the public support and economic benefits of such projects. Much of the recreation opportunities provided by these facilities take the form of water-based activities, including boating, swimming, and fishing, for which land-acreage data are not an adequate measure. State park systems total about 12.6 million acres, with county, regional, and municipal parks comprising perhaps another 10 million acres. A study by the Urban Land Institute and the Trust for Public Land reports enthusiastically that "the last five years [1995–1999] [seem] like another City Beautiful Movement: in the number of parks constructed or revamped, in the substantial amount of money invested in them, and, notably, in the public's stake in the park's success as a city emblem" (Harnik 2000). The study found a high degree of support for funding of city parks, with 70 percent of park bonds and referenda being approved, far exceeding other ballot issues.

A large but unquantifiable amount of private land is devoted to commercial recreation. Such lands include intensive-use facilities such as golf courses, ski resorts, tennis clubs, and private campgrounds as well as more extensive facilities such as private nature sanctuaries and membership camping and hiking parks. Schools and colleges provide additional recreational land on their grounds.

Acreage data, of course, do not adequately measure the potential value of a recreational site. Location, site design, amenities, and natural characteristics are usually more important than mere size in determining the functional utility of recreational land.

Wetlands

Wetlands are an important subset of the total land and water resources of the United States. Wetlands are generally characterized by the presence of water at or close to the surface, a predominance of saturated hydric soils, and a prevalence of vegetation adapted to wet conditions (Mitsch and Gosselink 1986, 15–16). Depending on their physical nature, size, and location, wetlands perform various natural functions such as providing natural habitat, flood storage, concentration of nutrients, absorption of pollutants, buffering of coastlines from storm waves, recharge of groundwater aquifers, and scenic amenity.

The National Wetland Inventory, conducted by the U.S. Fish and Wildlife Service, estimated total wetlands in the early 1980s to be approximately 99 million acres nationally (Dahl and Johnson 1991). Average annual loss of wetlands nationally due to dredging, filling, drainage, and conversion to agricultural or urban purposes is roughly estimated to be 290,000 acres (Dahl and Johnson 1991). About 87 percent of the wetlands losses between the 1950s and 1970s was due to agricultural drainage (which is not regulated under the federal Clean Water Act). The remaining 13 percent of losses was due to urbanization and other development (Tiner 1984, 31). Between the mid-1970s and the mid-1980s, agricultural drainage accounted for only 54 percent of the total loss of 2.6 million acres, of which 95 percent was freshwater wetlands and the remainder coastal wetlands (Dahl and Johnson 1991). Coastal Louisiana has been losing extensive areas of estuarine and freshwater wetlands annually due in part to land subsidence related to agriculture as well as to sea level rise.

Two regional wetland complexes, the Mississippi River Delta in Louisiana and the Florida Everglades, have attracted widespread attention (National Research Council 1992). Coastal Louisiana has lost an estimated 1,526 square miles of wetlands since the 1930s, with recent losses averaging about 17,000 acres per year. Much of this loss has been attributed to the reduction of sediment transported by the Mississippi River due to levees and dams to control floods and ensure navigability. Possibly even more important human factors have been the construction of canals through wetlands for transportation and oil and gas development, impoundments and failed land reclamation, and land subsidence due to withdrawal of oil and gas from subsurface strata. In 2002, the Southern Governors' Association proposed a multibillion-dollar federal-state program to reverse or at least slow the rate of coastal wetland loss in Louisiana.

The Florida Everglades, once one of the largest freshwater marshes in the world, is now considered one of the most threatened ecosystems anywhere due, like the Louisiana coastal wetland loss, to human interventions. In its natural state, the Everglades are a vast grassland extending south from Lake Okeechobee in central Florida about 100 miles to the Gulf of Mexico. Its unique ecosystem of sawgrass marsh, cypress hammocks, waterfowl, and crocodiles was dependent on the overflow of freshwater from the lake. This flow has been greatly diminished by flood control projects, navigation canals, and projects to divert water to agriculture and cities. Those changes in turn have displaced vast areas of grasslands, reducing the Everglades by about half (Douglas 1947; Caulfield 1971; Jaquay-Wilson 2000). Under pressure from environmentalists across the nation, Congress in 2000 created a long-term restoration program to be jointly conducted by federal and state authorities at a total cost of $7.8 billion, the largest environmental restoration project in U.S. history. Debate continues, however, regarding whether this investment will adequately protect and restore ecological integrity of the Everglades or instead primarily benefit urban development and agricultural interests (*New York Times* 2002).

Floodplains

Coastal and riverine floods affect about 6–8 percent of the land area of the contiguous ("lower") forty-eight states; more than 6.4 million structures are estimated to be located within flood-prone areas, or "floodplains" (Alexander 1991, 141). Floodplains are low-lying areas adjoining rivers, streams, lakes, and tidal waters that are occasionally inundated by high water levels due to storms, rapid snowmelt, or other causes. Floodplains are not a separate category of land use; when not submerged, they are typically utilized for cropland, grazing, recreation, forestry, or urban purposes. Many floodplains also are wetlands.

Floods are a chronic and costly threat to people, structures, and communities in their path. In the United States the number of lives lost in floods has declined in recent decades due to improved forecasting and warning capabilities, but the economic costs of floods have risen steadily as human investment at risk from flooding increases. Although annual loss estimates are notoriously unreliable, certain epic disasters have been closely analyzed. After the 1993 Midwest floods, the White House convened a special commission that estimated the total federal outlays relating to that event at approximately $4.2 billion. Total direct and indirect costs of that disaster have been estimated at $19 billion (Interagency Floodplain Management Review Committee 1994; Changnon 1996).

Floods take many forms: (1) *gradual riverine floods* like the 1993 Midwest flood, which inundated portions of fifteen states over a period of several months; (2) *flash floods* like the Rapid City, South Dakota, flood in 1972 that killed 232 people; and (3) *coastal storm surges* due to "northeasters" and tropical storm systems like Hurricane Fran in 1996 and Hurricane Floyd in 1999. Flooding also may result from dam breaks or local stormwater drainage problems. (For more information, see www.fema.gov.)

The United States has spent billions of dollars since the 1920s to reduce floods and their effects. From the 1920s through the 1960s, this effort primarily took the form of large flood control projects: dams, storage reservoirs, levees, and coastal protection projects. Research by geographers and others persuaded Congress in the late 1960s to shift to alternative strategies, such as land use planning, flood warning systems, relocation of structures and small communities at risk, and a national flood insurance program (Mileti et al. 1999; Platt 1999). (For further discussion of floodplain management, see Chapters 9 and 12.)

Globally, floods and other natural disasters inflict rising tolls of death and economic damage. During the period 1985–2000, nearly 561,000 people died in natural disasters around the world, 96 percent of them in less developed countries. Floods accounted for 28 percent of catastrophic events and about half the total loss of life. Measured in 1999 dollars, the 1990s experienced some $600 billion in economic losses from natural disasters, three times the 1980s total and fifteen times the level in the 1950s (Abramovitz 2001).

Urban Land

With its vast open spaces devoted to agriculture, forests, grasslands, and wilderness, the nation's land area is still predominantly *rural*. Yet the American people have been predominantly *urban* since the 1920s. As discussed in Chapter 6, about 80 percent of the U.S. population today lives in metropolitan areas (Figure 1-4), although some of these people live in fairly countrified surroundings in "McMansions," in rural slums, or somewhere in between.

Urban population growth is occurring in all regions of the country, but is much more intense in the newer "Sun Belt" urban regions of the West and South than in the older "Frost Belt" cities of the Northeast and Midwest (Table 1-3). This shift

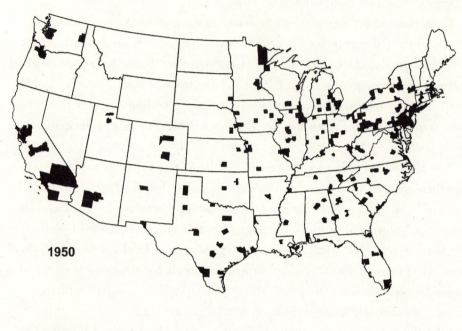

1950

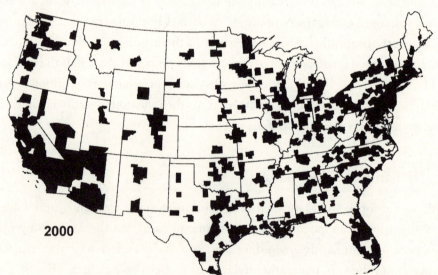

2000

FIGURE 1-4 Metropolitan regions of the United States, 1950 and 2000.
(Source: Gillham 2002, Fig. 1.18.)

reflects in part the flows of retirees from colder to warmer climates, the growth of high-tech and military-related industries in the Sun Belt states, and high rates of immigration from Latin America and Asia into the Southwest and West Coast States.

Whether urban population and land use change is rapid or slow, it is difficult to measure actual changes in *urban land* because the metropolitan landscape is such a patchwork of built and unbuilt areas fragmented among myriad ownerships. Rural lands—farming, forestry, grazing, and barren lands—tend to occur in large, relatively homogeneous spatial units that are easy to identify, although they may shift from one category to another over time. Also, because a large proportion of rural land is publicly owned, it is mapped and managed by government land agencies (federal, state, county, or local). The urban landscape, by contrast, is a vast mosaic of buildings, paved areas, parks, vacant land, private yards, and even residual agriculture and natural areas. How much of this crazy-quilt of land use is "urban"? Drawing a boundary between urban and nonurban areas is a matter of definition and subjective judgment.

Another problem is the scarcity of national-level data on urban land usage. Unlike European countries, which have very precise national land inventories, the United States considers land use to be largely a state, local, and private domain. Federal agencies, notably the USDA and the U.S. Department of the Interior, use remote sensing and geographic information systems (GIS) to track changes in rural lands relevant to their program missions. National-level data on urban land use, however, are much more spotty: Even the U.S. Department of Housing and Urban Development devotes little attention to the growth of urban areas (despite the second part of its title).

The exact amount of urban land is not that crucial; it is approximately 6–8

TABLE 1-3 U.S. POPULATION AND GROWTH RATES, BY REGION, 1960–2000 [IN MILLIONS]

REGION	1960	1970	1980	1990	2000	1960–2000 % CH.
Northeast	44.6	49.0	49.1	50.8	53.5	20.0%
Midwest	51.6	56.5	58.8	59.7	64.3	24.6%
South	54.9	62.8	75.3	85.4	100.2	82.5%
West	28.0	34.3	43.1	52.8	63.1	125.3%
Total	179.3	203.3	226.5	248.7	281.1	56.7%

SOURCE: *Statistical Abstract of the U.S.—2003.*

percent of the contiguous forty-eight states. Far more interesting are the rate of growth of urban land over time and the concomitant "loss" of farmland, forests, wetlands, and other categories of undeveloped land. The U.S. Bureau of the Census for several decades has been identifying *urbanized areas* (UAs) that approximate the area of built-up land for larger communities, but changes in UA definitions and lack of precise land area data impair their usefulness for tracking urban land trends from one census to the next.

Most metropolitan areas are expanding spatially much faster than they are adding population, according to a recent study by the Brookings Institution (Fulton et al. 2001). Between 1982 and 1997, the nation's urbanized areas increased by 47 percent, whereas the nation's population grew by only 17 percent (although, surprisingly, ten of the fifteen densest metropolitan areas in 1997 were located in California, Nevada, and Arizona). Overall, as land occupied by metropolitan areas has expanded faster than population, the average density has declined from 407 persons per square mile in 1950 to 330 in 2000 (ibid.).

Cities

Cities are at the core of urban and metropolitan America. Despite the proliferation of office parks and *edge cities* in suburbs, cities with traditional downtown *central business districts* (CBDs) are still very important economic and cultural foci of U.S. society. Cities are not just a subset of "urban land"; they are legal and political constructs, created under state law and modeled on medieval precedents. (See Chapters 3 and 8.) Among other functions, they are vested with various powers under state law to tax; spend; build and operate schools, parks, libraries, and water and sewage systems; and regulate the use of land and buildings. Cities are also socioeconomic organisms with disproportionate percentages of both rich and poor who are separated by an ever-growing economic chasm as well as by neighborhood of residence. Older cities house disproportionate numbers of people of color and ethnic minorities in comparison with suburbs. In 2000, 46 percent of central city population was black, Hispanic, or Asian, whereas the equivalent figure for suburbs was 23 percent.

About 200 U.S. cities have populations of more than 100,000. Most of these cities are *central cities* (also known as *core cities*), surrounded by wide belts of politically independent (and often hostile) suburbs. Beyond the suburbs, thousands of smaller cities, towns, and villages are scattered across rural America. For people living in *unincorporated areas* (i.e., outside any incorporated unit of local government), counties provide local services (Table 1-4). (These matters are discussed further in Chapter 8.)

At the global scale, the population of cities and their suburbs will soon exceed that of rural areas for the first time in human history. In 1900, only 16 cities had one million people or more, and only about 10 percent of the world's population lived in cities of any size. By the end of the twentieth century, at least 326 cities had over one million inhabitants, and 14 *megacities* exceeded ten million inhabitants (Brown 1999, 7). In September 1999, the world passed the six billion threshold of population, having added one billion people in only twelve years (Table 1-5). The 50

TABLE 1-4 *U.S. INCORPORATED PLACES BY SIZE, 2000*

POPULATION SIZE	NUMBER OF PLACES	POPULATION (MILLIONS)	TOTAL POPULATION OF INCORPORATED PLACES (%)
1 million +	9	22.9	13.2
500,000–1 million	15	12.9	7.4
250,000–500,000	37	13.3	7.7
100,000–250,000	172	25.5	14.7
50,000–100,000	363	24.9	14.3
25,000–50,000	644	22.6	13.0
10,000–25,000	1,435	22.6	13.0
< 10,000	16,772	28.7	16.6
Total	19,452	173.5	100.0

SOURCE: *Statistical Abstract of the U.S.—2001*, Table 32.

TABLE 1-5 *WORLD POPULATION GROWTH AND URBANIZATION*

YEAR	WORLD POPULATION	TIME TO ADD 1 BILLION	PERCENT URBAN
1850	1 billion	All prior human history	10%
1930	2 billion	80 years	20%
1960	3 billion	30 years	30%
1975	4 billion	15 years	40%
1987	5 billion	12 years	43%
2000	6.1 billion	12 years	48%
2050 est.	9.3 billion est.		> 50%

SOURCE: Brown 2001, p. 212; *The New York Times Almanac—2000*, p. 483.

percent urban threshold is expected to be passed by 2010, reflecting in part a natural population increase in cities, the migration of rural population to urban places, and the reclassification of villages as "urban" as they are enveloped by the advancing edge of metropolitan growth.

Continued rapid population increase in poor countries and the unplanned growth of the world's megacities are interconnected challenges to the sustainability of human society in coming decades (National Research Council 1999). The world is currently gaining eighty million people a year, the equivalent of *adding eighty cities the size of Dallas, Texas,* every year! Ninety-seven percent of this population increase will occur in less developed countries and regions of Asia, Africa, and Latin America. Large, fast-growing countries such as India, Pakistan, and Indonesia are today politically unstable and rife with religious fundamentalism and terrorism. The urban problems of new megacities in less developed countries include inadequate and unsafe water supplies, waste disposal, land degradation, deforestation, food supply, housing, natural hazards, infectious diseases (particularly AIDS and malaria), traffic congestion, and air pollution (Blaikie and Brookfield 1987; Mitchell 1999; National Research Council 1999; Brown 2001).

Conclusion

This chapter has summarized the status and usage of land resources in the United States at the beginning of the twenty-first century. A clear dichotomy exists between rural land uses on the one hand and urban and built-up uses on the other. Rural land, predominantly used for cropland, grazing, or forestry, is abundant in quantity to meet anticipated domestic needs. Adequacy in terms of international demand is difficult to assess in light of fluctuating currency exchange rates and global trade patterns. The overriding goal of public policy toward rural land should be to preserve the productive capacity or "sustainability" of such resources to meet future domestic and foreign demand. In particular, those lands deemed most or least suitable for specific uses should be identified, designated, and used accordingly by public and private land managers. Reversible conversion of rural land from one use to another is a normal response to changing economic circumstance. Irreversible transformation of productive rural land, either to a degraded condition (e.g., due to soil erosion, salinization, or inundation) or to an urban or built-up condition, poses important public policy issues.

The spatial growth of urban land is the mirror image of the loss of rural land to

BOX 1-1 *Policy Issues Related to Land Use*

INEFFICIENT USE OF LAND

- Development of prime agricultural land
- Loss or pollution of wetlands
- Overextension of public services
- Visual blight

ENERGY WASTE

- Traffic congestion
- Decline of public transportation
- Heating and air conditioning of small structures

WATER SUPPLY AND WASTEWATER TREATMENT

- Adequate quantity and quality of drinking water
- Conservation and protection of existing water sources
- Efficient irrigation practices
- Relating development to available infrastructure

LOSS OF BIODIVERSITY AND SPECIES EXTINCTION

- Habitat conservation plan

NATURAL HAZARDS

- Urban flooding
- Seismic risk
- Soil and slope instability
- Coastal storm hazards

SOLID WASTES

- Rising volume of wastes
- Shortage of landfill capacity
- Siting of new landfills and incinerators

PUBLIC RECREATION AND OPEN SPACE

- Spatial imbalance of supply and demand
- Multiple functions and constituencies
- Deterioration of older facilities

AFFORDABLE HOUSING

- Exclusionary zoning
- Inadequate public financing
- Conversion of rental units to condominiums
- Deterioration of older housing

development. The implications of such growth, however, are not limited to the loss of productive or potentially productive rural land. Urbanization involves a spectrum of public issues, including environmental quality, adequacy of water supply, equity in housing and economic opportunity, energy consumption, traffic congestion, visual blight, natural hazards, loss of biotic habitat and biodiversity, and rising public costs per capita for providing utilities and services to a vastly expanded region of urban habitation (Box 1-1).

References

Abramovitz, J. 2001. Averting Unnatural Disasters. *State of the World — 2001*. New York: Worldwatch Institute / W. W. Norton.

Alexander, D. A. 1991. *Natural Disasters*. New York: Chapman and Hall.

Blaikie, P., and H. Brookfield. 1987. *Land Degradation and Society*. London and New York: Methuen.

Brown, L. 1999. A New Economy for a New Century. *State of the World — 1999*. New York: Worldwatch Institute / W. W. Norton.

———. 2001. *Eco-Economy*. New York: W. W. Norton.

Caulfield, P. 1971. *Everglades*. New York: Sierra Club / Ballantine Books.

Changnon, S. A. 1996. *The Great Flood of 1993: Causes, Impacts, and Response*. Boulder, CO: Westview Press.

Clawson, M. 1963. *Land for Americans: Trends, Prospects, and Problems*. Chicago: Rand McNally.

———. 1983. *The Federal Lands Revisited*. Baltimore: Johns Hopkins University Press.

Crosson, P. R., and S. Brubaker. 1982. *Resource and Environmental Effects of U.S. Agriculture*. Washington, DC: Resources for the Future.

Dahl, T. E., and C. E. Johnson. 1991. *Status and Trends of Wetlands in the Conterminous United States, Mid-1970s to Mid-1980s*. Washington, DC: U.S. Department of the Interior, Fish and Wildlife Service.

Douglas, M. S. 1947. *The Everglades: River of Grass*. New York: Rinehart.

Fulton, W., R. Pendall, M. Nguyen, and A. Harrison. 2001. Who Sprawls Most? How Growth Patterns Differ across the U.S. (monograph). Washington, DC: Brookings Institution.

Gillham, O. 2002. *The Limitless City: A Primer on the Urban Sprawl Debate*. Washington, DC: Island Press.

Gleick, P. H. 2001. Making Every Drop Count. *Scientific American* 284 (2): 40–45.

Harnik, P. 2000. *Inside City Parks*. Washington, DC: Urban Land Institute.

Hillel, D. 1994. *Rivers of Eden: The Struggle for Water and the Quest for Peace in the Middle East*. New York and Oxford: Oxford University Press.

Interagency Floodplain Management Review Committee. 1994. *Sharing the Challenge:*

Floodplain Management into the 21st Century. Washington, DC: U.S. Government Printing Office.

Jacobs, H. M., ed. 1998. *Who Owns America: Social Conflict over Property Rights.* Madison: University of Wisconsin Press.

Jaquay-Wilson, S. 2000. Saving the Florida Everglades. Unpublished research paper prepared for the author.

Jehl, D. 2002. Dry California Cities Covet Farms' Full Glass. *New York Times,* Sept. 24, 1, A20.

Jefferson, T. 1785. Letter to Rev. James Madison. In *The Life and Selected Writings of Thomas Jefferson,* ed. A. Koch and W. Peder. New York: The Modern Library.

Mileti, D. S., et al. 1999. *Disasters by Design: A Reassessment of Natural Hazards in the United States.* Washington, DC: Joseph Henry Press.

Miller, C. 2001. *Gifford Pinchot and the Making of Modern Environmentalism.* Washington, DC: Island Press.

Mitchell, J. K., ed. 1999. *Crucibles of Hazard: Megacities and Disasters in Transition.* Tokyo: United Nations University Press.

Mitsch, W. J., and J. G. Gosselink. 1986. *Wetlands.* New York: Van Nostrand Reinhold.

National Research Council. 1992. *Restoration of Aquatic Resources.* Washington, DC: National Academy Press.

New York Times. 2002. Decision Time on the Everglades. Sept. 23, A26.

Platt, R. H. 1985. The Farmland Conversion Debate: NALS and Beyond. *Professional Geographer* 37 (4): 433–42.

———. 1999. *Disasters and Democracy: The Politics of Extreme Natural Events.* Washington, DC: Island Press.

Postel, S. 2001. Growing More Food with Less Water. *Scientific American* 284 (2): 46–51.

Tiner, R. W., Jr. 1984. *Wetlands of the United States: Recent Status and Trends.* Washington, DC: U.S. Government Printing Office.

U.S. Bureau of Statistics. 1996. *Statistical Abstract of the United States, 1995–1996.* Table no. 1122. Austin, TX: The Reference Press.

U.S. Council on Environmental Quality. 1984. *Environmental Quality—1984.* Washington, DC: U.S. Government Printing Office.

U.S. Department of Agriculture. 1974. *Our Land and Water Resources.* Misc. pub. no. 1290. Washington, DC: Economic Research Service.

CHAPTER 2   *The Interaction of*
Geography and Law

Taking control of the future ... means tightening the connection between
science and policy.
— **WILLIAM D. RUCKELSHAUS 1989, 167**

Chapter 1 summarized a number of types of land use but said little about *how* land is allocated among various uses and *who* has a voice in making that allocation. The conventional answer to both questions used to be: the private land market as expressed through the decisions of individual property owners. The eighteenth-century Scottish political economist, Adam Smith, along with David Ricardo, John Stuart Mill, and others, advocated the philosophy of *laissez-faire* in which the best interest of society was achieved by allowing private owners or entrepreneurs to maximize their personal profit from the use of land and other resources with minimal governmental involvement. As applied to land, property owners were considered to have "absolute dominion" over their land with the right to use it as they saw fit. This ancient doctrine of the English common law, as transplanted to America and other British colonies, was historically limited only by court-imposed doctrines of *nuisance* and *trespass* to protect property owners from unreasonable actions of one another or the general public. The absolute dominion doctrine was superceded by various forms of governmental limits and regulations in the twentieth century, although it still survives in the minds of property rights advocates, particularly in the American West. (See Chapters 3, 8, and 10 for more on these concepts.)

28   *Land Use under* Laissez-Faire

For the sake of discussion, let's assume that property owners have absolute dominion. In such a case, how do they decide how to use their land? The nineteenth-century German geographer Johann Heinrich Von Thunen translated classical *laissez-faire* principles into a theory of land economics to explain the broad patterns of land use he observed in his day (Wartenberg 1966; Jordan-Bychkov and Domosh 1999). According to Von Thunen, the use of land depends on the profitability of alternate uses, known as *economic rent*, as determined by the land's location in relation to the larger pattern of towns and countryside. Disregarding physical differences in land (a big qualification!), he postulated that urban places were surrounded by belts of rural land uses resulting from the influence of distance from the nearest market town or city. Dairy, meat, and vegetable products, being perishable, bulky, and in daily demand, required production sites close to cities to minimize the costs and time of transportation to market. In economic terms, these intensive agriculture activities paid the highest "economic rent" for suitable land located closest to towns and cities. Farther out was a wider belt of country devoted to more extensive production of crops such as wheat, barley, and maize, and grazing of livestock for meat and wool. Beyond that, the outermost belt was devoted to forestry, fishing, and gathering of mushrooms and berries or was essentially undisturbed. Such remote lands were the least productive in the economic sense and generally remained in their natural state until modern technology claimed them for intensive forestry, water projects, mining, agriculture, recreation, and other rural development activities.

Von Thunen's principle of *location* or distance from urban centers resonates in today's metropolitan real estate markets. Real estate agents recite the mantra that the three most important variables in urban land value are "location, location, and location." Of course, location must be understood in terms of distance or travel time to specific destinations (the produce markets inside the city walls in Von Thunen's time). Today, location is understood in terms of accessibility to a variety of elements of the larger urban system, including places of employment, transportation routes, entertainment opportunities, and public services such as schools, parks, health care, police and fire services. In addition, as commuters stuck in traffic well realize, location is not measured merely by the shortest distance to be traveled but also by the time and nervous energy required to reach a particular destination.

Although Von Thunen ignored physical variation to isolate the influence of location, the importance of physical geography on land use cannot as easily be disregarded. Compared with the featureless German plain of Von Thunen's model, the real world offers dramatic diversity in physical geography, including landforms, soils, surface and groundwater hydrology, vegetation, biota, and climate. Traditional geography texts used to distinguish between *site* characteristics of a tract of land—its physical geography attributes—and its *situation* or its location relative to the larger regional context. Both were and are important geographic variables in explaining the use of particular land.

Of course, the influence of location, combined with technology, may in fact overcome physical site limitations. Boston's fashionable Back Bay district was built on wetlands filled by steam dredges in the 1860s. The U.S. Gulf of Mexico coast historically was a swampy, snake-infested wilderness that was bypassed by earlier westward settlement. With air conditioning and the attraction of beaches, fishing, and retirement living, the Gulf Coast after the 1960s became a hot real estate market. Houston, Texas, a sweaty and humid small city a century ago, became the fourth largest city in the United States in 2000, thanks to the oil industry, air travel, air conditioning, and political clout in Washington, D.C. Although building homes on very steep slopes is usually viewed as hazardous and a poor investment, the hills of Oakland, California, with views of San Francisco Bay are lined with enormous new homes clinging precariously to steep slopes prone to wildfires and earthquake hazards (Figure 7-2 and Platt 1999, Chap. 8). Similarly, the city of Scottsdale, Arizona, had to purchase steep mountain slopes to prevent builders from perching homes on them. And the shores of low-lying barrier islands along the Atlantic Ocean and the Gulf of Mexico are lined with upscale vacation homes in the face of hurricanes, flooding, and shoreline erosion (Figure 7-3; Platt 1999, Chap. 6).

Indeed, the doctrine of "absolute dominion," if applied literally today, would allow no effective public limits on private developers' zeal to maximize short-term economic profit through building wherever and however they choose. Metropolitan America is justly faulted today for its chaotic and wasteful land use patterns, its visual blight, its vulnerability to natural hazards, and its unequal access to housing and employment. Consider, though, how much worse the situation would be if "absolute dominion" still reigned supreme, if it ever did. Fortunately, it does not. Private land use decisions in the United States (and other countries where private ownership of land prevails) are not entirely a matter of the owner's personal or corporate whim. The public through its governmental institutions has an important voice (or chorus of voices) concerning how land may or may not be used. Law and the legal/political system play a subtle but critical role, along with geographic variables of location and physical site characteristics, in shaping the contemporary human landscape.

Recognition that law influences the allocation and use of land is scarcely new. In 1689, John Locke noted that a primary purpose of an organized society is to use law to facilitate the efficient and productive use of land:

I cannot count upon the enjoyment of that which I regard as mine, except through the promise of the law which guarantees it to me. *It is law alone which permits me to forget my natural weakness*. It is only through protection of law that I am able to enclose a field, and to give myself up to its cultivation with the sure though distant hope of harvest. (Locke 1689/1952, 71; emphasis added)

Although the value of land inherently relates to its physical characteristics and its regional location ("site and situation"), such geographical factors may be rendered moot by the inability of owners to be assured of enjoying the fruits of their labor or financial investment in the land. Security of investment expectations is the province of law that confirms property rights in a capitalist society and thereby helps ensure that land will be put to productive use. Furthermore, if Locke had lived in the twenty-first century rather than the seventeenth, he would surely have mentioned the additional role of law as a means to control harmful or stupid uses of land that impose unfair costs (*externalities*) on neighboring property owners or the general public. Thus law theoretically both *encourages* and *restrains* the profit-seeking behavior of private property owners. To walk that tightrope is a challenging legal balancing act!

To make it even more interesting, land use law necessarily must reflect the "geography" of the land in question, its physical site characteristics, and its location with reference to the larger land use context, again its "site and situation." As shown in Chapter 10, the *constitutionality* of land use regulations in the United States depends greatly on their *reasonableness* in light of the character of the land and the public objective to be served. So it is a "chicken and egg" problem: geography and law jointly influence the use of land and, to some extent, each other.

The main purpose of this book, then, is to examine this interactive relationship of geography and law as they jointly shape human landscapes. Although the fields of geography and law may seem initially to be quite unrelated, where land use is concerned they are logical and necessary allies with much to contribute to each other. If geography is defined as the science of spatial organization of human activities, land use geography seeks to explain the functional interrelationships of units of land area to one another and to larger systems of human settlement, such as neighborhoods, communities, regions, nations, and the planet.

Five Questions

To borrow the familiar clichés of journalism, we may pose five fundamental questions about land use: (1) *What* is a tract of land like (its "site")? (2) *Where* is it located with respect to other places or land uses (its "situation")? (3) *Why* is it used in a particular way? (4) *How* can it be better utilized to avoid harmful externalities and promote favorable ones? (5) *Who* has the authority to cause beneficial changes in land use practices? These questions span both geography and law. The first two restate the traditional geographical perspectives on land use. The third involves policy judgments based on physical and social science, and the fourth and fifth slide into the domain of law. Land use law is very much concerned with protecting owners and the public from unreasonable land use actions of others and with *how* that protection may be assured through the legal and political process. Law is concerned with the *process* by which land is allocated for various purposes through the recognition and exercise of private rights and public powers affecting land use.

Law is both a social construct *dependent* on perception of the natural and built environment and also as an *independent* variable that itself shapes that environment in sometimes unexpected ways. A model that describes this interactive relationship is discussed later in this chapter. First, however, the geographical and legal "landscapes" are examined to draw some important contrasts and points of contact between the two fields. After that, the role of law in the shaping of human landscapes, for better or worse, is considered.

The Geographical Landscape

The field of geography is inherently eclectic. Its two major branches, physical geography and human geography, are in turn divided into a number of subfields. Where land use is concerned, the principal physical geography subfields include geomorphology, hydrology, biogeography, and climatology. On the human geography side, the relevant subfields are urban, political, economic, cultural, and social geography. Land use bridges both the physical and human sides of the geographic field, particularly where natural hazards or other physical site limitations are of concern.

It has been said that geographers have more in common with their colleagues in other related disciplines (e.g., geology, economics, political science, urban planning) than they do with one another. Indeed, geographers used to worry about whether they have a field of their own. Playing devil's advocate, the noted geographer Richard Hartshorne (1939, 125) wrote, "Defined not in terms of a particular set of facts, but in terms of causal relationships presumed to exist, [the field of geography] could have but a parasitic character." Hartshorne, however, went on to argue that geography's unique interest in such "causal relationships" that explain observed spatial distributions of various phenomena (the perennial "Why?") distinguishes it as a separate discipline.

Certain organizing themes, models, and concepts characterize the geographic perspective and method. For present purposes, the following pertinent concepts are briefly summarized: (1) spatial organization, (2) scale, (3) function, and (4) externalities.

Spatial Organization

A common denominator that traditionally unites geographers is a fundamental concern with *spatiality*, the spatial organization or discernible patterns of physical and human phenomena as diverse as water resources, agriculture, banking institutions, language and religion, housing markets, ski resorts, poverty, and wealth (James and Martin 1981, Chap. 15). Spatiality is to geographers what spirituality is to the ministry and health is to the physician.

In particular, geographers seek to identify, delineate, and interpret spatial patterns of diverse phenomena, notably including land use and landscape (Morrill 1970). To *identify*, spatial data are derived from field surveys, interviews, government reports, remote sensing, and other sources. To *delineate*, geographers use maps, photographs, and computer-generated graphics to represent spatial patterns and relationships. (Cartography, the development and preparation of maps suitable for particular tasks, is itself a subfield of geography and is now primarily computer-based.) To *interpret* spatial patterns requires analysis and inference, including such tools as statistical analysis, digital geographic information systems (GIS), field research, modeling, historical knowledge, and scholarly intuition. As a simple example, the pattern of large green circles within square fields visible when flying over the West, as noted in the Preface, can be explained in terms of the interaction of the Federal Land Survey (which accounts for the squares) and the application of center-pivot groundwater irrigation (the circles) (Figure I-2). Thus the geographer interprets an unusual human landscape in terms of the interaction of multiple sets of data, in this case those relating to climate, groundwater, soils, legal context, and technology.

After the causes of a particular spatial phenomenon are discerned, the land use geographer turns to issues and problems for public policy. To carry the above example a step further, it may be observed that many of the circles are brown during the growing season. Such browning implies that irrigation of some fields has been suspended for any of a number of possible reasons, such as drought or inadequate groundwater, high cost of electrical power to pump the water, low commodity prices, a federal land conservation program, or soil restoration.

Spatial patterns of land use may be broadly analyzed in terms of the interaction of three overlapping categories or layers of spatial data consisting of (1) physical phenomena, (2) human (socioeconomic and cultural) patterns of land use, and (3) patterns of ownership and political authority affecting the use of specific land.

The *physical geography* of a particular site, locality, or region may be described and interpreted in terms of its patterns of bedrock and landforms, soils, hydrology, natural vegetation and wildlife (biogeography), and climate. The geographer draws on the findings of the appropriate field to the level of detail necessary to resolve the problem under consideration.

The *human geography* of land use includes systems of rural activities—agriculture, forestry, and mining—as well as urban settlements ranging from hamlets to metropolitan regions. Some human landscapes primarily reflect the influence of past economic activities, such as degraded coal mining regions of Pennsylvania and West Virginia, and old paper and lumber mill towns of the Kennebec and Penobscot valleys in Maine. Other landscapes may reflect the economies of the present (i.e., Silicon Valley) or even the future (wind-generating "farms" in San Bernadino Pass east of Los Angeles and on the Oakland Hills). Other human landscapes reflect cultural roots and meanings (Indian burial sites, battlegrounds, cemeteries, Ground Zero in Lower Manhattan). Each of these variants of human landscapes lends itself to delineation and interpretation through geographical analysis.

Both economic and cultural landscapes comprise fragments of larger spatial systems. Spatial analysis of these systems involves (1) the identification of *nodes* or points of activity (e.g., mines, factories, power plants, sacred or historical sites) and (2) *linkages* or connections between nodes (e.g., transportation corridors, pipelines, and communications networks, migration pathways, routes of historic military maneuvers). Such linkages serve as conduits among activity nodes for a variety of dynamic commodities, including materials, nutrients, energy, goods, information, people, capital, and pollution.

The geography of *legal and political authority* may be described as a series of jurisdictional templates overlying land, representing the layers of authority that collectively influence the use of land in the United States (Figure 2-1):

- ▸ Ownership (private or public)
- ▸ Minor civil divisions (municipalities, special districts, counties)
- ▸ States
- ▸ Federal government

Units of authority at each level in the hierarchy are bounded by precise, if irregular, territorial limits that define the geographic reach of their legal power over land. Moreover, units at different levels in the hierarchy influence the use of land within their jurisdictions in different ways according to their respective legal, political, and fiscal capabilities. The use of individual parcels of land thus reflects a complex interaction among the various levels of land managers who share jurisdiction over a given site. Broader patterns of land use result from the aggregation of use characteristics of individual parcels.

Legal and political boundaries of course are invisible to observation unless marked by a sign, fence, or other visual indicator. The presence of institutional boundaries, however, may often be inferred from observation of abrupt changes in land use patterns, as from a high-end, low-density elite residential district to an adjoining area of dilapidated housing, abandoned storefronts, and visual blight. The capricious location of legal and political boundaries—the result of long-forgotten historical reasons—strongly influences land use patterns (Whittlesey 1935; Clark 1985), sometimes with strange results. State lines are often marked by

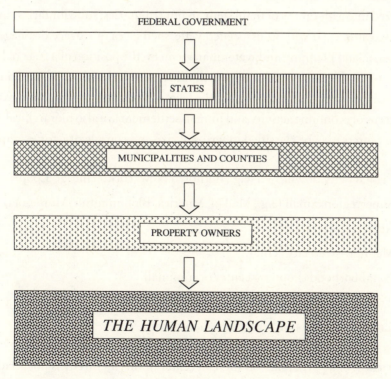

FIGURE 2-1 Diagram of hierarchy of authority over land use in the United States.

huge outlets selling fireworks, liquor, or other goods legally available in one state but not the other. Many casinos, like Foxwoods and Mohican Sun in eastern Connecticut, have erupted on tribal lands that are legally exempt from gambling laws of the state or town that surrounds them. Towns that ban liquor outlets ("dry towns") are certain to spawn liquor stores just across the town line in the next municipality.

Of course, legal and political boundaries are not totally independent variables in shaping the human landscape. The municipal boundaries of many newer suburbs tend both to reflect, and in turn to reinforce, the spatial patterns of housing markets, economic activity, and locational preferences of house buyers. This relationship is explored in later chapters.

Scale

Scale or "hierarchy" is fundamental to geographic analysis of spatial organization. Physical, economic, and legal/political systems may be viewed as nested subsets of smaller units within larger ones. A river drainage system, for instance, is physically organized into a hierarchy of main stem, major tributaries, subtributaries, and tiny source streams, each with its associated watershed (area of surface drainage). For purposes of land planning and water management, the position of a tract of land in relation to this hierarchy of drainage is significant in terms of quality and quantity of surface flow past the site, as well as the level of flood risk to which it is exposed.

Patterns of economic activity and human settlement are also hierarchical. Commercial centers may be classified in terms of size and complexity, for example:

1. Primary city downtown (e.g., midtown New York, Chicago Loop)
2. Superregional mall (e.g., Mall of America, Bloomington, Minnesota)
3. Regional shopping center
4. Medium-sized city center
5. Neighborhood shopping center or minimall
6. Traditional village center
7. Crossroads gas pump and convenience store

The status of a particular commercial center in this hierarchy is not accidental. Geographers have developed numerous theories and models to account for the spatial organization of urban and economic systems (Berry and Parr 1988). Central place theory, in particular, relates the size and spacing of commercial centers to the distance consumers are willing to travel to obtain certain goods and services. Thus gas, beer, bread, and milk are normally purchased from the nearest neighborhood or convenience store, whereas one travels farther for a full-scale supermarket or specialty outlet such as an organic food market. New cars and banking, legal, and health services are obtained from larger ("higher-order") centers, whereas rare art objects, major corporate financing, and open-heart surgery are likely to be sought in a major city like Boston, Denver, or Seattle. Commercial centers at each higher level thus provide a wider array of goods and services to consumers from a broader geographic area or *hinterland*. Concomitantly, the size and diversity of a commercial center is limited by its proximity to competing centers of the same or higher order (Palm 1981, Chap. 8).

The geographic location of a tract of land in relation to the hierarchy of urban places, like its position in a drainage system, bears an important relationship to its suitability for particular uses. The history of land settlement in the United States is rife with examples of speculative land ventures that failed to achieve the shining prosperity predicted by their promoters, in part because they were too close to a better situated place that attracted available settlers and commerce. New Haven, Connecticut, for instance, despite its early settlement has always been overshadowed by New York as a port and business center, just as Portland, Maine, plays second fiddle to Boston. For every successful Chicago or St. Louis, there have been many a disappointed Michigan City, Indiana, or Cairo, Illinois, that were eclipsed by their more prosperous (and better located) rival. Today's counterpart is the proliferation of "dead malls" that have become redundant as newer, larger, and flashier regional shopping complexes have usurped their customers (or the region is financially hard-pressed and cannot support as many shopping outlets). Park Forest, Illinois, a planned postwar suburb outside Chicago, originally boasted the first shopping center in its area. Subsequent development of much larger malls in the vicinity forced the Park Forest center to close (although it later was "reinvented" as economical space for certain specialty businesses and services). Park Forest segues into the concept of *function*, which is essential to the existence of communities, shopping centers, and uses of land.

Function

The raison d'être of a town or city and its size and rank in the central place hierarchy are directly related to the functions that it performs. An urban place without a function is a virtual nullity, regardless of what laws or promoters may say. Colonial legislatures of Virginia and Maryland attempted to encourage the growth of towns by laying out sites adjoining rivers and granting them special port privileges. The region, however, shipped its products directly from river landings at each plantation and needed no port towns. In the pithy words of Thomas Jefferson, a geographer among his many talents, "The laws have said there shall be towns; but nature has said there shall not, and they remain unworthy of enumeration" (1784/1944, 227). This statement illustrates a common practice today: trying to promote economic growth through legal means without considering the geographical context. (For a contemporary example, see Box 12-1 about a failed proposal for a container port at Sears Island, Maine.)

Urban economic functions may be *primary* (e.g., agriculture, forestry, mining), *secondary* (manufacturing), *tertiary* (retail, service, information based), or a combination of these functions. Some urban places are characterized by a single dominant function, as in the case of seaports or lake ports, transportation hubs, governmental centers, academic towns, recreational resorts, and retirement communities. Larger cities usually encompass more than one major function in addition to a variety of subsidiary activities (e.g., shopping, banking, medical care, car sales).

Urban functions change over time with technological innovation, patterns of economic investment (domestic and international), demographic and lifestyle trends, shifts in political power, and changing public perception or "image." Thus cities may lose or gain in their range of functions with corresponding change in their demographic size, wealth, and status in the region, state, or nation. Old "smokestack cities" like Detroit, Buffalo, and Pittsburgh lost much of their population and economic importance beginning in the 1960s with the decline of their major industries such as automobile manufacturing and steel production. While such "Rust Belt" cities lost population and wealth newer "Sun Belt" places like Orlando, Phoenix, and San Diego flourished as meccas for tourism, retirement, and high-tech industry. More recently, however, single-function high-tech regions like Silicon Valley in California stumbled with the dot-com collapse of the early 2000s. Meanwhile, older industrial cities like Pittsburgh are developing new functions as centers of culture, higher education, urbane living, and a wider range of affordable housing stock than the "geek ghettos" of the 1980s.

Another way of explaining the size of cities is to realize that the larger the region dependent on an urban place (e.g., for jobs, shopping, entertainment), the stronger the economy of that city and the greater its own population and prosperity are likely to become. Thus urban places traditionally have grown or dwindled in relation to the extent to which they functionally serve a wider public (hence the concepts of *core* and *hinterland*).

As mentioned earlier, the position of a city in the hierarchy of urban "central places" depends on the size and wealth of the hinterland that a core urban place functionally serves. New York City became the largest U.S. city due in part to the opening of the Erie Canal in 1825, followed by railroads lines, which made it the cheapest port for shipping midwestern grain abroad (a function later preempted by New Orleans with the advent of cheap barge transport on the Mississippi and its tributaries). Of course, New York's continuing economic functions as a world center of finance, fashion, the arts, entertainment, education, and medicine have ensured its continued status at the pinnacle of the U.S. hierarchy of urban places.

The notion of "function" applies not only to urban places but also to individual tracts of land. Each unit of land may be viewed as functioning within larger physical and human systems. Ecologically, land in its natural state supports biological diversity, stores and releases surface and groundwater, transmits moisture and carbon dioxide to the atmosphere through evapotranspiration, concentrates energy through photosynthesis, and supports the formation of soils. Within the agricultural system, land use functions include cropland, pasture, fallow, horticulture, woodlot, and farmstead. Urban land functions as building sites for homes, business, industry, institutions, and transportation while, it is hoped, some unbuilt land is retained to function as parkland and ecological preserves.

Function is thus related to, but not synonymous with, the term *land use*. Function refers to the relationship between a parcel of land and the wider physical and socioeconomic spatial systems to which it belongs. Even vacant land that is unused in a market sense may function in a physical and social sense, and such functions may be either positive or negative in relation to surrounding areas. Thus a vacant urban lot may have no formal economic use but may function beneficially as a visual amenity, a perceptual buffer between neighborhoods, a play space for children, an informal parking area, or a habitat for wildlife. Negatively, it may serve as a dumping site for trash, junk cars, or hazardous wastes, or as a refuge for drug abusers or various illicit activities.

Externalities

No parcel of land is an island unto itself. Land use functions, by definition, affect surrounding areas or a broader public. Such *externalities* may be either beneficial or harmful. Beneficial externalities include jobs created in the surrounding community or region from a new industrial plant or commercial firm. An attractively landscaped site or an architecturally pleasing home benefits passersby aesthetically and may increase the values of neighboring homes. Although society seeks to encourage such *positive* externalities from the use of land, though, *negative* or harmful externalities are a far greater concern.

Adverse externalities arise from the failure of land use managers at various scales (e.g., property owners, corporations, municipalities, states, nations) to recognize the negative impacts of their site-based actions on persons or land outside their area of control. Such effects may be physical or socioeconomic in nature, or both. Adverse *physical* externalities take such forms as air and water pollution; flooding; effects on fisheries, birds, and other wildlife; depletion of water supplies; littering and dumping of wastes; noise; and visual blight. Each of these types of externalities spreads geographically according to the physical process involved; examples are water pollution and flooding extending downstream in drainage systems and air pollution traveling where the wind blows. Negative *socioeconomic* effects resulting from geographic shifts in economic patterns may cause loss of jobs, retail sales, and tax revenue along with increased burdens on schools and other public services in adversely affected jurisdictions. Relocation of economic activities to outer suburbs causes the loss of jobs and tax revenue to older, more central jurisdictions (socioeconomic externality) while also leading to higher levels of ground-level ozone and other traffic-related pollution from traffic passing through such disadvantaged areas (physical externality) (Bullard, Johnson, and Torres 2000).

The problem of harmful externalities reflects the spatial noncorrespondence of relevant geographic variables: physical, socioeconomic, and institutional. Although the authority of land owners and political units is confined to the geographic space defined by their jurisdictional boundaries, the geographic diffusion of consequences of their actions (both beneficial and adverse) depends on the way those three sets of geographic systems interact spatially (Figure 2-2).

The nature, extent, and economic consequences of externalities may vary widely by type and magnitude of effects, yet the fundamental problem is the same: How can favorable externalities be encouraged and adverse externalities be suppressed or mitigated? Furthermore, some externalities are "serious enough" to justify higher-level governmental intervention such as flagrant air pollution and hazardous waste dumping. Others are simply left for the victims to endure, as with a noisy party next door or loss of tax revenue and jobs due to a new mall in the next

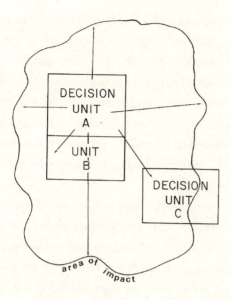

FIGURE 2-2
Diagram of spatial impacts
of externalities on adjacent
and nonadjacent land.

town. The determination of which is which, and what if anything should be done about it, poses legal and political questions. *The geographer, having framed the problem, refers its solution to the law*.

The Legal Landscape

The legal landscape is very different from that of the geographer. Although the latter is a composite of several interacting types of spatial phenomena—physical, economic, social, and legal/political—the law is primarily concerned with the last category, legal and political authority over land, and only secondarily with the others. Where the *geographical* model of the land economy identifies systems of nodes, linkages, flows, hierarchies, and functions, the *legal* counterpart may best be described as a battlefield on which private property interests struggle against one another (the *private law* context) as well as against governmental constraints (the *public law* context). This landscape is crisscrossed with the fortifications of entrenched legal interests: property owners, tenants, public agencies, neighbors, civic and environmental groups. The battlefield is littered with the shell craters of past legal salvos and is fraught with anxiety about assaults by smart zoning lawyers representing Wal-Mart and other agents of community change.

The adversarial and pragmatic perspective of law contrasts with the positivist orientation of geography. To the lawyer, land use patterns are the collective outcome of myriad individual cases, conflicts, appeals, administrative rulings, and political actions to which geographical notions of scale, function, and central place theory may seem irrelevant abstractions. The holistic, systematic perspective of geography yields to the particularistic, adjudicative focus of the law. To this focus, substantive outcomes, particularly broad-scale, long-term applications, are secondary to constitutional issues of fairness and reasonableness of the process by which conflicts are resolved. (As discussed in Chapter 10, however, the constitutionality of public land use measures is strongly related to the *reasonableness* of their impact, which raises geographical questions.)

A fundamental dichotomy in land use law lies between *ownership* (private or public) and *jurisdiction* (public). Ownership represents a set of rights and duties that "belong" to a property owner, by definition. Jurisdiction represents the power of a governmental body to oversee and regulate private activities within its political boundaries that affect the general public interest, such as land use. (Confusingly, both the public authority and the geographic territory within which it is exercised are referred to as "jurisdiction.")

The recognition of competing interests is itself an important difference between geography and law. Geography identifies various spatially differentiated "clusters" of common interest (e.g., immediate neighbors, neighborhood, ethnic community, business district, watershed, metropolitan housing market). In contrast to this open-ended approach, the law focuses on *parties in interest* who possess legal *standing*, which qualifies them to seek legal intervention. Classes of parties with legal standing in land use disputes normally include property owners directly affected by a decision, immediate neighbors, certain nongovernmental organizations (NGOs), and local, state, and federal governmental bodies having jurisdiction over the site. Other spatial constituencies such as the neighborhood, downstream residents, and the metropolitan region generally lack legal standing except to the extent that an organizational surrogate may successfully claim to represent their interests. Thus when Mount Laurel, New Jersey, was accused of practicing exclusionary zoning (one of hundreds of suburban communities doing so), the National Association for the Advancement of Colored People (NAACP) successfully filed suit on behalf of people prevented from living in the township due its use of zoning laws. (See Chapter 10.)

The rigidity of traditional legal rules regarding "standing" has somewhat eased since the 1970s in tacit recognition of geographically diffuse "parties in interest." Environmental and civil rights organizations and other interest groups have been fairly successful in asserting standing on behalf of their constituencies in a variety of lawsuits over the decades. In addition, *class actions* have afforded another way to assert standing on behalf of a large number of similarly affected individuals, as in product liability cases.

The complex hierarchies of political geography, however, are collapsed into a monolithic "public" for purposes of land use litigation. Typically, lawsuits involving land are filed by one or more private property owners(s) as *plaintiffs* against a unit of government, the *defendant*. The defendant government may be at the municipal, county, state, or federal level, or even a combination of levels. In the process, however, geographical distinctions are blurred. The plaintiff and defendant are the "parties" to the lawsuit and diverse other stakeholders—individuals neighborhoods, communities, regions, states, or NGOs—are conveniently ignored (unless one or more such stakeholders "intervenes" in the legal proceedings on behalf of the plaintiff or defendant).

Disputes over land use usually fall into three general classes: (1) owner *versus* owner, (2) owner *versus* public, and (3) public *versus* public. Disputes of the first type are usually settled by a court through application of *common-law* doctrines such as nuisance and trespass derived from past judicial decisions in the United States and Great Britain, considered in more detail in Chapters 3 and 7. The second class of disputes involves *constitutional* issues governing the respective rights of private and governmental interests as discussed in Chapter 10. The third class may involve disputes either between peer governmental units on the same level (e.g., between adjoining towns or states) or between units at different levels as when a city is sued by the federal government or state for failing to carry out a statutory or constitutional responsibility. Most land use cases fall under the second class, namely constitutional disputes.

Disputes between the federal government and one or more states present issues of *federalism*, the dynamic and contentious relationship between the national and the state levels of government. Disputes between a state and a local government involve the extent of municipal autonomy under express or implicit grants of state authority or *home rule* (Clark 1985). Federal-local disputes also arise in connection with enforcement of federal environmental, civil rights, and other action-forcing legislation. For instance, the U.S. Environmental Protection Agency is exerting considerable legal pressure on New York City and Boston to comply with the federal Safe Drinking Water Act (see Chapter 12).

Like private individuals, governmental bodies are primarily concerned with their own welfare. Accordingly, they seek to resist harmful externalities inflicted on them while disregarding those they may inflict on their neighbors. As the phrase goes, local governments follow the Ungolden Rule: "Do unto others before they do unto you." In the contentious atmosphere of municipal rivalry for growth, jobs, and taxes, a genuine public interest tends to be lost in the fray. Courts are thus often at a loss to determine which geographical public to protect. For instance, in a suit by a home construction association challenging the growth management program of Petaluma, California, a federal district court favored the right of a *local* government to plan its future. That view, though, was overturned by the federal court of appeals, which held the city to be unconstitutionally impairing the *regional* housing market. (See the discussion of *Construction Industry Assn. v. City of Petaluma* in Chapter 9.)

With all the contrasts indicated above, can it be said that land use geography and law occupy any common ground? The answer is an emphatic "Yes." It was suggested earlier that the problem of externalities is an area of overlap between the geographical and legal frames of reference. Externalities, which represent friction among components in the geographer's *macro* view of the land economy, are in fact the central concern of the lawyer's *micro* view. If there were no externalities among land use management units, there would be little or no need for land use law. *The central problem of land use law is that of externalities, and that problem is fundamentally geographical.*

A Short Digression: The Legal Process

Before proceeding further, it is important that the nonlawyer reader understand how the law of land use is articulated in the United States. What is loosely referred to as "the law" is a complex mosaic of rules and principles expressed in various forms of documents, including the following:

1. *Constitutions* (federal and state)
2. *Legislative acts* (also known as *statutes* or *legislation*)
3. *Judicial decisions* in court cases (also known as *case law*)
4. *Administrative regulations* issued by regulatory agencies

To simply list the major sources of legal authority is scarcely to convey the complexity of the relationships among them. Clearly, the starting point is the Constitution of the United States, which was stated by the nation's founders to be "The Supreme Law of the Land." The U.S. Constitution established the basic balance of powers among the executive, legislative, and judicial branches of the federal government. The nature and extent of individual rights, including the right to own property, are set forth in the Bill of Rights (the first ten amendments passed in 1791) and later amendments. State constitutions perform essentially the same functions as the federal constitution and are subordinate to it (notwithstanding the old Southern segregationist rhetoric of "states rights"). Of particular importance to the land use context, the Fifth Amendment to the U.S. Constitution declares: "No person shall be ... deprived of life, liberty, or property without due process of law, nor shall private property be taken for public use without just compensation." (This troublesome "takings clause" is discussed in more detail in Chapter 10.)

Legislation—laws adopted by Congress and state legislatures—must be consistent with the U.S. Constitution, as determined by the courts. The Constitution was silent on the ability of courts to overrule legislative acts thought to be contrary to the Constitution. This power was asserted in the famous 1803 U.S. Supreme Court decision by Chief Justice John Marshall in *Marbury v. Madison* (5 U.S. 137), which established the principle of *judicial review* under which courts may determine the constitutionality of federal, state, and local laws in cases in which that issue is presented.

In deciding cases presented to them, courts customarily draw on *precedent*, namely previous rulings by courts in cases presenting issues similar to the one now to be decided. Lower courts normally defer to the prior decisions of higher courts, but often there is precedent on both sides of a dispute from diverse prior decisions. Much of the legal process involves reconciling inconsistent decisions from diverse courts and contexts. Law students are taught how to present their cases to resemble precedents that support their clients and distinguish other precedents that lean the other way. In politics, it is called "spin"; in law, it is called earning your fee!

Finally, administrative agencies are created by federal and state legislation and are authorized to adopt and enforce *regulations* to carry out specific programs and purposes. Such agencies are creatures of legislation and may not exceed the express or implied powers delegated to them by legislation. Administrative regulations are of course subject to review by courts to determine their constitutionality or consistency with the applicable legislation.

Laws and policies concerning land use are usually developed by each state rather than at the federal level (subject to the U.S. Constitution). States in turn have delegated most of their land use authority to local governments through planning and zoning enabling acts. Since 1970, however, many states have reclaimed authority over certain types of land use actions, such as those involving affordable housing, floodplains, wetlands, or historic sites (Kusler 1985; DeGrove and Stroud 1987).

The United States maintains two parallel systems of courts: federal and state. Land use cases are usually brought to the courts of the state in which the land is located. Cases may be initiated in, or transferred to, the applicable federal court when a federal constitutional issue or statute is involved (federal question jurisdiction) or when the parties are located in different states (diversity jurisdiction). In either case, threshold levels of economic harm must be involved for a case to be accepted in the federal courts.

In the typical land use case, the court is asked by the plaintiff to resolve whether a challenged statute or regulation is "constitutional" and fairly applied to the plaintiff by the defendant unit of government. In such cases, the plaintiff asks the court to nullify the measure and the defendant seeks to have its action upheld. Many land use cases, however, are decided on procedural grounds without reaching the merits of the case. Others are found to be "fairly debatable" on their merits, and courts then normally apply a *presumption* that the public action is valid. In a third set of decisions, courts are persuaded by the plaintiff that the public measure is "discriminatory, arbitrary, or capricious" and the measure is held invalid, at least as applied to the plaintiff. Examples of these types of rulings are seen in cases discussed throughout this book.

Relatively few land use disputes actually reach the courts, and even fewer are appealed by the losing party to a higher ("appellate") court. Very rarely, cases of major significance are submitted for review by the U.S. Supreme Court, which is very selective in cases it accepts. Only about a dozen land use decisions have been issued by the U.S. Supreme Court since 1980, but they are quite familiar to land use lawyers as well as, one hopes, land use geographers. State supreme courts collectively account for most significant decisions in land use law. Their decisions apply directly only to the state in which they arise but are disseminated nationally to provide guidance to courts considering similar cases elsewhere. State court decisions on matters of state law are "precedent" within the state where they are issued (unless overruled); elsewhere they have persuasive value in similar cases but are not necessarily treated as precedent.

Land use case law in both the state and federal court systems is a rich archive of judicial perspectives on the relationship of law and geography. Judicial opinions apply applicable legal authorities (e.g., prior case law, statutes, treatises) to the facts of the case. It is the role of the attorneys for each party to portray applicable legal authority and the facts of the case favorably to their respective positions. The court in turn forms its own opinion of the state of the law and the facts of the case and

BOX 2-1 *A Note on Legal Citations in This Book*

Formal expressions of law include, in addition to the federal and state constitutions: (a) *legislation* adopted by the U.S. Congress and state legislatures (also referred to as *statutes*); (b) *judicial decisions* issued by federal and state courts; and (c) *administrative regulations* issued by federal, state, or municipal agencies pursuant to legislative authority. All these legal documents may be obtained either in bound volumes in a law library or via Lexis/Nexis on the Internet.

Forms of citation of these and other legal documents are prescribed in *The Bluebook: A Uniform System of Citation* (*Bluebook*) available in any law library and many bookstores. In the interest of simplification, this book does not adhere strictly to *Bluebook* rules of style. Federal statutes here are usually cited by their *Public Law* (P. L.) number, which refers to the text of a law as originally adopted by Congress. For example, the National Environmental Policy Act of 1969 (P.L. 91-190) was the 190th act to be passed by the 91st Congress.

The Public Law text of a statute of course does not usually reveal how it may have modified earlier legislation and obviously does not include later amendments. The current version of a federal statute, reflecting all additions and deletions by various public laws passed at different times, is "codified" by subject matter in the *U.S. Code Annotated* (USCA). In addition to the current text of a statute, USCA provides a wealth of additional information on legislative history, changes in language, court decisions, and law review articles that discuss the statute.

Discussion of land use law in this book is primarily historical, focusing on the evolution of public response to perceived societal needs. The use of Public Law citations is appropriate for this purpose, as we are interested in the language of a law as adopted at a particular time. For anyone who wishes to research the current status of a federal law, however, the USCA must be consulted. It is indexed by subject matter and by popular name of statutes. State laws follow the same twofold form of citation, namely by (1) chronological order of adoption (*session laws*) and (2) subject matter (*annotated code*).

Judicial opinions are published in a series of "Reporters" by West Publishing Co., which are available in law libraries and on-line. The standard form of citation used in this book is as follows:

Plaintiff v. Defendant Volume No., Reporter Abbreviation, First Page (State, Year)

For example, *Just v. Marinette County* 201 N.W.2d 761 (Wis., 1972) is found in Volume 201 of the Northwest Reporter, Second Series, beginning at page 761. Consult a law librarian for explanation of other reporter abbreviations.

reaches a decision accordingly. The legal outcome therefore reflects in part the court's perception of the geographic context.

Judges, being human, do not necessarily view the circumstances of a land use issue in the same way (Clark 1985). Judicial disagreement may arise (1) among individual judges on a multijudge court (as expressed in dissenting opinions), (2) between a lower and higher court reviewing the same case, (3) between courts in different states or federal jurisdictions reviewing similar cases, and (4) between courts considering a similar issue at different points in time. The last category is particularly important in weighing the role of geographical perspective in the judicial process. Law is a flexible and dynamic institution. The adjudicative process permits reinterpretation of legal principles over time in response to actual or perceived changes in society and its needs. As stated by the U.S. Supreme Court in *Village of Euclid v. Ambler Realty Co.* (272 U.S., at 365 [1926]):

> While the meaning of the constitutional guarantees never varies, the scope of their application must expand or contract to meet the new and different conditions which are constantly coming within the field of their operation. (272 U.S., at 386)

Leading decisions on similar land use issues over time may thus reflect shifts of legal response to "new and different conditions" among which geographical circumstances loom large.

Law as an Agent of Urban Form

We now turn to consideration of the imprint of legal and political authority on the human landscape. As once stated rather elaborately by political geographer Derwent W. Whittlesey:

> Political activities leave their impress upon the landscape, just as economic pursuits do. Many acts of government become apparent in the landscape only as phenomena of economic geography; others express themselves directly. Deep and widely ramified impress upon the landscape is stamped by the functioning of effective central authority. (1935, 85)

The "impress" or impact of law, however, differs from place to place, from one historical period and social order to another, and among different districts within the same city. Old cities like London, Tokyo, and Boston have historic core areas where there seems to be no order or plan in the layout of local streets and buildings; they are irregular, assymetric, and picturesque to the contemporary eye. By contrast, some old cities were founded under military or imperial rule with strict control on the laying out of streets, markets, and building sites. Such disparate urban districts as the French Quarter of New Orleans, the Green in New Haven, Connecticut, the city of Kyoto, Japan, and central Beijing, China, were each laid out under some form of "central authority" that imposed control over the layout and size of streets and public spaces. The urban geographer James E. Vance Jr. (1977, 24) referred to the former unplanned urban pattern as *organic* and the latter as *preconceived* (Figure 2-3). Contemporary metropolitan development tends to be "preconceived" or planned at the scale of individual subdivisions and shopping malls, whereas the larger regional land use pattern appears "organic," if not outright chaotic!

Most urban landscapes lie somewhere between these two extremes, as preconceived plans and individual preferences mingle in ever-shifting combinations with physical site, economic context, culture, and technology to produce the cities of the world. Law as an instrument of both private rights and public authority is a subtle but ubiquitous agent in the evolution of urban form and is often discernible in the rural landscape as well, as in the checkerboard of square fields derived from the federal land survey visible from the air over much of the American Midwest.

Imposed Plans: The Ubiquitous Grid

The *orthogonal* or *grid* street plan provides a widespread instance of the "impress" of a preconceived plan on the human landscape. The use of the grid as a basis for land allocation and street layout has been traced back to the third millennium B.C. in the Indus Valley by geographer Dan Stanislawski, who cites such a plan, wherever found, as evidence of centralized control:

> This pattern is not conceivable except as a … whole. If the planner thinks in terms of single buildings, separate functions, or casual growth, the grid will not come into being; for each structure considered separately, the advantage lies with irregularity. History is replete with examples of the patternless, ill-formed town that has been the product of growth in response to the desires of individual builders. (1946, 28)

Similarly, Castagnoli (1971, 124) stresses the influence of governing authority in establishing a preconceived pattern of land allocation and usage:

> The regularity or irregularity of town forms depends entirely on the presence or absence of spontaneity in their birth and growth. The irregular city is the result of

FIGURE 2-3A Armani and laundry share an "organic" medieval street in Venice. *(Photo by author.)*

FIGURE 2-3B St. Mark's Square, Venice, a world-famous example of Renaissance city planning (as modified by Napoléon in the early nineteenth century). *(Photo by author.)*

development left entirely to individuals who actually live on the land. If a governing body divides the land and disposes of it before it is handed over to users, a uniformly patterned city will emerge.

The grid plan serves several administrative goals: equitability of land allocation, convenience of survey and house numbering, and ease of expansion into later settled areas. Its disadvantages include incompatibility with irregular terrain, problems of defensibility, excessive street length in relation to built-up land, and (to contemporary observers at least) monotonous regularity.

Grid street plans have been employed in many sociocultural contexts and periods of urban history. Beijing, Kyoto, Mexico City, Berlin, Buenos Aires, New York, and most U.S. cities west of the Appalachians employ grid street plans, at least in part. The grid has been particularly suited to the layout of colonial outposts and new settlements, from the *cardo* and *decumanus* of Roman enclaves in conquered territories (Grimal 1954/1983), to thirteenth-century *bastide* towns in France, Wales, and Ireland (Beresford 1967), to Spanish and French settlements in the New World following Roman standards (Stanislawski 1947). The grid also appears where a newly planned sector has been added to an earlier, unplanned city, as in James Craig's 1766 plan for Edinburgh's New Town, which faces the medieval Old Town across a beautiful park (once a sewer). London's elegant seventeenth- and eighteenth-century West End residential squares starkly contrast with the irregular labyrinth of streets in Soho and parts of The City (London's financial district). When part of Lisbon was destroyed by an earthquake in 1755, the district was rebuilt under royal supervision in the elegant baroque style then popular in Paris and London, providing a distinct contrast with the organic informality of the adjoining medieval Alfama district that escaped the earthquake (Mullin 1992).

The grid served as a standard pattern for new settlements established by land proprietors in colonial America such as William Penn's 1686 checkerboard plan for Philadelphia, James Oglethorpe's 1733 plan for Savannah, and the 1820 Mount Auburn subdivision in Boston (Reps 1969). The pervasive rectangularity of rural and urban land use in the United States west of the Appalachians results from one of the first sovereign acts of the new national government, the Land Ordinance of 1785. This ordinance initiated the federal rectangular land survey, which eventually covered much of the country west of the Appalachians (Figure 2-4), as further discussed in Chapter 7. Even near the East Coast, evidence of early rectangular surveys are found in many cities and in rural parts of northern New England and western New York State.

FIGURE 2-4 Boulder, Colorado: major east-west streets following Federal Land Survey
lines seem to converge in the distance. Diagonal highway at bottom connects
Boulder to Denver. *(Photo by author.)*

The grid plan unmistakably reflects the influence of central authority—royal,
military, land proprietor, national or local government—on the use of land. So also
do other geometric urban forms that conspicuously reflect an imposed plan, as in
the case of "round cities" of the Renaissance (Johnston 1983) and profusely orna-
mental "baroque cities" of Europe (Sitte 1945). Washington, D.C., is a composite
of a grid street plan and a baroque pattern of radial avenues and French-inspired
circles and squares, originally designed by the French engineer Pierre Charles
L'Enfant in 1792.

The urban-shaping role of law, however, is not necessarily as obvious or as geographically widespread as in these cases. It may operate more subtly and pro-
saically, as for instance in the width of streets; the size, spacing, construction, and
use of buildings; and the balance of built and unbuilt space. How are physical
differences among sections of the same city explained? To paraphrase landscape
architect Grady Clay (1973), we must "read the city" in terms of legal and institutional influences as well as economic, cultural, and physical factors.

EVOLUTION OVER TIME: THE CASE OF BOSTON

A short walk across central Boston traverses an archive of different stages of public involvement in the city-shaping process (Figure 2-5). Starting at the waterfront

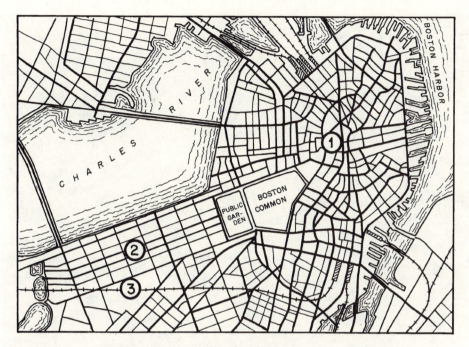

FIGURE 2-5 Locations of areas of Boston, Massachusetts, built in different historic periods: (1) the old colonial North End, (2) nineteenth-century Back Bay, (3) Prudential Center.

on Boston Harbor, one wanders through the North End and financial district where irregular street patterns date from Boston's earliest settlement in the 1630s. (According to local folklore, these streets originated as cow paths.) These streets lead eventually to the city's open core, the Boston Common, set aside by the colonial settlement in 1630, and the Public Garden, created two centuries later in the 1830s. Adjoining the Public Garden to the west are the rectilinear streets and bowfront brick rowhouses of Back Bay, Boston's mid-nineteenth-century expansion onto newly filled land bordering the Charles River. Crossing Boylston Street from Back Bay, one enters the high-rise complex of multiple-use structures in Prudential Center and adjacent areas (Figure 2-6). And in 2003, one cannot avoid the colossal construction project (known locally as the "Big Dig") to put the elevated highway called the Central Artery underground, which eventually will provide new greenspace through Boston's downtown.

How does one account for the obvious contrasts in urban structure among the North End, Back Bay, Prudential Center, and the Big Dig? These contrasting urban landscapes within Boston may be partly attributed to the *economic circumstances* of Boston at the time of their development. Thus the North End and

FIGURE 2-6 Aerial view of Boston's Back Bay (foreground) and
                Prudential Center, planned developments of the 1860s and 1960s,
                respectively. *(Photo by author.)*

financial district originally served as the core of a crowded, mercantile settlement
oriented chiefly to its wharves. Back Bay originated, and in part still serves, as an
elite residential quarter reflecting Boston's prominence as a center of education,
finance, and culture (Whitehill 1968). The Prudential Center involved the revitalization of a blighted site to enhance Boston's function as a corporation headquarters and convention site (Conzen and Lewis 1976, 50). And the Big Dig reflects a
belief of public officials in the 1990s that highway traffic and urban open space may
be mutually accommodated through urban reconstruction.

   Changes in *technology* also underlie some of the perceived contrasts in Boston.
Transportation has evolved from foot and sailing vessels in the seventeenth century, to trains and streetcars in the nineteenth century, to automobiles, trucks, and
elevators in the twentieth century. Construction technology has moved from the
era of clapboard and shingle, to brick and slate, to reinforced concrete, glass, and
steel, and most recently to the use of high-tech instruments such as lasers, global
positioning systems (GPS), and computer-enhanced design.

   In addition to economic function and technology, differences among urban districts may be attributed to the *legal context* at the time of their construction, particularly the extent and form of public intervention in the private building process. Boston's early growth was largely organic. Efforts by the town selectmen to constrain individual freedom in building were limited to measures concerned with fire, as in specifying materials to be used in roofing and chimneys and in requiring householders to possess fire-fighting implements (Bridenbaugh 1964, 55–61). Otherwise, the town placed few restrictions on the layout of individual structures and the cows had their way.

Back Bay, by contrast, was a totally preconceived expansion of Boston. New land created by filling of the malodorous swamps bordering the growing city was legally owned by the Commonwealth of Massachusetts, which historically holds tidelands in trust for the public. In 1856, a multipartite agreement to govern the filling and development of the fens was executed between the Commonwealth, the City of Boston, and various private proprietors (Whitehill 1968, 151). Pursuant to this agreement, the Commissioners on the Back Bay, a legal entity created by the legislature in 1852, exercised plenary control over the layout of streets and disposition of parcels. Purchasers of building lots were required to accept deed restrictions limiting the use, height, and external appearance of structures. Municipal land use zoning would not appear in Boston until after World War I. Meanwhile, deed restrictions provided strict legal control to ensure harmonious development of Back Bay.

The mid-twentieth-century Prudential Center legally resembles nineteenth-century Back Bay to the extent that public authorities promoted the development of an underutilized site (in this case a railroad yard) and controlled its form and usage through deed restrictions. Prudential Center, however, involved other legal devices as well. The site, including the *air rights* or space above the rail yard, had to be *condemned*, that is, purchased by a public agency from the previous owner at a price set by a court. It was then reconveyed at a lower cost to the redevelopment corporation. This reconveyance was required to provide an auditorium and convention hall, as well as public ways and parking spaces, as a condition to constructing private commercial space. A special state law deferred certain real estate taxes for up to forty-five years as a subsidy to the development's future profitability (Haar 1963, 181–82). Prudential Center thus resulted from a complex interaction of public and private initiatives characteristic of much contemporary metropolitan development (Platt 1994). Finally, the Big Dig has resulted from the politics and generous federal highway subsidies of the late twentieth century.

In summary, legal impacts on the human landscape assume many forms and operate in subtle and sometimes contradictory ways (e.g., laws favoring economic development versus laws to protect the environment). These laws interact with nonlegal constraints, such as site and situation, economic conditions, culture, and technology, in various combinations.

The relative influence of law differs from one time period to another and from site to site. For example, a further tour along the Boston waterfront reveals a highly differentiated geography of public and private legal interaction as one proceeds from the revitalized Faneuil Hall Market to the former Charlestown Navy Yard, the New England Aquarium, Rowe's Wharf, and the proposed Fan Pier and other projects on the South Boston waterfront. Simply the provision of new walkways and docks along the waterfront has a complex legal history involving a 1641 colonial ordinance, as applied by a court decision in 1979 (*Boston Waterfront Development Corp. v. Commonwealth* 393 N.E.2d 356), that led to amendments to the state waterfront law to require private developers to provide public access as a condition to construction on existing or former tidelands (under the so-called *public trust doctrine*) (Archer et al. 1994). Among the many legal devices applied to redevelopment of the Boston waterfront are flexible zoning provisions, historic restoration tax credits, tidelands building lines, endangered species laws, and accelerated depreciation.

A Model of the Interaction of Land Use and Society

The complexity of land use management—types of decision makers, the powers they exert, and the interactions between them—tends to obscure an understanding of the overall process: the "forest cannot be seen for the trees." Furthermore, the legal perspective on land use, as stated earlier, views the decision process as adversarial between private and public interests. In fact, both private and public land use decision makers jointly, although not always amicably, determine how a society uses its land resources for better or worse.

Figures 2-7 and 2-8 represent the interaction of the three sets of spatial data discussed earlier, namely (1) physical, (2) human/cultural, and (3) legal/political, in two ways. Figure 2-7 portrays these three "geographies" as templates or layers overlying and shaping the resulting landscape. The dynamic interaction of these three "geographies" over time is depicted in the land use and society model in Figure 2-8. Thus any place or tract of land may be analyzed in terms of the interaction of (1) the physical characteristics of the site itself, (2) the institutions that collectively determine how that land may or (or may not) be used, and (3) the resulting patterns of land and water usage (i.e., the human landscape). Specified units of land area (a state, town, farm, or building site, for example) may be analyzed in terms of these three sets of geographical variables.

The model (Figure 2-8) links the circles or data sets with arrows or vectors. The most important vector is labeled *resource management*, the process by which society organizes the use of land, water, and air. This vector represents the aggregate influence of both *private*-sector decisions (by owners, households, builders, financial institutions, etc.) as well as *public* authorities (local, state, federal, other) that jointly determine how land is used. The relative weight of the private sector versus the public sector varies greatly from one locality and state to another and from one type of land use to another. Disputes arising between the public and private sectors, as well as conflicts among members of those sectors (e.g., neighbor versus neighbor, town versus town), may be submitted to the court system for decisions, as discussed earlier. Resource management thus represents the collective output of the legal process, a result of possibly years of legal and political wrangling.

Two input vectors to the "legal circle" inform the decision makers within that

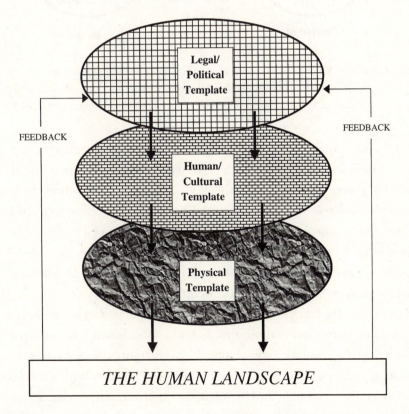

FIGURE 2-7 Three sets of spatial data (templates) for analyzing landscape:
(1) legal/political, (2) human/cultural, and (3) physical.

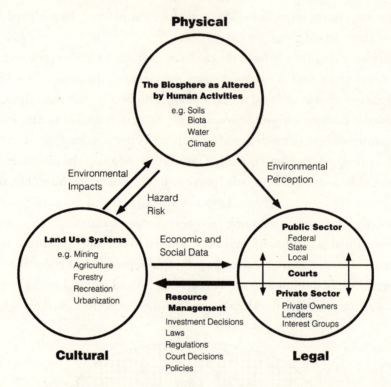

FIGURE 2-8 The Land Use and Society model: dynamic interaction of the three sets of spatial data. (This model is referenced throughout the book to describe societal response to perceived land use and environmental problems.)

circle and thus influence, to some degree, the resource-management output. One of these is *environmental perception*, a term used broadly to refer to the flow of information concerning the state of the physical resource, as modified by human activities (the *environmental impact* vector). Environmental indicators include data concerning the sustainability of particular land uses, risks posed by natural or technological hazards, and, in general, the actual or possible environmental effects of using land in a particular way. The *economic and social* vector represents feedback on the financial and social effects of a land use.

The process of feedback is not simple. Private and public decision makers weigh environmental and socioeconomic information very differently according to their specific objectives. Until the 1960s, economic profitability prevailed over resource degradation and social effects in decisions affecting land use. With the rise of the environmental movement in the late 1960s, the *environmental perception* vector has gained some weight in the United States, but its influence fluctuates with political commitment and the state of the economy. The social impacts of land use decisions have also received some recognition, as in *fees* charged to commercial developers to facilitate provision of affordable housing in the community.

Diverse agencies and levels of government may differ in their goals. For instance, a long-debated plan to renourish the beach at Fire Island, New York, pits two federal agencies against each other: the Army Corps of Engineers (which would oversee the project) advocates the plan to protect property and the local economy, whereas the U.S. Fish and Wildlife Service opposes the project due to its possible harm to the piping plover, an endangered species of beach bird (Platt 1999, Chap. 6). Likewise, property owners fight with their town or county governments, and often with their neighbors, over land use issues. The resulting outcome—which may be no action at all—ensues from the playing out of the "land use game" (a phrase adapted from Richard Babcock's 1966 book, *The Zoning Game*). Whatever the name of the game, the model's "legal circle" represents the playing field (or the battlefield).

The interactive loop of the model is completed by the *environmental impact* vector. This vector represents the modification of the physical environment by human activities, at either the macroscale or the microscale. In the agricultural context, row cropping on hilly terrain hastens soil erosion and causes sedimentation and pollution of downstream water bodies; irrigation may lead to salinization of the soil mantle or, where drawing from groundwater, to a lowering of aquifer levels. Such practices, if continued unchecked, may lead to a loss of productivity in the areas affected and eventually to a destruction of the physical resource. (See discussion of the "Tragedy of the Commons" in Chapter 3.) If and when the harm of existing practices is perceived by government, new laws and regulations may modify the way the land use activity is conducted. Or perhaps a well-informed private owner (individual or corporation) may institute more sustainable land use practices on land within his or her control, such as a timber company that practices selective harvesting rather than clear-cutting every tree in sight.

Thus the model in Figure 2-8 depicts a dynamic feedback process whereby a particular land use activity in the human/cultural circle may be modified by a new set of resource-management signals issued from the legal/political circle in response to new awareness of the impacts of existing practices on the physical world. This new awareness may result from a single dramatic catastrophe, which instantly leads to revision of the prevailing rules, as when the 1666 Great Fire of London led to a dramatic reform of building practices in the Act for Rebuilding London of 1667 (discussed in Chapter 3). Or it may result from a change in social values regarding an existing state of affairs that, previously acceptable or ignored, becomes intolerable and leads to legislative reform. Thus the sanitary reform movement of the 1840s and the progressive movement in the early twentieth century focused public attention on conditions of urban squalor and overcrowding and prompted the adoption of sanitary codes and zoning laws. (See Chapters 5 and 6.) The years since the 1960s have witnessed a proliferation of new environmental laws and programs in response to growing perception of environmental deterioration as documented by Rachel Carson, Barry Commoner, Lester Brown, Paul Ehrlich, Gilbert F. White, and many others.

Today, the feedback loop of the land use model is laboring to formulate legal response to the growing recognition of new threats to the biosphere in the form of global warming, stratospheric ozone depletion, and deforestation. The legal circle must expand geographically to embrace multiple nation-states and international institutions. A major success at that level was the 150-nation protocol to ban the use of chlorofluorocarbons (CFCs) that destroy the ozone layer. The agreement was stimulated by uncontrovertible scientific evidence of an "ozone hole" over Antarctica. This new "environmental perception" input thus elicited a change in "resource management" at the international level with measurable benefit. According to Lester Brown (2001, 255) of the Earth Policy Institute, "The negotiation of the Montreal Protocol and its implementation represent one of the finest hours of the United Nations." Thus the model sometimes works at the global scale. Yet the fate of the 1997 Kyoto Agreement on reducing greenhouse gases in 2003 remains in limbo for lack of U.S. leadership.

Over time, specific legal institutions and measures have thus emerged in response to the prevailing coalescence of political, social, and economic objectives regarding land use. As societal conditions and expectations changed, however, the broad legal concepts did not necessarily vanish, although specific applications may have been superseded. Like the woodstove and the windmill, the legal approaches of earlier eras remain available for subsequent rediscovery. Earlier practices, laws, and perceptions, however, may also impede social adaptation to new research findings. We must continually adapt our institutions for managing the use of land, air, and water at all scales so as to better respond to new knowledge and threats. In the words of William D. Ruckelshaus (1989, 167), former administrator of the Environmental Protection Agency, who also opened this chapter:

> Sustainability is the nascent doctrine that economic growth and development must take place, and be maintained over time within the limits set by ecology in the broadest sense—by the interrelations of human beings and their works, the biosphere and the physical and chemical [and geographical] laws that govern it.

References

Archer, J. H., D. L. Connors, K. Laurence, S. C. Columbia, and R. Bowen. 1994. *The Public Trust Doctrine and the Management of America's Coasts*. Amherst: University of Massachusetts Press.

Babcock, R. F. 1966. *The Zoning Game*. Madison: University of Wisconsin Press.

Beresford, M. 1967. *New Towns of the Middle Ages*. New York: Praeger.

Berry, B. J. L., and J. B. Parr. 1988. *Market Centers and Retail Location: Theory and Applications*. Englewood Cliffs, NJ: Prentice Hall.

Bridenbaugh, C. 1964. *Cities in the Wilderness: Urban Life in America 1625–1742*. New York: Capricorn Books.

Brown, L. 2001. *Eco-Economy: Building an Economy for the Earth*. New York: W. W. Norton.

Bullard, R. D., G. S. Johnson, and A. O. Torres. 2000. *Sprawl City: Race, Politics, and Planning in Atlanta*. Washington, DC: Island Press.

Castagnoli, F. 1971. *Orthogonal Town Planning in Antiquity*. Cambridge, MA: MIT Press.

Clark, G. L. 1985. *Judges and the Cities*. Chicago: University of Chicago Press.

Clay, G. 1973. *Close-Up: How to Read the American City*. Chicago: University of Chicago Press.

Conzen, M. P., and G. Lewis. 1976. *Boston: A Geographical Portrait*. Cambridge, MA: Ballinger.

DeGrove, J. M., and N. E. Stroud. 1987. State Land Planning and Regulation: Innovative Roles in the 1980s and Beyond. *Land Use Law* (March): 3–8.

Grimal, P. 1954/1983. *Roman Cities*. Trans. and ed. G. M. Woloch. Madison: University of Wisconsin Press.

Haar, C. M. 1963. The Social Control of Urban Space. In *Cities and Space*, ed. L. Wingo Jr. Baltimore: Johns Hopkins University Press.

Hartshorne, R. 1939. *The Nature of Geography*. Lancaster, PA: Association of American Geographers.

James, P. E., and G. J. Martin. 1981. *All Possible Worlds: A History of Geographical Ideas*. 2nd ed. New York: Wiley.

Jefferson, T. 1784/1944. Notes on Virginia. In *The Life and Selected Writings of Thomas Jefferson*, ed. A. Koch and W. Peden, 187–292. New York: Modern Library.

Johnston, N. J. 1983. *Cities in the Round*. Seattle: University of Washington Press.

Jordan-Bychkov, T. G., and M. Domosh. 1999. *The Human Mosaic: A Thematic Introduction to Cultural Geography*. New York: Addison-Wesley.

Kusler, J. A. 1985. Roles along the Rivers: Regional Problems Meet National Policy. *Environment* 27 (7): 18–20, 37–44.

Locke, J. 1689/1952. *Second Treatise of Government*. New York: Liberal Arts Press.

Morrill, R. L. 1970. *The Spatial Organization of Society*. Belmont, CA: Wadsworth.

Mullin, J. R. 1992. The Reconstruction of Lisbon Following the Earthquake of 1755: A Study in Despotic Planning. *Planning Perspectives* 7:157–79.

Palm, R. 1981. *The Geography of American Cities*. New York: Oxford University Press.

Platt, R. H. 1994. Commentary on "The Entrepreneurial City: Fabricating Urban Development in Syracuse, New York." *The Professional Geographer* 46 (2): 250–51.

———. 1999. *Disasters and Democracy: The Politics of Extreme Natural Events*. Washington, DC: Island Press.

Reps, J. 1969. *Cities of the American West: A History of Frontier Urban Planning*. Princeton, NJ: Princeton University Press.

Ruckelshaus, W. D. 1989. Toward a Sustainable World. *Scientific American* 261 (3): 166–70.

Sitte, C. 1945. *City Planning According to Artistic Principles*. New York: Random House.

Stanislawski, D. 1946. The Origin and Spread of the Grid-Pattern Town. *Geographical Review* 36 (1): 105–20.

———. 1947. Early Spanish Town Planning in the New World. *Geographical Review* 37 (1): 94–105.

Vance, J. E., Jr. 1977. *This Scene of Man*. New York: Harpers College Press.

Wartenberg, C. M., trans. 1966. *Von Thunen's Isolated State: An English Edition of* Der Isolierte Staat. Elmhurst, NY: Pergamon Press.

Whitehill, W. M. 1968. *Boston: A Topographical History*. 2nd ed. Cambridge, MA: Harvard University Press.

Whittlesey, D. W. 1935. The Impress of Effective Central Authority upon the Landscape. *Annals of the Association of American Geographers* 25:85–97.

PART II

*From Feudalism to
Federalism: The Social
Organization of Land Use*

CHAPTER 3

Historic Roots of Modern Land Use Institutions

*The common bell called the commons to the town from the common streets
and the green commons to the common hall and in common hall assembled
a common seal to release their common land, for which a fine is paid into
their common chest. All is common; nothing is public.*

—F. W. MAITLAND, TOWNSHIP AND BOROUGH, 1898, 32

The concepts of property rights and land use law in the United States owe much
to the legal systems of Great Britain, France, and Spain at the time of European
settlement of North America. In particular, the English "common-law" institutions of private property and local government were transplanted directly to
American soil with the founding of the Massachusetts Bay and Virginia colonies
and their offshoots in the early seventeenth century. Judicial precedent from the
courts of the home country were directly applied in the colonies, and most states
today still retain vestiges of the English common law relating to land. States originally settled under Spanish or French conquest, including Florida, Louisiana,
Texas, New Mexico, Arizona, and California, also reflect the influence of the "civil
law" tradition that prevailed in continental Europe dating to back to early Roman
and Germanic roots.

These two imports, common law and civil law, blended in various combinations
in different places with native land rights, religious laws, and local custom. As settlement moved westward, new legal doctrines were devised to adapt to different
geographic environments, most notably the "prior appropriation" water rights
doctrine that evolved in arid regions during the nineteenth century to ensure scarce
water for mining and agriculture. After the American Revolution, imported

65

colonial property law concepts coexisted (sometimes uneasily) with the property rights implications of the U.S. Constitution, as interpreted in legislation, court decisions, and administrative regulations to the present time.

This chapter reviews the evolution of English legal practice concerning land use from its origins in feudalism predating the Norman Conquest of 1066 through the dawn of modern public and private land use institutions in the seventeenth and eighteenth centuries. This discussion leads into Chapter 4, where some of the institutional origins and innovations of the industrial city and metropolis during the nineteenth century are examined.

The Feudal Commons: Sustainability in the Dark Ages

Private ownership of land is fundamental to modern capitalism, the dominant economic system in most developed and many developing countries today. *Capitalism*, according to *Webster's New University Dictionary*, is "an economic system marked by open competition in a free market, in which the means of production and distribution are privately or corporately owned." In terms of land, capitalism involves the fragmentation (or "parcelization") of land resources among multiple ownership units of diverse size and function. Aside from areas reserved in public ownership, the dominant "legal landscape" of capitalist countries today, as noted in Chapter 2, is a mosaic (or "battlefield") of large and small parcels of land held by diverse owners. *Ownership* implies freedom to use land as the owner wishes, subject to minimum legal constraints imposed by society to limit harmful externalities. (See Chapter 7.) A further attribute of capitalism is social inequity, whereby a small fraction of the population owns or controls most of the land while the rest of the population owns little or nothing. The transition from common rights to proprietary rights is illustrated in Figure 3-1.

The purpose at the moment is not to extol or condemn capitalism, but rather to contrast it with its predecessor, the *feudal commons*. Feudalism was the prevailing socioeconomic system of England and continental Europe from as early as the ninth century until approximately the seventeenth century. It prevailed in Japan into the nineteenth century and in parts of China and Russia into the early twentieth century.

Under feudalism, land was not privately owned in the modern sense, but rather was "held" by the Crown by virtue of inheritance, marriage, or conquest. The Crown allocated portions of his or her realm to faithful nobles or *lords* who in turn divided their shares (*fiefdoms*) among local aristocracy known in England as

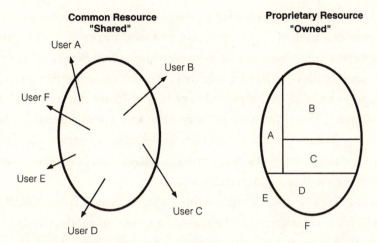

FIGURE 3-1 Diagram of common and proprietary (or capitalist) forms of land tenure. Note the inequality of resulting land holdings and the dispossession of some peasants under proprietary land tenure (right side of diagram).

barons. Supporting this pyramid of barons, lords, and Crown was the peasant class (also known as *villeins*, *commoners*, or *serfs*), which provided the labor to wrest food, fiber, and other necessities of life from the land.

Members of the peasantry were assured a minimal level of subsistence and safety provided they rendered a portion of the products of the land as *tribute* to support the households, courts, and armies of the nobility and Crown. Although thus assuring a "safety net" to the peasantry, who were essential to the entire system, feudalism was unquestionably oppressive. Like worker ants in an ant colony, the peasantry were bound to the land and sentenced to short lifetimes of labor, tedium, darkness, and ignorance, lightened only by visions of redemption offered by the church and copious consumption of beer and ale.

Despite its inequity, however, a land use system that endured many centuries in many regions of the world deserves a closer look. The system of mutual interdependence known as feudalism arose not from royal decree or statute but from practical necessity. The collapse of the Roman Empire throughout Europe after the sixth century A.D. ended centuries of urbanism, trade, and military protection, leaving the surviving populations to revert to a precarious agrarian existence. Mere survival against starvation, freezing weather, and hostile attack assumed paramount importance. In the words of Lewis Mumford (1961, 249): "From the eighth century to the eleventh, the darkness thickened; and the early period of violence, paralysis, and terror worsened with the Saracen and the Viking invasions. Everyone sought security."

Security was achieved, to the extent possible, through the evolution of the feudal hierarchy of authority. Petty monarchs and local warlords assumed transient control over particular districts only to be overthrown from time to time by invading "barbarian hordes" or jealous neighbors. To sustain continuous preparations for war and to indulge in the pleasures of riotous living during peacetime, the Crown exacted "tribute" from the nobility who in turn demanded the same from the peasantry. Tribute—the upward flow of resources in return for security—included a portion of the food and fiber produced by the serfs, monetary taxes, and able-bodied men to be slaughtered in battle.

The socioeconomic foundation of this entire system was the *feudal manor*, within which the commons was the prevalent system of productive land use. A manor typically consisted of an extensive tract of land divided into (1) *arable* or cropland, (2) *green common* or pasture, and (3) *waste*, including woods, ponds, wetlands, and uplands (Figure 3-2). The nucleus of the manor was a village settlement. This center was no borough or town, but merely a cluster of dwellings huddled near the baron's hall, a parish church, and a water-powered mill. The manorial village had no legal or corporate status but served as the domicile and socioeconomic nexus of the local baron and peasantry. The baron's manor hall served as gathering place and occasionally as court for the village (Trevelyan 1953, 199ff.).

Members of the peasantry shared access rights to the land "in common," that is, they held roughly equal rights to cultivate, graze, fish, and forage upon the common lands. Common rights in land differ markedly from private rights. In a commons, no individual has exclusive and permanent control (*proprietary rights*) over any particular land or resource. Instead, rights of usage (*usufructory rights*) are shared or exercised in common among members of a defined socioeconomic group such as a village or tribe whose members exercise exclusive control over a particular area of land.

The feudal manor in its ideal form represented a balance between population and resources. Use of the land required the limitation of individual greed and desire for short-term gain in the interest of long-term productivity. This situation in turn required a state of legal equilibrium in which all parties, nobility and peasantry alike, were bound by customary rules and constraints in the use of manorial resources.

The degree of control differed among the three classes of manorial lands: *arable*, *green common,* and *waste*. Apparently little regulation was needed regarding the

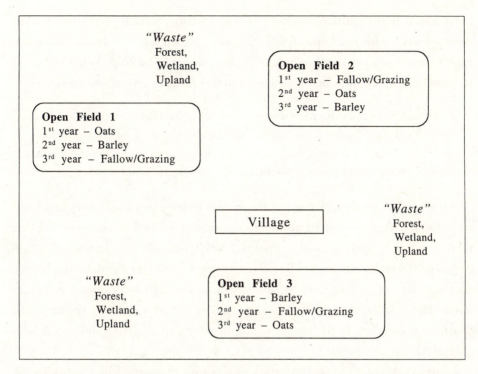

FIGURE 3-2 Diagram of land allocation in an English feudal manor. The use of each of the three "open fields" would rotate annually to ensure soil replenishment.

use of "waste." As long as population pressure was low, fish, game, and firewood were adequate (although the killing of wildlife in protected royal forests was a capital offense). "Green common" was normally subject to limitations on the number of livestock that each household, including the baron's, could graze.

Management of the arable was more complicated. A manor's cropland was usually divided into three large open fields. These three fields were rotated annually among wheat, oats, and fallow. This customary cycle allowed the soil to restore itself to ensure long-term productivity. Fertility was also maintained through the application of human and animal wastes. In its fallow year, a field was grazed by livestock to restore its soil nutrients, and "night soil" (human waste) was regularly deposited on all the fields.

Each open field was internally divided into small strips of approximately one acre each. Certain strips were reserved to support the baron's household and provide tribute to the higher nobility. The remaining strips were allocated among the tenants as *commoners*. Each commoner household was assured the use of about thirty 1-acre strips, from which it derived food and fiber for its own sustenance and for tribute to the baron. (Commoners also had to cultivate the baron's strips.) Allotments of strips within the open fields were interspersed side by side and end to end rather than being clustered in blocks under a single household. What this fragmentation lacked in productive efficiency, it theoretically gained in equity:

> It is probable that the strips were scattered in this way in order to give each [commoner] a little bit of the good land, a little bit of the indifferent, and a little bit of the bad. To allot to each owner a continuous area, compensating by extent of area for deficiency in quality, was beyond the powers of a primitive community. (Holdsworth 1927, 39)

Although internally apportioned, the open field was a species of commons. Individual strips were not fenced and were separated only by low ridges of soil that served as both boundaries and footpaths. During the fallow cycle, animals could be pastured without the need to be tethered within particular strips. Undoubtedly, conflicts arose regarding trespass, vandalism, or encroachment on one another's strips. These disputes were settled in a peculiarly feudal institution: the manorial court, an antecedent to the future courts of equity in England and its colonies (Trevelyan 1953, 173–76).

Land management in feudal England was thus dominated by the commons. Much of the manorial land was literally shared in common, and even allocated cropland in open fields was subject to a high degree of collective mutual involvement. The use of one's own strips was dependent on the compatible use of surrounding land. No one, not even the baron, was free to break out of this system and introduce new crops or fence in their strips, as whimsically described by the English legal historian F. W. Maitland in the quotation beginning this chapter.

The last sentence of that quotation ("All is common; nothing is public") is vital to understanding the early development of social control of land use. Under feudalism, there was no *public* regulation or management of land. The manorial system was symbolically subject to the power of baron, lord, and crown. In fact, none of these could tinker with the system of open fields and commons without toppling the entire delicately balanced structure. When William the Conqueror invaded England in 1066, he replaced the vanquished Saxon nobility with his own Norman followers and installed himself as king, but he did not tamper with the equilibrium of the existing system of manor and commons. Instead, he simply inventoried the assets and resources of each manorial unit of his realm. The record of that epic survey survives as the legendary *Domesday Book* of 1086, one of England's most important historic documents (Trevelyan 1953, 171).

This system was perhaps the best example in all history of a land management system that was self-perpetuating and sustainable:

> We underrate the automatism of ancient agriculture.... So far as the arable land is concerned, the common-field husbandry, when once it has been started, requires little regulation.... [By 1803 in Cambridge, England], for some centuries the common-field husbandry had needed no regulation; it had been maintaining itself. (Maitland 1898, 25)

Why was the commons so durable as a land-management institution? In early medieval England and Europe, there was no feasible alternative to the commons as a means of organizing land use to supply a reliable supply of food and fiber. Stability, however, does not necessarily imply efficiency or vitality. The stifling conformity of feudalism discouraged innovation and creativity. The arrival of the plague or "Black Death" in the fourteenth century killed a tenth of Europe's population (Tuchman 1978, Chap. 5). The ensuing depopulation of feudal manors placed increasing pressure on the labor-intensive commons system of land rights. Concurrently, as discussed later, the revival of trade and towns attracted the more enterprising of the peasantry to flee the manors. Trade with the Continent and the rise of wool production in England to serve the looms of the Low Countries stimulated members of the landed nobility to seek approval to *enclose* (fence off) common lands for sheep raising for their private gain.

Because common rights were protected by common law, they could be abridged only by statute. Beginning as early as 1235, Parliament adopted a long series of special acts authorizing specified tracts of land to be *enclosed* or "privatized" to the exclusion of commoners who were forced to choose between working as hired laborers or seeking employment elsewhere (Gonner 1966, 43). The commoners resisted this erosion of their livelihood and security as best they could, sometimes resorting to open violence, but with little success. The enclosure movement represented a gradual but distinct social and legal revolution in which common rights in land were slowly extinguished and replaced with the modern system of private rights in land, a process consistent with the general model of land-law interaction proposed in Chapter 2. Feudalism was thus gradually replaced in England with private ownership of land and its products, the hallmark of modern capitalism. Elsewhere, the end of feudalism was more abrupt, and sometimes led in directions other than capitalism (e.g., the Russian Revolution of 1918).

The early settlement of New England in the seventeenth century coincided with the last stage of the open field or commons system of land tenure in England.

Settlers originating in various districts of England initially established the system of land tenure that prevailed in their place of origin, either open field or private proprietorship. Sudbury, Massachusetts, for instance, followed the open field practice of Sudbury, England, for its first few decades (Powell 1963). Each family was granted by the original proprietors a small house lot and garden for personal use, together with rights to plant crops and graze livestock on the town's open or common fields. Eventually, in both Sudburys the open field system, a legacy of the vanishing feudal manor, yielded to private ownership of farmland.

A type of commons persists to the present time in England and the northeastern United States in the form of patches of green space in the centers of old towns. Yet could a citizen of Boston today cut firewood or graze a cow on Boston Common? Clearly the legal status, purposes, and usage regulations of these open spaces have changed. The village common is no longer common property of the inhabitants, but instead is owned and managed by the local municipal government for such allowed uses as recreation, farm markets, carnivals, and parking.

In a different sense, however, the modern world is awash in common resources: the oceans, major rivers and lakes, the atmosphere, outer space. Streets, parks, subways, and schools have elements of the commons. Traditional village and tribal societies manage fisheries, cropland, and forest resources in ways reminiscent of the feudal commons.

This use today suggests a critical problem concerning the viability of common property regimes, namely the degree to which users maintain control over the common resource and are able to limit or exclude additional users. Under feudalism, common land tenure worked because populations were small and social units were reasonably well defined by locality. Such arrangements are called a *closed-access commons*, and they are characterized by internal order and exclusivity. There are many forms of self-managed, closed-access commons today, such as tribal or village regimes regarding fishing, forestry, wildlife, and other shared resources (Ostrom 1990). Another example is the swimming pool of a YMCA. If open to anyone to use without supervision or rules, chaos and accidents would result and personal benefits would be minimal. By installing lane dividers and requiring lap swimming at peak times, the resource benefits are optimized.

Where access is not closed and potential users are indefinite in number (an *open-access commons*), lack of mutual restraint on overuse may lead to destruction of the resource. This dilemma is a chronic one in the twenty-first century in the context of global warming and degradation of oceans, lakes, and ecosystems. The threat of failure of open-access common resources has been termed the *tragedy of the commons* by the biologist Garrett Hardin (1968). According to Hardin's gloomy axiom, if shared resources are not regulated through group or social self-restraint, individual users will inevitably maximize their own gains to their eventual mutual harm:

> Ruin is the destination toward which all men rush, each pursuing his own best interest in a society that believes in the freedom of the commons. *Freedom in a commons brings ruin to all*. (Hardin 1968, 1244; emphasis added)

Since publication of "The Tragedy of the Commons," the notion of the "commons" has been associated with the threat of global and regional environmental disaster, overpopulation, and mutual genocide. The metaphor of the commons also has been applied to cyberspace, public information, gene pools, and other resources facing erosion through overuse and commodification (Bollier 2002). A central challenge of the twenty-first century may be defined as the avoidance of the tragedy of the commons through new social institutions to control the abuse and destruction of common resources of many kinds, achieving the sustainability of the feudal commons without consigning most of the world's population to serfdom. (See the Ruckelshaus quotations at the beginning and end of Chapter 2.)

Medieval Cities: The Municipal Idea

The feudal commons was essentially a rural institution that was ill-suited to the governance of urban communities. As the quote beginning this chapter so vigorously stated, the commons involved no concept of "public." All transactions were based on custom and personal status, not on formally adopted laws. The revival of towns and cities in England and the Continent starting in the early Middle Ages called for the development of new institutions more suited to the governance of closely built, nonagricultural settlements. One of those new institutions, the *municipal corporation*, has lasted from medieval times into the twenty-first century as the legal form of the modern city and suburb.

Conditions for Urban Revival

As described earlier, after the fall of the Roman Empire, feudalism blanketed England and Europe like a miasma, smothering commercial and artistic

exuberance and confining most of the population to a short, ignorant, pastoral existence. Only the Christian Church through its far-flung cathedrals and abbeys, as
well as Islamic sanctuaries in southern Europe and North Africa, preserved classical literature and art. The cultural deep freeze of the Dark Ages (approximately
the sixth through the twelfth centuries A.D.) was accompanied by the stagnation
and abandonment of once thriving Roman cities such as Paris, Rome, London, and
York.

The ancient walled cities would not forever remain moribund, inhabited by
monks, cats, and Roman ghosts. By the eleventh century, hints of a coming urban
revival could be detected. According to French historian Henri Pirenne (1952),
the prerequisite to this process was the revival of trade between regions that in
turn gave rise to the need for urban markets and cities in which to hold them.
This development would lead to the regrowth of a merchant class that would
inhabit cities and towns and give them political as well as functional importance.
Broadly speaking, the urban revival was characterized by (1) an increase in urban
populations largely due to migration from rural areas; (2) the reappearance of a
middle class engaged in manufacturing and commerce; (3) the construction of new
buildings both within and outside the old city walls; (4) the emergence of the *municipal corporation* (or *municipality*) as a new legal institution independent of feudalism;
and (5) the onset of urban problems such as water supply, disease, crime, and fire.

The market function of medieval cities involved both a *physical* space within the
protection of the walls and a *legal* climate within which trade could flourish. The
physical marketplace was typically a central open space at the heart of the old
walled city, surrounded by the cathedral, town hall, guild hall, and other civic
buildings. The marketplace was multifunctional; besides its commercial role, it
provided open space for ecclesiastic and civic ceremonies, social interaction, and
games (Mumford 1961). Today, many European marketplaces retain these functions, along with outdoor cafes, political demonstrations, street life, and parking.

For a marketplace to function, it had to be accessible. Streets leading from the
city gates to the market had to be wide enough for people, animals, and carts to
squeeze past one another. Given the scarcity of buildable land within the walls,
streets and the marketplace itself were subject to chronic pressure of encroachment
by adjoining property owners. This pressure was opposed, not by building laws,
which were rarely effective if they existed at all, but literally by the throng of
humanity and traffic: "Streets will be as narrow as they can be while allowing for
transit of goods and persons" (Saalman 1968, 30) (Figures 3-3 and 3-4).

FIGURE 3-3 Riverfront view of Frankfurt Am Main, 1646.
(Source: Saalman 1968, plate 38.)

FIGURE 3-4
Plan of Frankfurt
Am Main, 1646, a
classic late-medieval
walled city. Note bridge
over river connecting
the two parts of the city.
Wide streets and open
space in the lower part
of the city would be
crowded with market
activity. *(Source: Saalman
1968, plate 39.)*

In many cases, the demand for market space generated by growing trade simply outstripped available land within the city walls. As the threat of hostile attack declined, development of new markets and accompanying houses and workshops appeared outside the gates of many new cities. These areas, known in France as *faubourgs*, were the original suburbs. Pirenne (1952) stresses that their commercial functions were not limited to periodic markets or fairs but assumed the continuous nature of modern commercial districts. It is likely that commerce outside the walls was promoted in some cases by a desire to escape the restrictions imposed on trade within the walls.

Municipal Charters

The medieval city, like its modern counterparts, was both a geographic and a legal entity. Seldom of any great size in area or population, medieval cities nevertheless achieved a high degree of self-governance as virtual city-states. Legally independent of the onerous structure of feudalism, "the symbol of the city in the Middle Ages was eventually found in the sworn community which legally assumed the form of a corporation" (Weber 1899/1958, 105).

The origins of this "sworn community" are obscure. In England after the Norman Conquest in 1066, certain older towns obtained charters or grants of privileges from the Crown. Charters were either purchased or awarded as a token of royal favor. Some towns claimed the benefit of charters on the ground that they had been exercising certain powers of self-government "since time out of mind" (i.e., a very long time) and therefore such powers could not be withdrawn.

The effect of a charter was to release the town and its inhabitants from traditional feudal obligations to render tribute in money, goods, or military service. Municipal courts replaced the whim of the Crown or nobility in petty judicial matters. Persons attending the weekly market would be excused from paying a market toll to the lord, which was regarded by merchants as a hindrance to trade. In place of these feudal obligations, the town was authorized to appoint its own sheriff, raise revenue from any available sources, and render annual tribute in the form of monetary payment to the Crown:

> Charters appeared at the close of the Eleventh Century and for the next two centuries they increased both in number and in the extent of the privileges granted. The acquisition of charters finally made the majority of towns communities with extensive rights of self-government and helped to make the townsmen a distinct element in the political, social, and economic life of England. (Lunt 1956, 178)

Broadly speaking, the privileges bestowed by charter included:

- The right to hold a market
- The right to adopt municipal ordinances
- The right to establish a municipal court
- The right to organize a merchant guild
- Freedom from feudal tribute, except certain taxes
- The right to elect municipal officials
- The right to coin money and to regulate weights and measures

Citizens of towns (*burghers*) enjoyed not only commercial freedom but personal freedom as well. Even peasants who fled from their manors and resided in towns for a year and a day were legally released from their feudal bonds and gained the status of freemen:

> The status ... [of the individual under city law] was one of freedom. It is a necessary and universal attribute of the middle class.... Every vestige of rural serfdom disappeared within its walls. Whatever might be the differences and even the contrasts which wealth set up between men, all were equal as far as civil status was concerned. "The air of the city makes free," says the German proverb. (Pirenne 1952, 193)

The medieval town and countryside (*core* and *hinterland*, geographically speaking), however, maintained a symbiotic, not hostile, relationship. Towns depended on their rural hinterlands for the necessities of life as well as products to be traded in their markets. Rural manors needed markets as well as the genteel "night soil" (human waste) from well-fed burghers to fertilize the open fields. Amicable relations were often preserved with the local nobility and the church as well. In general, this period impresses the modern mind with its high degree of pragmatism and mutual interdependence among manor, aristocracy, church, and town.

Merchant Guilds

Guilds were organizations of merchants or craftsmen that wielded great influence within the medieval town and its economy. The guilds' economic and political power arose from grants of monopoly status conferred on them by the Crown. Thus the wool traders' guild could establish the place and hours of operation, standards of quality, weights and measurement, and terms of credit for all wool trading in the town. Nonmembers of the guild were either prohibited from wool trading in the town or were required to pay exorbitant fees to the guild. In addition, they could sell only to guild retailers; no nonmember middlemen were allowed (Stenton 1962, 178).

London by the early seventeenth century had more than fifty craft guilds ranging from apothecaries (druggists) to woodmongers, each with its own hall or meeting place. The leading members of the more important guilds were *ipso facto* leading citizens. The guilds provided a social and cultural dimension, and their halls were the scene of banquets, plays, and ceremonies. They also contributed to the physical development of the community. Street maintenance, construction or replacement of bridges, additions to hospitals, repair of fortifications, and most permanent of all, the building of cathedrals were all among the public-spirited works of guilds (Pirenne 1952, 186). The phrase "public-spirited" is deliberately chosen: for the first time since the fall of Rome, there was emerging a new sense of "public."

Ultimately, the influence of the guilds was reflected more enduringly in legal institutions than in bricks or mortar. Over time, medieval cities under their direction, and with the benefit of royal charters described above, assumed a new legal status as *municipal corporations*. As inventions of law, municipal corporations were vested with perpetual existence apart from the terms of particular office holders. They were empowered by charter to (1) own land and buildings, (2) sue and be sued, (3) adopt local laws, and (4) possess a corporate seal for attesting the official status of municipal documents (Holdsworth 1927). These legal characteristics of the municipal corporation have remained fairly constant from the Middle Ages to the present time. (See Chapter 8 for a discussion of modern municipal governments.)

In the medieval city, as in its modern counterpart, municipal authority extended to the entire area within the city walls, except possibly church buildings. This authority comprised public *jurisdiction*, not public *ownership*. The former was (and is) a general power to enact ordinances concerning such matters as land use and building practices within the geographic boundaries of the city. The latter is the authority of the city to directly own certain land and buildings, such as the town or city hall, police stations, schools, and public open spaces.

English municipal ordinances of the Middle Ages may be roughly divided into two classes. First were those concerned with public morals, health, and safety in the urban environment. London, for instance, had ordinances dealing with the removal of dung from stables, the lighting of streets, and "sweating houses, whereunto any lewd women resort" (Hearsey 1965, 11). These ordinances were at best unevenly enforced and, at worst, totally ignored.

The second class of ordinances dealt with offenses against trade and commerce, such as theft, overcharging, and sale of inferior goods. Penalties for these offenses, which struck directly at the economic welfare of the guilds, were swift and often harsh. For example, a baker caught selling bread of substandard weight was "strapped to a sort of low cart harnessed to a horse and dragged through the streets, accompanied by the City Minstrels playing on tabors and pipes, and finally brought back and released at his own door" (Pendrill 1937, 22). Breaches of the "market peace" such as theft or disorderly conduct were subject to far more brutal punishments:

> This city peace was a law of exception, more severe, more harsh, than that of the country districts. It was prodigal of corporal punishments: hanging, decapitation, castration, amputation of limbs. It applied in all its rigor the *lex talionis*: an eye for an eye, a tooth for a tooth. Its evident purpose was to repress derelictions through terror. (Pirenne 1952, 200)

Regulation of the urban environment was clearly of lower priority than deterring crimes against property. Petty theft of commercial goods in a public thoroughfare was a breach of the market peace and was punished severely. The permanent encroachment of private buildings into or above the same public way, however, was likely to be ignored (Saalman 1968, 30–31).

The existence of corporate jurisdiction over the medieval city therefore did not necessarily mean that such power was used effectively to regulate the placement, height, construction, or use of buildings. The resulting cityscape was characterized by narrow and twisting streets, overhanging upper stories, and prevalent use of wood as a construction material. Just as the casual disposal of human and animal waste and lack of clean water contributed to periodic epidemics, the unregulated crowding of buildings posed a constant and growing danger of citywide fire. As in modern times, reform and progress were the result not of enlightened foresight, but of bitter hindsight.

The Common Law of Property

The thirteenth century marked the dawn of the modern era of land law in England. The new era was characterized by the gradual replacement of feudal tenure with *freehold* or proprietary ownership, a process that would extend over the next six centuries (see Figure 3-1). As described earlier, feudal land was not "owned" in the modern sense, but instead was "held" by one party in subservience to another. The holder was essentially entitled only to mere right of usage (*usufruct*) in exchange for tribute rendered to someone of the next higher rank in the feudal hierarchy. A right of usage did not involve the right to sell, give, or devise the land to one's heirs. Nor, under the custom of the commons, could land be converted to different uses or removed from production: the automism of three-field agriculture simply plodded along until open fields were "enclosed" with fences and controlled by individual landlords to the exclusion of the commoners. This historic process in England, known as the *enclosure movement*, lasted over several centuries.

The transition from feudal tenure to freehold ownership of land first appeared in the reviving towns rather than the countryside. The breakdown of feudal control over land was a concomitant of the growth of personal freedom within city walls:

> With freedom of person there went on equal footing, in the city, the freedom of the land. In fact, in a merchant community, land could not remain idle and be kept out of commerce by unyielding and diverse laws that prevented its free conveyance and restrained it from serving as a means of credit and acquiring capital value.... Land within the city changed its nature—it became ground for building. It was rapidly covered with houses, crowded one against the other, and increased in value in proportion as they multiplied.... Cityhold thus became freehold. (Pirenne 1952, 194–95; emphasis added)

Just as "freehold" or private ownership was essential to city growth, feudalism had to break down in the countryside for innovation to flourish and personal wealth to be amassed (primarily by the landed aristocracy). The transformation of rural land from feudal tenure to freehold began in England with a statute of Parliament in 1290 that permitted the substitution of one landholder for another, subject to the same feudal obligations as the earlier holder. This change in effect legitimized the sale of land from one party to another on a monetary basis, which is the essence of property ownership (Dukeminier and Krier 1981, 358). Over time, feudalism withered away, and virtually all land came to be held by individual proprietors subject only to the obligation to pay taxes.

By the eighteenth century, the institution of private property ownership in both England and the American colonies was solidly established. The concept that "every man's home is his castle" was most forcefully stated by the jurist William Blackstone in 1768:

> There is nothing which so generally strikes the imagination, and engages the affections of mankind as the right of property; or that *sole and despotic dominion* which one man claims and exercises over the external things of the world, in exclusion of the rights of any other individual in the Universe. (Blackstone 1768/1863, 1; emphasis added)

Although tinged with hyperbole, Blackstone's view of private property stands the feudal tenure system on its head and exalts the landed aristocracy over the Crown. (In Great Britain today, much valuable urban land still remains under the control of landed estates that lease it for private development under long-term leases, thus helping the upper class afford their Rolls Royces.)

Yet as John Locke declared in a quotation presented in Chapter 2, private property is valueless unless the owner is secure in reaping the "harvest" or other benefits of ownership. Blackstone's proposition declares that the owner is protected from the Crown, but what about one's neighbors? The answer is found in the development of the common-law doctrines of *trespass* and *nuisance* under which a property owner could seek the protection of the courts from offensive conduct by other parties. As stated in Chapter 2, the English common law consists of the accumulated decisions of courts, based on principles declared in earlier cases involving similar issues ("precedent"). There have been innumerable common law precedents concerning trespass and nuisance.

The common law, however, has never been an efficient means of regulating the urban environment and land development practices as it only responds to actual cases brought by victims (*plaintiffs*) against alleged wrongdoers (*defendants*). If the victims are unable to bring their grievances to court, or if the wrongdoers are too numerous or unknown (e.g., as with water or air pollution), the lawsuit-driven common law is ineffective. For that reason, it was gradually supplemented (but not replaced) in the nineteenth and twentieth centuries by *public regulations* such as building laws and land use zoning (discussed in later chapters). Before the advent of such regulations, however, adjudication of disputes between private parties under the common law provided a crude means to control or punish flagrant abuses in the preindustrial urban community.

The most fundamental protection afforded by the common law was against *trespass*. Without security against unauthorized entry of unwanted persons, property ownership meant nothing. The essence of trespass was a physical entry on land or into a building by an individual who had no legal right to do so. Over time, courts expanded the doctrine of trespass to hold parties liable who allowed livestock or even water to enter on the property of another without permission. No proof of any actual damage was required because invasion of the plaintiff's premises is wrongful in itself. Anyone who enters someone else's property without the right to do so is said to be "strictly liable" and may be subject to fine or prison sentence (Prosser 1971, 357–64). The common-law doctrine of trespass since medieval times has always reflected the principle that one's home and land are sacred.

The doctrine of *nuisance* afforded additional protection to property owners under the common law. Unlike trespass, nuisance did not require any physical entry of a premises. Rather, it addressed the externalities of actions originating elsewhere—typically on adjoining land—that injured the beneficial enjoyment of the plaintiff's property. Typical forms of nuisance include blocking off a neighbor's light and air, causing bad odors and air pollution, loud continuing noises, and other externalities that impair the quiet enjoyment of nearby property. The medieval doctrine of nuisance—still cited today—was *Sic utere tuo ut alienum non laedas* (Use your property so as not to harm that of others).

This golden rule of nuisance has always been easier to express than to apply. In deciding nuisance cases, courts have traditionally attempted to *balance the equities*, that is, weigh the social benefits, if any, of the conduct complained of against the degree and type of harm suffered by the plaintiff(s). Courts usually favor the victim when the harm clearly outweighs the value of the activity. With the coming of industrialization, however, plaintiffs often lost cases in which the defendant was an industrial polluter that happened to supply a useful product and employ many people. Courts gradually became more creative in fashioning orders (*injunctions*) that limited the harmful effects of a particular enterprise without terminating it entirely.

Building Laws: Rebuilding London after the Great Fire

While medieval municipal authorities attempted to regulate urban building practices on a piecemeal basis, most rules were ignored. Part of the problem lay in the tragedy of the commons: each property owner viewed the streets and marketplaces as common property to be encroached on for private gain to the maximum extent possible. Such encroachment often took the form of overhanging second floors projecting over narrow streets with consequent loss of daylight and increased risk of fire spreading from one wooden building to another. After centuries of worsening urban congestion, London experienced a catastrophe—the Great Fire of 1666—that forced the king and Parliament to adopt and enforce the first modern building code: the Act for Rebuilding London of 1667.

London Before the Fire

Between 1400 and 1666, London's population grew from 50,000 to about 400,000 inhabitants. This eightfold demographic expansion reflected both an influx of rural laborers displaced by enclosure of common lands and immigration of persons fleeing persecution on the Continent. It was accompanied by physical expansion of London's housing stock both within and beyond the city's old Roman walls.

Queen Elizabeth I in 1580 attempted to halt the peripheral sprawl in a famous decree (anticipating the "greenbelt" laws of the mid-twentieth century) that ordered all persons to: "desist and forbear from any new buildings of any house or tenement within three miles from any of the gates of the said city of London" (quoted in Rasmussen 1934/1967, 68). This decree was a total failure as indicated by the continued growth of London outside its walls and gates. By 1666, the walled City of London was described as comprising only one-third of the total urbanized area of London: "The great urban spread had begun, and already a number of the better-off preferred to live outside the City where their work or business was" (Hearsey 1965, 2). What is now the chic West End Theatre District of London was then the rural-urban fringe with large homes interspersed among remaining common fields and small cottages.

The old Roman-walled core of London (now the financial district known simply as "The City") remained in 1666 solidly medieval in character. Prefire London was a labyrinth of narrow, twisting streets with pervasive overhanging upper stories. Wood was the usual construction material. Exterior walls were required to be of brick or stone, but "the precaution was very partially observed" (Bell 1920/1971, 11). The City was connected to the surrounding countryside by gates on the landward side and by the famous London Bridge across the Thames River. The walled City contained more than one hundred parish churches and some fifty guild or livery halls. The ancient gothic St. Paul's Cathedral, the largest in Europe, loomed above the smoky, crowded city (Hearsey 1965, 60).

The Fire

The Great Fire of September 2–7, 1666, was perhaps the first major catastrophe to be fully described by literate eyewitnesses (at least since Noah's flood!). Samuel Pepys's *Diary* relates the following:

> Jane comes in and tells me that she hears that above 300 houses have been burned down tonight by the fire we saw [the night before] and that it is now burning down all Fish-street, by London Bridge. So I made myself ready presently, and walked to the Tower, and there got up upon one of the high places, ... and there I did see the houses at that end of the bridge all on fire, and an infinite great fire on this and the other side.... So down with my heart full of trouble to the Lieutenant of the Tower, who tells me that it

begun this morning in the King's baker's house in Pudding-lane, and that it hath burned down St. Magnes Church [the first of 80 churches to be burned] and most part of Fish-street already. So I down to the water-side and there got a boat, and through bridge, and there saw a lamentable fire.... Everybody endeavoring to remove their goods, and flinging into the river, or bringing them into lighters that lay off; poor people staying in their houses as long as till the very flames touched them, and then running into boats, or clambering from one pair of stairs by the water-side to another ... and the wind mighty high, and driving it into the City; and everything after so long a drought proving combustible, even the very stones of the churches. (Pepys 1666/1898, 392–93)

In the absence of any effective water distribution system, the fire burned unchecked for three days and consumed most of London within the walls and a considerable area outside. Within this area, 13,200 houses were destroyed in some 400 streets and alleys. Over 100,000 were homeless and left camping miserably in fields outside the city. In terms of loss of life, the Great Fire of 1666 was vastly overshadowed by an outbreak of plague in London the previous year. Although 56,558 persons were reported to have died in the plague, only four deaths were attributed directly to the fire out of a population of 400,000.

The "First Modern Building Law"

The fire epitomized Hardin's (1968, 1244) adage: "Freedom in a commons brings ruin to all." Although London was scarcely a feudal commons, neglect of the urban environment under four centuries of municipal self-government had yielded disaster. Its public spaces were virtually an unregulated commons, with private structures clogging the narrow lanes and passageways and blocking access to the Thames River. In the absence of effective regulation of building size, location, and construction materials, the fire was inevitable. Without access to water, it could not be halted.

The point was not missed by certain leading minds of the time. While the ruins were still smoking, plans for the rebuilding of London were being prepared by Sir Christopher Wren, the city's leading architect, and several others (Bell 1920/1971, Chap. 13). Wren proposed to transform the city into a monumental imperial capital, much as Haussmann would later restructure Paris two centuries later (as described in Chapter 4). The prefire street alignments and property lines of London were to be abolished where necessary and replaced by an orderly, geometric network of major streets and open plazas with lesser streets leading into them. Churches, company halls, and other important buildings would be situated on the new squares or along the connecting arteries. The Thames embankment would be cleared and reserved for major buildings with open space between and in front of them. Dwellings would be confined to the lesser streets. The city should be rebuilt, according to Wren, along the lines of baroque Renaissance cities in Italy that he greatly admired.

Such a radical proposal for restructuring London, however, was incompatible with the mood of the times. First, the Crown was weakened after the English Civil War (1648–1660); the newly restored Charles II, returned from playboy exile in Europe, sought to avoid the fate of his father, Charles I, namely beheading. Second, Parliament and city authorities could not afford to pay property owners whose private lots would have been taken to implement the plan. Third, Wren's plan would take too long to implement. Finally, the plan was too grandiose and "non-English" to meet with approval of England's upper class (Hearsey 1965, 179).

A week after the fire had subsided, with the advice of Wren and others, Charles II issued a surprisingly modern-sounding proclamation calling for restraint and foresight in the rebuilding process, pending a full investigation of the causes of the disaster. The preamble to the proclamation combined seventeenth-century moralism and twentieth-century civic boosterism:

> And since it hath pleased God to lay this heavy Judgement upon Us … as evidence of His displeasure for Our sins We do comfort Our Self with some hope, that he will … give Us life, not only to see the foundations laid, but the buildings finished of a much more beautiful City than is at this time consumed. (Quoted in Rasmussen 1934/1967, 117)

The proclamation went on to address five practical city planning aspects of the rebuilding process (Rasmussen 1934/1967, 116–17):

1. Stone or brick was to be used for exterior facades in place of wood.

2. The width of streets was to be established in relation to their importance.

3. A broad quay or open area would be maintained along the Thames for access to water for firefighting.

4. Public nuisance activities such as breweries or tanneries should be removed from central London to more suitable locations.

5. Reasonable compensation should be determined and paid to property owners whose right to rebuild was curtailed by public restrictions.

Like a modern mayor or governor, the king then appointed a "blue-ribbon committee" of experts (including Wren) to draft a law to regulate the rebuilding of the city. The resulting Act for Rebuilding London was adopted on February 8, 1667, five months after the fire. What the law lacked in immediacy, it made up in detail. The act has been described as London's first "complete code of building regulations" (Bell 1920/1971, 251). It was long, detailed, and practical:

> [It] covered important aspects of the rebuilding program: first, the rearrangement of some of the worst features of the old plan, with its apparently wayward meanderings, jutting corners, and frequent bottle-necks; second, the partial standardization of the new buildings, particularly with a view to fire resistance; and third, the raising of money for the public ... buildings by a tax on coal. (Summerson 1962, 53)

By far the most lasting of the act's legacies dealt with the height and construction of dwellings to replace those burned in the fire. The size of a home that could be built on a site depended on the location and importance of the street or square on which it faced. The use of stone or brick for exterior walls was required. Thickness of walls, heights of ceilings, and other architectural details were also specified. Overhangs above the public way were prohibited. In short, the act "crystallized the best practice of the time" (Summerson 1962, 54). It was, in effect, a building code for the redevelopment of the burned area and a guide to new construction in surrounding areas. The act was farsighted in its provisions for permits and fines, a precedent for modern building codes. In addition, its regulations regarding the banishment of smoky or noxious activities to specified locations anticipated modern zoning laws.

The act was not uniformly effective, for indeed there was little experience or administrative structure to enforce its requirements. Furthermore, it did not purport to change building patterns or land usage to eliminate overcrowded alleys and courts behind other buildings. Working-class London sprang back to life still densely crowded and deprived of light and air. Such conditions would become increasingly intolerable over the next two centuries.

Although the exact influence of the act is difficult to discern from what might have occurred in its absence, it clearly marked a threshold between the medieval and the modern eras of urban land use. The lethal combination of overcrowding, use of flammable building materials, and abysmal sanitary conditions produced the twin perils of the medieval city: disease and fire, both of which struck London in tandem in 1665 and 1666. The Great Fire swept away not only the overhanging wooden houses and the rats they contained, but also the attitude of medieval neglect toward the urban environment. Charles II's moratorium on rebuilding, reinforced by the commission of experts, marked a sea change in governmental process from Elizabeth's useless edict of 1580. The Act for Rebuilding London represented the beginning of modern urban planning, although two centuries more would elapse before public building codes were widely adopted in England and the United States.

The Act for Rebuilding London exemplified the operation of the land use and society model presented in Figure 2-8: meaningful legal reform affecting the rebuilding of the urban environment resulted from improved perception of the causes of the disastrous Great Fire (Figure 3-5).

Private Land Use Restrictions

At the same time that London was being rebuilt under the 1667 act, the agricultural estates beyond the city's walls were undergoing development for the first time. The building boom north and west of the city proper (including what is now

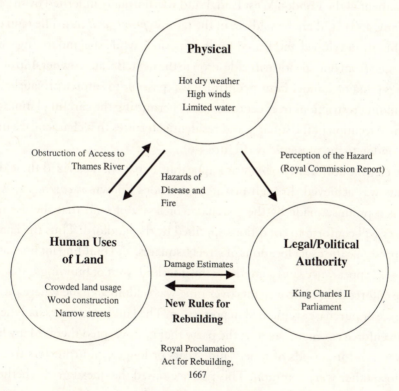

FIGURE 3-5 The land use and society model, as applied to the rebuilding of London after the Great Fire of 1666.

the fashionable West End district) was not subject to the act, but displayed never-theless a remarkable uniformity in land use pattern and architectural style. This uniformity was achieved not through governmental regulation, but through private deed or lease restrictions imposed by aristocratic landlords upon the building and occupance of new residential districts.

The building of London's residential squares between the 1630s and the 1820s provided new upper-class housing and neighborhoods near the royal palaces, clubs, offices, and social life of London. Much of this development occurred on land held by aristocratic families under ancient feudal grants or acquired when Henry VIII abolished monasteries and sold them to affluent buyers. In either case, the owners, including the royal family, were eager for land development profit. Landlords and upper-class lessees alike agreed that fashion required that the new neo-classical districts must maintain a uniform and haughty appearance to the rest of the world.

A quirk of English legal history was to determine the scale and quality of the development of the London West End. Land was normally inherited by the eldest son, if any, and could not be sold out of the family (*primogeniture*). The land could be profitably developed and leased for long periods while the underlying ownership passed from one spendthrift eldest son to the next. Because ownership of large holdings remained under family control, it was possible to enforce private land use and building restrictions over centuries, thus permitting the careful planning and uniform execution of the squares and residential terraces that characterize upper-class London to the present day (Figure 3-6).

The elegant uniformity of exterior appearance that characterized these developments was achieved through private restrictions known as *covenants*. A covenant is a promise made by the purchaser or lessee of land that the use of the premises will conform to conditions specified by the landlord. Thus the landlord could prescribe the exact locations of streets, squares, and building lot lines as well as the size, appearance, and sometimes the interior layout of buildings.

The enforceability of covenants over time was seldom an issue where the original lessee or purchaser remained in possession. The landlord always had the legal right to enforce covenants against the party that had accepted them. Many leases, however, ran for periods of ninety-nine years or longer, and transfers from one party to another were common. This practice raised the question of whether the covenants would still be enforceable against subsequent parties in possession who had not specifically accepted the restrictions. In 1848, an English court decision

FIGURE 3-6 Eighteenth-century townhouses at Bedford Square, London. Note the "to let" signs reflecting the practice of using long-term leases instead of outright sale to retain the property in the Bedford Estate. *(Photo by author.)*

(*Tulk v. Moxhay*, 41 Eng. Rep 1143) concerning London's Leicester Square ruled that covenants may be enforced against subsequent lessees or occupants of the premises. (In quaint legalese, covenants are said to *run with the land*.)

The neoclassical residential districts regulated through private covenants were the antithesis of medieval unplanned growth. They exuded wealth, conservatism, power, and control in contrast to the irregular, heterogeneous, human scale of older districts. James Craig's 1766 plan for the "New Town" in Edinburgh stands in startling contrast to the medieval Old Town. Although little of medieval vintage remains today in the Old Town, it retains a mysterious and romantic atmosphere amid the Scottish fog and gloom. Across a narrow linear park (formerly a fetid creek), Craig's eighteenth-century New Town stands elegant, symmetrical, and respectable, graced by its elegant townhouses and leafy squares, all protected by covenants (Figure 3-7).

In the United States, the English-style residential square inspired several counterparts, notably Louisburg Square in Boston's Beacon Hill, laid out by private developers in 1826, and New York City's Gramercy Park, established in 1832. Both

FIGURE 3-7
Neoclassical doorway by
Robert Adam in Edinburgh's
eighteenth-century "New
Town." The premises are now
a corporate office rather than a
home, but the external appearance
is protected by lease restrictions.
(Photo by author.)

of these squares still remain private parks, with keys available only to owners and tenants of adjacent buildings.

Today, private deed restrictions are widely used to control the use of land and buildings within subdivisions, condominium developments, and office parks, as considered in Chapter 7.

Improvement Commissions

Private deed restrictions served the needs of the wealthy to implant their concepts of style on their elite quarters. Industrial working-class districts, though, which began to grow rapidly in the eighteenth century, were a different story. London doubled from about 400,000 at the time of the Great Fire to 864,000 in 1801. Other British and Scottish industrial cities, including Manchester, Birmingham, Liverpool, and Glasgow, grew at comparable rates. Most of this population increase consisted of migration from the countryside and from Ireland and the Continent to the "satanic mills" of the industrial cities. This migration caused hideous overcrowding of existing dwellings and a proliferation of cheap, shoddy, unplanned tenement districts within walking distance to the factories and mills (Ashworth 1954).

To make matters worse, the old municipal corporations that nominally governed each city had stagnated by the eighteenth century. Municipal offices were allocated according to status and privilege, not experience or interest in reform or public service (a practice not unknown today). The corporations were unresponsive to what Ashworth (1954, 50) has termed "the increasingly lethal nature of the swelling towns." The result was a state of anarchy in the town building process in the eighteenth and nineteenth centuries, apart from elite areas developed under deed restrictions.

Not only the municipal corporations but also the courts were largely ineffectual in confronting the new circumstances. As stated earlier, abatement of *nuisance* through court intervention was limited to case-by-case treatment upon petition of the wronged party. Normally, the harm complained about had to be in existence; it was rare that courts would prohibit a prospective nuisance. In addition, the party seeking a remedy had to own the property, not be a mere tenant. Legal action was also expensive then as it is today. In theory, nuisance actions remained available, but in practice, the courts provided little restraint over the tenement-building process because the victims seldom were able to complain.

The abysmal working-class residential environment of eighteenth-century industrial England was described a century later by socialist reformers Sydney Webb and Beatrice Webb (1899/1963, 50) as follows:

> To begin with the houses—springing up on all sides with mushroom-like rapidity— there were absolutely no building regulations. Each man put up his house where and as he chose, without regard for building-line, width of street or access of light and air.... Streets of projecting houses nearly meeting at the top rooms with small windows never meant to open; and dirt in all its glory, excluded every possible access for fresh air.... The narrow ways left to foot and wheeled traffic were unpaved, uneven, and full of holes in which the water and garbage accumulated. Down the middle of the street ran a series of dirty puddles, which in time of rain became a stream of decomposing filth.

Members of the conservative ruling class in the eighteenth century—including the landed aristocracy and new capitalists—were generally disinterested in the fast-growing squalor within the cities. Creative and large-scale measures to address the crisis—for example, public sanitation and building laws, the public parks movement, urban redevelopment, and model planned towns—would not appear until the second half of the nineteenth century, as discussed in the next chapter.

One simple but practical stopgap measure, however, appeared in the late seventeenth century to address the need for better public services, namely *improvement commissions*. These commissions were established by Parliament to perform particular functions in specified cities. They were the forerunners of contemporary special districts and authorities in England and the United States. Like their modern counterparts, improvement commissions could overlie general-purpose units of government and indeed could serve more than one municipality. The first of these new institutions was the Commissioners of Scotland Yard established in 1662 to serve London. This commission was not a detective agency but rather was empowered to "make new sewers, enlarge old ones and to remove nuisances . . . to appoint public rakers or scavengers, who were to make daily rounds with 'carts, dungpots, or other fitting carriages' . . . and to remove encroachments upon public ways and to license hackney coaches" (Webb and Webb 1899/1963, 240).

Improvement commissions proliferated throughout England during the eighteenth century, numbering some three hundred by the early 1800s. They assumed many of the functions of modern local governments, such as "paving, cleansing, lighting, watching, and regulating" (Webb and Webb 1899/1963, 242). In addition, they engaged in activities of a more regional nature: building bridges and canals, improving drainage, enclosing commons, erecting markets and slaughterhouses, supplying water, and constructing highways.

Yet like the municipal corporations and courts, the improvement commissions were hampered by institutional constraints in their efforts to stem the deterioration of English cities. They were strictly limited to specified functions and geographic areas as established by Parliament. They had no general jurisdiction or "home rule" authority to address a wider spectrum of urban needs without parliamentary approval. Thus a commission responsible for paving and lighting in a particular district had no authority to deal with drainage or water supply, no matter how obvious the need. Furthermore, the improvement commissions lacked any authority to plan or regulate new building; they were largely limited to dealing with harmful conditions after the fact, not beforehand. By the early nineteenth century, these commissions:

> too often concentrated their attention solely on the middle-class districts of their towns, leaving the greater number of streets inhabited by the poorer classes wholly without essential services. However valiantly the improvement commissioners might struggle to cope with the flood-tide of urbanization—and few of them struggled very valiantly—they were fighting losing battles. [They were] constitutionally, financially, administratively, technically, and ideologically ill-equipped to cope with the frightening immensity of the task. (Flinn 1965, 17)

Improvement commissions were thus a temporary eighteenth-century expedient to remedy certain kinds of urban ills on a piecemeal basis until more sweeping public approaches were devised. They totally failed to restrain the continued proliferation of slums and the lethality of the working-class residential environment. The idea of the improvement commission, however, like the municipal corporation, was to become a permanent addition to the institutional fabric of urban and metropolitan government in Great Britain, the United States, and elsewhere.

Conclusion

The creativity of the English people and their legal system yielded a series of institutional innovations over several centuries to meet perceived needs to better organize and control the use of land. The source of each device differs considerably. Some of the institutions discussed in this chapter, such as the feudal commons and the municipal corporation, arose spontaneously from the "invisible hand" of social necessity. The doctrines of trespass and nuisance and later the recognition of private covenants as restrictions that "run with the land" were products of the English judicial system. The Act for Rebuilding London and the improvement commissions were the result of parliamentary legislation. Judicial and legislative actions continued to be the primary vehicles for reform of land use and building practices through the nineteenth and twentieth centuries. Each of these may be understood as crude efforts of society to understand and correct problems in the development of urban places, as described by the land use and society model of Figure 2-8. The historical narrative of this ongoing process from 1800 to the present time is the subject of the next three chapters.

References

Ashworth, W. 1954. *The Genesis of Modern British Town Planning*. London: Routledge & Kegan Paul.

Bell, W. G. 1920/1971. *The Great Fire of London in 1666*. Westport, CT: Greenwood Press.

Blackstone, W. 1768/1863. *Commentaries on the Laws of England* (Second Book). Philadelphia: Lippincott.

Bollier, D. 2002. *Silent Theft: The Private Plunder of Our Common Wealth*. New York: Routledge.

Dukeminier, J., and J. Krier. 1981. *Property*. Boston: Little, Brown.

Flinn, M. W., ed. 1965. *Edwin Chadwick's Report on the Sanitary Condition of the Labouring Population of Great Britain*. Edinburgh: Edinburgh University Press.

Gonner, E. C. K. 1966. *Common Land and Inclosure*. 2nd ed. London: Frank Cass.

Hardin, G. 1968. The Tragedy of the Commons. *Science* 162:1243–48.

Hearsey, J. E. 1965. *London and the Great Fire*. London: J. Murray.

Holdsworth, W. S. 1927. *An Historical Introduction to the Land Law*. Oxford: Clarendon Press.

Lunt, W. E. 1956. *History of England*. New York: Harper and Row.

Maitland, F. W. 1898. *Township and Borough*. Cambridge: Cambridge University Press.

Mumford, L. 1961. *The City in History*. New York: Harcourt, Brace and World.

Ostrom, E. 1990. *Governing the Commons: The Evolution for Collective Action*. New York: Cambridge University Press.

Pendrill, C. 1937. *Old Parish Life in London*. London: Oxford University Press.

Pepys, S. 1666/1898. *Diary*, ed. H. B. Wheatley. London: George Bell and Sons.

Pirenne, H. 1952. *Medieval Cities: Their Origins and the Revival of Trade*. Princeton, NJ: Princeton University Press.

Powell, S. C. 1963. *Puritan Village: The Formation of a New England Town*. Middletown, CT: Wesleyan University Press.

Prosser, W. L. 1971. *The Law of Torts*. 4th ed. St. Paul, MN: West.

Rasmussen, S. E. 1934/1967. *London: The Unique City*. Cambridge, MA: MIT Press.

Saalman, H. 1968. *Medieval Cities*. New York: George Braziller.

Stenton, D. M. 1962. *English Society in the Early Middle Ages*. Baltimore: Penguin Books.

Summerson, J. 1962. *Georgian London*. Baltimore: Penguin Books.

Trevelyan, G. M. 1953. *History of England*. Vol. 1. Garden City, NY: Doubleday Anchor.

Tuchman, B. W. 1978. *A Distant Mirror: The Calamitous 14th Century*. New York: Knopf.

Webb, S., and B. Webb. 1899/1963. *Statutory Authorities for Special Purposes*. Hamden, CT: Archon Books.

Weber, M. 1899/1958. *The City*. New York: Free Press.

CHAPTER 4 *City Growth and Reform*
in the Nineteenth Century

And did the Countenance Divine
Shine forth upon our clouded hills?
And was Jerusalem builded here
Among those dark Satanic mills?
—**WILLIAM BLAKE, 1809**

The modern industrial city came of age in Europe and North America over the course of the nineteenth century. The population and geographic size of the principal cities of industrial nations—London, Paris, Berlin, New York, Boston, and others—expanded at unprecedented rates with immigration from the countryside and from abroad. At the same time, small towns located near sources of water power or coalfields mushroomed into crowded "satanic" mill towns such as Manchester and Birmingham in England and Lowell, Massachusetts, and Scranton, Pennsylvania, in the United States. With rapid growth came a deluge of threats to life, health, and morality. In the early decades of the century, industrial tenements proliferated, sanitation collapsed, crime and disease flourished, and life expectancy declined. Gradually, the horrors of uncontrolled urbanization were recognized, at first by a few perceptive individuals and ultimately by a broader spectrum of society and its law-making bodies.

Fortunately, as cities expanded, so gradually did social capacity to equip and govern the modern city through innovation in such fields as civil engineering, social statistics, public health, finance, public administration, and landscape design. The primitive late medieval and colonial towns of 1800 became the nascent world cities of 1900.

Fundamental to the growing capacity to cope with urban problems were three primary avenues of reform that emerged in England, the European Continent, and the United States during that century of urban change:

1. *Regulation.* Beginning with the British Public Health Act of 1848, perception of squalor, overcrowding, and lack of basic sanitation yielded a series of public laws and regulations intended to gain some degree of control over the building of cities. These laws would lay an institutional foundation for the proliferation of land use and environmental regulations to appear in the twentieth century.

2. *Redevelopment.* Large cities underwent massive construction or modernization of urban infrastructure in the form of paved streets, lighting, water and sewer systems, urban drainage, mass transportation, schools, and urban parks. Such construction anticipated the urban redevelopment programs after World War II in Great Britain, the United States, and elsewhere.

3. *Relocation.* Late-nineteenth-century social reformers proposed encouraging people to move from overcrowded, unhealthy industrial cities to new model towns in outlying locations. These new towns were to be carefully planned, physically and socially, to uplift the spirit as well as to provide an honest living and healthful surroundings. Planned industrial towns, garden cities, and religious "New Jerusalems" that appeared between the 1830s and the early 1900s helped inspire large-scale "New Town" programs in many nations after World War II. They also contributed to the late Victorian ideal of suburban living that would metastasize into the vast metropolitan "nowheres" of today.

This chapter first summarizes the demographic and physical growth of cities and then considers these three fundamental avenues of urban reform in more detail. The stage will then be set for an overview of twentieth-century urbanization in the following two chapters.

Urban Growth during the Nineteenth Century

The increasing magnitude and concentration of manufacturing activities during the Industrial Revolution caused an astonishing increase in size and populations of cities in Europe and the United States during the nineteenth century (Table 4-1).

The growth of cities during that century was documented in 1899 by demographer Adna F. Weber in a study characterized in an anonymous preface as "the first really sound, comprehensive, and complete contribution to urban studies by an American" (1899/1963, 1). Weber identified three major elements of nineteenth-century urbanization: (1) the absolute and proportional increase of *urban population*; (2) the emergence of large numbers of *new urban places*; and (3) the phenomenal expansion of *very large cities* such as London, New York, and Paris. These elements are interrelated facets of the prevailing movement of people to urban places from the countryside and from other countries.

In England and Wales, large and small cities captured 80 percent of population growth between 1801 and 1891, and the urban proportion of the population grew from 16 percent to 53 percent. Urban places larger than 20,000 grew tenfold in total population from 1.5 million to 15.5 million (Weber 1899/1963, 43). In France, the number of people living in cities larger than 10,000 quadrupled from 2.6 million in 1801 to 9.9 million in 1891. The United States started the nineteenth century with a negligible urban population; by 1890, 18.2 million people lived in places

**TABLE 4-1 *NINETEENTH-CENTURY URBAN GROWTH:
ENGLAND AND WALES, FRANCE, AND THE U.S.***

ENGLAND AND WALES: URBAN PLACES EXCEEDING 20,000 INHABITANTS			
YEAR	NUMBER OF CITIES	TOTAL URBAN POPULATION (MILLIONS)	PERCENT OF NATIONAL POPULATION
1801	15	1.5	16%
1851	63	6.2	35%
1891	185	15.5	53%
FRANCE: URBAN PLACES EXCEEDING 10,000 INHABITANTS			
1801	90	2.6	9.5%
1851	165	5.1	14.4%
1891	232	9.9	25.9%
UNITED STATES: URBAN PLACES EXCEEDING 8,000 INHABITANTS			
1800	6	0.1	3.3%
1850	85	2.9	12.5%
1890	448	18.2	29.0%

SOURCE: Adapted from Weber (1899/1963).

exceeding 8,000, representing 29 percent of its population. (Urban population in the United States would exceed rural population by 1920.)

The shift of energy source from running water to coal, and later to electricity, facilitated the spread of manufacturing towns during the nineteenth century, resulting in the proliferation of new urban places. For instance, the number of towns with populations exceeding 8,000 in the United States rose from merely six in 1800 (Philadelphia, New York, Baltimore, Boston, Charleston, and Salem) to 448 in 1890.

Yet even though urbanization was spreading to smaller towns and cities in out-lying locations, the principal cities nevertheless attracted the major share of population growth, largely due to immigration. London's population expanded sixfold to 5 million during the century. New York City grew tenfold from 1800 to 1850 and then tripled again in the next four decades, reflecting the arrival of large numbers of immigrants from Ireland and Continental Europe. (In 1898, New York rose to 7 million with the addition of Brooklyn, Queens, the Bronx, and Staten Island to form the five-borough New York City of today.) Boston grew from a modest town of 24,900 in 1800 to a world-class city of about 450,000 in 1890 (Weber 1899/1963, 450). Paris quadrupled from 547,000 in 1801 to 2.4 million in 1891, rising from 2 percent to more than 6 percent of the nation's population. Berlin grew

TABLE 4-2 *GROWTH OF INDUSTRIAL AND DEVELOPING CITIES*

(a) INDUSTRIAL CITIES GROWTH 1800-1890

CITY	1800	1850	1890	1850-90 ANNUAL GROWTH RATE
London	860,000	1.7 mill.	5 mill.	4.8%
Paris	547,000	1.0 mill.	2.4 mill.	3.5%
New York	62,500	660,000	2.7 mill.	7.7%%
Boston	25,000	137,000	448,500	5.6%

(b) DEVELOPING CITIES GROWTH 1950-2000

CITY	1950	2000	1850-90 ANNUAL GROWTH RATE
Tokyo	6.9 mill.	26.4 mill.	5.6%
Mexico City	3.1 mill.	18.1 mill.	9.6%
Jakarta	3.0 mill.	11.0 mill.	5.3%
Cairo	2.4 mill.	10.6 mill.	2.5%
Bombay	2.9 mill.	18.1 mill.	6.8%

SOURCES: Adapted from (a) Weber 1899/1963 and (b) *New York Times Almanac—2003*, p. 472.

from 201,000 to 1.6 million between 1819 and 1890. These rates of growth rival those of large cities in Africa, Asia, and Latin America in the late twentieth century (Table 4-2).

Public Regulation: From Sanitary Reform to Urban Planning

Urban Squalor

The building of dwellings to accommodate the astronomic increase in urban populations in the industrializing nations during the nineteenth century lagged far behind demand. Overcrowding to inhuman levels was ensured by the prevailing building practices of the times. Unfettered by any public regulations, tenement building was a joint result of the need for tenants to be within walking distance to factories and mills and the builder's greed for profit. Thus dwellings were minute in size and packed together with space left unbuilt only to the minimum extent necessary to provide physical access to each unit.

A prevalent building pattern in English industrial cities during the first half of the century was the "courtyard system." Dwellings were constructed facing streets with a second row, back to back with the first row, which faced only onto an interior courtyard or alley. Narrow tunnels connected these interior courts with the streets and outside world (Figure 4-1). In the absence of any means for removing sewage and refuse from the premises, the courts, alleys, and the streets served as waste receptacles. With sunlight and ventilation blocked out, the stench and health hazards were unimaginable (Figure 4-2).

The socialist reformer Friedrich Engels described Manchester, England, in 1845 as follows:

> Here one is in an almost undisguised working-man's quarter, for even the shops and beer-houses hardly take the trouble to exhibit the trifling degree of cleanliness. But all this is nothing in comparison with the courts and lanes which lie behind, to which access can be gained only through covered passages, in which no two human beings can pass at the same time. Of the irregular cramming together of dwellings which defy all rational plan, of the tangle in which they are crowded literally one upon the other, it is impossible to convey an idea. And it is not the buildings surviving from the old times of Manchester which are to blame for this; the confusion has only recently reached its height when every scrap of space left by the old way of building has been filled up and patched over until not a foot of land is left to be further occupied.... He who turns [into the maze of passageways and courts] gets into a filth and disgusting grime the equal of

Dust
A
B
Passage
Cart Shed
LEWIS ST.
Totally enclosed court
Tunnel 2ft 10ins wide
LEWIS SQU
HARRINGTON ST.
Tunnel
To HART'S YARD.
RANCLIFFE ST.
Public House
House & Shop
SUSSEX ST.

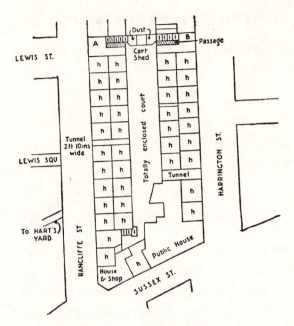

FIGURE 4-1

Diagram of tenement courtyard in Nottingham, England, circa 1840. *(Source: Benevolo 1967, Fig. 31.)*

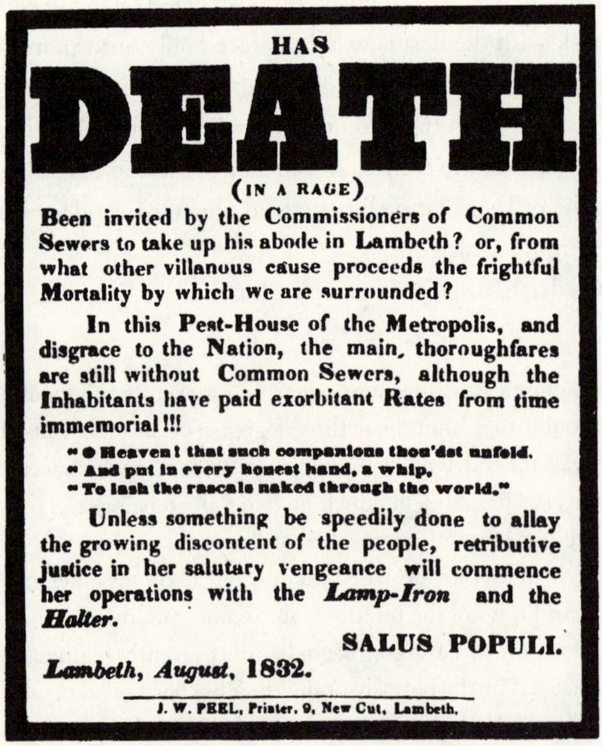

HAS
DEATH
(IN A RAGE)
Been invited by the Commissioners of Common Sewers to take up his abode in Lambeth? or, from what other villanous cause proceeds the frightful Mortality by which we are surrounded?
In this Pest-House of the Metropolis, and disgrace to the Nation, the main thoroughfares are still without Common Sewers, although the Inhabitants have paid exorbitant Rates from time immemorial!!!
"O Heaven! that such companions thou'dst unfold,
"And put in every honest hand, a whip,
"To lash the rascals naked through the world."
Unless something be speedily done to allay the growing discontent of the people, retributive justice in her salutary vengeance will commence her operations with the Lamp-Iron and the Halter.
SALUS POPULI.
Lambeth, August, 1832.
J. W. PEEL, Printer, 9, New Cut, Lambeth.

FIGURE 4-2

Broadside protesting inaction of improvement commissioners regarding sewerage, 1832. *(Source: Benevolo 1967, Fig. 30.)*

which is not to be found.... In one of these courts there stands directly at the entrance a privy without a door, so dirty that inhabitants can pass into and out of that court only by passing through foul pools of urine and excrement. Below it on the river there are several tanneries which fill the whole neighborhood with the stench of animal putre-faction. (Quoted in Benevolo 1967, 23)

Not only were the dwelling units pitifully small to begin with, but they were hopelessly overcrowded. Manchester in 1841 "had 1,500 cellars where three persons, 738 where four, and 281 where five slept in one bed" (Rosen 1958, 206), Liverpool, Bristol, Leeds, Glasgow, and London all contained sizable districts of similar nature. Liverpool in 1884 was reported to have certain districts with up to 1,210 persons per acre (Ashworth 1954, 10). In the United States, high-density tenement districts flourished in ports of entry for European immigrants. New York's Lower East Side had a density of 272 persons per acre in 1860, which doubled in the next thirty years as further waves of Irish and Italian immigrants arrived (Weber 1899/1963, 460).

Public Health Implications and Reforms

The pervasive overcrowding and absence of sanitation, potable water, fresh air, waste removal, and open space—combined with long working hours in unhealthy conditions—magnified human misery and shortened life expectancy. Tuberculosis (TB) or "consumption" was the leading cause of death in urban England during the nineteenth century. TB was inevitably associated with undernourishment, poor ventilation, and general debilitation (Flinn 1965, 11). TB, however, attracted little social consternation before the 1840s because it was viewed as an inevitable aspect of the working-class existence. Also, statistics on TB were unreliable due to the difficulty of diagnosing the disease and the absence of any governmental agency for collecting data on morbidity and mortality. As long as the elite were unthreatened by TB and its companion urban killer, typhus, nothing was done about it. (Perhaps Puccini in his 1895 opera *La Bohème* employed the death of Mimi to make the upper class more empathetic to the tragedy of TB.)

Cholera was another story. This Asian import struck London in 1831–1832 and reappeared several times thereafter. In terms of numbers of deaths and chronic level of threat, cholera was far less important than TB or typhus. Its effects, however, were not confined to poor districts. Cholera struck with particular force in the wealthy neighborhoods where plumbing and connection to (polluted) central water supplies facilitated its spread. Together with a growing incidence of crime against property, cholera galvanized consternation of the elite regarding the conditions of urban squalor in their midst: "Even if he were not his brother's keeper, every man of property was affected by the multiplication of thieves; everyone who valued his life felt it desirable not to have a mass of carriers of virulent diseases too close at hand" (Ashworth 1954, 47). And another pithy account:

> Cholera frightened people. It stirred even the moribund, degraded, unreformed municipal corporations into fits of unwonted sanitary activity. It was the clearest warning of the lethal propensities of the swollen towns of the new industrial era. (Flinn 1965, 8)

Cholera frightened the elite, but fear per se is a poor basis for public action. Converting fear into rational public response required not simply rhetoric but sound scientific investigation and documentation. The period between 1832 and 1860 marked the beginning of scientific sanitary surveys, which launched the modern public health movement (Rosen 1958, 213).

Besides the cholera scare, two other factors helped lay a foundation for sanitary reform. One was the development of the science of *statistics* and its application to the analysis of social problems. The first British Census was undertaken in 1801, partly to start a data base for the calculation of premiums for government-sponsored life insurance. The field of vital statistics was pioneered by William Farr, whose reports "provided the ammunition used in the campaigns against disease in the home, in the factory, and in the community as a whole" (Rosen 1958, 227).

The other factor was the appearance of a *liberal political philosophy* that urged government intervention to remedy social ills that impeded the economy. The necessary framework was provided by a small group of intellectuals headed by the energetic and enigmatic Jeremy Bentham (whose earthly remains dressed in his own clothes today reside in a hallway at University College, London). Among other reforms in the fields of law, education, and birth control, these reformers called for a review of the Poor Laws to centralize relief to the poor and to ensure that the system promoted rather than discouraged working for a living.

That the appointment of a Royal Poor Law Commission in 1832 would eventually lead to sanitary reform was in large part due to the driving force of a key individual: Edwin Chadwick. Like Robert Owen, Frederick Law Olmsted, and Ebenezer Howard, who are considered later in this chapter, Chadwick exemplified the nineteenth-century tradition of the inspired amateur. He would eventually be knighted for distinction in a field in which he had no formal training. Due to his association with Jeremy Bentham, Chadwick was appointed in 1832 as secretary to the new Poor Law Commission where he remained until 1847. In this capacity, he began to study the causes of public outlays for "poor rates" (welfare payments), which inevitably led him to the long-ignored problem of slum housing. Assisted by three physicians, Chadwick prepared a report in 1838 that linked for the first time the incidence of disease fostered by unsanitary living conditions to the economic costs borne by the nation through the payment of "poor rates" (i.e., welfare payments).

This report was the first of a series of sanitary surveys that applied the new science of statistics to the analysis of patterns of illness and death. Essential to this task was a geographic perspective. With reasonably accurate vital statistics supplied by William Farr, the spatial patterns of disease could be mapped and related to environmental factors such as water supply. For example, there were two thousand deaths from cholera in 1854 in Newcastle-on-Tyne, while in Tynemouth, 8 miles away, where new drainage regulations were in force, only four deaths occurred (Ashworth 1954, 61).

The importance of Chadwick's work to sanitary reform, and ultimately city planning, can scarcely be overstated:

> The year 1838, then, was an important turning-point in the history of the public health movement. Although its roots stretch back fifty years, the movement was, before 1838, unorganized, leaderless, and in a legislative sense—the only sense that mattered in the long run—aimless. Essential foundations had been laid, preconditions established, but, important as these were, effective action was missing. This is what Chadwick supplied. (Rosen 1958, 35)

In 1842, Chadwick wrote another seminal report: *Concerning the Sanitary Condition of the Labouring Population of Great Britain*. It reflected a broad investigation of the incidence and causes of disease in poor districts, as well as Chadwick's personal reading of scientific literature on epidemiology and urban health. The 1842 report was graphic in describing the squalor prevailing in Great Britain's industrial towns. It helped lay a foundation for future work in urban sociology as well as public health. Like the commission convened by Charles II after the Great Fire of London, it resembled the modern "blue-ribbon commission" as a means to educate decision makers about a serious social problem.

Although it examined the social, health and moral effects of urban slum conditions in unprecedented detail, the 1842 report was hesitant to recommend stronger building laws, occupancy limits, mandatory ventilation and collection of wastes, and limits on the number of dwellings per unit of land. Such restrictions on the private sector were still too controversial, and Chadwick evidently did not want to alienate his conservative audience by calling for governmental control of private land development. He did, however, perform a unique public service in documenting the nature, extent, causes, and economic implications of urban squalor.

In 1843, Parliament established a Royal Commission on the State of Large Towns and Populous Districts (Health of Towns Commission) to build on Chadwick's research and to propose necessary legislation. Chadwick wrote much of the commission's two reports in 1844 and 1845, including proposals to

- ▸ Delegate responsibility for sanitary regulation to local health authorities
- ▸ Prepare detailed sanitary surveys within a district before planning a drainage system
- ▸ Coordinate sewer construction with road improvements
- ▸ Establish minimum sanitary requirements for new dwellings
- ▸ Require ventilation and cleaning of existing dwellings
- ▸ Provide new public parks in industrial cities (Benevolo 1967, 91–93)

In 1848, faced with a new outbreak of cholera, Parliament finally adopted England's first comprehensive Public Health Act. This law was based on the 1845 Royal Commission Report that in turn drew heavily from the 1842 report, all drafted by Chadwick. Thus a major legislative reform was achieved in response to the perception of environmental threat documented in these and other investigative reports. Like the Act for Rebuilding London after the Great Fire of 1666, the 1848 Public Health Act demonstrated the capacity of the British legal system to respond (albeit belatedly) to the need for innovation in the face of disaster (Figure 4-3).

The 1848 act established a General Board of Health and authorized the creation of local district health boards. The latter, when locally established, were required to prepare "a map exhibiting a system of sewerage for effectually draining their district." Furthermore, new dwellings within health districts must be equipped with drains and a lavatory, a totally unprecedented public requirement. Other provisions dealt with refuse collection, removal of harmful wastes, inspection of slaughterhouses and lodging houses, the paving and upkeep of roads, the establishment of public gardens, water supply, and the burial of the dead (Benevolo 1967, 96–97).

It is of course one thing to pass a law, and another to bring about the physical changes desired:

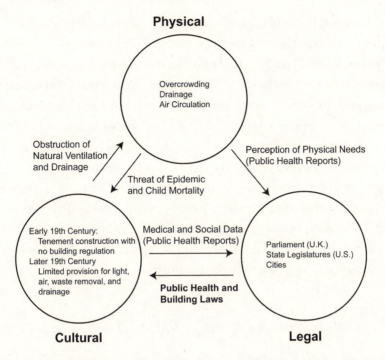

FIGURE 4-3 Land use and society model applied to nineteenth-century public health and sanitary reforms.

The Act of 1848 constituted a tentative and uncertain start to govern action in a major field.... Nevertheless, it had put a foot through a door which had hitherto defied all attempt at opening, and although the detailed administrative arrangements it laid down were scrapped within half a dozen years, its principle of state responsibility was not discarded. It was this principle which the [1842] "Sanitary Report" had sought to establish. (Flinn 1965, 73)

Chadwick's work and the resulting 1848 Public Health Act inspired further reforms in Great Britain as reflected in subsequent laws adopted in 1875 and 1890. The English reforms were watched closely in Europe and influenced parallel efforts in the United States where industrialization and immigration were rapidly overcrowding cities along the Eastern seaboard. By midcentury, sanitary investigations inspired by Chadwick's work were under way in New York, Boston, and other cities, with new public health laws soon to follow. The New York (State) Metropolitan Health Act of 1866 was the first major law in the United States in this field. (The U.S. federal government would play no major role in urban environmental issues until a century later.)

The sanitary reforms of the mid-nineteenth century launched not only modern public health but also the field of city planning. Three major results of nineteenth-century sanitary investigations that underlie modern town planning were (1) construction of urban sewers (and later, sewage treatment plants); (2) sanitary survey planning; and (3) townsite consciousness, as reflected in the urban parks movement (Peterson 1983). Sanitary reform and the early public health laws evolved gradually into the urban planning movement of the early twentieth century. The conduct of sanitary surveys helped develop the methodology of general planning investigations. The surveys also elevated the geographic scale of investigation from selected neighborhoods or problem areas to entire cities and even metropolitan regions. Ultimately, building and public health legislation, primitive though it was, laid a constitutional foundation for the acceptance of broader land use zoning and environmental regulations in the twentieth century.

Redevelopment: A Century of Municipal Improvements

Advent of Public Responsibility

New public health and building laws of the second half of the nineteenth century, however well intended, largely applied to new construction and had little or no effect on the teeming slum districts already in existence. Thus when progressive urban reformers called attention to the squalid conditions, proposals for more drastic public action—tearing down the worst slums, in particular—began to be heard. One of the first of such projects took place in the notorious district of the Lower East Side of Manhattan where population densities reached hundreds of people (mostly recent immigrants) per acre. The crusading journalist Jacob Riis in 1890 published a landmark report, *How the Other Half Lives*. With camera, maps, and pungent prose, Riis documented the appalling conditions of New York's slums, including crime, debauchery, disease, and high rates of mortality as compared with other areas of the city. He described the immigrant district known locally as Five Points as the "wickedest of American slums" and the "foul core of New York's slums" (quoted in Page 1999, 73). A 3-acre site named Mulberry Bend near Five Corners was torn down by the city in 1896, a direct result of Riis's disclosures and the first of New York's slum clearance projects (Page 1999, 76).

Nonetheless, cities in the nineteenth century lacked legal authority, money, and experience in directly attacking the problems of existing slums. London, which had possessed a municipal charter of self-government since 1193, well into the nineteenth century still lacked the authority or the will to provide basic urban ser-vices such as water supply, drainage, paving, and street lighting to most of its inhabitants. For those not fortunate enough to live in one of the privately planned estate developments, the haphazard activities of the local "improvement commis-sions" and a few widely ignored municipal regulations represented the extent of public interest in their welfare. Paris, which unlike London had not burned in recent history, remained medieval in its physical appearance and state of infrastructure.

Many of today's major parks and boulevards of European capitals originated as royal lands or were created by royal initiative. London's Hyde Park was a former royal hunting ground that was opened to public recreational use around 1640 (Ras-mussen 1967, 92). The Champs-Élysées, the primary boulevard of Paris, originated in 1670 at the direction of Louis XIV. The two great Paris parks, Bois de Boulogne and Bois de Vincennes, originated as royal land that was replanned for more dem-ocratic uses in the 1850s at the instigation of Emperor Louis-Napoléon (Jordan 1995). Berlin's central park, the Tiergarten, was another former royal hunting ground, and that city's grand boulevard, the Unter den Linden, was laid out by Emperor Frederick William in the mid-seventeenth century (Abercrombie 1913, 222).

No such legacies of royal lands and patronage boosted U.S. cities into the mod-ern era. City building in the United States, let alone the emergence of urban infra-structure and institutions, had scarcely begun in 1800. Urban historian Carl Bridenbaugh (1964) has documented the struggle of colonial towns to cope with chronic problems of water supply, fires, epidemics, and crime. Boston and New York, for instance, passed municipal laws during the seventeenth and eighteenth centuries requiring suitable construction and periodic inspection of chimneys. In the absence of a public fire department, each Boston householder was required to possess a bucket, ladder, and long-handled swab for extinguishing rooftop fires.

Necessary facilities in early American towns were usually provided through private initiative, often under a monopoly granted by the colonial legislature or municipal authorities. Boston's Mill Dam was constructed in the 1630s (at the present site of Government Center) by private citizens who leased sites for tidal-powered mills (Whitehill 1968, 5). The first bridge across the Charles River between Cambridge and Boston was privately constructed in 1768 under a law granting the builder a monopoly over river crossings, which was later rejected in a landmark court decision (Kutler 1971). Boston's first public water supply was established at Jamaica Pond by a private company in 1796.

The rapid demographic and spatial expansion of both European and American cities in the early nineteenth century rendered such *ad hoc* and profit-oriented solutions outmoded as responses to many urban needs. Although some services such as urban transportation, mills, and wharves continued to be provided through enfranchised private entrepreneurs, the urgent need to develop larger-scale facilities for common benefit such as water and sewer systems, parks, highways, and firefighting capabilities demanded that urban governments retool themselves, legally and technologically, to meet modern challenges. (Ironically, today some U.S. cities are reprivatizing their water and sewer systems, solid waste management, parks, libraries, and even schools.)

Transition in London: The Nash Improvements

To the delight of Anglophiles and the agony of traffic engineers, London historically has refused to be a planned city. From its 1666 Great Fire to the Nazi blitz of the 1940s, proposals for a sweeping redesign of the metropolis have failed to win popular support. Aside from the neoclassical geometry of the seventeenth- and eighteenth-century elite residential squares, the city as a whole has grown and evolved organically with a minimum of deliberate planning. One major exception to this history of incrementalism was the work of John Nash, the nineteenth-century successor to Christopher Wren as London's premier architect and planner:

> Once, and only once, has a great plan for London, affecting the development of the capital as a whole, been projected and carried to completion. This was the plan which constituted the "metropolitan improvements" of the Regency ... carried out under the presiding genius of John Nash. (Summerson 1962, 177)

Nash, born in 1752, was a prominent architect, society habitué, and close friend of the prince regent (who ruled England in place of his insane father George III from 1811 until the latter's death in 1820 and then in his own right as George IV until 1830). Nash was to be the leading architectural designer of "Regency London" whose works included Buckingham Palace and Trafalgar Square. Two legacies of this period were London's vast Regent's Park and the new Regent Street to connect the park to the center of the city. The program of urban improvement began in 1811 with the desire of the prince regent to develop a sizable tract of royal land at the northern edge of London known as Marylebone Park. This project was intended not for the social betterment of the lower classes, but to create a new sub-urb for the aristocracy and also to enrich the royal household.

A major obstacle to this concept was the isolation of Marylebone Park from cen-tral London and the royal palaces, offices, banks, clubs, and "low-life districts" where upper-class gentlemen spent much of their time. As the selected architect for the project, John Nash proposed the construction of a brand new street from what would become Regent's Park to the center of London (Figure 4-4). For the park itself, he proposed to convert the site into a vast picturesque landscape, punc-tuated by opulent "terraces" of aristocratic townhouses. Nash also proposed the creation of Trafalgar Square (Figure 4-5), the redesign of several streets in its vicin-ity, and the construction of Regent's Canal to serve as a navigation artery and water source for the lake and fountains of Regent's Park (Summerson 1962, 177). Alto-gether, it was for London a program of unprecedented magnitude.

The importance of this vast undertaking as a transition between *royal* and *pub-lic* initiative is apparent in the contrast between the ends and the means involved. The Prince Regent made no secret of his wish to eclipse Napoléon as an imperial city builder and to enhance the royal household income, but he lacked the finan-cial resources to accomplish the work, particularly to build Regent Street. To obtain an appropriation from Parliament, "there must have been some social aim in view, and the building of the new street was granted in 1813 as a means of improving the sanitation of the unhealthy quarters [along its route]" (Rasmussen 1967, 274).

The alignment of the new street was an early exercise of "scientific" city plan-ning. The route traversed the western edge of the shabby and cheap districts of Soho, directly adjacent to the more opulent Mayfair neighborhood. Thus Nash as *planner* eliminated some run-down housing while acquiring the right-of-way as cheaply as possible. The alignment close to the best district of London ensured that the frontage of the new street would be developed for elegant homes and businesses. In Nash's own words, the new street would provide "a boundary and complete separation between the streets and squares occupied by the nobility and gentry, and the narrow streets and meaner houses occupied by mechanics and the trading part of the community" (quoted in Davis 1966, 66). Like the U.S. urban renewal program of the 1950s and 1960s, Nash's Regent's Park and Regent Street projects benefited the wealthy while purporting to upgrade the condition of the poor.

Eager to please his royal patron and potential investors, Nash as *architect*

FIGURE 4-4
Regent's Park and Regent Street improvements in London designed by John Nash between 1812 and 1835. *(Source: Benevolo 1967, Fig. 13.)*

FIGURE 4-5 John Nash's Trafalgar Square, London, 1830. *(Photo by author.)*

designed elegant neoclassic facades for his Regent's Park terraces and Regent
Street frontage. Park Crescent, where Regent Street meets the park is a fine sur-
viving example of "pure Nash," a curving, colonnaded exterior of creamy stucco.
This stylish façade merges an entire row of townhouses into a continuous, majes-
tic unity, resembling John Wood's earlier "Royal Crescent" in the city of Bath,
England.

Finally, Nash as *landscape architect* achieved brilliance in the design of Regent's
Park itself. There was nothing democratic about the initial plan for the park; in
concept, it was simply a grandiose version of the West End squares laid out by
landed aristocrats for their peers. The general public was not admitted to Regent's
Park until 1838, and even then there was little to amuse the horseless working class
(Chadwick, 1966, 32). Over time, however, Regent's Park evolved from a garden
suburb for the wealthy to a public pleasure ground bordered by expensive townhouses. Today, Regent's Park is one of London's largest and most heavily used
parks and contains, among other amenities, the London Zoo.

Nash was associated with two other park projects in central London, both
designed to be public from the outset. One was St. James Park, a Crown property
since the reign of Henry VIII, which Nash redesigned in 1828. It was open to the

public but has remained crown property ever since (Chadwick 1966, 34). Trafalgar Square was, by contrast, public from the outset in both ownership and use (Figure 4-5). As London's equivalent to New York's Times Square, Trafalgar Square has always been the place for crowds to gather to protest governmental policies, to celebrate victories, or to welcome the New Year. That may not have been the intention of Nash, and certainly not of his royal patron, but in 1830, the latter died and the square opened, symbolizing the passing of royal privilege and the advent of planning for the people.

Haussmann's Transformation of Paris

The Nash "regency program" in London was but an appetizer to the banquet of urban and metropolitan improvements in Paris undertaken by Emperor Napoléon III and his technical administrator, Baron Georges-Eugène Haussmann. The rebuilding of Paris between 1853 and 1870, with work continuing until the outbreak of war in 1914, touched every inhabitant of Paris and its suburbs. It ingeniously blended the aesthetic with the functional. It pioneered new methods of finance and public administration. It converted Paris from an overcrowded, unhealthy medieval town into the fabled "City of Light."

The onset of comprehensive redevelopment of Paris coincided with the election of Louis-Napoléon as president of the Second French Republic after the Revolution of 1848. Returning from exile in England, this nephew of Napoléon Bonaparte immediately undertook to revive and continue the program of public works initiated in Paris by his uncle and carried on spasmodically thereafter. Perhaps influenced by the recent building of Regent Street and Regent's Park in London, Louis-Napoléon turned his attention first to the streets and parks of Paris. Following the coup d'état of 1851 and his assumption of the title of Emperor Napoléon III, in 1853 he selected Haussmann, then a rising lawyer and provincial administrator, to hold the office of "Prefect of the Seine":

> This was a very special post not only because the Seine was the richest and most densely populated Department in France, and Paris the hub of national political life, but also because on grounds of public policy, the Prefect of the Seine acted both as head of the Department and as municipal head of the city of Paris itself, two posts of immense influence and powers. (Chapman 1953, 179)

Haussmann's powers were civil and municipal in nature, not simply an extension of the Emperor whose authority was much diminished in comparison with the earlier Napoléon. While Louis Napoléon strongly promoted the redevelopment of Paris, the actual program was a joint undertaking of the state, city, and private sector, utilizing essentially modern forms of legal procedures, financing, and contracting. Regal in scale and inspiration, the rebuilding of Paris was civic and bourgeois in execution.

Napoléon III's motives for undertaking the program are subject to debate. The conventional wisdom ascribes the laying-out of the great boulevards and plazas at their intersections (most notably the Place de l'Etoile) to military considerations, namely the need to protect the government against the socialist rabble who flourished in the twisted streets of Old Paris (Peets 1927). Certainly the revolutions of 1830 and 1848 may have influenced the Emperor's thinking, but great boulevards are two-way streets, as the Germans demonstrated in 1871 and 1940. A more humanitarian view is that Napoléon III understood the "sociological and hygienic condition of modern civilization [which] ... forced upon him the sympathetic duty of making a suitable home for [his] people" (Smith 1907, 22). Another writer suggests three motives: (1) military considerations, (2) economic revitalization, and (3) "to make Paris into a capital city worthy of France, a capital provided with the light, beauty, and cleanliness essential to human dignity in cities" (Chapman 1953, 182).

Even before Haussmann arrived on the scene, his royal patron was already engaged in planning new avenues and redesigning Paris's great western park, the Bois de Boulogne. This area was a former royal hunting ground that the city of Paris took over from the Crown in 1848 on the understanding that the city would improve it as a public park: "The Emperor himself was vastly interested in the scheme, which he saw as a future rival to Hyde Park and the other royal parks of London which he had known earlier as a refugee in England" (Chadwick 1966, 153).

With the appointment of Haussmann in 1852, the urban rebuilding program began in earnest. Haussmann's first act was to order the preparation of an accurate survey of the city, using temporary timber towers to provide clear sight lines over the tops of buildings. The first phase of construction, approved by the legislature in 1855, involved new north-south and east-west avenues that followed the routes of the ancient Roman road crossing at the city's heart (Smith 1907, 25). The great boulevards laid out under this and later phases of work are the most familiar and cherished elements of post-Haussmann Paris (Jordan 1995) (Figure 4-6). Clearly inspired by neoclassical and baroque precedents, notably Louis XIV's Palace of Versailles, the Haussmann boulevards were widely acclaimed and set the style for ambitious cities around the world. For example, an ecstatic American architectural critic wrote in 1907:

FIGURE 4-6 Bird's-eye view of two Haussmann boulevards, Paris, circa 1870s. *(Source: Benevolo 1967, Fig. 51.)*

The *Avenue Napoléon,* now [Avenue] *de l'Opéra,* is a perfect modern French street; not too long, spacious, well-built and furnishing axial vista to a fine symmetrical monument. This is the culmination of the classic scheme of axial symmetry, conceived in the Hellenic period, more perfectly suggested in the Roman, carried a little farther in the Renaissance, fully understood by the Bourbon designers in France and brought to an ideal and complete realization by Haussmann in the Avenue de l'Opéra. (Smith 1907, 36)

To a greater extent than Regent Street in London, Haussmann's avenues and boulevards extended from point A to point B through whatever lay in their path. Not simply a widening of existing streets, these projects involved the acquisition, demolition, and replacement of the adjoining frontage on both sides of the new street. Today, the boulevards Sébastopol, de Saint-Michel, and de l'Opéra, among others, are broad, tree-lined avenues separated into through-traffic lanes, local-service access lanes, and broad pedestrian sidewalks, often clogged with parked motor scooters. The avenues are bordered by uniform facades of stylish, balconied *Second-Empire* buildings (Figure 4-7). Unlike West End London where residential districts are unsullied by shops, the frontage buildings in Paris have always been multipurpose. The ground floor is devoted to shops, cafés, banks, and restaurants; the next two or three floors contain elegant apartments for the upper middle class.

FIGURE 4-7 Street scene along a Haussmann Paris boulevard. *(Photo by author.)*

Above them, the attics beneath the mansard roofs contain artists' studios and gar-ret rooms (possibly now converted to condominiums) (Saalman 1971, 26–27).

The frontage bordering the new avenues experienced a phenomenal increase in value as Haussmann expected. It was his hope that the city would retain owner-ship of the frontage and lease or sell it on the open market to capture the increase in value and thereby defray part of the cost of building the streets. This creative use of *excess condemnation,* however, was opposed by the financial community and was finally prohibited by the Council of State in 1858, which ordered that frontage lots, once cleared, should be returned to their previous owners (Benevolo 1967, 135–36). This promoted a lively speculation in land expected to be acquired for new streets. Construction of the new frontage buildings proceeded under private auspices but with uniformity of style ensured by a combination of public building restrictions and the aesthetic taste of the time. The construction of Back Bay in Boston at about the same time mimicked the legal and technical approach of Haussmann in Paris, but with a somewhat different architectural aesthetic.

The architectural critic Sigfried Giedion (1962) disliked the "great length" of Haussmann's boulevards, which he suggested were overly dominated by traffic concerns. But he praised the architectural treatment of the façades:

> Haussmann showed his sagacity in refusing to allow any tricks to be played with facades. Simply and without discussion, he spread a uniform facade over the whole of Paris. It featured high French windows, with accents provided by lines of cast-iron bal-conies like those used in the Rue de Rivoli under Napoleon I. He employed, unobtru-sively, Renaissance shapes of a pleasantly neutral nature. A last touch of the unity which marked baroque architecture can still be felt. The neutral facades and the general uni-formity make Haussmann's enormous work of rebuilding better than any other exe-cuted in or after the fifties of the nineteenth century. (Giedion 1962, 672)

Another Haussmann legacy was a new system of parks and open spaces in Paris. The smallest of these were carved out of the existing medieval clutter at the junc-tions of major streets. These green spaces have since provided oases of foliage, gar-dens, playgrounds, and park benches. Three larger parks and the gardens of the Champs-Élysées provide a middle scale of parks within the city. The regional parks of the Bois de Boulogne in the west and Bois de Vincennes in the east were elaborately redesigned to serve the well-to-do and the working-class populations of Paris on holidays. This three-tiered hierarchy of public open spaces qualifies Haussmann to be honored as "the creator of the first real urban park system" (Chadwick 1966, 152). Other Haussmann improvements included the markets of

Les Halles (since demolished for an underground shopping mall), the Opera, the completion of the Place de l'Etoile, several churches and theaters, major additions to the Louvre and Sorbonne University, hospitals, and schools Chapman 1953, 185).

In addition to these many visible embellishments of Paris, Haussmann oversaw the construction of critical infrastructure to improve the public health of Parisians. Between 1800 and 1850, the population inside the old Paris walls doubled from 547,000 to 1,170,000, while areas just outside the walls quadrupled. "The density of [the central core of Paris] was higher than on the lower East Side of New York in the 1930s" (Jordan 1995, 95):

> All the basic urban services collapsed under this burden. Water, sewers, hospitals, police, transportation, education, commerce—nothing functioned adequately. Pedestrians and carts could no longer use the same space.... Then came the ghastly cholera epidemics of 1832 and 1849. (Ibid.)

Like his counterparts in London and New York, Haussmann and Napoléon III sought to combat the public health menace through establishment of a regional water supply system to replace local wells, cisterns, and the foul Seine as water sources. And like Robert Moses, New York's legendary "power broker" of a later generation (Caro 1974), Haussmann was adroit at skirting the law to achieve his purpose: "He quietly went ahead with his plans for new aqueducts, his surveys, and the buying of sites, so that when finally permission was obtained he could immediately begin operations" (Chapman 1953, 186). By 1870, when both the emperor and Haussmann had departed from office, work was under way on two aqueducts to bring freshwater to Paris from the Aisne and Loire river basins, far from the city. (This project was in part influenced by New York City's new Croton River reservoir and aqueduct described later in this chapter.)

The other fundamental Haussmann contribution to public health was the Paris sewer system, a network of underground canals varying in width from 4 to 18 feet and totaling some 600 miles in length. Principal interceptor sewers and galleries were laid beneath the new avenues as those arteries were constructed (a practice more farsighted than was the case with most urban highway construction in the United States since World War II). The canals conducted street drainage and raw sewage to an underground reservoir beneath the Place de la Concorde from which it flowed to the Seine, a few miles downstream from the city (which polluted that river for the next century).

In terms of public works both seen and unseen, Paris was thus transformed during the period 1850–1870. Despite rancor over Haussmann's high-handed financial schemes, work continued on many of his projects under subsequent governments until World War I. The result was a Paris transformed into the City of Light, flamboyant in style and functionally habitable:

> Haussmann's Paris was a city of luxury, commerce, banking, railroads, capitalism, government, administration, and pleasure, whether licit or illicit, popular or socially restricted. Its most obvious physical characteristic was the boulevard and movement. The wealthy and new west end dominated the older neighborhoods, and whatever the actual percentages of workers and artisans in the city, its overall flavor was bourgeois. Uniformity of scale and similarity of design proclaimed orderliness. (Jordan 1995, 163)

As important as the physical results of Haussmann's Improvements program, however, were its political and institutional innovations. The rebuilding of Paris was a unique, pathbreaking experience that bridged the gap between the cities of the eighteenth and twentieth centuries. Its legacies to modernizing cities elsewhere may be summarized under five headings: (1) aesthetic style, (2) functionalism, (3) metropolitanism, (4) finance, and (5) administration.

AESTHETICS

The architecture and plan of Haussmann's rebuilt Paris were widely celebrated as the ideal translation of classical and Renaissance principles into "modern" city planning (Smith 1907, 38). The broad boulevards terminating in monumental focal points, the small and large parks, the statuary and fountains, and the atmosphere of wealth and power all set the model for aspiring cities around the world. Paris was imitated in late-nineteenth-century redevelopment in Vienna, Berlin, Barcelona, London, Rome, Budapest, and many other European national and regional capitals. In the United States, Haussmann's design principals were imitated in the "city beautiful" movement, beginning with the 1893 Chicago World's Fair. Daniel H. Burnham, the principal architect of the fair, also drew on Haussmann precedents profusely in his 1902 plan for the Washington, D.C., park system and his 1909 *Plan of Chicago*. (See Chapter 5.)

FUNCTIONALISM

Less acclaimed than Haussmann's visible Paris improvements, a major contribution to modern city-building was his integration of urban infrastructure into the process of redevelopment. Thus the "City of Light" also became the "City Functional." The impressive new avenues were pathways, not only for surface traffic, but also for sewers, gas mains, water conduits, and, by the end of the nineteenth century, subway tunnels and stations (Le Metro). All the elements of modern cities were addressed somewhere in Haussmann's plans: housing, communications, food, water, gas, sewerage, commerce, education, culture, recreation, hospitals, cemeteries. Haussmann thus was a towering figure in the development of modern city planning.

METROPOLITANISM

In two respects, Haussmann promoted a metropolitan or regional approach to urban governance. The first was his development of regional water, sewer, and later transportation systems serving Paris and some of its suburbs. The other was his successful effort to expand the city geographically by annexing surrounding neighborhoods just outside the old city walls. In 1859, eleven communes containing some 400,000 inhabitants (many living in industrial tenements) were legally annexed to Paris, yielding its present territory. The annexed neighborhoods then had to pay taxes to the city but in turn received urban public services. Similar enlargements of municipal territories occurred in London in 1888, in New York City in 1898, and in Berlin in 1923. In the twentieth century, however, annexations to central cities tapered off as metropolitan systems to provide water and other services to both central cities and suburbs became widespread.

FINANCE

A fourth Haussmann legacy was his development of modern fiscal approaches to urban redevelopment. About two-thirds of the total cost of improvements under his direction was derived from national and municipal grants and the sale of public lands. The municipal contribution was facilitated by the significant rise in tax revenues attributable to the improvements themselves. The remaining one-third was financed through borrowing from private banks and other lenders. This "deficit financing," so familiar today, was novel and controversial in Haussmann's time. His optimistic expectations were proven accurate, however, and the loans were repaid (Chapman and Chapman 1957, 236–37).

ADMINISTRATION

Finally, the Haussmann era marked an administrative revolution, the advent of the modern technocrat. With objectives established by higher authority—emperor, state council, or city council—it was Haussmann's role to carry out the will of his superiors:

> Precisely because he did have the Emperor's support, Haussmann was always able to avoid having to justify his actions politically and could present them as technical and administrative measures deriving from objective necessities.... Haussmann set the pattern for the town-planner as a specialist worker who declines all responsibility for initial choice, and therefore in practice for the town-planner who is at the service of the new ruling class. (Benevolo 1967, 134)

The transformation of Paris under Haussmann's direction was unparalleled in world history, apart from rebuilding after war or natural disaster. Haussmann's closest twentieth-century counterpart was New York's Robert Moses (Caro 1974). Although Haussmann's program was high-handed, expensive, elitist, and unpopular at the time with many Parisians, it created one of the world's most elegant, beloved, and (in the absence of war damage) enduring monuments of neobaroque city planning. Post-Haussmann Paris was a unique blend of the human and the majestic. On the one hand, its alleys, garrets, cafés, and universities nurtured literary and artistic exuberance—the Paris of Renoir, Monet, Stein, Fitzgerald, and Hemingway. On the other hand, it served as exemplar of the baroque world capital with its boulevards, parks, museums, and visions of grandeur. And beneath it all lay the sinews of a modern metropolis.

Water Supply for New York and Boston

Urban communities in the United States in 1800 were few in number, small in size, and coastal in location. The colonial period left each of these settlements with a primitive preindustrial infrastructure, including streets (mostly crooked and unpaved), docks, a town meeting hall, some common open spaces, firefighting implements, a constabulary and jail, and foul water supplies. As population growth began to soar in the early decades of the eighteenth century, the inadequacy of potable water was perceived to be the chief liability and limitation on urban health and prosperity.

The water problem for both New York and Boston was especially acute. Situated respectively on an island (Manhattan) and a peninsula (Shawmut), both cities were bordered by tidal, brackish water with no available freshwater streams. The citizens of each city were already dissatisfied with their existing sources in 1800. The water table aquifers on which they depended were easily contaminated with wastes from privies. Wells close to the shore could become brackish due to salt-water intrusion. In addition, with limited surface recharge of local groundwater, the reliable yield of springs and wells was insufficient. Rainwater cisterns added little to the general supply. By 1830, New York had grown to 200,000 inhabitants and Boston to more than 58,000. In that year, Thomas Crapper invented the flush toilet, and thenceforth water consumption per capita would rise rapidly as water-borne sewerage gradually replaced on-site privies and "night soil" collection (Weidner 1974, 55).

During the early decades of the nineteenth century, the provision of urban water supply was regarded as a private rather than a public function (Blake 1956, Chap. 4). New York, Boston, Baltimore, and several small towns relied initially on enfranchised private companies in preference to assuming the burden directly. An exception was Philadelphia, where recurrent outbreaks of yellow fever at the turn of the nineteenth century prompted a more aggressive municipal response. In 1801, Philadelphia constructed at public expense a pumping plant on the Schuylkill River powered by two steam engines. This project was designed and promoted by the noted engineer Benjamin Latrobe. It marked a dual break-through, first in *technology* (the use of the steam engine to pump water) and second *institutionally* (the use of public taxation to finance a municipal water supply) (Blake 1956, 33).

In Boston, the Jamaica Pond Aqueduct Company was chartered in 1796 to sup-ply that town with water. It laid a 4-mile-long hollow-log pipe from Jamaica Pond in Roxbury (then an independent town) to Boston. This early example of an extraterritorial water supply, however, was inadequate for firefighting or to meet the needs of the growing Boston population (Nesson 1983, 1–2).

Similarly, in New York, the Manhattan Water Company was chartered in 1799 with an exclusive franchise to supply the city with water. It initially constructed a reservoir in lower Manhattan to supply 400 families from local groundwater: "But this water proved both scarce and bad;... and it was not long before the new works were voted a failure" (Booth 1860, 666). In 1811, a plan for the future expansion of New York was prepared by a special commission established by the state leg-islature. The "Commissioners' Plan" projected future streets marching miles into the countryside of upper Manhattan as far as "155th Street." The plan was an accurate, if monotonous, forecast of the spatial growth of the city. The opening of the Erie Canal in 1825, which connected the Hudson River with the Great Lakes, established the city's economic preeminence in the nation and doubled its population to 200,000 in the decade 1820–1830. Local water sources were hopelessly inadequate to serve this rapidly growing population. Various schemes were debated fruitlessly.

Finally, catastrophes in the form of fires (1828 and 1835) and cholera (1832) forced an end to the dithering. Colonel DeWitt Clinton Jr. was retained by the city to assess the water crisis and propose a solution. His report predicted that Manhattan would reach a population of one million by 1890 (he was late by twelve years). His proposal was simple in concept and vast in magnitude, namely, to tap the Croton River 40 miles north of the city to obtain a reliable supply of 20 million gallons per day (gpd) of pure upland water. (Clinton assumed per capita demand of 20 gpd, not foreseeing the impact of the flush toilet.) The elevation of a Croton River reservoir at 200 feet above sea level would permit the water to flow by gravity through an aqueduct to be constructed with enough pressure to serve the needs of taller buildings and firefighting (Weidner 1974, 28–31).

The Croton River project required the construction of storage and conveyance facilities unprecedented since the Roman Empire. With the total cost estimated at several million dollars, the project was too large and too important for private enterprise. Accordingly, the city of New York, under authority from the state legislature, undertook to plan and execute the Croton River project directly. A water commission was quickly appointed, financing was approved by the city's voters in 1835, and construction began in 1837.

The project involved five major structural elements: (1) a masonry dam impounding a reservoir with a storage capacity of 600 million gallons; (2) a 40-mile-long covered masonry aqueduct to the city; (3) a 1,450-foot-long arched bridge to convey the aqueduct across the Harlem River into Manhattan; (4) a 35-acre receiving reservoir within what would become Central Park; and (5) a 4-acre, masonry-walled distributing reservoir located on the present site of the New York Public Library at Fifth Avenue and 42nd Street. The first Croton River water arrived in Manhattan on July 4, 1842, an event celebrated with church bells, cannon, and a 5-mile-long parade (Weidner 1974, 45–46).

Six years later, Boston would hold a similar celebration. In 1845, John Jervis, who directed the Croton River project and was "America's foremost water supply engineer" (Nesson 1983, 4), was hired to study Boston's water crisis. He recommended adoption of an earlier plan to create a water supply at Long Pond (later

Lake Cochituate) in Natick, 17 miles from Boston. The Massachusetts legislature in 1846 authorized the Long Pond project to be constructed by the city of Boston and provided state backing of municipal bonds to finance it (Nesson 1983, 9). The project was completed in two years and the westward march of Boston's quest for water was under way. By 1860, Boston was using the entire safe yield of that source. With legislative backing, the city developed a new reservoir in Chestnut Hill and six smaller reservoirs in the Sudbury River watershed to augment the Long Pond supply. By 1878, Boston had tripled its supply to about 63 million gpd.

These early water projects set the precedent for later expansions of the New York and Boston water systems extending farther into their rural hinterlands (Figure 4-8). In 1898, Greater New York was consolidated into a single city of 3.5 million inhabitants. Despite enlargement of the Croton River system with a new aqueduct completed in 1891 and a new, much larger dam in 1906, the city required new sources of water. Between 1907 and 1929, it developed a series of reservoirs and a new aqueduct to draw water from the Catskill Mountains, 100 miles north of the city. The Catskill Aqueduct crossed the Hudson River by means of an "inverted siphon" 3,000 feet long and 1,100 feet below the surface of the river (Weidner 1974, 161). This spectacular feat was repeated in the 1940s when the city reached out more than 100 miles to the Delaware River headwaters in central New York State. Today, the combined systems supply New York City with over 1.4 billion gallons per day, of which 90 percent is derived from sources west of the Hudson River and the rest from the Croton River (see Figure 4-8a).

Meanwhile, Boston was pursuing a similar strategy under a different governmental framework. Whereas New York City itself established and continues today to operate its water supply system even in upstate New York, Boston's system in 1895 was sold to a newly created regional authority, the Metropolitan Water District, which was charged by state legislation to develop new water supplies to serve Boston and its immediate suburbs. In 1908, the Metropolitan Water District completed Wachusett Reservoir in central Massachusetts, connected by an 18-mile aqueduct to the earlier Sudbury reservoirs. In the 1930s, Boston's principal water source, the 400-billion-gallon Quabbin Reservoir, was constructed in central Massachusetts. The metropolitan Boston water system today serves 2.5 million people in the city and forty-three suburbs (Platt 1995) (see Figure 4-8b).

Thus during the nineteenth century, the water supply systems of both New York City and Boston evolved from dependence on primitive, privately constructed local sources to large-scale, regional systems constructed and operated by governmental agencies. The transition reflects both the advance of modern

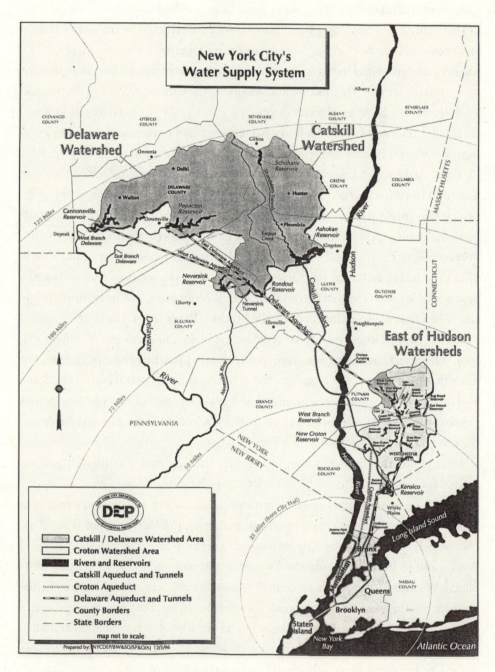

FIGURE 4-8(a) Map of New York City water supply system. *(Source: New York City Department of Environmental Protection.)*

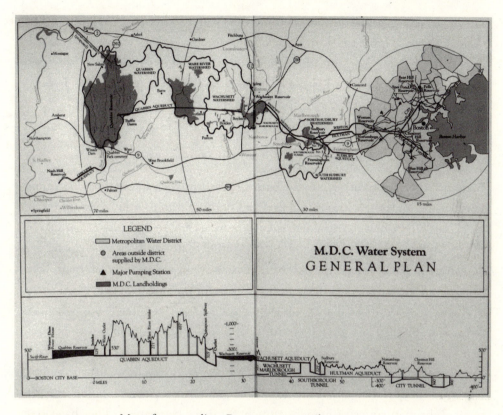

FIGURE 4-8(b) Map of metropolitan Boston water supply system.

technology (e.g., the ability to construct underground aqueducts with high-pressure siphons) as well as the evolution of municipal and regional institutions capable of serving the public interest. As in Paris, the emergence of these institutions was characterized by the development of new forms of finance, the application of modern concepts of eminent domain (land taking), and the administrative skills of technical experts.

The development of the New York and Boston water systems, each based on diversions from distant upland sources, would influence many other U.S. cities. Some cities, of course, did not require long-distance diversions; for example, Great Lakes cities found an ample source at their doorstep. (Chicago, however, had to dig a diversion channel to avoid polluting Lake Michigan—its source of drinking water—with sewage.) Los Angeles through devious means gained control of agricultural water from Owens Valley and constructed a 120-mile aqueduct to convey it to the orange groves of the San Fernando Valley (Reisner 1986). San Francisco after its 1906 earthquake and fire battled successfully against John Muir to dam the

Hetch Hetchy Valley in the Sierra Nevada as a water source (see Chapter 11). The basic strategy behind these and other long-distance urban water projects was learned from New York and Boston: employ modern technology and political power to obtain pure upland water from hinterland sources at high enough elevation to allow it to flow by gravity to where it is needed.

Urban Parks in America: The Olmsted Legacy

Imagine New York City without Central Park, Philadelphia without Fairmont Park, San Francisco without Golden Gate Park, Boston without its "Emerald Necklace," and Chicago without its lakefront parks. How impoverished would be the urban habitat of the older cities of the United States without their distinctive and spacious parks, their "green lungs" as park advocates used to call them. The existence of the great city parks is perhaps taken for granted today by the residents of those cities. Yet like urban water supply systems, parks did not simply happen to fall into place. They were established through deliberate public action, often amid controversy. Their creation during the second half of the nineteenth and early twentieth centuries required vision, money, political power, artistic genius, legal innovation, labor, and technology. The great urban parks were the embodiment of the maturing city as an instrument for social betterment. They have long been its most visible, accessible, and sometimes most neglected artifacts.

The advent of the U.S. parks movement may be traced to 1853, the year that New York's Central Park was authorized by the New York State Legislature. Central Park represented several firsts: (1) the first deliberately planned urban park in the United States (Chadwick 1966, 190), (2) the first park project of Frederick Law Olmsted, (3) the first accomplishment of landscape architecture as a profession in the United States (Fabos et al. 1968), and (4) perhaps the first use of land-value increment taxation to finance a portion of the costs of a public improvement.

In just two decades of immigration from the political turmoil in Europe between 1840 and 1860, Manhattan gained about half a million new inhabitants. In 1845, Dr. John C. Griscom published *A Brief View of the Sanitary Condition of the City,* which, like Chadwick's studies in England, documented the abysmal conditions of overcrowding and incidence of disease in the city's tenement districts (Rosen 1958, 236). One implication of the growing crisis had already been addressed in the development of the new Croton River water supply, which reached the city (but certainly not all its households) in 1842. Another need identified in Griscom's report, as in most sanitary reform literature of the time, however, was for public parks and open spaces where the working class could devote their few hours of leisure time to outdoor recreation and exercise.

In 1853, New York possessed only a handful of small parks, totaling about 117 acres. These parks were supplemented by a few privately developed "pleasure gardens": urban oases of cafés, music, and flower gardens modeled on Vauxhall Gardens in London or Copenhagen's Tivoli Gardens. By 1850, though, these places were disappearing as their site value for building increased. The only other open spaces available were cemeteries (Olmsted and Kimball 1928/1973, 20–22).

The proposal to establish a large central park in New York actually arose not from the sanitary reformers but from the city's literary and artistic community. During the mid-nineteenth century, the urban upper class became enthralled with the transcendent beauty of nature and wildness through the work of artists such as John James Audubon, Thomas Cole, and Frederick Church, writers such as George Perkins Marsh and Henry David Thoreau, and poets such as William Cullen Bryant and Henry Wadsworth Longfellow. Thus began social action to protect and restore remnants of "nature" within cities and their hinterlands. In 1844, William Cullen Bryant, whose day job was editor of the *New York Evening Post,* wrote, "If the public authorities, who expend so much of our money in laying out the city, would do what is in their power, they might give our vast population an extensive pleasure ground for shade and recreation" (Olmsted and Kimball 1928/1973, 22). Bryant's appeal was reinforced by landscape architect Andrew Jackson Downing whose journal *The Horticulturist* urged that New York should emulate English cities in the creation of large public parks.

Without a legacy of royal lands as Nash had to work with in London, however, New York had to purchase land for a park from private owners. To obtain a sizable tract of land at a reasonable cost, it was necessary to look beyond the limits of the existing built-up city—about 34th Street in 1850—to the still rural precincts of upper Manhattan. At that time, the proposed site of Central Park was a messy landscape of squatters, goats, mud, and rubbish, a thirty-minute walk from the existing city. Its advocates, however, correctly anticipated that all Manhattan would soon be paved and built over, and thus the park would be central indeed.

After prolonged lobbying by Bryant, Downing, and others, the New York State Legislature in 1853 authorized the city to establish Central Park. It was originally to comprise a rectangle of 770 acres, including space for two reservoirs to receive water from the new Croton system. The park was later expanded to 110th Street on the north, bringing its total area to 843 acres, about 0.5 mile east and west by 2.5 miles north to south.

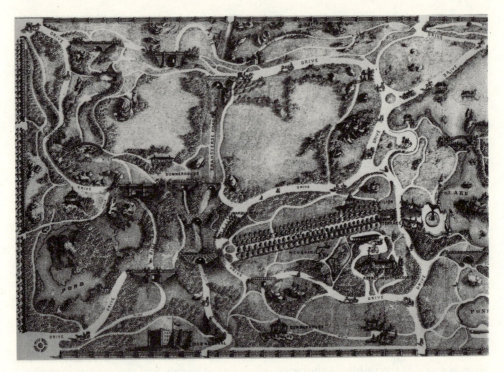

FIGURE 4-9 Excerpt from "Greensward Plan" for New York City's Central Park by
Olmsted and Vaux, 1858. *(Source: Fabos, Milde, and Weinmayr 1968.)*

The conversion of this huge and squalid tract of land into one of the world's
great urban parks was the triumph of Frederick Law Olmsted. Olmsted possessed
no particular training for landscape architecture, a field that he would soon dom-
inate. Born in 1822, he studied agricultural science and engineering at Yale and
then devoted himself to farming, travel, and writing. He moved from his farm on
Staten Island directly to the post of superintendent of the new Central Park project in 1857 (Sutton 1971, 7). In collaboration with Calvert Vaux, he prepared the
winning plan in a design competition for the park. In 1858, he was appointed
Architect in Chief to execute their plan.

Olmsted and Vaux's *Greensward Plan* for Central Park (Figure 4-9) was
influenced by English "picturesque" landscape designs, particularly Nash's
Regent's Park in London and Joseph Paxton's Birkenhead Park in Liverpool
(Chadwick 1966, 71–72). The essence of this style was deliberate informality, contrast between open meadow, groves of woods and water, and attention to the park's
borders with the surrounding city. Although as carefully planned and engineered
as a formal baroque park such as Versailles, the picturesque style sought to create
the illusion of an artificial "countryside." Olmsted wrote in 1872 that his purpose

in designing Central Park was "to supply to the hundreds of thousands of tired workers, who have no opportunity to spend their summers in the country, a specimen of God's handiwork that shall be to them, inexpensively, what a month or two in the White Mountains or the Adirondacks is, at great cost, to those in easier circumstances" (Olmsted and Kimball 1928/1973, 46).

A distinctive feature of Central Park, later widely imitated, was the separation of different forms of circulation. Pedestrians were removed from the path of equestrians and carriages, and internal bridle paths and carriage roads were isolated from cross streets for through traffic. Where routes serving different purposes met, Olmsted provided under- or overpasses to eliminate stopping points and to enhance the illusion of open countryside.

The building of Central Park was the largest public work yet undertaken in the city of New York, involving thousands of jobs and millions of dollars. The city's political machine known as "Tammany Hall" hampered Olmsted in the execution of his plans during the twenty-five years of his official connection with Central Park. He actually resigned from the project five times (Sutton 1971, 9). The park has continued to spark civic controversy ever since, as in the "Tavern on the Green" battle in the 1960s when Parks Commissioner Robert Moses ordered bulldozers to clear trees for a restaurant parking lot within the park that was opposed by park advocates (Caro 1974).

Despite its political travails, Central Park was a spectacular financial success. The total cost of acquiring its site of 843 acres from private owners was $7.4 million. The cost of improvements to the site was about $8.9 million (Olmsted and Kimball 1928/1973, 54, 95). The project was self-funding through increases in property tax collections on surrounding land. In the 1870s, the annual increase in such taxes was estimated to exceed the annual interest on the park project costs by over $4 million (Olmsted and Kimball 1928/1973, 95). Today, condominiums with a view of Central Park cost several million dollars apiece, with city tax revenues enriched accordingly.

From its inception, Central Park was also a practical success. In 1871, usership of the park amounted to some 30,000 visitors per day and more than 10 million per year (Olmsted and Kimball 1928/1973, 95), or about ten visits per capita for the entire population of Manhattan! Olmsted and Vaux sought to encourage active use in many ways, such as horseback riding, boating, carriage driving, skating, cycling, and strolling. Picturesque informality dominates most of the park plan, with the exception of a formal baroque-style mall. Open meadows, rocky outcrops, wooded areas, and water surfaces encourage spontaneity and the sense of freedom that

FIGURE 4-10 Enjoying Central Park on a fine June day, 2003. *(Photo by author.)*

provided, then and now, a charming facsimile of a rural landscape in the very heart of the nation's largest city (Figure 4-10).

Olmsted was not reticent about his achievement. In 1880, he wrote:

> To enjoy the use of the park, within a few years after it became available, the dinner hour of thousands of families permanently changed, the number of private carriages kept in the city was increased tenfold, the number of saddle horses a hundredfold, the business of livery stables more than doubled, the investment of many millions of private capital in public conveyances made profitable. It is often said, How could New York have got on without the park? Twelve million visits are made to it every year. The poor and the rich come together in it in larger numbers than anywhere else and enjoy what they find in it in more complete sympathy than they enjoy anything else together. The movement to and from it is enormous. If there were no park, with what different results in habitat and fashions, customs and manners, would the time spent in it be occupied.
>
>   And the Park of Brooklyn [Prospect Park] . . . is sure, as the city grows, to be a matter of the most important moulding consequence—more than the great bridge [Brooklyn Bridge], more so than any single affair with which the local government has had to do in the entire history of the city. (Quoted in Sutton 1971, 255)

The use of the term *moulding* [*sic*] suggests two meanings. First, Central Park and its counterparts in other cities were designed to "mould" the physical form and structure of the surrounding city. Parks were conceived to be oases of open space and bucolic scenery around which the city would grow. Second, parks were intended to "mould" the moral character of the populace. Olmsted frequently pontificated on the benefit of open space and outdoor recreation on the physical and mental health of the city dweller. These views became articles of faith in twentieth-century urban and regional planning. Today, Central Park has been substantially restored under the direction of Elizabeth Rogers, a landscape architecture historian and recently the administrator of the park and head of the Central Park Conservancy (www.centralparknyc.org). A parallel upgrading of Olmsted and Vaux's Prospect Park in Brooklyn (www.prospectpark.org) has been led by Tupper Thomas.

Perhaps Olmsted's most important contribution to modern city planning was the recognition of parks and open space as integral elements of the urban system:

> The success and popularity of Central Park started a trend, and city administrators throughout the country woke up to the advantages of open spaces. The land they were willing to purchase and sacrifice for this purpose, however, was usually some site undesirable for commercial or residential buildings, and in no way integral to the established patterns of city life, for example: the Fens in Boston; the mountain in Montreal; the swamps in Buffalo; the marshlands in Chicago. In general, the officials adopted simplistic notions of a park, separating it in their minds from the activities of the city. *Olmsted's effort was to integrate the two.* (Sutton 1971, 10–11; emphasis added)

The Emerald Necklace plan for the Boston park system, formulated in the 1880s, was a logical progression from the concept of Central Park (Figure 4-11). It comprised a series of major and minor open spaces, some existing and some proposed, to roughly encircle central Boston on its landward side. One anchor for the necklace was the old Boston Common and the new Public Garden (laid out in 1839). The other terminus of the necklace was the proposed Franklin Park. These parks were to be connected by a series of parkways and greenways bordering local streams. The achievement of these links was to be incorporated within the ongoing development of new land created by draining the Back Bay marshes in the 1860s. Commonwealth Avenue, a broad parkway, formed the main axis of the fashionable new Back Bay district and simultaneously served as a link in the Emerald Necklace.

The next link was less obvious. Olmsted urged that a remaining stretch of marsh bordering the humble Muddy River, a tributary to the Charles River, be set aside as open space rather than be filled like the rest of Back Bay. Viewed in isolation, the Muddy River Fens were befouled with rubbish and sewage and were generally unpromising as urban park space. Olmsted, though, enumerated multiple benefits to be achieved in rehabilitating the swamp: (1) abatement of a "complicated nuisance," (2) "reconciliation of convenient means of general public communication through the adjoining districts of the city," (3) "dressing and embellishment of the banks," and (4) an element of a "general scheme of sylvan improvement for the city" (quoted in Sutton 1971, 227). Olmsted's Fenway is today sadly overshadowed by an elevated highway. It is chiefly known for its namesake, Fenway Park, the home of the Boston Red Sox, and for its community gardens planted and tended by neighborhood residents (Figure 4-12).

The two paradigms of Olmsted's legacy were thus reflected in Central Park and the Emerald Necklace. The former involved the use of open space as the "working man's White Mountains" and the latter the use of a series of connected open spaces to interrupt or buffer the spread of urbanization. Olmsted enjoyed a wealth of opportunities to apply these two paradigms in various cities of North America. In contrast to Haussmann, who dealt with all planning elements of a single city, Olmsted specialized in a particular city element—parks and open space—in more than a dozen major cities. Olmsted is most celebrated for his achievements under the first paradigm, the creation of the great urban parks, but few more of them were established in the United States in the twentieth century as the white middle class fled to the suburbs, turning its back on cities. The second paradigm—interruption of urban sprawl with greenbelts and other systems of green spaces—would become a prominent theme of the conservation movement of the 1960s and thereafter (Platt 1994, 2000).

No appraisal of Olmsted would be complete without mention of his contributions to urban planning. In 1869, he and Calvert Vaux designed the prototype "garden suburb" at Riverside, Illinois, just west of Chicago (Jackson 1985, 79–81). Riverside's curvilinear streets, common greenways, and spacious residential lots impressed Ebenezer Howard, who visited there in 1876 and incorporated these characteristics into his influential garden city concept that in turn would influence twentieth-century American planning advocates like Lewis Mumford. Olmsted returned to Chicago in 1890 as landscape architect to the Columbian Exposition of 1893. He planned the lakefront site for this world's fair (which today is Jackson

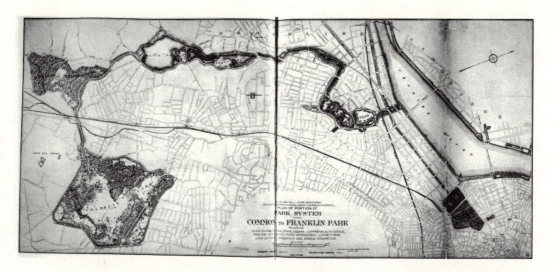

FIGURE 4-11 Olmsted's "Emerald Necklace" plan for the Boston park system, ca. 1885. *(Source: Fabos, Milde, and Weinmayr 1968.)*

FIGURE 4-12 Community gardens in the Fenway, Boston, with Prudential Building in background. *(Photo by author.)*

Park) to accommodate great pavilions and exhibition halls amid open courts, lagoons, reflecting pools, and statuary. Alongside this beaux arts "White City" was a touch of pure Olmsted, a wooded island "to contrast with the artificial grandeur and sumptuousness of the other parts of the scenery" (Sutton 1971, 194).

Behind the grandiose stage set of the White City, the 1893 exposition was admired for its applications of modern technology and planning. Transportation, food, lighting, water supply, waste disposal, and mechanical energy were all incorporated into its design. To highlight its function as a showcase for electricity, President Grover Cleveland activated its lighting and fountains by pushing a button in Washington, D.C. (to the strains of Handel's "Hallelujah Chorus" sung by a chorus of one thousand!). Thus even though the exposition looked backward to Haussmann, Versailles, and antiquity for its architectural inspiration, it looked forward to the next century in its application of technology to the design of a new community, albeit a temporary one. The contrast between the planned environment and what lay beyond its borders was widely noted:

> The [Exposition] was an artificial city that conflicted with the actual city in almost every important element. Where the American metropolis was chaotic and disorganized, the Exposition was planned and orderly; while the real city was private and commercial, the ideal was public and monumental; where Chicago was sooty and gray, the White City was clean and sparkling. (Mayer and Wade 1969, 193)

Olmsted as landscape architect was of course not responsible for the functional arrangements of the fair, but he may be credited for having successfully assimilated the demands of technology and aesthetics in his site design. This design was in effect a land use plan incorporating both the built and the unbuilt elements of a "city." The application of this integrative approach to actual cities and their surrounding regions, most notably in the 1909 Plan of Chicago, would be the work of Daniel H. Burnham, a Chicago architect and director of works for the fair. In effect, the torch of national preeminence in the art of planning cities passed from Olmsted to Burnham at the 1893 exposition. This summary of Olmsted's contributions to the U.S. city appropriately ends with a tribute to him by his successsor, Daniel Burnham:

> The genius of him who stands first in the heart and confidence of American artists.... He who has been our best adviser and our common mentor. In the highest sense he is the planner of the Exposition. No word of his has fallen to ground since first he joined us.... An artist, he paints with lakes and wooded slopes; with lawns and banks and

forest-covered hills; with mountain-sides and ocean views. [We honor him] not for his deeds of later years alone, but for what his brain has wrought and his pen has taught for half a century. (Quoted in Chadwick 1966, 196)

Relocation: The Ideal Communities Movement

This chapter has so far considered two broad avenues of public response to eighteenth-century urban crowding and squalor, namely *regulation* of building and sanitary conditions and *redevelopment* and expansion of urban infrastructure. These two approaches went hand in hand: the first yielded building and sanitary codes to be applied by local public authorities to new construction; the second fostered the development of new streets and residential districts, water systems, sewers, parks, and other infrastructure. The regulatory and the redevelopment approaches addressed the ills of existing cities directly, with gradual, uneven, but sometimes positive results.

There was, however, a third approach to the problem of urban squalor proposed by a handful of eighteenth-century utopians and progressives, namely *relocation* of workers to new, planned industrial villages in rural settings. Such communities, it was argued, would promote health, happiness, productivity, and morality. Several public-spirited individuals in Europe and the United States put their beliefs into practice and created model villages to inspire wider imitation. Although they did not succeed in the latter goal, the experimental communities and the theories of socioeconomic organization that prompted them have deeply influenced twentieth-century planning ideology.

The remainder of this chapter considers the experience of three early proponents of ideal communities. To list them is to indicate that this was no tightly circumscribed school or movement, but rather a diverse collection of individualists who were motivated by very different goals and assumptions. Those considered here are the Welsh-born utopian Robert Owen, the Chicago sleeping-car magnate George Pullman, and the stenographer-turned-progressive Ebenezer Howard. These and their like-minded contemporaries had little in common except for a repugnance for large cities, an impatience with conventional reforms, and a faith in environmental determinism.

An important heritage that influenced the planning of model industrial communities was the spiritual utopia movement that proliferated in the United States and elsewhere beginning in the late eighteenth century. The movement included

a few long-lasting and economically viable communities such as the Shaker villages of New England and New York, the Oneida settlement in New York, the
Amana Colonies in Iowa, and the Mormons in Illinois, and later, Utah. They also
included a variety of more ephemeral utopian experiments whose religious or
philosophical objectives perhaps overshadowed economic and functional practicality, as with Brook Farm in Massachusetts or the thirty *phalanxes* established in
the United States between 1843 and 1858 by followers of the French utopian
philosopher Charles Fourier (Hayden 1976, 149). Concepts for spiritual utopias
floated in the wind of mid-nineteenth-century America like cottonwood seeds.
According to Ralph Waldo Emerson in 1840, "Not a reading man but has a draft
of a new community in his waistcoat pocket" (quoted in Hayden 1976, 9).

Utopian settlements established for religious or philosophical purposes were by
definition limited to adherents to those beliefs, whereas industrial model towns
were intended for the laborers working for particular companies. The spiritual
communities valued total isolation from mainstream society, whereas the industrial communities required access to main transportation routes (obviously a
sleeping-car factory had to be connected to mainline railroads). Religious communes, however, undoubtedly influenced the concept and form of industrial
model towns and garden cities. Fundamental elements of both types of communities included (1) centralized control over the use of land and structural development (usually through ownership of the site by sect or corporation); (2) proximity
of work and residence; (3) population limits with overflow to be accommodated in
new settlements in the vicinity; (4) a rural setting with much open space within and
surrounding the community; and (5) facilities and programs for social, cultural,
and moral betterment.

Owen: From Practice to Theory

Robert Owen (1771–1858) and Ebenezer Howard (1850–1928) symmetrically
opened and closed the nineteenth century. Owen moved from practical experience
gained in a preexisting community—New Lanark, Scotland—to articulate a general theory of cooperative socioeconomic organization. Howard first formulated
his theory of the *garden city* and then successfully applied it in the establishment
of new communities at Letchworth and Welwyn. Both men proselytized public
opinion but with quite different styles and results. Howard's "peaceful path to
reform" promised a humanitarian experiment involving "no direct attack upon
vested interests" (Osborn, 1945/1965, 131). He was rewarded with a knighthood in

FIGURE 4-13 Robert Owen's New Lanark, ca. 1818. *(Source: Reproduced by permission of New Lanark Conservation Trust.)*

1927. Owen's more strident advocacy of labor organization earned him the adulation of subsequent socialists but no knighthood. Discussion of each of these visionaries, together with the pragmatic American industrialist George Pullman, will conclude this chapter.

The laboratory for Robert Owen's far-ranging theories was New Lanark, a village founded in 1783 as a site for cotton-spinning mills on a rapids of the Clyde River in south central Scotland (Figure 4-13). Upon marrying the daughter of one of the founders in 1800, Owen assumed the position of manager of the mills, which then employed more than 1,100 workers, two-thirds of them children. Owen devoted the next fourteen years and much of his personal profits to the improvement of New Lanark, both physically and institutionally. Living conditions first attracted his attention:

> The great bulk of their houses ... consisted of one single room, and before the door of that room was, as often as not, a dung-heap. One of Owen's first acts was to build another story to each of these houses, thus giving the family two rooms, and to remove the dung-heaps to a less unhealthy and unsightly position. (Cole 1953, 54)

Owen also had the streets cleaned and paved and reorganized the provision of food and coal to the inhabitants, but his chief contribution to New Lanark was in the area of education. He espoused the view, remarkable at the time, that children should be in school rather than in the mills, at least until the age of ten! His

Institute for the Formation of Character opened in 1816 in collaboration with the radical philosopher Jeremy Bentham. The institute provided child care and instruction beginning when a child could walk. It was designed to provide a balance of classroom teaching, exercise, and training in music and the arts (Benevolo 1967, 40).

No more humble than Haussmann or Olmsted, Owen referred to New Lanark as "the most important experiment for the happiness of the human race that has yet been instituted at any time in any part of the world" (Allen 1986, 3). The scope of his increasingly utopian schemes, however, was rapidly expanding beyond the possibilities for practical implementation in the "experimental cell" of New Lanark (Ashworth 1954, 119). In response to a national inquiry into the problem of unemployment and public unrest after the close of the Napoleonic Wars, Owen articulated his vision for "villages of cooperation" to accommodate workers displaced from their former jobs, who now were crowding the cities and depending on meager relief. (This idea might resonate in the United States today.)

Owen envisioned villages of about one thousand inhabitants who would chiefly be occupied in farming, although some "manufactories" would also be provided. Like a feudal manor, each village would be largely self-sufficient in food (Cole 1953, 110). He specified the size, use, and arrangement of buildings for communal living, dining, education, and relaxation. Supportive facilities included churches, stables, slaughterhouses, breweries, and corn mills. Missing from this list were courts of law and prisons, which he deemed superfluous!

According to his son, Owen's "one ruling desire was for a vast theater on which to try his plans of social reform" (Owen 1874, 211). He became convinced that such a theater could be found not in Britain but in the hinterland of the United States. The site of his second practical experiment in social organization was New Harmony, Indiana, on the Wabash River. In 1825, Owen purchased a communal village already established there by followers of the utopian George Rapp, together with 20,000 acres of alluvial farmland and forest. He and his son moved there to establish a "village of cooperation."

The enterprise was a failure. Unlike New Lanark, New Harmony lacked an existing economic base to undergird its social principles. Furthermore, Owen attempted to carry these principles much further than at New Lanark, to make every adult settler an equal partner in the ownership, operation, and economic yield of the land and manufacturing assets of the village: "Liberty, equality, and fraternity, in downright earnest!" (Owen 1874, 254). This goal, to which Owen pledged his personal wealth, was defeated by the unsuitability of the people who were attracted to settle there "a heterogeneous collection of radicals, enthusiastic devotees to principle, honest latitudinarians, and lazy theorists, with a sprinkling of unprincipled sharpers thrown in" (Owen 1874, 254). In 1827, Owen declared the project a failure and returned to England, having lost four-fifths of his own wealth.

New Harmony was Owen's last attempt to found or restructure a social community himself; subsequent experiments of this kind were conducted by his Owenite disciples (with similarly disastrous results). Owen devoted the remainder of his life to the cause of trade unionism and the advocacy of worker cooperatives.

Pullman: The Perils of Paternalism

George M. Pullman (1831–1897), one of the United States' most prominent union busters, was an incongruous successor to Robert Owen in the field of ideal town building. Like the early Owen of New Lanark, Pullman was a capitalist entrepreneur who recognized that a worker is likely to be more productive if he or she is well housed, well fed, healthy, and entertained. Yet whereas Owen departed from the profit motive to explore the possibilities of pure socialism at New Harmony, Pullman remained a stalwart industrialist. Ironically, despite the apparent success of his town in terms of bricks and mortar, Pullman's experiment in socioeconomic engineering was ultimately defeated by his obstinate *capitalism* as surely as Owen's obstinate *socialism* proved *his* undoing at New Harmony. Pullman, Illinois, is probably better known for the great labor strike that occurred there in 1894 than for its physical plan and amenities. Perhaps the underlying similarity of both men was their inability to compromise.

George Pullman invented the railroad sleeping car that bore his name in 1864 and thereafter dominated the construction and operation of such cars on railroads throughout the United States. (Readers who have never heard of, let alone traveled on, a "Pullman Car" are referred to the Marilyn Monroe film *Some Like It Hot* for a sense of the experience!) To establish a new factory for his burgeoning Pullman Palace Car Company, Pullman in 1880 purchased 4,000 acres of prairie and boggy wetland adjoining Lake Calumet, 20 miles south of downtown Chicago. This site was certainly not selected as a rural utopia, but rather for the sound reasons of cheap land and accessibility to mainline railroads. There was, however, nowhere for a workforce to live without a long train ride. Making a virtue of necessity, Pullman undertook to build a brand-new town as a model of enlightened corporate planning and good employer-employee relations (Figure 4-14).

There were few precedents to draw on. Since New Lanark, only a handful of industrial model towns had actually been constructed in Europe and the United States (Ashworth 1954, 126). The best known were Titus Salt's woolen-mill town Saltaire in England, completed in 1871, and the Massachusetts towns of Lowell and Holyoke, which produced textiles and paper, respectively. With the help of a New York architect Pullman essentially designed his town personally.

The basic elements of the town were the car factory, the residential district, a commercial and cultural arcade, a covered market, parks, a hotel, a theater, and an interdenominational church. All were built and owned by Pullman through a holding company. In physical terms, it was progressive, humane, and "ideal." Housing of diverse size and rental cost was provided to accommodate both laborers and managers. Even the lowest-cost units consisted of brick row houses lining paved streets at densities of eight to ten per acre, far less crowded than usual at the time (Saltaire in England had thirty-two houses per acre). Human wastes were collected and conveyed by pipeline to agricultural land south of the town that produced commodities for sale in the local market. Consistent with Owen, and later, Howard, alcoholic beverages were banned from sale in the town, but schools, a

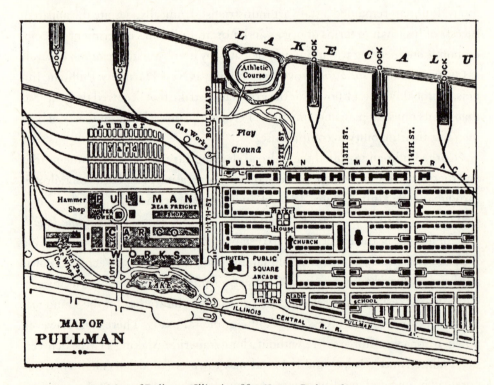

FIGURE 4-14 Map of Pullman, Illinois, 1885. *(Source: Buder 1967.*
Reproduced by permission of Oxford University Press.)

library, a theater, and other morally uplifting amenities were provided at Pullman's expense.

The town attracted immediate public attention:

> From 1880 to 1893, the town was intensely surveilled [*sic*]. Hundreds of thousands saw this most modern and novel of communities and an overwhelming majority left impressed.... Here was an American utopia that people wanted to succeed. (Buder 1967, 92–93)

The town was touted at the company's exhibit at the 1893 world's fair in Chicago as a place "where all that is ugly, and discordant and demoralizing is eliminated, and all that inspires to self-respect, to thrift and to cleanliness of thought is generously protected" (Buder 1967, 148).

Unfortunately, similar protection was not extended to the right to form a labor union or to object to company policies on wages, hours, and costs of rent, water, and food in the company store. The paternalism that benefited the eight thousand inhabitants in prosperous years became their scourge when recession forced wage cuts and layoffs in 1894. The hand that fed them could also starve them. The resulting strike lasted three months and provoked the first use of federal troops in U.S. labor history. George Pullman died three years after the strike, vilified by those whom he thought he was helping. The town, severed by legal action from the company in 1904, gradually deteriorated into obscurity until gentrification set in during the 1960s. Pullman's worker row houses rebounded as solid investments for Chicago yuppies.

Howard: From Theory to Practice

It was perhaps inevitable that an Ebenezer Howard should appear at the close of the nineteenth century. England and the United States were rife with utopian and progressive outrage concerning the state of large cities. Someone had to synthesize the many strands of thought, word, and deed into a practical program. That was Howard's contribution. In his own words, "I have taken a leaf out of the books of each type of reformer and bound them together by a thread of practicability" (Osborn 1945/1965, 131).

In effect, Howard blended Owen's New Lanark cooperative socialism with Pullman's bricks-and-mortar paternalism (although neither are discussed in his book). He incorporated impressions of landscape design experienced during his visit to Olmsted's Riverside, Illinois, community. He was influenced by Henry

George's theory of a single tax on land rent to recoup undeserved profits of land ownership for the public welfare. He was enthralled with Edward Bellamy's 1889 socialist tract *Looking Backward,* which envisioned American society recast on Owenite principles with centralized planning, cooperative enterprise, and equality of income (Fishman 1977, 33).

There was in fact very little that was original in Howard's garden city proposal, but the assimilation of these and other intellectual "leaves" yielded his influential little book, *To-morrow: A Peaceful Path to Real Reform* (published in 1898 and reissued in 1902 as *Garden Cities of To-morrow*). According to Lewis Mumford in his preface to the 1965 republication the book, "*Garden Cities* ... has done more than any other single book to guide the modern town-planning movement and to alter its objectives" (Osborn 1945/1965, 29).

Howard was the last of the great nineteenth-century self-taught urban reformers. By trade, he was a court stenographer and inventor, implying an ability to record faithfully the statements of others and to assemble components into a workable machine. Both skills, his admirers have noted, served him well in formulating his garden city theory, first in assimilating the ideas of the time and second in visualizing a community as a system or "machine." Frederick J. Osborn, Howard's chief disciple and publicist, described him as "not a political theorist, not a dreamer, but an inventor" (Osborn 1945/1965, 21). Another biographer identifies a trait of "Americanism" in Howard's personality:

> The special inheritance of the Puritan as we see it philosophically in Emerson, practically in [Henry] Ford, is a real conviction that mind triumphs over matter, that a clear idea tends to actualize itself by the inherent force that is in it. The mind of old England works from the concrete to the abstract—the New Englander works from the ideal to the real. (MacFadyen 1933/1970, 11)

Although Howard was scarcely a New Englander, the analogy is apt: in contrast to Owen, he effectively moved from theory to the practical.

The garden city idea was represented by Howard's famous magnet metaphor (Figure 4-15) wherein *town* and *country* are opposed. The former affords economic opportunity and culture at the expense of health, high prices, and crowding, whereas the latter provides a healthy environment but also boredom, poverty, and "lack of society." Howard's remedy was represented by a third magnet, *town-country,* which incorporated the advantages and minimized the negative features of the other two. It was Howard's fundamental synthesis, which appealed strongly to the Hegelian spirit of the time: "thesis, antithesis, synthesis."

Howard's magnet metaphor had additional significance. He rejected compulsion by a central authority as a means of accomplishing resettlement of population to the new garden cities. He viewed migration as a voluntary, individual decision. Thus his proposed garden city(ies) would offer inducements—social, environmental, and economic—that would draw working-class people away from the miserable conditions of the large cities and would intercept rural migrants headed toward the same cities. In Howard's diagram, " 'The People' are poised like iron filings between the magnets" (Fishman 1977, 39).

The physical plan of the garden city reflected Howard's "central idea that the size of towns is a proper subject of conscious control" (Osborn 1945/1965, 10). His recommended population size was about 32,000 people, sufficient to attract industry and sustained cultural and social activities but small enough to retain a healthy and uncrowded environment. Such a community was to be situated on a tract of about 6,000 acres, of which the town itself would occupy a central core of 1,000 acres. The remainder would be devoted to a circumferential *greenbelt* of agriculture and other rural activities (Figure 4-16). Garden cities were to be located within convenient rail distance of a central metropolis (e.g., London) but should develop a local economic base to discourage long-distance commuting to work.

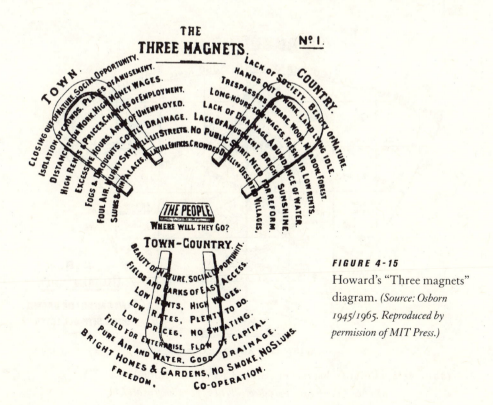

FIGURE 4-15

Howard's "Three magnets" diagram. (*Source: Osborn 1945/1965. Reproduced by permission of MIT Press.*)

Internally, the garden city would provide a range of housing opportunities to attract families of different socioeconomic levels (as in Pullman). Dwellings were to be situated along broad sylvan boulevards or local interior streets. The center of the town would be devoted to a community park surrounded by a "crystal palace" or enclosed shopping arcade, together with a "town hall, principal concert and lecture hall, theater, library, museum, picture-gallery, and hospital" (Osborn 1945/1965, 53). Privately tended gardens and common open spaces would interlace with the village core and residential areas (the Olmsted factor). An outlying industrial district would accommodate smokeless, "nonsweat" industry (Figure 4-17).

Crucial to the importance of Howard's proposal was its means of accomplishment. The entire site of the garden city, including its agricultural greenbelt, was to be acquired, planned, and managed in perpetuity by a limited-dividend (nonprofit) charitable corporation or trust. This entity would raise capital from philanthropically inclined private investors in exchange for a modest, fixed rate of return. The trust would derive all its revenue from rents on land used for residence, business, industry, and agriculture. Any revenue accruing to the trust over and above the dividend to investors and operating costs would be returned to the community for beneficial purposes (the Henry George factor). As owner of the

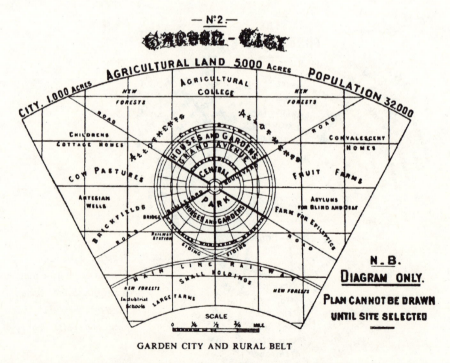

GARDEN CITY AND RURAL BELT

FIGURE 4-16 Howard's diagram of Garden City and its "Rural Belt."
(Source: Osborn 1945/1965. Reproduced by permission of MIT Press.)

land, the trust would strictly control land use and development according to a community master plan.

Limitation of population size would be achieved by limiting the supply of dwelling units and by establishing additional garden cities at a suitable distance. Howard envisioned that the prototype community would lead to a cluster of such towns, separated by their greenbelts, that in time would become a formidable "magnet" drawing the working-class populace out of the cities.

Howard and his supporters actually built two garden cities: Letchworth, starting in 1903, and Welwyn in 1920. Of the two, Letchworth is the more faithful to Howard's principles and the more widely admired. Its present population is about 32,000 as Howard had envisioned. Its residential district is graced by "cottage picturesque" architecture set amid gardens, parks, and grassy commons. The town plan of 1903 by Barry Parker and Raymond Unwin smoothed the rigid symmetry of Howard's diagrams in favor of a more organic, informal design. It includes prototypical suburban *cul-de-sacs* as well as a network of footpaths. The commercial core lacks the central park and crystal palace of Howard's imagination but instead provides retail spaces ranging from a Victorian arcade (reminiscent of Pullman), to a linear shopping street narrowed into a pedestrian and bus mall, to a

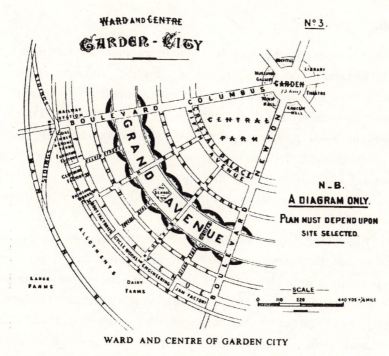

WARD AND CENTRE OF GARDEN CITY

FIGURE 4-17 Howard's diagram of Garden City's "Ward and Centre."
(*Source: Osborn 1945/1965. Reproduced by permission of MIT Press.*)

contemporary shopping center. Letchworth remains protected by an agricultural greenbelt, albeit comprising only about 2,000 acres now.

In 1963, the original Letchworth corporation was replaced by a public corporation created by an act of Parliament at the request of the town inhabitants. The new corporation performs the same role as its predecessor as trustee for the local public welfare. Every year, it allocates sizable sums from excess land rents to social and cultural organizations in Letchworth.

Howard's hope that garden cities would proliferate once their potential was demonstrated was dashed by depression, war, and the spread of less planned suburbs in Great Britain and the United States. The garden city thesis, as promoted by F. J. Osborn and the Town and Country Planning Association, however, substantially influenced the global postwar New Towns and Greenbelt programs. The British New Towns and their counterparts in France, India, the Soviet Union, Hong Kong, and elsewhere scarcely resemble Letchworth in scale or form of organization. They are predominantly high-rise, publicly constructed communities with populations far exceeding 32,000. Yet the elements of unified ownership and control of land, their mixture of functions, and their goal of metropolitan decongestion are faint echoes of Howard's third magnet.

Conclusion

This chapter has surveyed three approaches to the problems of rapid urbanization during the nineteenth century: (1) regulation of building and sanitary conditions, (2) redevelopment and expansion of urban infrastructure, and (3) relocation of factory workers to planned model communities in nonurban settings. The first two approaches involved primarily governmental actions. The third approach involved private initiatives taken by well-meaning individuals of widely differing backgrounds and motivations. All three, however, required the development of new legal measures, authorities, and doctrines to modify the existing abusive practices of urban development.

Each of these three approaches in turn served as precedent for more expansive intervention into the private land market by government during the twentieth century. Regulation would lead directly to the zoning movement that began just after World War I and continues today. Regulation also proliferated in the various public programs of environmental management concerned with clean air and water, wetlands, toxic wastes, pesticides, and many other issues. Redevelopment emerged after World War II as the focus of the public urban renewal programs and its various offshoots. Relocation has been the self-selected strategy of millions of central city residents who have moved to suburban areas or back to the hills and byways of rural America. Although not overtly a governmental policy, many laws and programs (e.g., the interstate highway system and federal tax benefits for home ownership) have contributed to the impetus to abandon older central cities. The next two chapters continue this chronology of the evolution of cities, land use, and society through the twentieth century.

References

Allen, N. 1986. *David Dale, Robert Owen, and the Story of New Lanark.* Edinburgh: Moubray House Press.

Ashworth, W. 1954. *The Genesis of Modern British Town Planning.* London: Routledge and Kegan Paul.

Benevolo, L. 1967. *The Origins of Modern Town Planning.* Trans. J. Landry. Cambridge, MA: MIT Press.

Blake, N. M. 1956. *Water for the Cities.* Syracuse, NY: Syracuse University Press.

Booth, M. L. 1860. *History of the City of New York.* New York: W. R. C. Clark and Meeker.

Bridenbaugh, C. 1964. *Cities in the Wilderness.* New York: Capricorn Books.

Buder, S. 1967. *Pullman: An Experiment in Industrial Order and Community Planning, 1880–1930.* New York: Oxford University Press.

Caro, R. A. 1974. *The Power Broker.* New York: Knopf.

Chadwick, G. F. 1966. *The Park and the Town: Public Landscape in the 19th and 20th Centuries.* New York: Praeger.

Chapman, B. 1953. Baron Haussmann and the Planning of Paris. *Town Planning Review* 24:177–92.

Chapman, J. M., and B. Chapman. 1957. *The Life and Times of Baron Haussmann: Paris in the Second Empire.* London: Weidenfeld and Nicolson.

Cole, M. 1953. *Robert Owen of New Lanark.* London: Batchworth Press.

Davis, T. 1966. *John Nash: The Prince Regent's Architect.* London: Country Life.

Fabos, J. Gy., G. T. Milde, and V. M. Weinmayr. 1968. *F. L. Olmsted, Sr.: Founder of Landscape Architecture in America.* Amherst: University of Massachusetts Press.

Fishman, R. 1977. *Urban Utopias in the Twentieth Century.* New York: Basic Books.

Flinn, M. W., ed. 1965. *Edwin Chadwick's Report on the Sanitary Condition of the Labouring Population of Great Britain.* Edinburgh: Edinburgh University Press.

Giedion, S. 1962. *Space, Time, and Architecture.* Cambridge, MA: Harvard University Press.

Hayden, D. 1976. *Seven American Utopias: The Architecture of Communitarian Socialism, 1790–1975.* Cambridge, MA: MIT Press.

Jackson, K. T. 1985. *Crabgrass Frontier: The Suburbanization of the United States.* New York: Oxford University Press.

Jordan, D. P. 1995. *Transforming Paris: The Life and Labors of Baron Haussmann.* New York: Free Press.

Kutler, S. I. 1971. *Privilege and Creative Destruction: The Charles River Bridge Case.* New York: W. W. Norton.

MacFadyen, D. 1933/1970. *Sir Ebenezer Howard and the Town Planning Movement.* Cambridge, MA: MIT Press.

Mayer, H. M., and R. C. Wade. 1969. *Chicago: Growth of a Metropolis.* Chicago: University of Chicago Press.

Nesson, F. L. 1983. *Great Waters: A History of Boston's Water Supply.* Hanover, NH: University Press of New England.

Olmsted, F. L., Jr., and T. Kimball. 1928/1973. *Forty Years of Landscape Architecture: Central Park.* Cambridge, MA: MIT Press.

Osborn, F. S., ed. 1945/1965. *Ebenezer Howard's Garden Cities of To-Morrow.* Cambridge, MA: MIT Press.

Owen, R. D. 1874. *Threading My Way.* London: Turner.

Page, M. 1999. *The Creative Destruction of Manhattan: 1900–1940.* Chicago: University of Chicago Press.

Peets, E. 1927. Famous Town Planners: Haussmann. *Town Planning Review* 12:181–90.

Peterson, J. A. 1983. The Impact of Sanitary Reform upon American Urban Planning 1840–1890. In *Introduction to Planning History in the United States,* ed. D. A. Krueckeberg, 13–39. New Brunswick, NJ: Rutgers Center for Urban Policy Research.

Platt, R. H. 1994. From Commons to Commons: Evolving Concepts of Open Space in North American Cities. In *The Ecological City: Preserving and Restoring Urban Biodiversity*, eds. R. H. Platt, R. A. Rowntree, and P. C. Muick, 22–39. Amherst: University of Massachusetts Press.

———. 1995. The 2020 Water Supply Study for Metropolitan Boston: Demise of Diversion. *Journal of the American Planning Association* 61 (2): 185–99.

———. 2000. Ecology and Land Development: Past Approaches and New Directions. In *The Practice of Sustainable Development*, ed. D. R. Porter, 25–52. Washington, DC: Urban Land Institute.

Rasmussen, S. E. 1967. *London: The Unique City.* Cambridge, MA: MIT Press.

Reisner, M. 1986. *Cadillac Desert: The American West and Its Disappearing Water.* New York: Penguin.

Riis, J. A. 1890/1972. *How the Other Half Lives.* Williamstown, MA: Corner House.

Rosen, G. 1958. *A History of Public Health.* New York: MD Publications.

Saalman, H. 1971. *Haussmann: Paris Transformed.* New York: George Braziller.

Smith, E. R. 1907. Baron Haussmann and the Topographical Transformation of Paris under Napoleon III. *Architectural Record* 21–38.

Summerson, J. 1962. *Georgian London.* Baltimore: Penguin.

Sutton, S. B., ed. 1971. *Civilizing American Cities: A Selection of Frederick Law Olmsted's Writings on City Landscape.* Cambridge, MA: MIT Press.

Weber, A. F. 1899/1963. *The Growth of Cities in the Nineteenth Century: A Study in Statistics.* Ithaca, NY: Cornell University Press.

Weidner, C. H. 1974. *Water for a City.* New Brunswick, NJ: Rutgers University Press.

Whitehill, W. M. 1968. *Boston: A Topographic History.* 2nd ed. Cambridge, MA: Harvard University Press.

CHAPTER 5 *Building a Metropolitan Nation: 1900–1945*

Make no little plans. They have no magic to stir men's blood and probably themselves will not be realized. Make big plans; aim high in hope and work.
—DANIEL H. BURNHAM, 1907 [AS QUOTED IN WRIGLEY, 1983, 71]

The United States entered the twentieth century still predominantly a rural nation. Of its total 1900 population of 76 million, 40 percent (30.4 million) lived in cities, and the other 60 percent (45.4 million) in smaller towns and rural areas. The 1920 U.S. Census was the first to report that city dwellers exceeded rural population, and the urban population has continued to increase absolutely and proportionately ever since. By 2000, the total U.S. population had almost quadrupled from 1900 to about 281 million, of whom about four-fifths (229 million) lived in metropolitan areas (as discussed in Chapter 6) with only one-fifth (52 million) living in rural areas. The nation had about 7.5 times more urban residents in 2000 than in 1900 (Table 5-1). At the global scale, cities in 1900 contained about 160 million inhabitants, only one-tenth of world population (Table 5-2). Today, one of every two humans lives in urban regions (about 3 billion people), and 90 percent of projected population growth is expected to be urban, mostly living in less developed nations (O'Meara 1999, 5).

These bland numbers scarcely capture the drastic, colorful, and ominous changes the United States and the world underwent during the twentieth century. At its opening, railroads, steamships, and telegraph were commonplace, telephones and typewriters were beginning to appear, and aviation was just about to be born. A century later in developed nations, highway transportation has eclipsed rail service, personal computers and the Internet are ubiquitous, air traffic has reached saturation in many cities, and carbon dioxide emissions have increased

150

TABLE 5-1 U.S. POPULATION, 1900–2000

YEAR	U.S. POPULATION (MILLIONS)	PERCENT URBAN	PERCENT RURAL
1900	76.0	40%	60%
1910	92.4	46%	54%
1920	106.4	51%	49%
1930	123.0	56%	44%
1940	132.4	57%	43%
1950	152.2	60%	40%
1960	180.6	63%	37%
1970	205.0	74%	26%
1980	227.7	74%	26%
1990	249.9	75%	25%
2000	281.4	81.5%[a]	N.A.

[a] Metropolitan area population; "Urban" and rural population not available for the 2000 U.S. Census at time of writing.

TABLE 5-2 POPULATION OF THE WORLD'S LARGEST METROPOLITAN AREAS, 1900 AND 2000

CITY	1900 POPULATION (MILLIONS)	CITY	2000 POPULATION (MILLIONS)
London	6.5	Tokyo	26.4
New York	4.2	Mexico City	18.1
Paris	3.3	Bombay	18.1
Berlin	2.7	São Paulo	17.8
Chicago	1.7	New York	16.6
Vienna	1.7	Lagos	13.4
Tokyo	1.5	Los Angeles	13.1
St. Petersburg	1.4	Calcutta	12.9
Manchester	1.4	Shanghai	12.9
Philadelphia	1.4	Buenos Aires	12.6

SOURCE: Brown 2001, Table 9-1.

twelvefold—from 0.5 billion metric tons worldwide in 1900 to more than 6 billion in 2000 (one-fourth of which originates in the United States)—raising fears of global warming and sea level rise (Brown 2001, Fig. 2-1).

American society over the twentieth century displayed a love-hate relationship with its cities. The first three decades of the century were a time of exuberant city building, both upwards and outwards. The Great Depression and World War II suspended city evolution for fifteen years. After that war, government and industry switched from military to consumer production, and a massive boom in home construction resulted. Over fifteen million new homes were built during the 1950s, more than twice the total for the 1940s and six times the number built in the 1930s (Rome 2001, 35). Most of these were single-family homes built on farmland and hillsides in suburbs surrounding the older core cities. Most were purchased by white middle-class families leaving older city neighborhoods behind. This dual phenomenon of "urban sprawl" and "white flight" was aided and abetted by federal housing subsidies and highway construction programs and, in the early postwar years, deliberate policies that favored white households and communities (Jackson 1985).

Meanwhile, the federal urban renewal and highway programs were tearing down older neighborhoods, leaving the nonwhite and the poor to compete for space in overpriced surviving housing or in sterile and isolated public housing projects. Challenged by critics like Jane Jacobs and Herbert Gans, the urban renewal program gradually faded away with President Johnson's "War on Poverty" in the late 1960s, leaving vast areas of vacant land and abandoned neighborhoods in older industrial cities.

Migration from central city to suburb in the 1950s through the 1970s was overshadowed in the 1980s by population flows of professionals and retirees from "Frost Belt" to "Sun Belt" regions of the South and West, and in the 1990s to fast-growing desert cities of the interior West: Las Vegas, Yuma, and Phoenix were, respectively, the first, third, and eighth fastest-growing of the nation's 280 metropolitan areas during the 1990s. New wealth in the 1980s and 1990s fueled both a resurgence of glitzy downtown construction and peripheral "edge cities" (Garreau 1991) to meet the demand for upscale dining, shopping, and entertainment. Meanwhile, the "downscale" side of American society (e.g., those below the national median family income of $50,800 in 2000) went relatively unnoticed and unserved under both Republican and Democratic administrations alike after 1980. The corporate scandals and dot-com crash, soon followed by the terrorist attacks of September 11, 2001, left the nation tottering into the new century with no sense of direction on domestic priorities. All too often, older communities are strapped for money to maintain existing facilities and services, while developers of "green-field" sites beyond the urban fringe demand public subsidies for new schools, roads, water and sewer facilities, and other infrastructure.

With this thumbnail sketch as a road map, this chapter and the next will examine twentieth-century urban growth and decline in the United States in more detail.

American Cities circa 1900

The close of the nineteenth century offered many portents for the new urban century to come. The Chicago Columbian Exposition of 1893, a landmark among world's fairs, established that city as a world center of commerce, culture, and civic pride in its rebound from its Great Fire of 1871. In 1898, the city of New York responded to Chicago's challenge by consolidating Manhattan, Brooklyn, the Queens, the Bronx, and Staten Island to form the colossus "Greater New York": "over three million strong, over three hundred square miles huge, larger than Paris, gaining on London, New York was ready to face the twentieth century" (Burrows and Wallace 1999, 1235). Meanwhile, San Francisco, unaware of the catastrophic earthquake and fire about to happen in 1906, was achieving greatness at the turn of the century according to an ecstatic booster:

> The great triangle of the Pacific is destined to have its lines drawn between Hong Kong, Sydney, and San Francisco. Of these three ports, Hong Kong will have China behind it, Sydney, Europe, and San Francisco, America; and with America for a backing, San Francisco can challenge the world in the strife for commercial supremacy. (Keeler 1903, 94)

Not to be outdone, the next tier of cities of the Northeast and Middle West were flourishing to an extent hard to imagine in light of their decline later in the twentieth century (and partial revival in some cases). Many medium-sized cities rose and fell with the fortunes of a particular industry or company: examples are Detroit (automobiles); Hartford (insurance); Springfield, Massachusetts (fire-arms); Waterbury, Connecticut (clocks); and Rochester, New York (cameras). Buffalo, the country's eighth largest city in 1900, was the scene of the 1901 Pan-American Exposition (remembered chiefly as where President William McKinley was assassinated, followed by the inauguration of President Theodore Roosevelt). Prosperous cities of 1900 such as Buffalo, Hartford, Providence, Pittsburgh,

Cleveland, and Baltimore, despite later social and economic turmoil, still are well endowed with museums, parks, concert halls, hospitals, and universities provided by wealthy benefactors a century ago.

While large and small cities proudly built their downtown office towers, public buildings, and cultural facilities, the migration of their white middle class to the suburbs was already under way. Beginning just after the Civil War, horse-drawn streetcars, and later electric railways and subways, began to foster the development of new suburban towns within convenient commuting distance of downtowns (Warner 1978). Some of these places, like Roxbury and Dorchester, Massachusetts, were initially separate towns that joined the central city, to gain access to Boston's water system in their case. Other suburbs like Brookline and Newton, also in the Boston area, fought to remain independent of the central city. The struggle over the political geography of municipal territory would be a dominant issue in metropolitan governance throughout the twentieth century (Teaford 1979; Rusk 1999).

Meanwhile, the continued festering of slums and tenements in the late nineteenth century outraged social reformers and progressive journalists (known as "muckrakers"). In 1890, Jacob Riis's *How the Other Half Lives* documented through prose and photography the hideous state of New York's tenement districts. The moral implications of urban overcrowding were deplored by the Reverend Josiah Strong in his 1898 tract *The Twentieth Century City*: "the new civilization is certain to be urban; and the problem of the twentieth century will be the city" (quoted in Teaford 1993, 1). In 1904, Lincoln Steffens, a socialist journalist, scrutinized big-city bossism and corruption in *The Shame of the Cities*. Upton Sinclair's 1906 book *The Jungle* exposed the abuses of the meatpacking industry. Between 1903 and 1912, more than two thousand articles on social conditions in U.S. magazines and newspapers (Ciucci et al. 1979, 188). Immigration, however, continued to overcrowd urban ghettos in the major East Coast ports of entry. Arriving immigrants reached an all-time high of 1.3 million persons in 1907, and as of 1910, 13.3 million foreign-born persons were living in the United States, making up one-seventh of the nation's total population (Hofstadter 1955, 176). Around 1890, the social worker Jane Addams established Hull House on Chicago's West Side to administer to the needs of the poor immigrants of the neighborhood. Hull House would be the model for the "settlement house movement" in many cities in the early 1900s (Mayer and Wade 1969, 160).

By the dawn of the twentieth century, the major fault lines of city versus city, city versus suburb, rich versus poor, and "native" versus foreign-born were well established. Many of the same debates of that time continue today: unequal distribution of wealth, corporate greed and irresponsibility, and disagreement over the responsibility of government to help the less fortunate. The names of the stakeholders have changed: Standard Oil, railroads, and "Big Steel" in 1900, but Enron, WorldCom, and Time Warner in 2003; Irish, Germans, and Italians in 1900, but Hispanics, Cambodians, and Somalians today. As a polymorphous nation, however, the social and economic divisions of the United States have always been reflected in, and often reinforced by, patterns of land use and urban geography. The character of American society, for better or worse, may be read in its urban, political, and socioeconomic landscape. Concomitantly, efforts of various subgroups—both rich and poor, white and nonwhite—to improve their status have frequently taken the form of proposals and programs to manipulate the use and design of urban space.

The City Ascendant: 1900–1933

The first third of the twentieth century—roughly marked by the inaugurations of President Theodore Roosevelt in 1901 and his distant cousin Franklin D. Roosevelt in 1933—was the golden age of the American city. It was a period of tall new "skyscrapers," high-speed and luxurious intercity railroads, convenient and affordable commuter rail service, the spread of national radio networks, the advent of big-city professional sports, and the convenience of buying and selling stocks via "wire" or telephone. After the nation's two-year involvement in World War I, followed by a raging influenza pandemic, the nation's cities rebounded as the stage sets for the "Roaring 20s" and the "Jazz Age." Organized crime flourished, as did real estate speculation, big-city political machines, corruption, vice, and "speakeasies." This era was memorialized in F. Scott Fitzgerald's *The Great Gatsby*; George Gershwin's *Rhapsody in Blue*; the cubist paintings of Picasso, Matisse, and Leger; soaring art deco office buildings and stock prices; and unlimited optimism in a permanent state of peace and prosperity. The exuberance of the period lingered even into the Great Depression in the striking (but empty) 102-floor Empire State Building and Rockefeller Center (Okrent 2003) in New York and the 1933 Chicago "Century of Progress" Exposition. The nation was 56 percent urban according to the 1930 census, and the preponderance of those city dwellers—rich, poor, and middle class—still lived in the nation's large central cities.

The urban problems inherited from the nineteenth century—poverty, slums, infectious disease, labor exploitation, nativism, racism, and corporate greed—

continued unabated in the early 1900s. Also continuing in the new century were the three strands of social adaptation to squalor and epidemic identified in Chapter 4, namely *regulation*, *redevelopment*, and *relocation*. These three approaches would respectively underlay twentieth-century urban reform efforts, as discussed in later chapters: (1) land use zoning and environmental regulations; (2) urban redevelopment, revitalization and gentrification; and (3) suburbanization, as promoted by federal policies on taxation, housing, and highways.

In 1900, land use and building practices were still largely the result of private market decisions by landowners, lenders, public transit companies, and utility providers (Warner 1978). Public involvement in the planning of cities and suburbs was virtually nonexistent as the doctrine of laissez-faire dominated the political and economic culture of the United States. Similarly, government had little voice in the growing monopolies of steel, oil, railroads, banking, and other industries; labor reform and consumer protection also lay in the future.

The first two decades of the century, however, would yield remarkable changes in the respective roles of government and the private market concerning the evolving nature of cities and suburbs. The first National Conference on Planning was held in 1909, and the nation's first zoning ordinance was adopted by New York City in 1916. These two changes in turn led to widespread adoption of planning and zoning legislation in many states, and in the 1920s, a full-fledged planning and zoning movement swept the country.

This dramatic social and legal change in the role of government in relation to urban development (consistent with the land use and society model; see Figure 2-7) may be ascribed to the convergence of at least four contemporary cultural influences on the political establishment at the turn of the century: (1) the city beautiful movement, (2) the garden city movement, (3) nuisance and building regulation, and (4) the progressive movement. Collectively, these developments contributed to public acceptance of, and demand for, limited governmental intervention in the private land market to foster orderly, safe, and functional spatial patterns of urban land use and to curtail abuses by property owners affecting their neighbors or the wider public.

The City Beautiful Movement

The City Beautiful movement influenced the design of city centers and public architecture in the United States between the 1890s and the 1950s (Hall 1988, Chap.

6; Wilson 1990). The movement was inspired by the architecture and urban spaces of ancient Greece and Rome, as reinterpreted in palaces and city plans of the late Renaissance in Europe, most notably Louis XIV's extravagant Versailles Palace of the late seventeenth century. Georges Haussmann's redevelopment of Paris in the mid-nineteenth century was strongly influenced by Versailles and other archetypes of neoclassical design. The ornate style of architectural design popularized by Haussmann's Paris, known as the *beaux arts,* in turn spread to the United States, making its debut in the 1893 Chicago Columbian Exposition. The vast colonnades, fake temples, reflecting pools, and statuary of that exposition were in jarring contrast to the more indigenous "prairie school" architectural style being developed by Louis Sullivan and Frank Lloyd Wright. The pseudo-classicism of the exposition, later called a "great leap backward" by the architectural critic Sigfried Giedion (1962), nevertheless shaped the opinions of civic leaders across the country that anything that looked "old" and "European" was superior to homegrown American architectural styles. Thus city halls, libraries, museums, government offices, banks, and other downtown buildings were embellished with columns, porticos, arches, and stonework. City plazas were relentlessly geometric and focused on statues or fountains (or both as in Chicago's Grant Park) surrounded by formal gardens and paved pedestrian spaces. From Washington, D.C., to Cleveland to Denver to Seattle, the nation's older city centers are still dominated by public spaces and pompous architecture from the city beautiful era (Figure 5-1): ancient Egypt, Greece, and Rome meet Main Street!

The twentieth century opened with the commissioning in 1900 of what would be a showcase of the city beautiful style: the McMillan Commission Plan for the Washington, D.C., park system (named after its Senate sponsor James McMillan). A special "blue-ribbon panel" was appointed that included four principals of the 1893 Columbian Exposition: architects Daniel H. Burnham and Charles F. McKim, landscape architect Frederick Law Olmsted Jr. (who had assumed his ailing father's practice), and sculptor Augustus Saint-Gaudens. The original 1792 plan for Washington, D.C., was drawn by Pierre L'Enfant, a French military engineer, who provided the future "Capital of Democracy" with an ironic resemblance to the seventeenth-century Versailles Palace and formal grounds designed for the despotic Louis XIV. The growth of the city during the nineteenth century generally conformed to the L'Enfant plan, but with much clutter and encroachment on public spaces. By 1900, Congress believed that the nation's capital needed a facelift.

In search of inspiration, the commission traveled to various European capitals and particularly Paris. The commission's report (U.S. Congress 1902) proposed a monumental redevelopment program later described as "an inspiring set piece of the city beautiful movement that was to sweep the nation" (Gutheim 1976, 38). The Mall, as the city's major axis, was to be redesigned, replanted, and extended to include the future reflecting pool and Lincoln Memorial. It was to be cleared of encroachments and embellished with new public buildings, fountains, gardens, and statuary (Figures 5-2 and 5-3). Most of the commission's Mall improvements were subsequently carried out, including the replacement of an ill-placed rail terminal with the gleaming beaux arts Union Station constructed in 1903 (which today is also the site of a three-level shopping concourse).

Chicago architect Daniel Burnham was to be the "high priest" of city beautiful architecture and city planning after his successes in the Columbian Exposition and the McMillan Commission plan. The latter were quickly followed by plans for Cleveland (1903), San Francisco (1905), and Manila (1905) (Wilson 1990). Burnham's masterpiece, however, was the 1909 *Plan of Chicago* (Burnham and Bennett 1909). In the course of preparing that plan, Burnham allegedly uttered the most

FIGURE 5-1
The City Beautiful in Buffalo: Egyptian obelisk in front of art deco government building with Grecian columns and frieze, ca. 1920s. *(Photo by author.)*

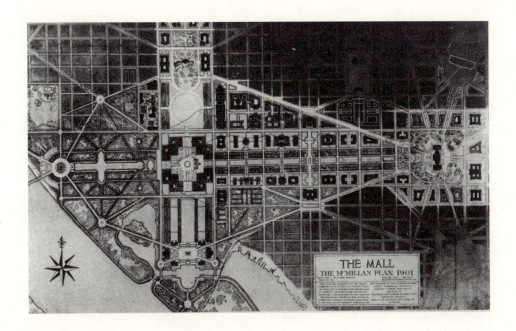

FIGURE 5-2
(*above*) The 1901 McMillan
Commission Plan for the
Mall in Washington, D.C.
(*Source: Gutheim 1976, Fig. 16.*)

FIGURE 5-3
(*left*) The Mall in Washington,
D.C., 2002. (*Photo by author.*)

famous adage in U.S. city planning history that appears at the beginning of this chapter.

The *Plan of Chicago* in fact marked a transition from the city beautiful to more functional approaches to city planning. Its most city beautiful element—a baroque civic center flanked by Haussmann-style building facades—was (fortunately) never built (Figure 5-4). The functional elements of the plan, however, would reshape the face of the city over succeeding decades, including parks and forest preserves, streets and boulevards, bridges, rail, and port facilities. As popularized in a school textbook, the plan influenced a generation of Chicago taxpayers to support such projects as the completion of the city's lakefront park system; the double-decking of Wacker Drive and a traffic bridge across the rail yards south of the central business district; the consolidation of rail terminals; and, at a regional scale, the establishment of the Cook County Forest Preserve system (Figure 5-5).

The *Plan of Chicago* thus marked a major leap beyond earlier city beautiful plans dominated by pompous aesthetics and dubious practicality. Like its predecessors, however, the Chicago plan still disregarded needs other than public improvements, such as housing and neighborhood planning. A later critic observed that a defect of all city beautiful plans was "the lack of legitimation of any public control over the private actions that were decisive in setting the quality of the urban environment. The early planners merely avoided the issue when they made 'planning' coterminous with parks, boulevards, and civic centers" (Goodman 1968, 22). Even more acerbic was the indictment of the city beautiful by the urban historian Lewis Mumford (1955, 147), who wrote, "Our imperial architecture is an architecture of compensation: It provides grandiloquent stones for people who have been deprived of bread and sunlight."

Some public spaces of the city beautiful era, like Chicago's Grant Park and the Washington, D.C., Mall, are enormously popular and functional today. The latter serves as the nation's parade ground for all sorts of social movements and demonstrations as well as daily use by joggers, strollers, tourists, and gawkers. Other plazas from that era, like Denver's Civic Center, are simply windy open areas, either too hot or too cold, to be crossed as quickly as possible. Although many such city beautiful legacies today seem pompous and unecological, they resulted from well-meaning partnerships between the public and private sectors that invested in public buildings and city spaces. While its physical legacies are a mixed blessing, the spirit of that age and its civic pride should inspire today's efforts to revive older city centers from Portland, Maine, to San Diego.

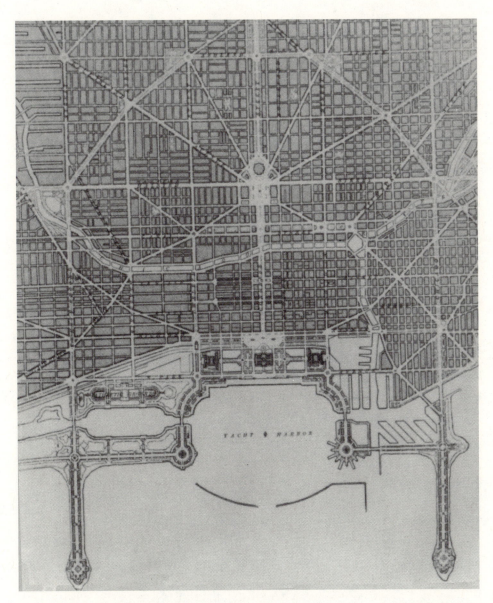

FIGURE 5-4 Burnham and Bennett's 1909 *Plan of Chicago*: proposed downtown and harbor improvements (unimplemented in part). *(Source: Mayer and Wade 1969, 277.)*

FIGURE 5-5 Burnham and Bennett's 1909 *Plan of Chicago*: proposed parks and forest preserves (mostly implemented). *(Reproduced from the original plan.)*

The Garden City Movement

A very different vision of a planned community was provided by Ebenezer Howard's book *Garden Cities of To-morrow* and the founding of Letchworth in 1903, as discussed in Chapter 4 (Hall 1988, Chap. 4). American admirers of Howard's theories established the Garden Cities Association of America (GCAA) in 1906, which attracted the "same kinds of civic and political leaders who had supported Howard's ideas in England" (Schaffer 1982, 32). This organization proposed to house 375,000 families in a series of garden communities to be constructed in several eastern states, but without result. F. L. Olmsted Jr.'s 1912 design for Forest Hills, New York, sponsored by the Russell Sage Foundation, however, reflected Howard's garden city principles (a reciprocal tribute to Howard's admiration for Olmsted Sr.'s design for Riverside, Illinois).

The GCAA was dissolved in 1921 and replaced two years later by the much more influential Regional Planning Association of America (RPAA), of which the young Lewis Mumford was a charter member. This group successfully promoted several garden city-style projects, most notably Radburn, New Jersey, in 1927 (Parsons 1994). Rexford Tugwell, another RPAA member and New Dealer, oversaw the construction of three "greenbelt towns" during the 1930s, as discussed later in this chapter. Direct interest in building garden cities on Howard's principles was, however, limited to these experimental communities and did not mature into a national movement in the United States.

Although the *process* of garden city establishment was relatively unfamiliar before the 1920s, the *form* of the garden city—particularly its emphasis on the sylvan, low-density residential neighborhood and the separation of homes and commerce—resonated perfectly with the iconography of early suburbia in the United States. Lacking the control provided by a unified land trust of the Letchworth type, it was natural for the new suburbanites to seek a legal means of perpetuating the bucolic environment that they had fled the cities to attain. Land use zoning, as upheld by the U.S. Supreme Court in 1926, would serve that purpose (discussed in Chapters 9 and 10).

Nuisance and Building Regulation

In 1915, the U.S. Supreme Court upheld an unusual Los Angeles city ordinance that prohibited brickyards within a 3-square-mile district recently annexed to the city. The measure was challenged by the owner of a clay pit and brick kiln that predated both the ordinance and the annexation of his site by the city. The Court upheld the regulation against the charge that it substantially reduced the value of the property and did not apply to similar businesses elsewhere in Los Angeles (*Hadacheck v. Sebastian* 239 U.S. 394). This decision today seems harsh and arbitrary in destroying a previously legal business, but it reflects growing social acceptance of government regulation to regulate activities that create a "public nuisance" (in this case, air pollution and possibly noise).

Hadacheck was consistent with a line of Supreme Court decisions extending back to the 1870s that upheld state and local regulation of particular uses of private property without compensation. These cases differed from the prevailing doctrine of laissez-faire, which opposed even minimal public intervention in the business economy, as reflected in the Court's disapproval in 1905 of a New York statute regulating child labor in *Lochner v. New York* (198 U.S. 45 [Toll 1969, 16–18]). When a private use of land or economic activity threatened the public interest, as opposed to the interest of individual workers, the Court was remarkably proactive. As early as 1872, a New Orleans ordinance that vested a monopoly in livestock slaughtering in one enterprise and banned all competitors without compensation was upheld by the U.S. Supreme Court with the following resounding declaration:

> Unwholesome trades, slaughter-houses, operations offensive to the senses, the deposit of powder, the application of steam power to propel cars, the building with combustible materials, and the burial of the dead, may all … be interdicted by law, in the midst of dense masses of population, on the general and rational principle that every person ought to use his property as not to injure his neighbors; and that *private interests must be made subservient to the general interests of the community. This is called the police power.* (Slaughterhouse Cases, 16 Wall 36, 1872; emphasis added)

In 1887, the Court upheld a Kansas law that prohibited the manufacture and sale of alcoholic beverages and closed existing breweries (*Mugler v. Kansas,* 123 U.S. 663), stating:

> A prohibition simply upon the use of property for purposes that are declared by valid legislation to be injurious to the health, morals, or safety of the community, cannot, in any just sense be deemed a taking or an appropriation of property for the public benefit [in violation of the Fifth Amendment to the U.S. Constitution]. Such legislation does not disturb the owner in the control or use of his property for lawful purposes nor restrict his right to dispose of it. (123 U.S., at 667–68)

These and other nuisance decisions reflected a growing use by states and local governments of laws to limit or even prohibit harmful private activities before they occurred, rather than after the fact, and without compensation to the affected private party. This role of government is known as the *public regulatory power* or simply the *police power.* A key element of the developing doctrine of the police power at the turn of the century was the recognition of the need for prospective regulation of private activity rather than simply taking action after harm had occurred:

> The common law of nuisance deals with nearly all the more serious and flagrant viola-tions of the interests which the police power protects, but it deals with evils only after they have come into existence, and it leaves the determination of what is evil very largely to the particular circumstance of each case. *The police power endeavors to prevent evil by checking the tendency toward it and it seeks to place a margin of safety between that which is permitted and that which is sure to lead to injury or loss.* This can be accomplished to some extent by establishing positive standards and limitations which must be observed, although to step beyond them would not necessarily create a nuisance at common law. (Freund 1904; emphasis added)

The proposition that the police power might address conditions that would not necessarily constitute a traditional common-law nuisance opened the door to the introduction of public regulation of the use of land and buildings. Furthermore, there was growing precedent for the establishment of different regulations for different geographical districts of a community, that is, incipient zoning. *Hada-check,* for instance, involved restriction on land use applicable to a particular area of Los Angeles.

Regulation of the heights of new buildings was approved by the 1909 U.S. Supreme Court opinion in *Welch v. Swasey* (214 U.S. 91). *Welch* involved a Mas-sachusetts law that imposed a limit of 125 feet for new buildings in designated com-mercial districts of Boston and lesser heights in residential districts. The Court upheld the measure, assuming that the legislature had good reasons for making such a distinction. (It suggested that women and children are more likely to be at risk from fire in residential areas and so buildings should be smaller there.)

These decisions reflect the degree of judicial tolerance toward public regula-tions affecting the use of private property prior to the advent of comprehensive planning and zoning in the 1920s. Supreme Court opinions are only the "tip of the iceberg" of what is happening in the society at large: for each disputed measure reviewed by the High Court, dozens were resolved in lower courts and hundreds went unchallenged. Height limitations, for instance, were quite widespread by the time of the *Welch* decision. As early as 1889 a height limit was imposed in

Washington, D.C. to enhance views of the Washington Monument and the Capitol. Due to that measure, Washington remains strikingly horizontal today in contrast to the vertical profiles of other U.S. central cities. By 1913, twenty-two U.S. cities had some form of height controls (Delafons 1969, 20).

The Progressive Movement

The first decade of the twentieth century spawned a wave of public interest in progressive reform as personified in President Theodore Roosevelt. The essence of the progressive movement in the words of historian Richard Hofstadter (1955, 5) was

> that broader impulse toward criticism and change that was everywhere so conspicuous after 1900. . . . While Progressivism would have been impossible without the impetus given by certain social grievances, it was not nearly so much the movement of any social class, or coalition of classes, against a particular class or group as it was a rather widespread and remarkably good-natured effort of the great part of society to achieve some not-very-clearly-specified self-reformation. *Its general theme was the effort to restore a type of economic individualism and political democracy that was widely believed to have existed earlier in America and to have been destroyed by the great corporation and the corrupt political machine*; and with that restoration to bring back a kind of morality and civic purity that was also believed to have been lost. (Emphasis added)

With respect to cities, progressives were greatly concerned with the twin evils of overcrowding and political corruption. Both were products of the continuing surge of immigration to eastern seaboard cities from Europe. The highest-ever annual level of immigration to the United States was recorded in 1907 when 1.3 million foreigners arrived. In 1910, 13.3 million foreign-born persons were living in the United States, making up one-seventh of the nation's total population (Hofstadter 1955, 176). These destitute and largely non-English-speaking refugees readily supported big-city politicians who offered them jobs and food in exchange for votes.

Such reformers as Jacob Riis, Lincoln Steffens, Josiah Strong, and Upton Sinclair forcefully called for urban reform in many sectors: political, housing, sanitation, education, and public morals. Particular outrage was focused on "saloons" and their perceived contribution to violence and immorality, leading to adoption of the Eighteenth Amendment to the U.S. Constitution in 1919 prohibiting the manufacture, sale, and transportation of alcoholic beverages. ("Prohibition" was repealed in 1933 as part of President Franklin Roosevelt's campaign to rally the nation's spirits, so to speak, in the middle of the Depression.)

Apart from the issue of corruption in city governments, the most politicized urban concern of progressives was *congestion*. That term included a variety of ills: disease-ridden tenements, mobbed streets in office districts, loss of light and air, and inadequate open space for recreation. Congestion was the rubric under which progressive ideology was translated into practical city planning measures, such as land use zoning.

One of the first progressives to advocate planning to achieve social reform was Frederick C. Howe, whose 1905 book, *The City: The Hope of Democracy*, urged the adoption of German city planning practices. Howe's book strongly influenced Benjamin C. Marsh, a young social activist, who in 1907 was appointed executive secretary to the newly formed Committee on Congestion of Population in New York City. Like James Chadwick, who launched the British sanitary reform movement by writing reports for prestigious committees, Marsh made good use of his position. In 1908, he organized an exhibition on the evils of congestion, which was displayed at the American Museum of Natural History in New York. In the following year, after travels in Europe, Marsh privately published *An Introduction to City Planning* (1909), which opened with the adage "A City Without a Plan is like a Ship Without a Rudder." Marsh urged U.S. cities to imitate German planning techniques, such as public control over street location and design and the zoning of urban land to regulate building height and volume. Unlike Burnham and Bennett's *Plan of Chicago* of the same year, which largely called for public improvements, Marsh advocated public regulation of private land development.

In 1909, Marsh organized the First National Conference on City Planning and Congestion in Washington, D.C. The conference proceedings, published as a Senate Document (U.S. Congress 1910), summarized the state of planning at the time:

> The forty-three conferees met in an air of excitement and hope. Many of the nation's leaders in urban affairs attended, including Frederick Howe, Jane Addams,... John Nolen, [and] Frederick Law Olmsted, Jr.... Representatives of municipal art, social work, architectural, civil engineering, and conservationist groups also attended. The meeting vividly reflected the many interest groups concerned with city planning at the time. (Kantor 1983, 69–70)

City planning was deemed critical to national survival, no less, by financier Henry Morgenthau:

There is an evil which is gnawing at the vitals of the country, to remedy which we have come together—an evil that breeds physical disease, moral depravity, discontent, and socialism—and all these must be cured and eradicated or else our great body politic will be weakened. This community can only hold its preeminence if the masses that compose it are given a chance to be healthy, moral, and self-respecting. (U.S. Congress 1910, 230)

The city beautiful movement was vilified as impractical and elitist by landscape architect Robert Anderson Pope (Daniel Burnham was not present):

We have rushed to plan showy civic centers of gigantic cost, ... brought about by civic vanity, ... when pressing hardby we see the almost unbelievable congestion with its hideous brood of evil, filth, disease, degeneracy, pauperism, and crime. What external adornment can make truly beautiful such a city? (U.S. Congress 1910, 75)

Instead of "showy civic centers," Pope urged (1) decentralizing and more equitable distribution of land values, (2) widening of streets and establishment of radial and belt thoroughfares, and (3) the adoption of land use zoning as practiced in Germany to regulate "building heights, depth of blocks, number of houses per acre, and land speculation with all its attendant evils" (U.S. Congress 1910, 75). Like Morgenthau, Pope expressed a remarkable belief among urban reformers at this time that city planning was essential to national and ethnic survival:

The average recruit in the German army is much taller, stronger, and heavier than the British soldier, spends less time in hospital, and has a lower death rate.... The modern tendency toward congestion in cities and the increase of unhealthful living conditions have been so ably combated in Germany that no real impairment of her manhood can be detected.... While it is admitted that many causes have contributed to this result, city planning is known to be a very important factor. (Ibid., 77)

Subsequent national conferences on city planning provided an annual forum for the development of the planning profession. Thenceforth, "congestion" receded as a rhetorical theme, to be replaced by more emphasis on "data, statistics, techniques, management, standards, efficiency, and evaluation" (Kantor 1983, 71). Social progressives joined with city design practitioners to prepare a fertile soil for the advent of modern land use planning and zoning in the 1920s.

High-minded ideals and aesthetics aside, however, the nation's acceptance of public intervention in private land use decisions began in New York City with two motivating causes, one immediate and newsworthy, the other gradual and self-ish. The first was a tragic fire that devastated the Triangle Shirtwaist Company on March 25, 1911, gutting the 10-story building and killing 146 young female employees. Movie film of the disaster, one of the first to be so recorded, appalled the national public with views of trapped young women jumping to their deaths in the absence of usable fire escapes and rescue equipment (a horror to be repeated in the collapse of the World Trade Center ninety years later). Although the working conditions of "sweatshops" would not be addressed until much later (and never fully), the fire prompted calls for public regulation of the height and safety of multistory buildings. (Another twenty-first-century parallel was the pair of nightclub tragedies in early 2003 that prompted inspections and review of codes for such establishments across the nation.) The year after the Triangle Shirtwaist tragedy, the British steamship *Titanic* hit an iceberg and sank with the loss of 1,503 passengers and crew members while attempting to win a ribbon for the fastest crossing of the Atlantic for its corporate owner, the White Star Line. That well-publicized disaster further aroused the American and British people to the perils of *laissez-faire* in the face of technological change and corporate arrogance.

The second, less sensational, impetus to the advent of city planning and zoning was a growing sense of overcrowding on the streets of downtown Manhattan. The Singer, Metropolitan, and Woolworth towers of the early 1900s were early exemplars of the skyscraper style: ornate, slender, tapering to a pyramid or cupola, they fairly reflected the mood of exuberance and prosperity of prewar America. At street level, though, these and their bulkier neighbors cut off light and air from business districts and flooded the sidewalks with office workers. Adding to that concern was the outright hostility of influential merchants along the New York's premier retail street, Fifth Avenue, toward encroachment by garment factories and offices (Toll, 1969). Since the unwanted activities generally occupied taller buildings, the merchants urged adoption of controls on building size by district to protect existing commercial property values. Thus began the long tradition of using zoning to reflect what is now called the NIMBY ("not in my backyard") syndrome. Pursuant to the reports of two city commissions established at the behest of the Fifth Avenue merchants, a zoning enabling act was adopted by the New York State Legislature, which led to the adoption of the nation's first zoning ordinance in New York City in 1916. As recounted in Chapter 9, zoning rapidly spread to hundreds of other cities and in 1926 received the blessing of the U.S. Supreme Court, which held it to be constitutional (overruling a lower court decision declaring it to be elitist and economically discriminatory).

Three years later, the stock market crash of October 1929 slowed new urban construction, along with most other economic activity. Cities then entered a state of suspended animation until the late 1940s as the nation and the world were preoccupied by the Great Depression and World War II.

The 1930s: Public Works and Grand Visions

Cities became poorer during the 1930s but changed little in outward appearance. According to Jon C. Teaford (1993, 74): "A tourist visiting New York City, Chicago, Philadelphia, or Boston in 1931 who returned fourteen years later would find few changes in the cityscape. Virtually no new skyscrapers soared overhead, the same hotels catered to travelers, and the leading department stores had changed little but their window displays." Fortunately, by the 1930s the major U.S. cities of that time were already endowed with infrastructure—streets, parks, schools, sewer and water systems, mass transit lines, electricity, gas, and telephone utilities, museums, medical facilties, and government buildings—constructed over the previous half-century of public improvements.

Public Works

Although the *private* sector was in retreat in the 1930s, the Depression would actually stimulate *public* construction and modernization of city and regional infrastructure across the nation. The inauguration of President Franklin D. Roosevelt on March 4, 1933, marked the beginning of New Deal programs to combat unemployment through federally funded public works. The Civil Works Administration and the Public Works Administration employed the jobless to repair streets, modernize schools, build post offices, install streetcar systems, and lay new sewers. The Works Progress Administration employed artists to design and embellish public buildings. New Deal–era buildings such as the Department of Interior headquarters in Washington, D.C., and post offices across the country are embellished with art deco details and historic lobby murals by artists like Thomas Hart Benton. Visitors to national and state parks today still widely use roads, trails, restrooms, lodges, and other amenities constructed during the Depression by the Civilian Conservation Corps.

Certain immense projects begun or planned in the 1920s were completed in the middle of the Depression, such as New York's George Washington Bridge (1931), San Francisco's Golden Gate Bridge (1937), and Hoover Dam (1936). In New York City, the hyperactive and abrasive Robert Moses oversaw the construction of the

Triborough Bridge, the Queens Midtown Tunnel, and Jones Beach State Park, among countless other public works during the 1930s (Caro 1974). In the tradition of Georges Haussmann in Paris, Moses was a modern "technocrat" who used (some would say abused) federal, state, and local funds to pursue his vision of an automobile-based metropolis.

One of the most durable legacies of the New Deal, the Tennessee Valley Authority (TVA), was chartered by Congress in 1933 as a public corporation to focus federal resources on an impoverished and environmentally stressed region, namely the watershed of the Tennessee River including portions of six southeastern states. The TVA is best known for its series of mainstem dams that control the river for power, navigation, recreation, and flood control. The TVA also, however, developed pioneering programs in soil erosion management, reforestation, economic development, and improvement of housing, medical care, schools, and recreation. It proved to be an internationally important experiment in governmental resource management. Although no other similar agencies were established in the United States, the idea of promoting regional development through comprehensive river basin management was demonstrated (White 1969).

After devastating floods in 1935, 1936, and 1938, Congress authorized a national program of flood control projects—dams, reservoirs, levees, seawalls—to be constructed by the Army Corps of Engineers. Although adding more projects and jobs to the public works mission, such projects later would be criticized for transforming natural rivers into sterile concrete channels and in some cases for inviting unwise development of floodplains that resulted in higher losses in catastrophic floods that exceeded the project's design limits (Platt 1986).

Along with sponsoring public construction projects, the New Deal also sought to stimulate city, regional, and national planning to guide future investment in public works and other government activities. A series of national committees culminating with the National Resources Planning Board (NRPB) were established by the White House during the 1930s to conduct and promote "scientific" planning on many public policy topics, including cities, housing, transportation, economic development, agriculture, soil erosion, and water resources (Clawson 1981). The NRPB and its predecessors attracted expertise from the nation's top universities (so-called brain-trusters) and prepared reports that laid a foundation for later initiatives to conserve land, improve cities, and protect the environment in the 1960s and 1970s. So influential were Roosevelt's brain-trusters in blocking certain "pork barrel" projects desired by politicians that Congress abolished the NRPB by statute in 1943.

Visions of the Future

Although most freight still traveled by rail in the 1930s, private automobiles by then held a sacrosanct position in American society. Thanks to Henry Ford, cars were affordable and fun. Thanks to city planners like Robert Moses from the 1920s on, they would become a necessity, even within cities having excellent streetcar and subway systems. The General Motors *Futurama* exhibit at the 1939 New York World's Fair foretold a society totally dependent on highways and motor vehicles, which became a self-fulfilling prophecy.

The celebrated American architect Frank Lloyd Wright in the 1930s developed a model plan for a "democratic" future American metropolis that he named *Broadacre City* (Wright 1958; Fishman 1977, Part 2). Wright envisioned a metropolitan nation of sprawling low-density residential districts surrounding compact commercial centers connected by limited-access highways. Conveniently ignored in this utopian vision were heavy industry, the poor, the nonwhite, and those who preferred urban clutter and convenience to sprawling pseudo-agrarian suburbia. The influence of Broadacre City, or at least its prescience, in the patterns and car dependence of postwar U.S. metropolitan growth is unmistakable.

The 1930s also produced another utopian urban construct—*La Ville Radieuse* (Radiant City)—by the French architect Le Corbusier (Hall 1988, Chap. 7; Fishman 1977, Part 3). No less arrogant than Wright, Le Corbusier proposed exactly the opposite metropolis. His concept would house the urban populace in glistening high-rise apartment towers, set within walking distance of one another amid common open spaces devoted to parks and open spaces. Mobility within the urban system was by public transportation and elevator; automobiles presumably were only needed to get to the countryside. Like *Broadacre City,* Le Corbusier's *Ville Radieuse* influenced urban designs for "new towns" in Great Britain, Europe, and Asia.

In the United States, however, *Ville Radieuse* primarily influenced the design of postwar government housing projects for the poor, with disastrous results. One of the most notorious was the 1950s-era Robert Taylor Homes project on Chicago's South Side: 4,512 units in twenty-eight sixteen-story buildings facing a major expressway yet isolated from downtown jobs (Teaford 1993, 124). Urban critics such as Jane Jacobs in the 1960s excoriated such misguided "projects" and stimulated a search for alternative forms of urban housing, including revamping existing neighborhoods. Among many failings of the *Ville Radieuse* paradigm, as blindly applied in U.S. cities, was the pervasive use of open space between buildings not for parks but for parking, junk cars, litter, and gang "turf." Somewhat

FIGURE 5-6 Co-Op City, Bronx, New York, a 1960s middle-income apartment development loosely modeled on Corbusier's *Ville Radieuse*. (*Photo by author.*)

more successful has been Co-Op City, a Le Corbusier-inspired development of subsidized middle-class housing constructed by a state housing authority in the 1960s (Figure 5-6).

The 1930s yielded one further notable experiment in progressive community planning, the Greenbelt Towns Program of the Resettlement Administration, directed by Rexford Tugwell. As discussed earlier, Ebenezer Howard's garden cities movement in England stimulated a counterpart effort among progressive urban thinkers in the United States during the 1920s whose best-known legacy was Radburn, New Jersey. Radburn in turn influenced the design of three "greenbelt towns" built under Tugwell's direction: Greenbelt, Maryland; Green Hills, Ohio; and Greendale, Wisconsin. Each was designed and built by the federal government for a population of about 20,000, of whom virtually all would be white and middle class with families. The greenbelt towns, as with Letchworth Garden City, were intended as models for enlightened investors and builders to emulate. Instead, they became isolated legacies of New Deal idealism, largely ignored after 1940 (Hall 1988, Chap. 4).

Far more influential in shaping the postwar metropolis was the Federal Housing Administration (FHA) established in 1934, whose function was to insure loans on new homes to promote middle-class home ownership. The FHA and the Veterans Administration home loan program would jointly fuel postwar home construction and urban sprawl. Yet even before the war, the FHA had adopted the invidious practice, started by the Home Owner Loan Corporation, of *redlining* neighborhoods by class and race (Jackson 1985). Federal policy, as expressed through these and many other programs, was to preserve existing community and neighborhood character rather than promote integration, diversity, or equal access to housing (Teaford 1993). These racist elements of national housing policy would infuse the post–World War II explosion of home building to yield the "separate and unequal" geography of metropolitan America in the second half of the twentieth century.

References

Brown, L. 2001. *Eco-Economy: Building and Economy for the Earth*. New York: W. W. Norton.

Burnham, D. H., and E. H. Bennett. 1909. *Plan of Chicago*. Chicago: Commercial Club.

Burrows E. G., and M. Wallace 1999. *Gotham: A History of New York City to 1898*. New York: Oxford University Press.

Caro, R. 1974. *The Power Broker: Robert Moses and the Fall of New York*. New York: Knopf.

Ciucci, G., F. Dal Co, M. Manien-Elia, and M. Tafuri. 1979. *The American City: From the Civil War to the New Deal*. Cambridge, MA: MIT Press.

Clawson, M. 1981. *New Deal Planning: The NRPB*. Baltimore: Johns Hopkins University Press.

Delafons, J. 1969. *Land-Use Controls in the United States*. 2nd ed. Cambridge, MA: MIT Press.

Fishman, R. 1977. *Urban Utopias in the Twentieth Century: Ebenezer Howard, Frank Lloyd Wright, Le Corbusier*. New York: Basic Books.

Freund, E. 1904. *The Police Power*. Chicago: Callahan.

Garreau, J. 1991. *Edge City: Life on the New Frontier*. New York: Doubleday Anchor.

Giedion, S. 1962. *Space, Time, and Architecture*. Cambridge, MA: Harvard University Press.

Goodman, W. I. 1968. *Principles and Practice of Urban Planning*. Chicago: International City Managers Association.

Gutheim, F. 1976. *The Federal City: Plans and Realities*. Washington, DC: Smithsonian Institution Press.

Hall, P. 1988. *Cities of Tomorrow*. Oxford: Basil Blackwell.

Hofstadter, R. 1955. *The Age of Reform*. New York: Knopf.

Howe, F. C. 1905. *The City: The Hope of Democracy.* New York: Scribner's.

Jackson, K. 1985. *Crabgrass Frontier: The Suburbanization of the United States.* New York: Oxford University Press.

Kantor, H. A. 1983. Benjamin C. Marsh and the Fight over Population. In *The American Planner: Biographies and Recollections,* ed. D. A. Krueckeberg, 58–74. New York: Methuen.

Keeler, C. A. 1903. *San Francisco and Thereabout.* San Francisco: California Promotion Committee.

Marsh, B. C. 1909. *An Introduction to City Planning.* New York: Benjamin C. Marsh.

Mayer, H. M., and R. C. Wade. 1969. *Chicago: Growth of a Metropolis.* Chicago: University of Chicago Press.

Mumford, L. 1955. *Sticks and Stones: A Study of American Architecture and Civilization.* New York: Dover.

Okrent, D. 2003. *Great Fortune: The Epic of Rockefeller Center.* New York: Viking.

O'Meara, M. 1999. *Reinventing Cities for People and the Planet.* Worldwatch Paper 147. Washington, DC: Worldwatch Institute.

Parsons, K. C. 1994. Collaborative Genius: The Regional Planning Association of America. *Journal of the American Planning Association* 60 (4): 462–82.

Platt, R. H. 1986. Floods and Man: A Geographer's Agenda. In *Geography and Environment, Vol. II: Themes from the Work of Gilbert F. White,* ed. R. W Kates and I. Burton, 28–68. Chicago: University of Chicago Press.

Riis, J. A. 1890/1972. *How the Other Half Lives.* Williamstown, MA: Corner House.

Rome, A. 2001. *The Bulldozer and the Countryside: Suburban Sprawl and the Rise of American Environmentalism.* New York: Cambridge University Press.

Rusk, D. 1999. *Inside Game/Outside Game.* Washington, DC: Brookings Institution Press.

Schaffer, D. 1982. *Garden Cities for America: The Radburn Experience.* Philadelphia: Temple University Press.

Steffens, L. 1904/1957. *The Shame of the Cities.* New York: Hill and Wang.

Strong, J. 1898. *The Twentieth Century City.* New York: Baker and Taylor.

Teaford, J. C. 1979. *City and Suburb: The Political Fragmentation of Metropolitan America: 1850–1970.* Baltimore: Johns Hopkins University Press.

———. 1993. *The Twentieth Century American City.* 2nd ed. Baltimore: Johns Hopkins University Press.

Toll, S. 1969. *Zoned American.* New York: Grossman.

U.S. Congress. 1910. *City Planning.* 61st Cong., 2nd sess. Senate Doc. no. 422. Washington, DC: U.S. Government Printing Office.

Warner, S. B., Jr. 1978. *Streetcar Suburbs: The Process of Growth in Boston (1870–1900).* Cambridge, MA: Harvard University Press.

White, G. F. 1969. *Strategies of American Water Management.* Ann Arbor: University of Michigan Press.

Wilson, W. H. 1990. *The City Beautiful Movement.* Baltimore: Johns Hopkins University Press.

Wright, F. L. 1958. *The Living City.* New York: Mentor Books.

Wrigley, R. L., Jr. 1983. The Plan of Chicago. In *Introduction to Planning History in the United States,* ed. D. A. Krueckeberg, 58–72. New Brunswick, NJ: Rutgers Center for Urban Policy Research.

CHAPTER 6

The Polarized Metropolis:
1945–2000

*The ultimate effect of the suburban escape in our time is, ironically, a low-grade
uniform environment from which escape is impossible.*
—LEWIS MUMFORD 1961, 456

*All Americans pay for sprawl with increased health and safety risks, worsening air
and water pollution, urban decline, disappearing farmland and wildlife habitat,
racial polarization, city/suburban disparities in public education, lack of
affordable housing, and the erosion of community.*
—ROBERT D. BULLARD 2000, 2

Post–World War II America was far more interested in building houses than in
planning, conservation, or social justice. Politicians and the media demanded federal housing programs to provide returning veterans and their families with
affordable new homes. According to environmental historian Adam Rome (2001,
34–35), even such a conservative business magazine as *Fortune* "published dozens
of articles in 1946 and 1947 on the housing shortage. In a rare editorial—'Let's
Have Ourselves a Housing Industry'—the editors supported a handful of government initiatives to encourage builders to operate on a larger scale ... as the best
defense against socialism."

Congress rose to the challenge. In the late 1940s and early 1950s, it created a variety of new housing stimulus programs under the aegis of the Federal Housing
Authority and the Veterans Administration. These programs helped fuel a construction boom of some 15 million new housing units during the 1950s; in every year
from 1947 to 1964, housing starts would exceed 1.2 million (Teaford 1993, 100).

Most of these millions of new units were single-family homes built on agricultural or wooded land outside the older central cities. Most were deliberately marketed to middle-class white families. The expansion of suburbia was further subsidized by the federal Interstate Highway System authorized by Congress in 1956 and by federal tax deductions for mortgage interest, local property taxes, and accelerated depreciation for commercial real estate investments. Thus the federal government through its housing, highway, and tax policies actively supported, and to a certain extent mandated, an *apartheid* United States with middle-class whites in the new suburbs and the poor and nonwhites relegated to the inner-city neighborhoods abandoned by departing whites (Jackson 1985; Suarez 1999; Teaford 1993).

As reinforced by migration of southern blacks to northern cities, the racial impact on central cities was dramatic:

> Whereas the white population of New York City declined 7 percent between 1950 and 1960, the black population soared 46 percent. In Chicago, the white total dropped 13 percent while the number of blacks rose 65 percent, and in Philadelphia there were also 13 percent fewer whites in 1960 than in 1950 but 41 percent more blacks. Overall, the black population in central cities having over 50,000 inhabitants rose 50 percent, climbing from 6,456,000 in 1950 to 9,705,000 ten years later. (Teaford 1993, 115)

Over the rest of the twentieth century, the central city *versus* suburb contrast blurred somewhat as nonwhites moved into the older "inner ring" of suburbs abandoned by whites and as newer central cities of the Sun Belt attracted mostly white migrants. For instance, the 2000 black population of the city of Phoenix was 5.1 percent and in San Diego it was 7.9 percent, compared with New York City at 26.6 percent black and Chicago at 36.8 percent black. For older central cities, white flight continued through the 1990s: the top 100 cities in the United States changed from being 52 percent white in 1990 to 44 percent in 2000, reflecting the net migration of 2.3 million whites to the suburbs, the Sun Belt, and elsewhere (Katz 2001). Central cities, however, maintained fairly stable population numbers during the 1990s with a growth of 43 percent (3.8 million) in Hispanic population, along with smaller increases in other ethnic minorities (ibid.).

For those left behind in the central cities by the postwar white exodus, Congress adopted laws in 1949 and 1954 that created the federal urban renewal program to clear and redevelop "blighted areas." As noted in Chapter 5, the standard model for urban renewal in the 1940s and 1950s was total site clearance followed by construction of high-rise public or subsidized apartment projects loosely modeled on

Le Corbusier's *Ville Radieuse*. Such projects provided low-cost rental apartments but usually not ownership units. Occupants were thus ineligible for federal tax deductions for home mortgage interest and local property taxes, assuming they had income against which to claim deductions. They also lacked the opportunity to build equity in the rising value of an owned unit. The best of these apartment complexes, such as Metropolitan Life's Stuyvesant Town and Peter Cooper Village in Manhattan were privately sponsored with government assistance. The worst, such as the infamous Pruitt-Igoe project in St. Louis and the Robert Taylor Homes in Chicago, both now demolished, were built by public housing authorities.

Cracks in the Picture Window

The inequity of national programs for white and black, middle class and poor, was not immediately challenged. During the 1950s, the nation was distracted by the Cold War, the Korean War, and McCarthyism, while basking in the afterglow of winning World War II and pride in the Marshall Plan to rebuild West Germany and Japan. President Dwight Eisenhower with his famous grin and campaign slogan "I Like Ike" presided over the United States from 1952 until 1961 like a genial grandfather. The onset of the civil rights movement required the more activist climate of the Kennedy Administration (1961–1963) and especially the aggressive stance on civil rights abuses by Robert F. Kennedy as attorney general. The Civil Rights Act of 1964 and the Fair Housing Act of 1968, both products of President Lyndon B. Johnson's "War on Poverty," were not yet on the radar screen in the 1950s, nor was the environmental movement that began in the late 1960s.

Although social inequity was scarcely noticed in the 1950s, there were rumblings of dissent on certain aspects of rapid urban growth that foretold the more violent storms of controversy that would sweep the nation in the following decade. One dissonant chord was struck by William H. Whyte and his colleague Jane Jacobs in their early writings on suburban sprawl and its converse, inner-city redevelopment. A second whiff of dissent concerned the "ecological" effects of urbanization, as summarized by Lewis Mumford, Carl Sauer, and others in a landmark 1955 symposium on *Man's Role in Changing the Face of the Earth* (discussed later). Third, the growing challenge of devising regional solutions to the needs of the increasingly fragmented *Megalopolis* was raised by the geographer Jean Gottmann. These three counterpoints to the smugly self-righteous 1950s are summarized next.

The Exploding Metropolis

In 1957, *Fortune* magazine, which had helped promote the postwar building boom, published a series of essays, republished as a book, challenging some of the basic assumptions of the nation's urban policies. Under the polemic title *The Exploding Metropolis: A Study of the Assault on Urbanism and How Our Cities Can Resist It* (Editors of *Fortune* 1957), the authors were "people who like cities" (Whyte 1957). The lead editor, William H. Whyte, was already famous for his sociological study, *The Organization Man* (1956), which examined the lifestyle and suburban habitat of young corporate executives and their families. Whyte would later expand his *Exploding Metropolis* essay on "Urban Sprawl" into a bible of suburban land conservation techniques entitled *The Last Landscape* (1968). Jacobs's essay "Downtown Is for People" challenged prevailing approaches to urban renewal, a theme she expanded in her classic, *The Death and Life of Great American Cities* (1961).

The Exploding Metropolis challenged the prevailing wisdom of postwar building practices on both aesthetic and functional grounds. Patterns of land development on the urban fringe were ugly and wasteful (Whyte), just as redevelopment in the urban core was ugly and unsafe (both Whyte and Jacobs). In Whyte's words, concerning the former:

> Aesthetically, the result is a mess. It takes remarkably little blight to color a whole area; let the reader travel along a stretch of road he is fond of, and he will notice how a small portion of open land has given amenity to the area. But it takes only a few badly designed developments or billboards or hot-dog stands to ruin it, and though only a little bit of the land is used, the place will *look* filled up.
>
> Sprawl is bad esthetics; it is bad economics. Five acres are being made to do the work of one, and do it very poorly. This is bad for the farmers, it is bad for communities, it is bad for industry, it is bad for utilities, it is bad for the railroads, it is bad for the recreation groups, it is bad even for the developers. (Editors of *Fortune* 1957, 116–17)

And concerning central city housing, Whyte wrote:

> The scale of the projects is uncongenial to the human being. The use of the open space is revealing; usually it consists of manicured green areas carefully chained off lest they be profaned, and sometimes, in addition, a big central mall so vast and abstract as to be vaguely oppressive. There is nothing close for the eye to light on, no sense of intimacy or of things being on a human scale. (Ibid., 21)

The Exploding Metropolis, like most urban writings of that time, deplored the outward sprawl of urban growth while overlooking the racial and class inequities in national policies that promoted it. The preferential treatment of the white middle class over nonwhite poor in federal housing and tax policies, as well as the use of exclusionary zoning by suburban communities, went unnoticed. Even Donald Seligman's essay "The Enduring Slums" in the same volume blandly observed that "the white urban culture they [poor nonwhites] might assimilate *into* is receding before them; it is drifting off into the suburbs" (Editors of *Fortune* 1957, 97). "Drifting off" is certainly a nonjudgmental way to describe the process of white flight in response to the *pull* of government incentives for suburban development and the reciprocal *push* of central city neglect.

During the 1950s, the central cities of the twenty largest metropolitan areas gained only 0.1 percent in population while their suburbs grew by 45 percent (Teaford 1993, 98). Whether people "liked cities" or not was often secondary to whether they would pay the economic and emotional price of staying in them (especially if they had children) *versus* fleeing to what a recent *New Yorker* magazine cover slyly termed "Outer Perturbia." Obviously, most chose the latter, whether out of choice or necessity. Federal policies implicitly, and sometimes explicitly, tilted in that direction, further polarizing the metropolis between haves and have-nots.

Subject to this important qualification, however, *The Exploding Metropolis* was fairly revolutionary for its day in at least four respects. First, it rejected the conventional wisdom that suburbs are necessarily preferable to "real cities." Second, it urged that cities should be thought of as "habitats for people," not simply as centers of economic production, transportation nodes, or grandiose architectural stage sets. Third, it challenged the prevailing notion that population density ("crowding") is necessarily bad. Fourth, it established a precedent for more searching critiques of urban policies and programs in the coming decades, including but by no means limited to those of Whyte and Jacobs themselves. It marked the emergence of journalists as urban critics and the rediscovery of the city as a "place," not just a complex of systems. In short, *The Exploding Metropolis* was the first round of the debate over the nature, purpose, and design of city space that continues today in the Smart Growth movement, New Urbanism, and other efforts to make cities and suburbs more habitable.

Man's Role in Changing the Face of the Earth

Another important exception to the prevailing euphoria concerning "growth" during the 1950s was the 1955 Wenner-Gren Conference held at Princeton

University on *Man's Role in Changing the Face of the Earth*. This symposium and the volume that ensued from it (Thomas 1956) marked a scholarly watershed in thinking about the environmental impact of human activities. Seventy-six distinguished scholars described "the multiple impacts of human beings as agents of vast and often fearsome change in the world" (Kates 1987, 529). *Man's Role* focused on degraded landscapes of the world: soils, forests, water, and biotic species, with new attention to cities, climate, and wastes.

Lewis Mumford (1956), the distinguished urban historian and conference co-convenor, warned that modern metropolitan development tends:

> to loosen the bonds that connect [the city's] inhabitants with nature and to transform, eliminate, or replace its earth-bound aspects, covering the natural site with an artificial environment that enhances the dominance of man and encourages an illusion of complete independence from nature. (Mumford, 1956, 386)

> Within a century, the economy of the Western world has shifted from a rural base harboring a few big cities and thousands of villages and small towns, to a metropolitan base whose urban spread ... is fast absorbing the rural hinterland and threatening to wipe out many of the natural elements favorable to life which in earlier stages balanced off against the depletions of the urban environment. (Ibid., 395)

The formidable proceedings volume from the conference was appropriately dedicated to George Perkins Marsh, the inquisitve Vermonter whose 1864 book *Man and Nature* documented the pervasive effects of human activities on the natural world. (See Chapter 11.) *Man's Role* also anticipated by fifteen years the adoption of the National Environmental Policy Act in 1970 and related environmental laws considered in Chapter 12.

Megalopolis

Like his fellow countryman Alexis de Tocqueville—author of *Democracy in America* 130 years earlier—the French geographer Jean Gottmann helped the United States better understand itself. His landmark study entitled *Megalopolis: The Urbanized Northeastern Seaboard of the United States* (1961) defined a new kind of urban region he named "Megalopolis" that comprised the 400-mile corridor of cities and suburbs extending from north of Boston to Washington, D.C., spreading across parts of eight states (later expanded to include southern Maine and northern Virginia). Fragmented by geography and political jurisdictions, Megalopolis was found to be unified by a dense network of linkages—economic, social, cultural, commercial, and communication and information—and by its concentration of world leadership in finance, culture, and government.

In contrast to urban growth skeptics like Mumford, Whyte, and Jacobs, Gottmann admired Megalopolis as "a stupendous monument erected by titanic efforts" (1961, 23). Summarizing the region's history, geography, economy, and land use, his findings were generally upbeat, as in "*on the average*, [Megalopolis is] the richest, best, educated, best housed, and best serviced [urban region] in the world" (ibid., 15; Gottmann's emphasis). Issues such as poverty and pollution did not interest him, as for instance the laconic statement that Megalopolis "attracts large numbers of in-migrants from the poorer sections ... especially Southern Negroes and Puerto Ricans, who congregate in the old urban areas and often live in slums" (ibid., 66).

His chapter entitled "The Symbiosis of Urban and Rural," however, reinforced some of Whyte's concerns on urban sprawl:

> In Megalopolis, the fully urbanized and built-up sectors are many and of impressive size, but there still remains a great deal of thinly occupied space devoted to woods, fields, and pasture.... On closer examination, however, we shall find that present and future use of these green spaces within Megalopolis is completely dependent on the march of urbanization. We shall also discover that, while the actual crowding is still localized and open land is available on a much larger scale than is usually recognized, *present trends indicate an urgent need for new policies if Megalopolitan populations are not to find themselves even more fenced in than are the people in other highly urbanized regions of the world.* (Gottman 1961, 218; emphasis added)

The need for *intergovernmental cooperation* was among Gottmann's key themes. As a new kind of urban complex straddling myriad state and local boundaries, new broad-scale approaches are required to provide regional needs such as transportation, water and sewer service, pollution abatement, and education. The penultimate chapter, "Sharing a Partitioned Land," reviewed a number of models for pragmatic intergovernmental arrangements such as annexation by central cities, special districts and regional authorities, and regional governments. The development of cooperative regional approaches still challenges the political leadership of Megalopolis and its analogs elsewhere such as Detroit-Chicago-Milwaukee, San Diego-Los Angeles-San Francisco, London-Birmingham-Manchester in England, and Tokyo-Kyoto-Osaka in Japan.

Deconstructing Metropolitan America

Metropolitan Statistical Areas

Megalopolis is a bold and resounding term, but it lacks precision as a geographic unit suitable for regional analysis of such spatial variables as demography, land use, housing, economics, and environmental change. To assess regional status and trends without having to combine data from large clusters of cities, towns, counties, and states, the federal Office of Management and Budget since 1950 has designated regional units now called *metropolitan statistical areas* (MSAs) for which it publishes a variety of demographic, housing, and economic data. Since 1950, the geographic size and number of designated MSAs have been expanded to reflect metropolitan growth (Figures 1-4 and 6-1).

MSAs are generally defined to include the following:

1. One or more *core cities* of at least 50,000 inhabitants each, or an *urbanized area* of that size (as defined by the Census Bureau), plus

2. The county or counties that contain such core city(ies) or urbanized area, plus

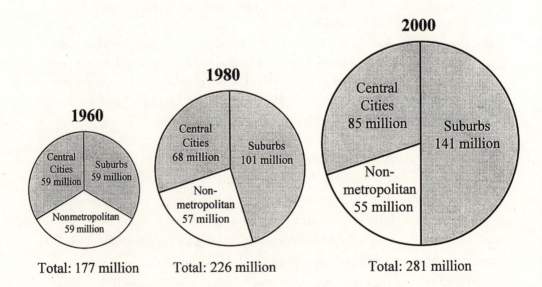

☐ Metropolitan Areas

FIGURE 6-1 Distribution of U.S. population: 1960, 1980, and 2000.
(Source: Adapted from U.S. Census data.)

3. Any adjoining counties in which at least 50 percent of the population lives within the defined urbanized area, plus

4. Any additional counties that are closely associated with the core city and its county in terms of commuting and other criteria (Wright 2003, 242).

In New England, MSAs are defined as clusters of closely related cities and towns, rather than counties. Table 6-1 summarizes the distribution and growth rate of metropolitan populations in 2000 by size class of MSA.

Urban regions of more than one million inhabitants may be designated as *consolidated metropolitan statistical areas* (CMSAs). Within them, subareas eligible for MSA status are designated *primary MSAs* (PMSAs). The number of designated MSAs and PMSAs has grown from 169 in 1950 to 331 in 2000. Of the latter, 73 are PMSAs that compose 18 CMSAs. Since MSAs are often enlarged by adding counties (or New England towns) to reflect ongoing growth, care must be taken when making statistical comparisons from one census to another to consider intervening changes in area of MSAs.

Metropolitan Growth and Sprawl Since the 1950s

Despite the early warnings of *The Exploding Metropolis* and its progeny, the United States is more urban and more sprawling than ever. Since 1950, metropolitan areas designated by the Bureau of the Census have increased in number from 169 to about 331, in population from 84 million (55 percent of U.S. total) to 226 million (80 percent), and in size from 9 percent to about 18 percent of the nation's land area (Table 6-2). Suburbs have grown from 55 million residents in 1950 to more than 141 million in 2000 and now are home to slightly more than one-half of the entire U.S. population. Metropolitan areas as a whole (including central cities) today account for four-fifths of the nation's population areas; the other one-fifth of the population lives in smaller cities, towns, on farms, and in the "boondocks." By comparison, central cities, suburbs, and nonmetro areas in 1960 each represented about one-third of the nation's population (Figure 6-1).

About two-thirds of metropolitan residents (147 million people) live in MSAs of more than one million inhabitants (first two rows of Table 6-1). Population constantly shifts within metro areas, among different metro areas, and between metro and nonmetro areas. Beginning in the 1970s, there has been a noticeable rise in the populations of some attractive rural areas—Vermont, Maine, the Appalachians,

TABLE 6-1 METROPOLITAN STATISTICAL AREAS BY SIZE, 2000

SIZE CLASS	NUMBER[a]	POPULATION (MILLIONS)	METRO POPULATION (%)	PERCENT CHANGE 1990–2000
2.5 million +	18	79.8	35	37.1[b]
1.0–2.5 million	43	66.9	30	10.7
500,000–1.0 million	42	28.3	13	3.0
250,000–500,000	79	28.4	13	3.2
100,000–250,000	129	20.8	9	3.4
< 100,000	20	1.7	1	−15.0
Total	331	226.0	100	14.7

SOURCE: *Statistical Abstract of the U.S.—2001*, Tables 29 and 30.

[a] Includes 331 MSAs and PMSAs defined by the Bureau of the Census as of June 30, 1999.

[b] Five MSAs moved into the "over 2.5 million" category between 1990 and 2000, accounting for the apparently high rate of growth of this size level.

TABLE 6-2 CONTRASTS IN METROPOLITAN AMERICA, 1950 AND 2000

	1950	2000
U.S. population	152 million	281 million
Number of metropolitan areas	169	> 331
Metropolitan population	84 million (55% of U.S.)	226 million (80% of U.S.)
Number of metropolitan areas > 1 million	14	39 (1990)
Population of metropolitan areas > 1 million	45 million (30% of U.S.)	125 million (50.2% of U.S.)
Metropolitan percentage of U.S. land area	9%	18%
Average metropolitan population density	407 persons/sq. mile	330 persons/sq. mile
Central city population	49 million (32% of U.S.)	85 million (30% of U.S.)

the Sierra foothills—representing an exodus of "yuppies" and "back to the land" enthusiasts from large urban areas. Yet rural America nevertheless lost two million inhabitants between 1980 and 2000. The Great Plains region, in particular, has lost substantial population and has been proposed for the "world's largest nature park" (Popper 1987).

As discussed in Chapter 1, MSAs are not very useful for measuring changes in *urban land*. Land area within MSAs has risen from about 207,000 square miles in 1950 (6 percent of the United States) to more than 650,000 square miles (19 percent) in 2000. The total area of land within MSAs, however, vastly overstates the quantity of land actually devoted to urban purposes. Because MSAs are defined according to county jurisdictions (or cities and towns in New England), they include much undeveloped rural land that happens to remain within those political jurisdictions. The U.S. Department of Agriculture (1987, 3–12) estimated in 1987 that metropolitan areas contain 20 percent of the nation's cropland and 20 percent of

FIGURE 6-2 Cartoon: "The Plan." *(Source: TOLES © The Buffalo News. Reprinted with permission of UNIVERSAL PRESS SYNDICATE. All rights reserved.)*

the land with potential for conversion to cropland (currently in forest, pasture, or other rural use).

Metropolitan America has sprawled far beyond the wildest imaginings of *The Exploding Metropolis* authors in the 1950s. A recent report by the Brookings Institution found that "most metropolitan areas are consuming land for urbanization much more rapidly than they are adding population" (Fulton et al. 2001, 1). The study calculated the growth in urban land in relation to population growth between 1982 and 1997 for every MSA. While the nation's metropolitan *population* grew by 17 percent between 1982 and 1997, *urbanized land* within metropolitan areas grew by 47 percent, from 51 million acres to 76 million acres (equal to 118,000 square miles or about 6.2 percent of the nation's land area, excluding Alaska). Average metropolitan density accordingly declined from 5.0 persons per urbanized acre in 1982 to 4.22 in 1997 (ibid., 7).

Surprisingly, the Brookings study found that new development in the West is *more dense* (i.e., less sprawling) than new growth surrounding the supposedly more compact northeastern and midwestern metropolitan areas. This density appears to be due to the high cost of buildable land in the West and the constriction of urban sprawl by federal lands, mountain ranges, and the Pacific Ocean.

Between 1950 and 2000, central cities collectively gained 73 percent in population while suburban residents have tripled in number. This statistic, however, understates the actual shift away from older cities to their suburbs and elsewhere. The category of "central cities" as designated by the Bureau of the Census includes a number of new or greatly enlarged Sun Belt cities that are predominantly suburban in character; examples are San Diego, whose population grew by 75 percent between 1970 and 2000; Phoenix (+145 percent); Los Angeles (+28 percent); and Las Vegas (+220 percent). The considerable expansion in area and population of these southern and western cities masks the heavy losses in the populations of many older northern cities whose boundaries are essentially inelastic and unable to expand to embrace new areas of development (Rusk 1999). Between 1970 and 2000, Chicago lost about 14 percent of its population (although it gained back 4 percent during the 1990s). Washington, D.C., lost 24 percent and Boston lost 8 percent during the same period. New York City lost about 800,000 people or 10 percent of its population during its economic downtown in the 1970s but more than regained that loss during the 1980s and 1990s, largely through Hispanic and Asian immigration (Katz 2001).

Race and Poverty

When race is considered, the contrast is even more stark. At the national scale, black population in 2000 accounted for 21 percent of central-city residents and 8 percent of suburban population. People of Hispanic origin, including both white and nonwhite, were about evenly divided in number between central cities (16.4 million) and suburbs (15.7 million), making up 19.2 percent of the population of the former and 11 percent of the latter.

Again, national-level data mask great contrasts among cities and regions. Although changing census categories impair exact comparison, the nonwhite (black, Asian, or nonwhite Hispanic) population of New York rose from 60.5 percent in 1990 to 82.2 percent in 2000. By contrast, the population of the retirement mecca of Scottsdale, Arizona, which grew by 47 percent in the 1980s and 56 percent in the 1990s, was only 15 percent "other than non-Hispanic white" in 2000.

Journalist Ray Suarez in his book *The Old Neighborhood* (1999, 10) documents the reversal of racial composition for some of the nation's largest cities:

Between 1950 and 1990, the population of New York stayed roughly level, the white population halved, and the black population doubled. As Chicago lost almost one million people from the overall count, it lost almost two million whites. As the population of Los Angeles almost doubled, the number of whites living there grew by fewer than ninety thousand. Baltimore went from a city of three times as many whites as blacks in 1950 to a city that will have twice as many blacks as whites in the year 2000. All this happened while the number of blacks in the United States has stayed a roughly constant percentage, between 11 and 13 percent.

Racial change is not *per se* a bad thing if it results in greater access to decent housing and jobs for nonwhites over time. That, however, is not the case. To begin with, blacks are more likely to be poor than whites. In 1993, the percentage of white families below the federal poverty level was 9.4 percent, compared with 31.3 percent of black families. Both of these proportions had increased since 1979 when they stood at 6.9 percent for white families and 27.8 percent for black households (U.S. Bureau of the Census, 1995–1996, Table 752). Thus with blacks making up a rising proportion of city population and poverty afflicting a rising proportion of black households and individuals, it follows that black poverty is heavily concentrated in central cities.

Such concentration, however, tragically does not translate into improved housing or economic opportunities for lower-income nonwhites by virtue of living in cities. Housing in "ghetto" neighborhoods is notoriously dilapidated but nevertheless costly to rent because poor tenants seldom have anywhere else to turn. David Rusk (1999, 70–71) quotes a bitter indictment by Oliver Byrum, former planning director of Minneapolis:

> Low-income people and poverty conditions are concentrated in inner city areas because that is where we want them to be. It is, in fact, our national belief, translated into metropolitan housing policy, that this is where they are supposed to be. Additionally, they are to have as little presence as possible elsewhere in the metropolitan area.... Cheap shelter is to be mostly created by the devaluation of inner city neighborhoods.

Furthermore, poverty itself is not color-blind. In 1990, poor whites in metropolitan areas about equaled the total of poor blacks and Hispanics combined. Yet even though three-quarters of the poor whites lived in "middle-class, mostly suburban neighborhoods," the same percentage of poor blacks and Hispanics inhabited inner-city low-income neighborhoods (Rusk 1999, 71). Whites of all income classes decreased from 52 percent to 43 percent of the total population of the nation's largest one hundred cities, a decline of 2.3 million people, while the Hispanic component rose from 17 percent to 23 percent, representing an increase of over 2 million people (Table 6-3).

Despite the civil rights, open housing, and equal opportunity laws adopted during the 1960s, central cities are more racially and economically challenged than ever. Consider Hartford, the state capital of Connecticut, the wealthiest city in the United States after the Civil War, and home to Mark Twain, Louisa May Alcott, Trinity College, and the Travelers Insurance Company. Hartford was recently described by the *New York Times* as "the most destitute 17 square miles in the

TABLE 6-3 ETHNIC COMPOSITION OF THE 100 LARGEST CITIES IN THE UNITED STATES, 1990 AND 2000

	1990	2000
White (non-Hispanic)	52%	43%
Black	25%	24%
Hispanic	17%	23%
Asian	5%	7%
Other	1%	3%

SOURCE: Brookings Institution 2001, as adapted from Gillham 2002, Fig. 3.13.

nation's wealthiest state, and a city where 30 percent of its residents live in poverty. Only Brownsville, Texas has a higher figure" (Zielbauer 2002, B4).

Adding to the downward spiral of older central cities, new jobs have been predominantly created in suburban locations, thus requiring employees living in the inner city to have a car and time for a lengthy reverse commute (Figure 6-3). In the case of Atlanta, sociologist Robert D. Bullard writes that the city's share of the metropolitan job market dropped from 40 percent in 1980 to 19 percent in 1997. From 1990 to 1997, the central city gained only 4,503 new jobs, just 1.3 percent of all jobs created in the region during that period, while 295,000 jobs or 78 percent of all jobs were added to Atlanta's northern suburbs (Bullard, Johnson, and Torres 2000, 10–11).

Suburbs

Despite the stereotypes of suburbia offered by novelists such as John Cheever, and John Updike, and movies like *The Ice Storm* and *Far from Heaven*, suburbs come in many sizes, shapes, and flavors. The earliest true U.S. suburbs were the late-nineteeth-century "streetcar suburbs" studied by the urban historian Sam Bass Warner (1978). With the advent of the automobile, suburbs proliferated rapidly until the Great Depression. After World War II, the nation embarked on its twin booms: babies and building suburban homes. In the mid-1980s, historian Kenneth T. Jackson (1985, 5) observed that "American suburbs come in every type, shape, and size: rich and poor, industrial and residential, new and old." This statement remains true today as more than half the U.S. population (141 million people in 2000) live in political units other than central cities within MSAs (see Figure 6-1).

Suburbs may be roughly classified among four general types. Of course, some suburbs may not fit neatly into any of these categories and some may straddle more than one. The following types are suggested merely as ways to perceive the considerable social and economic differences among communities that share metropolitan areas with central cities and each other. (See Chapter 7 regarding the legal nature of municipal governments.)

First, many older suburbs would be considered *full-fledged cities* but for their proximity to a much larger city. Suburbs like Evanston, Illinois; Boulder, Colorado; Framingham, Massachusetts; and White Plains, New York, have sizable territories, populations, and range of economic functions and land uses. Some, such as White Plains, shared in the economic boom of the 1990s, whereas others,

FIGURE 6-3 Chronic traffic congestion in both directions in Los Angeles.
(Photo by author.)

such as Newark, New Jersey, have experienced the opposite phenomenon: disinvestment, declining economic base, pervasive social and ethnic problems, and a crumbling infrastructure (Jackson 2000).

Second, white-collar and predominantly white-complexioned *bedroom suburbs*—some very wealthy such as Grosse Pointe, Michigan; Lake Forest, Illinois; and Lincoln, Massachusetts—represent the archetypal suburb caricatured by fiction writers and films. Such communities are characterized by large lots, huge homes, manicured lawns, an absence of manufacturing, and a lack of multifamily housing (except perhaps a few luxury condominiums for "empty nesters"). Municipal autonomy has permitted these suburbs to insulate themselves, legally, fiscally, and often racially, from the central cities from which their wealth arises.

Third, *blue-collar communities*—such as Chelsea, Massachusetts; Elizabeth, New Jersey; Hamtramck, Michigan; and Blue Island, Illinois—are embedded within metropolitan areas. These communities may have originated as industrial enclaves or as working-class land subdivisions oriented to mills or factories long since closed. They are likely to be ethnically and racially diverse, and they are often afflicted by poverty, unemployment, and inadequate schools and other public facilities. Although sharing many of the social, economic, and environmental ills of the central cities, they often lack the resources and technical sophistication to qualify for federal and state assistance.

Fourth, metropolitan areas are splattered with what might be called *splinter suburbs* of negligible size and population. According to the Advisory Commission on Intergovernmental Relations (1969, 75): "The overwhelming majority of metropolitan local governments are relatively small in population and geographic size.... About half of the nearly 5,000 municipalities in [MSA's] have less than a single square mile of land area, and only one in 5 is as large as 4 square miles. Two-thirds of them have fewer than 5,000 residents; one-third fewer than 1,000." Many splinter municipalities were created for reasons relating to morality, to allow liquor sales, gambling, and prostitution. According to Jon Teaford (1979, 20), the emerging fragmented metropolis of the early twentieth century "resembled a moral checkerboard with alternating squares of state law." In Minnesota, for instance, a law allowing municipalities to own and support themselves from municipal liquor stores gave rise to a number of incorporations involving only a city block, a few hundred persons, and (surprise) a liquor outlet. Avoidance of taxing and zoning policies of neighboring jurisdictions is another motive for defensive incorporation.

Suburbs of the traditional "bedroom" variety, of course, have changed in many respects and today are unlikely to resemble the lily-white "organization man" suburbs that Whyte (1956) described in the 1950s (except that many are still white). Many suburbs are more diverse in terms of life style and household status: the nuclear family stereotype of Ozzie and Harriet has been supplanted in many places by increasing numbers of singles, gays, elderly, and single-parent households. Both Ozzie and Harriet have jobs, if they are lucky, and may be divorced or separated with some sort of shared custody of Ricky and the other kid. Another Brookings study reports that in 2000, suburban nonfamily households—mostly young singles and elderly living alone—outnumbered traditional households consisting of married couples with children (Frey and Berube 2002). This study also found that suburbs grew faster in every household type than their respective central cities during the 1990s.

In affluent communities at least, the stereotype of vapid cultural life and humdrum shopping and entertainment available in suburbia is outdated. David Brooks in his book *Bobos in Paradise: The New Upper Class and How They Got There* (2000) parodies the suburban proliferation of trendy coffee bars, health food outlets, multicultural galleries, and other attributes loosely associated with "urbanism." These sites are the outward trappings of the stock boom of the 1990s as translated into cultural preferences of the new elite, which Brooks labels *Bobos* (short for "Bourgeois Bohemians"). Starbucks and Barnes and Noble may be solidly established in the upscale suburbs and shopping malls of the United States, but a mall is still a mall. Although they gain more ethnic flavor and cater to the wider diversity of suburbia itself, malls remain private enclaves where commercial occupancy and personal behavior are highly regulated and the uniform building design, controlled climate, and background "elevator music" is similar from coast to coast. In the words of Robert Kaplan (1998, 45), "Each future city seems likely to consist of the same borrowed fragments: standardized corporate fortresses, privately guarded housing developments, Disneyfied tourist bubbles, restaurants serving the same eclectic food, and so on."

Highway congestion has become a familiar and costly side effect of the outward sprawl of homes, jobs, shopping, and other necessities of metropolitan life. Mass transit, including streetcars, commuter and mainline railways, subways, and bus lines, evolved to convey people to and within central cities. Mobility among suburban locations is poorly suited to public transportation, leaving personal vehicles as the only way to get around. The construction of the 57,000-mile Interstate Highway System beginning in 1956 (90 percent financed out of federal highway taxes) encouraged suburbanization at the expense of central cities, but even those routes originally radiated to and from urban downtowns. Over the next four decades, perimeter highways like the Washington, D.C. Beltway and its counterparts across the country, along with various feeder highways, encouraged commuting among suburban locations without the need ever to "go downtown."

When proposed, the Interstate Highway System and other limited-access highways resembled *Broadacre City*, Frank Lloyd Wright's utopian American landscape of the 1930s. In reality, however, the "dream highways" of the 1950s became the nightmares of suburban living today. The problem stems from the unfeasibility of continuing to build new highways in already crowded areas, while vehicle ownership per capita continues to grow. Since 1970, the U.S. population has grown by 40 percent, while the number of registered vehicles has nearly doubled. *Private vehicles have thus proliferated more than twice as fast as people have*, and the average vehicle has grown larger and heavier with the craze for sport utility vehicles (SUVs). Meanwhile, since 1970, road capacity increased by just 6 percent (Seabrook 2002), and according to the Bureau of the Census, 76 percent of commuters drive alone (Fay 2001). The result, of no surprise, is that time and fuel wasted in getting from point A to point B is becoming unacceptable in many metropolitan regions of the United States. In Atlanta, the average commuter spent 25 hours a year stuck in traffic in 1992 versus 72 hours in 2000 (Seabrook 2002).

Edge Cities

Some malls are practically, but not quite, cities. Since the 1980s, metropolitan America has spawned dozens of megadevelopments popularly known as *edge cities* (Garreau 1991) or *urban villages* (Leinberger and Lockwood 1986). (Perhaps they should be called *mushburbs* due to their tendency to erupt practically overnight like mushrooms!) Edge cities may begin as a rural crossroads like Tyson's Corner, Virginia, a small farm village, or simply a tract of rural land near the advancing metropolitan fringe. Private investments affecting the area are usually triggered by public decisions concerning highway interchanges, new water or sewer service, or commuter mass transit stops (as with some suburban stations on the Washington, D.C., metrorail system). Given the necessary financing and legal approvals, the site erupts from its bucolic state into an instant "Emerald City" complete with glistening office towers, huge shopping malls, and big-name hotels with conference facilities, all set amid manicured landscaping and parking facilities.

Joel Garreau's provocative 1991 book, *Edge City: Life on the New Frontier*, defined "edge city" as a newly developed cluster having at least 5 million square feet of office space and 600,000 square feet of retail space, He identified more than 200 such complexes across the United States. In the early 1990s, those edge cities collectively contained two-thirds of all U.S. office space and in fact eclipsed conventional urban "downtowns." More office space is found in the edge cities of New Jersey than in the Financial District of Manhattan (Garreau 1991, 5). South Coast Mall in Orange County, California, does more business in a day than all of downtown San Francisco (ibid., 63), or at least it did when Garreau conducted his research.

Edge cities are not governmental units. They are tightly controlled islands of private development amid the general web of municipal, county, and state authority that interlace metropolitan America. Although they generate taxes and jobs that benefit the wider region, they may also harm the central city economy in competition for conventions, retail, and restaurant trade (Leinberger and Lockwood 1986). Also, they usually lack affordable housing, schools, public parks, and a sense of civic identity. An archetypal New Jersey edge city called "287 and 78" (an interstate highway intersection) "has no overall leader, no political boundaries that define the place. It is governed only by a patchwork of zoning boards and planning boards and county boards, and townships boards ... swirling like gnats—not any elected ruling structure" (Garreau 1991, 46).

Like William H. Whyte's study of Park Forest, Illinois, in *The Organization Man*, Garreau weighed the impact of the new edge cities on the well-being of their inhabitants. For those in the right age group (thirties and forties) and profession (finance, information, high tech) and who are childless, they appear to work well, despite their conspicuous lack of history or community. Those who do not qualify by reason of age, ethnicity, or skills are left behind (literally and politically) in the older central cities and suburbs.

Gated Communities

Metropolitan growth since the 1980s increasingly has reflected what architectural critic Paul Goldberger (2000, viii) terms the "triumph of the private realm." Many public elements of traditional urban life such as streets, parks, transportation, neighborhoods, schools, recreation, and shopping districts are now widely provided by the private sector to those who can afford the price. The most conspicuous products of this trend are *gated residential communities*. As edge cities are to regional shopping malls, gated communities are to traditional subdivisions. As discussed in Chapter 9, *subdivisions* are residential developments planned by a developer, reviewed and approved by the local government. The traditional subdivision merges into the surrounding community. Its streets are usually conveyed to the local government for maintenance and thus become public rights-of-way. Its interior green spaces may eventually become neighborhood miniparks and playgrounds for wider use. In many states, subdividers may be required to donate sites for future schools or parks related to the development or pay fees in lieu of actual land donations.

By contrast, gated communities do not merge into the surrounding community. Ownership of their interior streets, greenspaces, and other infrastructure is conveyed to a private homeowner or condominium association, not to the local government. They often feature golf courses, tennis courts, clubs, and other membership amenities. Access to a gated (and often walled) community is through actual gates policed by actual security guards or electronic access systems.

In their study of gated communities, *Fortress America: Gated Communities in the United States*, planners Edward J. Blakely and Ellen Gail Snyder estimated that there were by 1997 "as many as 20,000 gated communities, with more than 3 million units. They are increasing rapidly in number, in all regions and price classes" (Blakely and Snyder 1997, 7). They are most often found in affluent outer reaches of Sun Belt metropolitan areas in California, Arizona, Texas, and Florida. Large numbers are also found in wealthy suburbs of Chicago, New York, and other older cities.

A concomitant of the "triumph of the private realm" is the decline of community, at least outside the gates of the private development, private resort, and private school. Sociologist Robert D. Putnam (2000) in his book *Bowling Alone* chronicles the loss of community spirit, volunteerism, and sociability in the contemporary American metropolis.

Downtowns

This chapter now ends with a few observations about downtowns of U.S. cities, referred to more primly by planners and geographers as *central business districts* (CBDs). As in the 1960s Petula Clark song "Downtown," the city center traditionally offered the promise of escape, excitement, bright lights, and fun. Amid the glitz of postmodern offices and plazas, downtowns today often retain hints of the history, economy, and regional culture of the city. To many people, especially suburbanites and tourists, downtowns *are* the city: where you go for holiday shopping sprees, museums, theater, and major business transactions. Convention centers, sports arenas, railroad stations, and major hotels are usually located in or near downtown, as are those compulsively funky "olde town" districts of bars, eateries, and high-end clothing shops that cater to conventioneers and tourists. So important is the perception of a lively downtown that Las Vegas plans to invent one for itself (Gorman, 2001)!

Urban downtowns experienced a checkered history over the twentieth century. The heyday of downtowns, like cities overall, occurred during the period of approximately 1890–1929 when many of the museums, orchestra halls, railway stations, skyscrapers, civic buildings, and parks of the City Beautiful era were built, as discussed in Chapter 5. Many monuments of that period survive today, such as Chicago's Art Institute and Field Museum and New York's Grand Central Station, Public Library, and Carnegie Hall. Others such as New York's old Pennsylvania Station and Chicago's Stock Exchange, have been lost to the demolition ball. Many more buildings would have been razed but for the historic preservation movement and legislation it prompted in the 1960s triggered by the impending demolition of Grand Central Station. (See further discussion in Chapter 10.)

During the Depression, downtown city streets were often thronged with the unemployed lined up for job opportunities, for soup kitchens, or simply to use public restrooms. Downtowns have always been refuges for the destitute and homeless, where public assistance, companionship, and sometimes a job may be found. People who could afford the price sought escape in the great downtown movie palaces, "legitimate" theaters, and "speakeasies" that replaced bars during Prohibition. Jazz musicians from the South like Louis Armstrong performed in backstreet dives close to downtown Chicago, St. Louis, Kansas City, and New York. Wartime brought new vitality to downtowns as business retooled for national defense, women entered the labor force, and young soldiers and sailors, passing through, squandered their scarce liberty hours and money on booze and loose women.

The postwar home building boom turned its back on urban downtowns. Although "organization men" still commuted downtown by rail or car in the 1950s, other functions such as education, shopping, and recreation were increasingly pursued in suburbs with weekend trips downtown relegated to occasional "special occasions." Very large city downtowns maintained their role as centers of business, specialized shopping, and cultural activities, but elsewhere downtowns generally began to decline as suburban shopping opportunities expanded.

The archetype for the modern shopping mall was the Moorish style Country Club Plaza in Kansas City built in 1925 as part of a larger fashionable new district. Houston's Galleria located within the city limits but far from downtown opened in 1970 complete with ice-skating rink (Rockefeller Center comes to Texas). The next year, Woodfield Mall opened with 2 million square feet of retail space in the village/edge city of Schaumberg, Illinois, outside Chicago (Rybczynski 1993). The Mall of America in Bloomington, Minnesota, opened in the early 1990s with 4.2 million square feet, rivaling all of downtown Minneapolis. As malls proliferated in number and size, many premier downtown stores such as Wanamakers in New York and Philadelphia, and Hudson's in Detroit closed or moved to the suburbs. Three department stores closed in Pittsburgh between 1958 and 1960, reducing downtown retail space by a million square feet (Teaford, 1993, 111). A few landmark stores like Marshall Fields in the Chicago Loop and Jordan Marsh and Filenes in Boston retained their downtown stores while also opening suburban branches. With the loss of many "anchor" stores, however, thousands of smaller downtown businesses also folded or relocated, and downtowns other than in the largest cities began to look deserted by the early 1960s (Figure 6-4).

Further hastening the decline of downtowns, urban renewal programs in the 1950s and 1960s cleared older apartment buildings and neighborhoods close to the central business district. When the expected private redevelopment never materialized, the land remained unused except for parking; today, many CBDs are encircled by a forbidding belt of parking lots and pavement. as residential structures were razed in and near downtowns, many downtowns became mostly

FIGURE 6-4 Downtown Buffalo on a Sunday morning, 2003. Note light-rail and sidewalk improvements to encourage pedestrian use. *(Photo by author.)*

deserted in the evening and over weekends. Even weekday business declined as white-collar employment also migrated to the suburban office parks and edge cities. As mentioned earlier, the city of Atlanta's share of its metropolitan area's job market dropped from 40 percent in 1980 to 19 percent in 1997; 98.7 percent of all new jobs were created outside the city and its downtown (Bullard, Johnson, and Torres 2000, 10–11).

Beginning in the 1970s, many cities sought to emulate suburban malls in redevelopment schemes. New office, hotel, and residential complexes were constructed on top of multistory parking structures that absorbed cars and SUVs directly off the adjacent interstate highways. Once parked, the visitor would be encouraged to circulate on foot through interior shopping malls equipped with escalators and sometimes connected across streets by "sky bridges." Where feasible, historic structures were converted to shopping and eating complexes (e.g., Union Station and the Old Post Office in Washington, D.C., and Pittsburgh's Station Square). "Festival marketplaces" appeared in many cities modeled on James Rouse's pathbreaking adaptive reuse designs for Boston's Quincy Markets, New York's South Street Seaport, Baltimore's Inner Harbor, and San Francisco's Ghirardelli Square during the 1970s and 1980s.

FIGURE 6-5 Downtown sidewalk in Los Angeles on a busy weekday. *(Photo by author.)*

Apart from such showcase successes, however, many downtowns, especially in small- to medium-sized cities like Springfield, Massachusetts, Hartford, Buffalo, and Detroit, failed to regain vitality. Even where downtown life was reviving indoors, the street scene was moribund if not actually threatening. As documented by William H. Whyte in *City: Rediscovering the Center* (1988), a successful downtown depends in part on encountering other people, many of them different from oneself in safe, amenable public spaces. Yet downtowns, Whyte observed, have been rebuilt for the convenience of drivers, not pedestrians. Streets are lined with blank walls, shaded windows, or banal advertising (Figure 6-5). Would-be urban pedestrians are deprived of the simple pleasures of people-watching, window shopping, and baby- or dog-admiring, not to mention interesting routes for serious walking or jogging. Street life in the form of storefronts, sidewalk vendors, and impromptu entertainment for tips was missing from the late-twentieth-century American downtown. By contrast, many European cities, rebuilt after World War II, closed certain streets and squares to traffic so as to promote such street life and activity; American visitors to urban downtowns in Great Britain, France, Germany, Poland, the Czech Republic, and elsewhere find this terribly quaint. Like

FIGURE 6-6
Ice skating rink in downtown
Providence, Rhode Island.
(Photo by author.)

the McMillan Commission in 1902, urban design professionals brought bring
images of European downtowns to re-create in the United States, with mixed success (e.g., Beatley 2000).

The 1990s witnessed a renaissance for some older downtowns across the United
States from Providence, Rhode Island (Figure 6-6) to Oakland, California (Figure
6-7). Lessons learned in Europe and from urban design firms like Project for Public Spaces, Inc. (www.pps.org), founded by Whyte, helped shape the design of new
downtown development to incorporate outdoor and indoor public spaces, more
interesting streets, and convenient (sometimes free) public transit (Figure 6-8).
Zoning density bonuses are awarded in many cities in exchange for providing and
maintaining public plazas and other amenities at the developer's expense. This
strategy has yielded over five hundred "privately owned public spaces" in New
York City alone, albeit with a mixed record of public benefit (Kayden 2000).

The development of light-rail systems in some cities (Denver; Portland, Oregon; and San Diego, for instance) has helped encourage people to return to downtowns for work, shopping, or pleasure while leaving their vehicles behind. New
residential construction and conversion of old lofts and industrial buildings to

FIGURE 6-7
Downtown plaza in Oakland,
California, at lunch hour
(live jazz is playing).
(Photo by author.)

FIGURE 6-8
A lively Chapel Street in New
Haven, Connecticut, opposite
Yale University campus.
(Photo by author.)

apartments and condominiums have helped revive the resident downtown population in dozens of cities (Birch 2002). Even such car-dominated cities as Los Angeles, Denver, and Houston are reporting a growing population of downtown residents, which in turn provides patronage for local businesses and makes the streets livelier as well as safer.

Conclusion

This chapter summarizes the evolution of urban and metropolitan America since World War II. This brief overview suggests certain obvious contradictions and issues for public policy. One is the *social inequity* of national housing programs that have discriminated shamelessly between the white middle class and the nonwhite poor. Although the blatant bias of mortgage subsidy programs in the 1950s and 1960s has been eliminated, the effect of property tax and mortgage interest deductions under federal tax law still favors home ownership as compared with rental. In addition, local zoning laws in thousands of suburbs still favor single-family homes over multiple-family development. Both of these practices discriminate

FIGURE 6-9 "Affordable" new housing under construction
in Riverside, California, 2002. *(Photo by author.)*

against those less able to qualify for ownership of a single family home due to
income, color, age, or employability (Figure 6-9).

Closely related is the issue of *housing affordability*. With 107 million households
and 122 million dwelling units in the United States, it would appear that there is
enough housing in place and in the pipeline to accommodate the entire population
somewhere (Doyle 2002). Housing affordability, though, varies enormously from
place to place and from one housing market to another. In Buffalo, median family
income is about $49,500 and the median house valuation is $91,000, so it takes 1.8
years of family income to buy a typical house. In Boston, New York City, Los
Angeles, and many other "hot" housing markets, however, median house prices
are many times median income. Hence, a teacher earning, say, $50,000 in Los
Angeles faces median home prices ranging from about $200,000 to about $600,000
for most of the city (excluding the lowest and highest zip codes) (*Los Angeles Times*
2003). These prices represent four to twelve times that person's annual income,
probably out of reach unless a significant down payment is made. This situation
accounts in part for the long-distance commuting by so many metropolitan residents as they seek to maximize the housing they can afford at the cost of travel time

to work. Local preference for large-lot single-family homes, often in "exclusive" gated communities, drives up median house prices, thereby shutting out increasing numbers of middle-class households of all races.

Increasing flood and other *natural hazards losses* are a further result of metropolitan growth in vulnerable areas. As prime building sites are fully built out, developers turn to marginal sites to provide additional, possibly more affordable, housing. Thus, if the state and local governments concur, building may be located in floodplains, on unstable slopes, on filled wetlands, or on known earthquake faults. Natural disaster losses to private and public property have increased relentlessly since World War II in the United States and around the world. Some remedial measures, like the National Flood Insurance Program, are discussed in Chapter 12.

Finally, as Lewis Mumford and William H. Whyte both observed in the 1950s, metropolitan growth entails loss of open spaces, agricultural land, and contact with nature. It degrades water quality of streams, ponds, lakes, estuaries, and coastal waters through both *point sources* (e.g., inadequately treated sewage and industrial discharges) and *nonpoint sources* (e.g., failing septic systems and sedimentation from construction sites). As Gottmann noted in *Megalopolis*, the solution of these and other problems inherent to metropolitan growth requires a governance process capable of overcoming political fragmentation and offering regional approaches at the geographic scale appropriate to the nature of the problem.

References

Advisory Commission on Intergovernmental Relations. 1969. *Urban America and the Federal System*. Washington, DC: Author.

Beatley, T. 2000. *Green Urbanism*. Washington, DC: Island Press.

Birch, E. L. 2002. Having a Longer View on Downtown Living. *Journal of the American Planning Association* 68 (1): 5–21.

Blakely, E. J., and M. G. Snyder. 1997. *Fortress America: Gated Communities in the United States*. Cambridge, MA: Lincoln Institute of Land Policy and Brookings Institution Press.

Brooks, D. 2000. *Bobos in Paradise: The New Upper Class and How They Got There*. New York: Simon and Schuster.

Bullard, R. D., G. S. Johnson, and A. O. Torres, eds. 2000. *Sprawl City: Race, Politics, and Planning in Atlanta*. Washington, DC: Island Press.

Doyle, R. 2002. Affording a Home. *Scientific American*, Sept., 32.

Editors of *Fortune*. 1957. *The Exploding Metropolis*. New York: Doubleday Anchor.

Fay, W. D. 2001. Letter to *The Washington Post*, Oct. 25, 14.

Frey, W. H., and A. Berube. 2002. *City Families and Suburban Singles: An Emerging Household Story from Census 2000*. Washington, DC: Brookings Institution, Center on Urban and Metropolitan Policy.

Fulton, W., R. Pendall, M. Nguyen, and A. Harrison. 2001. Who Sprawls Most? How Growth Patterns Differ Across the United States (Survey Series Monograph). Washington, DC: Brookings Institution, Center on Urban and Metropolitan Policy.

Garreau, J. 1991. *Edge City: Life on the New Frontier*. New York: Doubleday Anchor.

Goldberger, P. 2000. Foreword to *The Essential William H. Whyte*, ed. A. LaFarge, vii–ix. New York: Fordham University Press.

Gorman, T. 2001. Real Downtown? Vegas Bucks the Odds. *Boston Sunday Globe*, April 8, 3.

Gottmann, J. 1961. *Megalopolis: The Urbanized Northeastern Seaboard of the United States*. Cambridge, MA: MIT Press.

Jackson, K. T. 1985. *Crabgrass Frontier: The Suburbanization of the United States*. New York: Oxford University Press.

———. 2000. Gentleman's Agreement: Discrimination in Metropolitan America. In *Reflections on Regionalism*, ed. B. Katz, 78–106. Washington, DC: Brookings Institution Press.

Jacobs, J. 1961. *The Death and Life of Great American Cities*. New York: Vintage.

Kaplan, R. D. 1998. *Empire Wilderness: Travels into America's Future*. New York: Vintage.

Kates, R. W. 1987. The Human Environment: The Road Not Taken; The Road Still Beckoning. *Annals of the Association of American Geographers* 77 (4): 525–34.

Katz, B. 2001. The New Metropolitan Agenda. Speech to the Southwestern Pennsylvania Smart Growth Conference, June 9.

Kayden, J. 2000. *Privately Owned Public Space: The New York City Experience*. New York: Wiley.

Kristof, N. D. 2003. Make Way for Buffalo. *New York Times,* Oct. 29, A25.

Leinberger, C. B., and C. Lockwood. 1986. How Business Is Reshaping America. *Atlantic Monthly* 258 (4): 43–52.

Los Angeles Times 2003. L.A. County Median Sales for January. Feb. 23, K1, K6.

Mumford, L. 1956. The Natural History of Cities. In *Man's Role in Changing the Face of the Earth*, ed. W. L. Thomas Jr., 382–398. Chicago: University of Chicago Press.

———. 1961. *The City in History*. New York: Harcourt, Brace, and World.

Popper, F., and D. Popper. 1987. The Great Plains: From Dust to Dust. *Planning* (Dec.): 12–18.

Putnam, R. D. 2000. *Bowling Alone*. New York: Touchstone.

Rome, A. 2001. *The Bulldozer in the Countryside: Suburban Sprawl and the Rise of American Environmentalism*. New York: Cambridge University Press.

Rusk, D. 1999. *Inside Game, Outside Game: Winning Strategies for Saving Urban America*. Washington, DC: Brookings Institution Press.

Rybczynski, W. 1993. The New Downtowns. *Atlantic Monthly*, May, 98–106.

Seabrook, J. 2002. The Slow Lane. *New Yorker*, Sept. 2, 120–27.

Suarez, R. 1999. *The Old Neighborhood: What We Lost in the Great Suburban Migration: 1966–1999*. New York: Free Press.

Teaford, J. C. 1979. *City and Suburb: The Political Fragmentation of Metropolitan America: 1850–1970*. Baltimore: Johns Hopkins University Press.

———. 1993. *The Twentieth-Century American City*. 2nd ed. Baltimore: Johns Hopkins University Press.

Thomas, W. L., Jr. 1956. *Man's Role in Changing the Face of the Earth*. Chicago: University of Chicago Press.

U.S. Bureau of the Census. 1995–1996. *American Almanac: Statistical Abstract of the United States*. Austin, TX: Reference Press.

U.S. Department of Agriculture. 1987. *The Second RCA Appraisal: Soil, Water, and Related Resources on Nonfederal Land in the U.S.* Washington, DC: Author.

Warner, S. B., Jr. 1978. *Streetcar Suburbs: The Process of Growth in Boston (1870–1900)*. 2nd ed. Cambridge, MA: Harvard University Press.

Whyte, W. H. 1956. *The Organization Man*. Garden City, NY: Simon and Schuster. (Republished 2002 by University of Pennsylvania Press.)

———. 1957. Urban Sprawl. In *The Exploding Metropolis*, ed. Editors of *Fortune*, 115–139. Garden City, NY: Doubleday Anchor.

———. 1968. *The Last Landscape*. Garden City, NY: Doubleday. (Republished 2002 by University of Pennsylvania Press.)

———. 1988. *City: Rediscovering the Center*. Garden City: Doubleday.

Wright, J. W., ed. 2003. *New York Times Almanac — 2003*. New York: Penguin.

Zielbauer, P. 2002. Poverty in a Land of Plenty: Can Hartford Ever Recover? *New York Times*, Aug. 26, 1, B4.

PART III

Discordant Voices:
Property Ownership,
Local Government,
and the Courts

CHAPTER 7 *Property Rights:*
The Owner as Planner

The true founder of civil society was the first man who, having enclosed a piece of land, thought of saying "This is mine" and came across people simple enough to believe him.

— JEAN-JACQUES ROUSSEAU, 1755, AS QUOTED IN BROMLEY 1998, 29

In most Western countries, including the United States, land is conceptualized, fictionalized, as a bundle of rights ... which the owner may use, sell, trade, lease, and/or bequeath. It is this bundle of rights that society recognizes as ownership.

— HARVEY M. JACOBS, 1998, X

The property owner is the primary land use decision maker. The public sector in the United States—primarily at the local level—essentially reacts to the decisions of the property owner. It is the owner who determines *how* to use his or her land in light of geographic, economic, legal, and personal circumstances. It is also the owner who determines when a change in existing land use should occur.

This chapter is devoted to a summary of the institution of *real property owner-ship* and the role the owner plays in the unfolding pattern of land usage. This discussion sets the stage for review of the regional, state, and federal roles respecting the land use decision process in later chapters.

What Is Real Property?

The legal concept of property in the United States and Great Britain (and other nations that retain the English *common law* as the basis of their property law system) distinguishes between two classes of property: real and personal. *Real property* includes physical land, buildings, vegetation, subsurface minerals, and, in some states, water rights pertaining to specific tracts of land. *Personal property* consists of "chattels" or physical objects owned by an individual—such as furniture, works of art, computers, motor vehicles, livestock, clothing—virtually anything other than real property that can be owned. The distinction between real and personal property is important in several ways: (1) they are taxed differently, (2) they are bought and sold with different formalities, and (3) a buyer of real property is not necessarily entitled to personal property of the previous owner located on the premises. (Normally, appliances that are attached to the structure or land, such as a furnace, gas stove, hot water heater, and perennial shrubs and trees, are *fixtures* that pass to the buyer of real property, whereas furnishings and appliances that are easily unplugged may be removed and retained by the seller.) A tract of land held in one ownership (whether or not it has buildings on it) is referred to as a *parcel* of real property or real estate.

Ownership of urban land is highly fragmented. Much land in cities is publicly owned in the form of streets, parks, school sites, fire and police stations, public works facilities, and so on. Land that is not in *public* ownership is by definition *private,* including homes, commercial and industrial facilities, malls, and hotels. Downtown redevelopment today often involves complex intertwining of public and private investment in multiuse development such as megamalls, sports arenas, and convention centers.

Owners of private real property (land and buildings) must pay property taxes to the applicable local government and other taxing districts. Property taxes are based on the *assessed value* of the site as set by the municipal or county tax assessor's office. Many cities have thousands of acres of derelict and abandoned properties that were once private but have reverted to public ownership due to failure of the owner to pay property taxes.

The concept of land as real property is three-dimensional. A classic legal cliché states: *Cujus est solum, ejus est usque ad coelum ad infernos* (roughly translated: "Whomsoever owns the soil, owns also to heaven and to hell"). It means that the ownership of real property extends both *horizontally* across the surface area of the site but also *vertically* downward and upward to the limits of practical or legal feasibility. Thus real property ownership may include subsurface *minerals rights* (e.g., oil, gas, coal, or valuable minerals) as well as *air rights* above the surface, at least to a height allowed by local zoning and air traffic regulations (Figure 7-1).

Land ownership is described in law school as a *bundle of green and red sticks.* The "green sticks" represent rights or benefits that owners possess to use their property

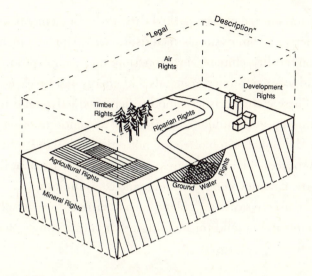

FIGURE 7-1
The geography of
legal rights in land:
Elements of real
property ownership.

for economic gain or personal use. "Red sticks" are the burdens required of the owner, like payment of property taxes, in exchange for the right to enjoy the green sticks. Thus in addition to the market cost of acquiring a parcel of real property, society places property owners under various obligations to use property in specified ways and to contribute to the public costs of maintaining local services. Naturally, owners want maximize their green sticks and minimize red sticks, which leads to the property rights debate to be discussed later. Meanwhile, a closer look at the bundle of sticks is needed.

Green Sticks: The Benefits of Property Ownership

Value may be derived from land in various ways. Some people or organizations acquire land purely as an investment, hoping to resell it to someone else for more money than they paid for it. This practice, known as *land speculation,* involves a complex set of variables, include the general economy, the local land market, tax laws, and public zoning and environmental regulations. Like the stock market, much money has been made and lost in land speculation. Also like stocks, which are shares in actual business ventures, the value of land ultimately depends on the actual or potential economic gain to be realized from its use. (Both stocks and land may be vastly overvalued under conditions of what in Japan has been called a "bubble economy," whose fate is self-evident from the term itself.)

Uses of land may be conveniently grouped in two general categories: *physical* and *spatial.* These categories reflect the dual nature of land as a wedge of the physical material of the earth and alternatively as a volume or space that can be enclosed by structures or used for storage of, say, parked cars. Physical elements of land value are principally derived from its site characteristics (see Chapter 2), including subsurface geology, soil fertility, climate, elevation, slope and solar exposure, surface water and groundwater resources, minerals and energy resources, ecology, and scenic amenity. These characteristics support such productive land uses as agriculture, forestry, mining, and outdoor recreation (not to mention *ecological services* on which all life depends but too often are not reflected in land valuation) (Daily 2000). Physical sources of land value are prevalent in rural areas, by definition, with relatively little land devoted to buildings and communities.

In and near urban areas, physical uses of land such as farming are usually displaced by more profitable use of land for buildings, thus substituting spatial for

BOX 7-1 *Who Owns Water?*

No one actually *owns* water in place. Water in its many natural states—rivers, lakes, wetlands, groundwater, the oceans, glacial ice, and the atmosphere—is a *common resource*. Like the common fields in feudal times, societies have developed complex legal regimes to use water for human benefit, with belated recognition that ecology also has a claim on water resources. In cities, we pay water and sewer fees for the right to use water (*water rights*) for certain purposes like drinking, bathing, toilet flushing, lawn watering, manufacturing, beer brewing, and fire fighting. In rural areas, households may derive water from on-site wells. In neither case, however, is the water actually owned by individual user. Unlike private land, water is not a proprietary commodity, except to the extent that it is bottled and sold as a beverage.

The concept of water rights is tricky; it differs among nations, states, and regions,

and it also differs according to the proposed use of water as well as its physical state (surface or ground, fresh or salt, navigable or nonnavigable). In the United States, two water law doctrines historically prevailed according to relative abundance of rainfall: *riparian rights* in states where precipitation is usually abundant, primarily east of the Great Plains, and *prior appropriation* in arid western states.

"Riparian" refers to land adjoining a stream, lake, or tidal body of water. Owners of riparian land in states following this doctrine may withdraw or store water flowing over or past their land for domestic, industrial, or agricultural purposes. Changes in stream flow (through dams or diversions) and water quality (through discharge of pollutants and reduction of flow) had to be *reasonable* in relation to the needs of other riparian users downstream. The respective rights of riparians sharing a physical sources of land value. Recall from Chapter 2 that real estate agents say that the three most important variables in land value are *location, location,* and *location.* Location and accessibility in relation to the larger spatial pattern of urban development are critical in determining when a parcel of land is more valuable for spatial than for physical uses, that is, for development rather than farming or forestry.

Development involves the structural enclosure of a portion of the air space above the land surface (*grade level*), as well as the excavation of additional space below the surface, for such purposes as homes, offices, hotels, factories, shopping malls, and parking. Physical site characteristics are relevant to the form and intensity of spatial development, but given sufficiently high locational value, physical site impediments may be overcome through technology. Portions of most cities

water source could, when necessary, be settled by a court, but that was a clumsy mechanism for regulating private use of water resources. During the second half of the twentieth century, public regulatory programs such as the Federal Clean Water Act and its state counterparts have largely superceded the riparian doctrine as tools for protecting and restoring water quality.

In arid and semi-arid *prior appropriation* states such as Colorado and Wyoming, water rights are legally separate from the ownership of land, and riparian rights are generally not recognized. Historically, this practice resulted from the needs of mining and agriculture to overcome the scarcity of local water sources by preempting large quantities of water at the nearest available source and conveying it by pipe or ditch to locations where it would be beneficially used. Under the prior appropriation system, legal claims to specific sources and quantities of water are formally registered with the state; the older

the date of original appropriation (its *seniority*), the stronger the claim to water from a particular source in times of scarcity, vis-á-vis later-filed (more *junior*) claims.

In prior appropriation states, water rights may be bought and sold separately from land transactions. Because little water remains unappropriated in many parts of the West, it is common today for urban developers and urban water suppliers to purchase registered water rights in the open market. When sold, a water right retains its date of seniority; thus the more senior the right, the more secure and therefore the more expensive it is to purchase today. Of course, prior appropriation states also are subject to federal and state laws regulating pollution, aquatic habitat, filling of wetlands, flood hazard reduction, and other functions of water resource management that transcend traditional doctrines of both riparian rights and prior appropriation.

FIGURE 7-2 Building on a slippery slope above the Hayward Fault in Oakland, California. *(Photo by author.)*

have been constructed on physically unpromising sites, like the Back Bay marshes in the case of Boston and the boggy lake plain of Chicago. Canyons of the San Gabriel Mountains bordering Los Angeles are filled with expensive homes that occasionally are destroyed in chaparral fires or debris flows from upslope (McPhee 1989). The willingness of Californians to risk seismic hazards in their locational decisions is well known (Palm 1986). As urban sprawl occupies areas of serious physical limitations, unwary investors sometimes experience unforeseen economic and psychic costs from such hazards as urban flooding, earthquake damage, and slope instability (Burby 1998).

The private real estate market is very clever at devising ways to profitably divide up the three-dimensional space represented by a parcel of real property. Buildings are sometimes elevated above the ground on pilings or stilts to retain the surface for a different use such as railroad tracks or a highway. Structures so elevated are referred to as *air rights development*. Downtown or "edge city" developments also excavate far below grade level to accommodate underground shopping concourses, parking garages, and other nonresidential uses. The below-grade geography of cities is a complex and often unmapped *terra incognita* just beneath our feet. For instance, the clearance of debris from the huge "Pit" after the destruction of the

FIGURE 7-3 Buildings threatened by coastal erosion, North Carolina. *(Photo by author.)* Also see Figure 12-2.

World Trade Center on September 11, 2001, laid bare a vast subterranean labyrinth of subways, utilities, pipes, parking garages, and building machinery spaces.

Multiunit development is of course commonplace in more densely developed communities. Traditionally, attached residential units are rented to tenants as apartments. Since the 1970s, the practice of selling attached housing units as *condominiums* has become very widespread, and in some cities former apartment complexes have been converted into separately owned "condos." Condominiums above the first floor are parcels of real property that "float" in midair supported by the framework of the building. Ownership of a condominium also involves a proportional share of the common elements of the overall building, such as its basement, exterior walls, roof, stairs, and elevators. Those facilities are maintained by a condominium association whose costs are paid from monthly assessment fees charged to each condo owner.

Red Sticks: The Burdens of Property Ownership

Owners of real property enjoy the array of physical and spatial rights to gain value from their investments, or they may profit from someone else's use of the property through rental or sale of the premises. Inherent to ownership of real property, however, are obligations to one's neighbors, to the community, and to society at large. These obligations or "red sticks" are the opposite side of the coin of property ownership.

In countries sharing the British common-law tradition, the most ancient obligation of real property ownership, as discussed in Chapter 3, is to refrain from creating a *nuisance* that interferes with the rights of adjoining property owners and the general public. Nuisance may be either private or public. A *private nuisance* is a harmful externality inflicted primarily on the occupants of neighboring property, such as air pollution, sickening odors, excessive noise, obstruction of light and air, overflow of storm drainage, accumulation of wastes, or allowing trash or dust to blow onto neighboring property. Nuisance is a flexible concept that has been adapted by court decisions to embrace such disturbing activities as vibration, loud parties, floodlighting, jet skis, racetracks, and animal feedlots. In 1990, for instance, a trial court in Massachusetts decided that ringing of a church bell every hour all night long was a nuisance to adjoining homeowners who had moved there when the clock was inoperative.

A *public nuisance* is one that affects a wider area or the public at large, as in the emission of air or water pollution; conducting an immoral or antisocial business, such as maintaining a "crack house"; or dumping hazardous wastes. The borderline between a private or a public nuisance is not always clear. Public nuisances, however, may be defined by state or local law and thus are criminal offenses (Prosser 1971, Chap. 15). Violation of an environmental statute, such as on hazardous waste disposal, may be both a public and a private nuisance. The growing use of obnoxious audio systems in personal vehicles ("boomcars") will, one hopes, soon be declared a public nuisance in communities that attract them.

Nuisance law terminology, which dates back to medieval England, is both quaint and colorful. When an injured party (*plaintiff*) files a lawsuit against the party causing the injury (*defendant*) through an unreasonable use of land, a court may issue an *injunction* that orders the defendant to stop causing such harm to the plaintiff and others. Courts have wide latitude to *balance the equities* in terms of weighing the relative impacts on the parties and on the larger community of banning a the offending activity, modifying it, or allowing it to continue. A defendant may also be required to pay monetary *damages* and legal expenses to the plaintiff to compensate for past or ongoing harm. If the plaintiff moved to the vicinity after the harmful activity was under way, the court may deny relief because the plaintiff *came to the nuisance*. Plaintiffs who wait too long to file a suit may be barred by the doctrine of *laches,* and if they are creating a nuisance themselves, the defendant will ask the court to dismiss the case due to the plaintiff's *unclean hands*!

PROPERTY TAXES

Another unpleasant duty of a property owner is to pay all taxes and special assessments levied against the real estate. These payments include *ad valorem* taxes (based on assessed property values) levied annually by the local municipality, county, and special districts within which the property is situated. One-time *special assessments* are also the responsibility of the property owner. Special assessments are often charged for public improvements that benefit the real property in question, as in the case of sidewalk or street reconstruction, new sewers, water lines, or other facilities of localized, as distinct from citywide, benefits. (Taxes are discussed further in Chapter 8.)

PUBLIC REGULATIONS

Beyond nuisance and tax obligations, the landowner must comply with land use and building regulations imposed at the local, state, and federal levels. Such measures can include building codes, zoning laws, subdivision regulations, wetland restrictions, seismic design requirements, floodplain regulations, and public nuisance laws. These regulations are considered in more detail in later chapters.

Types of Owners and Legal Interests

Real property may be owned by many types and combinations of owners. Private ownerships may involve one or more individuals (related or not), partnerships, trusts, estates, corporations (business or nonprofit), and other legal entities. Real property may also be publicly owned by federal, state, or local governments or by special units such as school districts. When private ownership is divided among multiple parties, each owns an undivided fractional interest. For example, one-third of a tract of land might be owned by a family partnership and the other two-thirds by two spouses as *joint tenants* (when one dies, the other succeeds to his or her share). Over time, the legal identity of ownership changes with the sale, gift, or bequest of interests in the property and other changes in status. Real property ownership is usually subject to additional claims or rights of usage by nonowners

BOX 7-2 *Nuisance: When Should "the Law" Step In?*

Many land use practices disturb neighbors or the community but are nevertheless perfectly legal. Development of open land itself may bother earlier arrivals who seek to protect their bucolic surroundings. Land use zoning, discussed in Chapter 8, seeks to maintain some degree of compatibility among developed land uses. Apart from whether a use of land conforms with local zoning, however, neighbors may still raise objections that they are unreasonably harmed by an existing or prospective use of land, arguing that it should be enjoined as a *nuisance*.

The question then is, When do bothersome effects of land uses in a *geographical* sense make up a nuisance in a *legal* sense? Some external "harms" may simply deprive the plaintiff of an external benefit previously enjoyed gratuitously, such as the view of a tree on someone else's property that is chopped down. Or the harm may be insignificant and the plaintiff viewed as unreasonably sensitive or fussy, such as complaining about a window air conditioner in the house next door. Some "harms" are simply part of life in modern society and fall into the common-law category of *damnum absque injuria*, or "harm without remedy."

Consider the following hypothetical scenario (also illustrated in Figure 7-4). Assuming that no public zoning or other public regulations are in effect, *when should a court intervene to declare A's conduct to be a nuisance*?

1. Homeowner B enjoys the proximity of landowner A's woods next door. B benefits from the shade, the privacy, and the bird life as well as the opportunity for her children and pets to cavort in A's woods, and to gather firewood.
2. A, after discovering B's unauthorized use of his property, builds a fence that deprives B's family of their access to the woods. B is thus "harmed," but can she complain legally of being denied the right to trespass?
3. A cuts down his woods, thus additionally depriving B of the external benefits of shade and natural surroundings. Should the law prevent this externality?
4. A constructs a house similar to that of B, who now loses her privacy and whose property declines in value. Should A be prevented from doing that?
5. Instead of a house, A builds an animal hospital that will involve traffic, inces-

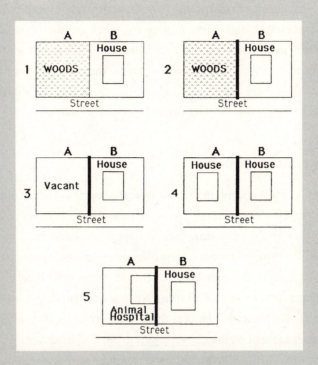

FIGURE 7-4 Externalities and nuisance: a hypothetical scenario.

sant barking, floodlights at night, and the stench of the furnace in which decreased pets are cremated. Is this use a nuisance?

Actions 1 through 4 would most likely be considered *damnum absque injuria*; that is, no legal relief would be available to B. Action 5, however, would probably be viewed as an unreasonable use of A's land causing damage to B that would be enjoined in a court (if B files a suit). In the absence of public regulation or legal complaint by B, A would be free to continue the animal hospital. If B sues, however, a court might try to avoid closing the business entirely (such facilities serve a useful purpose) by ordering changes in the hours of operation, soundproofing of the dog kennel, perhaps a landscape buffer, and moving the crematorium to a nonresidential location.

who have a legal interest in the premises, such as mortgage lenders, holders of easements, tenants, contractors owed money for work on the premises, and parties entitled to farm, mine, cut timber, or extract other resources from the land.

To better appreciate the complexity of ownership, which may plague the best-laid plans for the future use of particular land, the following discussion summarizes the types of legal interests that may be encountered.

Fee Simple Absolute

The highest and most complete interest in real property is known as the *fee simple absolute,* also known as the *fee simple* or just the *fee*. This concept is encompasses both the physical and spatial connotations of real property, the actual substance of the land and the volume of space extending above and below the parcel of land. It also includes a temporal dimension: fee simple ownership theoretically lasts forever. Real property owned in fee simple may be sold, rented, given away, or devised to heirs by means of a will. It "denotes the maximum of legal ownership, the greatest possible aggregate of rights, powers, privileges and immunities which a person may have in land" (Moynihan 1962, 29).

In practice, fee simple ownership usually involves dividing the total bundle of rights in various ways: (1) physical partition, (2) severance of specific usage rights, and (3) division in time. Physical partition of the land into two or more parcels allows a portion to be sold or given away and the rest to be retained. Farmers sometimes split off roadside building lots to raise cash or may give them to offspring as home sites or for resale, thus lowering the eventual inheritance taxes on the overall farm. Usage rights may be sold or leased to other parties to, for example, extract minerals such as oil or coal or cut timber. In such cases, the owner is divested of the right to exploit these resources in exchange for a one-time payment or a series of royalty or lease payments over time. Finally, the fee simple may be split into time periods, creating both present and future interests held by different persons. Some examples follow.

Life Estates and Future Interests

Students of property law are exposed to the complexities of *future interests* and *life estates*. Such interests in real property result from dividing the fee simple ownership into discrete time periods or "estates" by means of a will or a trust, or under state law. Typically, a will may specify that, upon the death of the owner, property will pass to the spouse for that individual's lifetime and then pass to surviving children as *heirs* who inherit the *remainder* interest. When one spouse dies, the other has a life estate for the rest of his or her lifetime, and the children own future interests in the property they will inherit. When the surviving parent dies, the children inherit the property as fractional owners in fee simple. (An only child heir would of course hold the entire fee simple.) If the family wants to sell the property, all family members having a life estate, future interest, or fractional present interest must sign the deed of sale so as to convey the entirety of fee simple ownership to the buyer. Spouses often hold real property as *joint tenants* with rights of *survivorship*. Even without a will, when one joint tenant dies the other automatically owns the property in fee simple (subject to any existing leases, liens, or other limitations).

Thus ownership of property may be divided among multiple parties, some with present and some with future interests, some possessory and some contingent on a future event. All parties must be ascertained through a *title search* when the property is sold.

Leaseholds and Tenancies

Owners of real property may obtain income by *renting* or *leasing* it for various purposes (those terms are used interchangeably). In either case, a written agreement between the landlord on the one hand and tenant or lessee on the other specifies the duration of the arrangement and the rights and duties of each party. In the case of an apartment rental, the landlord normally must provide clean, livable space while the tenant promises to keep the unit in good order and to pay the specified rent on time. Provision for utilities and heat should be specified in the rental or lease agreement. The owner remains liable for the payment of property taxes and compliance with local zoning and other public regulations. Either party may withdraw upon notice to the other party according to the terms of the agreement. Shorter rental agreements such as a "month-to-month" contract may be verbal rather than written. Such a contract leaves the tenant with no protection against eviction or rent increase, subject to a month's notice.

Farmland is frequently rented on a year-to-year basis where the owner does not wish to farm the land but wants to keep it available for sale when needed. Rental also helps the tenant farmer who needs extra land but cannot afford to buy it. Longer-term leases are used for mineral extraction, recreational facilities, and forestry where the lessee needs greater security to protect a major investment in equipment and labor.

A less formal, temporary arrangement is a *license* under which the owner may allow someone to occupy or use the land indefinitely by virtue of friendship, family relationship, or other personal reason. Normally, a written document is not used and rental payments may or may not be involved. The distinguishing feature of a license as compared with a formal rental or leasehold is that the occupant may be required to leave at any time by the owner. This situation is sometimes called a *tenancy at will*.

Easements

Easements are limited interests in real property held by parties other than the owner, or by the general public. Easements are most easily described in terms of the purposes they serve. *Utility easements* (corridors for utility lines, pipelines, or other purposes) may be established permanently across private land through purchase of easements providing rights of access along a defined narrow strip or right-of-way. *Easements of access* (building lots lacking frontage on a public way) may be accessible by means of an easement to cross intervening property owned by another person. (Zoning laws, however, may prohibit construction on a lot with inadequate frontage, regardless of easements.) *Recreation easements* (public access to rivers, coastal shorelines, ponds, or upland areas) may require easements of access across intervening private land.

Each type of easement involves a formal conveyance of a right of access to some party, such as a power company, a neighbor, or recreational users. In the absence of such an easement, the desired access could occur only by illegal trespass or by license, which could be revoked at any time. To obtain legal access on a continuing basis, the party desiring such benefit may offer to purchase an easement from the property owner. As with a lease, an easement is expressed in a formal written document that states the terms of the agreement, its duration, the obligations of each party, and how it may be terminated. An easement cannot be revoked by a subsequent buyer of the property: it is said to *run with land* until it legally expires. Easements must be recorded at the local Registry of Deeds to be enforceable against subsequent buyers of the property.

Scenic easements (also known as *conservation easements*) are commonly used to protect landscapes, farmland, and areas of high amenity value. A scenic easement does not necessarily involve public access, but it does involve a binding commitment by the owner not to develop or subdivide the land covered by the easement. Timber cutting may also be limited to necessary maintenance.

Scenic or conservation easements are commonly used to preserve the natural or open character of particular land while leaving legal title in the original owner. A community land trust or other conservation organization may offer to pay owners to convey a scenic easement or solicit an easement as a gift. Existing uses such as a home, farming, and woodlot management may continue. Property tax valuation of the land is usually reduced to reflect the severing of development rights from the land. If the owner is willing to donate a scenic easement to a charitable or public entity, a federal tax deduction may be claimed.

Covenants

Covenants are commitments or promises in a legal agreement (contract of sale or lease) affecting the ownership of real property. Developers usually include various restrictive covenants in deeds transferring the ownership of building lots. By accepting covenants, the buyer promises to use the property in a specified manner, for example, to construct a single-family home, to install and maintain landscaping, to refrain from causing nuisances, and in general to use the land in an orderly and predictable manner. Because each lot buyer in a subdivision must agree to an identical set of covenants, each may enforce covenants against the others, even after the developer has moved on. The lot buyers are then said to be *third-party beneficiaries* of the original agreement between each buyer and the developer. Like easements, covenants run with the land and are enforceable against subsequent purchasers of the property to which they apply. (The buyer is presumed to have notice of any covenants, easements, or other restrictions that have been properly recorded with the registry of deeds.)

Covenants are a powerful tool of private land use control because they are created by voluntary but irrevocable agreement between a buyer and a seller. They may reinforce public zoning and may in fact go far beyond zoning in regulating such matters as architectural style, landscaping, parking, trash, pets, lawn ornaments, and the decibel level of entertainment systems. Some retirement-oriented communities even ban children as residents!

Liens

Liens are claims against real property asserted by parties to whom the owner owes money relating to the premises. If local property taxes are unpaid, then the municipal or county government may file a *tax lien* against the property and eventually seize it for sale. Contractors such as painters or plumbers may file a *mechanic's lien* against property on which they have done work without being paid. Like a tax lien, the mechanic's lien may eventually be enforced by a court order requiring the property to be sold to satisfy the debt. Anyone purchasing real property must be careful that unsatisfied liens are cleared by the seller before transfer of the property so that the buyer will not acquire the outstanding debts.

Options

An *option* is a contract between an owner and a prospective buyer under which the latter has a right to buy the property at an agreed price within a stated time period. An option allows a potential buyer to seek financing, zoning, and other approvals while ensuring that the price cannot be raised or the property sold to someone else during the option period. The cost of an option is a small fraction of the total price, perhaps 5 percent, which is applied to the full sales price. It is not refunded, however, if the full price is not paid within the agreed time period.

Options are useful to public and private land conservation agencies. If a parcel of land is about to be subdivided or developed, an agency may seek to purchase an option to maintain the status quo for a few weeks or months to see if funding can be obtained to buy the tract outright. A helpful owner might voluntarily give an option (or *right of first refusal*) to a land conservation agency or land trust and might also ask for a less than market price (*bargain sale*) to have the land protected as open space.

Acquisition and Disposition

Real property is *alienable,* meaning that it may be transferred from one party to another. The usual ways in which real property may be alienated, either voluntarily or involuntarily, are by (1) purchase or sale, (2) gift, (3) inheritance, (4) involuntary forfeiture, and (5) eminent domain (condemnation).

The marketability of real property through purchase or sale is critical to its value as an economic asset. The law of property seeks to promote marketability by providing an orderly and secure process by which title may be transferred from one party to another. The conveyance of ownership of real property is usually a two-stage process. The first stage involves the execution of a *contract* between the buyer and seller specifying the property in question, the price to be paid by the buyer, and any covenants or commitments to be performed by either party. The second stage is the *closing,* when the legal deed to the property is transferred to the buyer in exchange for the purchase price.

Buyers typically borrow a significant part of the purchase price from a bank or other lending institution. To secure its loan, the lending institution requires a *mortgage* or contract by the borrower to repay the lender in regular monthly installments. Failure to do so will result in *foreclosure* by the lender and sale of the property to recover the outstanding balance of the loan plus interest. Thus the mortgage agreement between the buyer and bank must occur prior to the closing between the buyer and seller. Immediately after the closing, the deed and mortgage instrument are *recorded* at the registry of deeds office so that the respective interests of the lender and buyer are protected.

Real property may be gifted to anyone whom the owner selects. Frequently, property belonging to a parent may be conveyed as a gift to children or other relatives. Real property may be donated to nonprofit organizations for charitable or conservation purposes. It may also be donated to a governmental agency. In the case of a gift to a public agency or a qualified private organization (for example, Massachusetts Audubon Society, Trust for Public Land, or The Nature Conservancy), the value of the gift may be deducted from the donor's taxable income. To be valid, a gift of land must be legally accepted by the recipient. Occasionally, land may be offered to a public entity that is unwilling to accept it due to future maintenance costs and loss of tax revenue. No gift occurs in that case.

Real property, like personal property, may be *devised* by the owner through a *last will and testament,* known simply as a *will.* A will must be properly signed and witnessed. Where no valid will can be found, property is inherited by *next of kin* under state law. If no relatives can be found, property automatically passes (*escheats*) to the state.

The value of inherited property is reduced by *death taxes* levied by federal, state, and sometimes local governments. A branch of property law involves the establishment of trusts and other devices for conserving the value of the decedent's estate by minimizing taxes.

One form of involuntary forfeiture is *foreclosure* by a lender when a borrower fails to make mortgage payments on time. Foreclosure is, unfortunately, common during periods of economic recession. Similarly, the county or municipal government may foreclose on property that is subject to unpaid taxes.

A different kind of forfeiture occurs through the process of *adverse possession,* namely the occupancy of land by a nonauthorized individual (e.g., a squatter) for a lengthy period of time. If the occupancy is *open and notorious,* and without consent of the owner, the adverse possessor may claim legal ownership after a period of years specified by state law. The purpose of adverse possession is to recognize *squatter's rights,* where the owner takes no interest in the land and someone else works hard to put it to productive use. This doctrine chiefly affects rural land.

A *prescriptive easement* is a form of adverse possession asserted by the general public rather than a private occupant. It arises when the public uses a footpath, vehicular right-of-way, beach, or other private land without permission of the owner. If continued for the statutory period, the owner may be precluded from interfering with the continuation of the public trespass. The public right so gained, however, is limited to the particular right-of-way or tract itself and does not extend to the rest of the owner's property.

Eminent domain (also known as *condemnation*) is the taking of title to private land by a public agency or publicly regulated utility company. This topic is discussed in connection with public acquisition in Chapter 9.

Pinpointing the Land: Legal Boundary Descriptions

Given that the value of an acre of land ranges from thousands of dollars for productive rural land to millions of dollars in downtowns or edge cities, it is vital to be able to specify the exact boundaries of each parcel. Similarly, public land managers and political jurisdictions need to know the precise geographical boundaries of the areas within their control. *Legal descriptions* are used to define in writing the exact location of legal and political boundaries. With an accurate legal description, surveyors using a variety of instruments such as a global position system (GPS) can fix boundaries on the ground with great accuracy.

Uses of Legal Descriptions

Legal descriptions of property and political boundaries serve several purposes. First, legal descriptions permit precise delineation of the *boundaries* and extent of private property. Such delineation is crucial to anyone investing in real property, who must know exactly what land is owned. At many dollars per square foot on the urban fringe and much more in prime building locations, buyers must be assured that they are receiving all the land for which they bargained. Similarly, mortgage lenders must be assured that the real property that is security for a loan is exactly the same land that the borrower is buying. Where doubt exists, a survey must be made to delineate the boundaries of the site.

A second use of legal descriptions is to *avoid disputes* between adjoining property owners regarding their common boundaries. Third, accurate boundary delineation also promotes *efficiency* in the use of land. Adjoining property owners may use their entire land area to the parcel boundaries without fear of trespassing on neighboring land.

Finally, legal descriptions identify the ownership of land for purposes of *property taxation*. Without precise boundary descriptions, some land might be taxed to more than one person and other land might escape taxation altogether.

Types of Legal Descriptions

Three types of legal descriptions are prevalent in the United States: (1) *metes and bounds*, (2) descriptions based on the *Federal Land Survey*, and (3) lots numbered on recorded *subdivision plats*. All three types are used today in various locations and circumstances.

METES AND BOUNDS

Metes and bounds define the perimeter of a parcel of land through a series of straight line segments and references to physical features (Figure 7-5). Typically, the survey directions begin at one corner of the parcel, which is marked at the time of survey by a stone monument, iron pin, or other device. From this starting point, each straight line segment is defined by a precise compass direction and distance (usually expressed in surveyor's measurement units of chains, rods, and links). Corners or points where the boundary changes direction may be marked by further monuments or pins. Physical features such as streams, roads, and railroads may be mentioned in an older metes and bounds description. Questions may thus arise concerning changes in stream channel, shorelines, or road alignments.

Two further difficulties with early metes and bounds surveys appear in this description of the western boundary of Massachusetts, prepared in 1787:

> Beginning at a monument erected in 1731 by commissioners from Connecticut and New York, distant from the Hudson River twenty miles, and running north 15 degrees, 12' 9" east 15 miles 41 chains and 79 links to a red or black oak tree marked by said commissioners, which said line was run as the magnetic needle pointed in 1787. (Quoted in U.S. Geological Survey 1976, 13)

First, the reference to a "red or black oak tree," besides being botanically uncertain, leaves the boundary unmarked with the eventual disappearance of said tree.

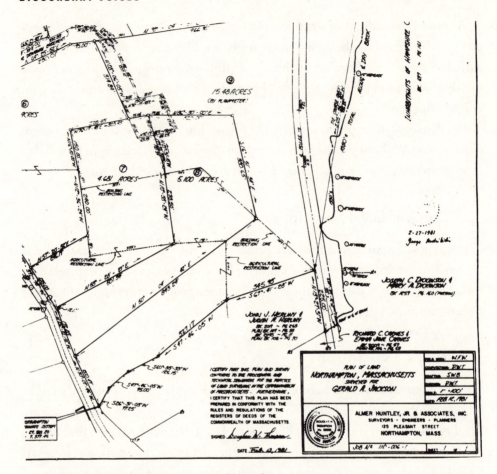

FIGURE 7-5 Excerpt from a metes and bounds property survey.

Second, the use of magnetic compass directions, which was universal at that time, left uncertainty as to the degree of compass error or divergence between magnetic north and true north, which varies from one place to another and changes over time.

Metes and bounds legal descriptions thus present many problems when old boundaries are resurveyed. Error arises from various sources, including inaccuracy of instruments, careless procedures, change of physical conditions, and illegibility of early field notes, yet property and political boundaries laid out in early times must be followed as faithfully as possible. The modern surveyor is armed with an array of new technology, including astronomical triangulation, satellite imagery, GPS, inertial guidance vehicles, and laser beams. Despite all this paraphernalia, when an ancient boundary must be redrawn, the modern surveyors must attempt to follow exactly in the footsteps of their pioneer predecessors.

Metes and bounds descriptions are cumbersome and susceptible to mistakes. A small error in direction—"west" instead of "east," for instance—will send the boundary off into the blue, and no area is thereby enclosed. A major source of error is simply the copying by hand or typing of a metes and bounds description. The metes and bounds system was too laborious to serve the needs of settlers of the trans-Appalachian public domain. Accordingly, at the dawn of its existence, the nation quickly devised a new and simpler system: the Federal Land Survey.

THE FEDERAL LAND SURVEY

The Land Ordinance of 1785, which established the *Federal Land Survey* (FLS) was probably the most lasting and influential achievement of the Congress of the Confederation. It also provided the most visible evidence of the influence of the national government on land use in the United States west of the original thirteen states. The basic principles for the Federal Land Survey were established in the Land Ordinance of 1785 and the survey itself commenced in that year. From its "point of beginning" where the Ohio River crosses the western border of Pennsylvania, the survey eventually extended westward as far as the Aleutian Islands of Alaska and southward to Key West, Florida (U.S. Geological Survey 1976).

The basic geographic unit of the federal survey is the *township*. In its ideal form, a township is a rectangle of six miles on each side, divisible into thirty-six *sections* of 1 square mile each. Townships under the FLS are identified with respect to *principal meridians* and *baselines,* which are designated for each state in which the survey is used. Townships are located with reference to their positions east or west of a principal meridian and north or south of the designated baseline (Figure 7-6).

Principal meridians and baselines may continue across several states. The fortieth parallel is the baseline for part of Illinois and also for Kansas and Nebraska, which it divides. Further west, the same parallel serves as the baseline for Colorado (Boulder's Baseline Street lies on this parallel). In some areas, local principal meridians and baselines were established to serve the needs of early mining or other settlements; examples are at Grand Junction, Colorado, and the Mormon region bordering Great Salt Lake in Utah.

The rectangular FLS has been described as "a striking example of geometry triumphant over physical geography" (Pattison 1970, 1). The curvature of Earth dictates that townships will be trapezoidal, not square, because their northern boundaries must be shorter than their southern borders. This problem is resolved by offsetting the north-south boundaries of ranges of townships at periodic intervals

BOX 7-3 *The Federal Land Survey*

By way of illustration, let us determine the legal description of parcel X in Figure 7-6. First, the fractional portion of section 24 is expressed as follows:

The north half of the southeast quarter of the northeast quarter of section 24 *plus* the southwest quarter of the southeast quarter of the northeast quarter of section 24.

Next, the township containing section 24 must be located with reference to the

overall survey grid: "Township 2 south, Range 3 east of the principal meridian." The full legal description abbreviated as per custom is as follows:

N. 1/2 of the S.E. 1/4 of the N.E. 1/4 of sec. 24 plus the S.W. 1/4 of the S.E. 1/4 of the N.E. 1/4 of sec. 24 of Twp. 2S, Range 3W of the Principal Meridian in County, State of , an area of 30 acres.

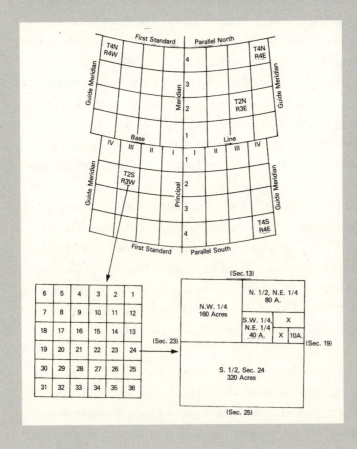

FIGURE 7-6
Hypothetical excerpt from the Federal Land Survey.

north and south of the baseline. Other problems arise from natural obstacles such as large bodies of water and mountain ranges.

Despite these complications, the Federal Land Survey proved indispensable to the disposition and management of the federal lands. (See Chapter 11.) Altogether, some 700 million acres have been transferred out of the public domain, most in areas covered by the federal survey. The FLS permits reasonably precise legal descriptions of parcels of land to be expressed in terms of township, section, and fractions of sections. The 640-acre section is an ideal unit for land transfer and subdivision into fractional parcels.

Obviously, this system is far superior to metes and bounds for describing large tracts of land in sparsely settled areas. The FLS has been most useful in the settlement of level or moderately hilly lands between the Appalachians and the Rocky Mountains. Anyone flying over the nation's heartland on a clear day witnesses the physical legacy of the federal survey in the infinite pattern of rectangular farms, fields, road systems, and urban development, all conforming to the pattern of townships and sections, baselines, and meridians.

Local variations require departures from the strict use of federal survey directions. Legal descriptions for land bordering rivers, lakes, or tidal waters may refer to that feature as a boundary. Metes and bounds may be used where necessary to describe irregular tracts that do not fall precisely into survey fractions.

Urbanization of land earlier settled under the federal survey is indelibly shaped by that all-pervading grid pattern. Streets of older midwestern and western cities follow section and half-section boundaries, relentlessly running north-south and east-west. Development after the 1950s, however, was more oriented to the new Interstate Highway System, which cut through cities without regard to the survey grid. The monotonous grid street plans of earlier communities yielded to the more curvilinear pattern of postwar suburbs. Reflecting the influence of the garden city movement, this new look emphasized curving streets, irregular lot shapes, and abundant landscaping and greenery.

THE SUBDIVISION PLAT

The *subdivision plat* was devised to serve the need for convenient means of bounding individual lots in subdivisions. A subdivision plat (or plan) is literally a map of a tract of land that is to be divided into smaller lots for sale to individual buyers (see Figure 7-5). Subdivisions usually anticipate residential development, although

BOX 7-4 *Property Analysis Report*

This box describes an exercise to introduce students to the various kinds of information that can be obtained about land through public sources without asking the owner. Students are asked to choose a parcel of land, obtain the requested information from public sources or observation, and prepare a professional-looking summary of their findings. Three or four weeks are given to allow time to get to the relevant public offices.

Each student should choose a piece of vacant land that is *privately owned*, preferably by someone unknown. It is all right if the parcel has some older, obsolete structures as long as it is substantially undeveloped or underutilized and therefore may be available for a new use in the future. The site may be located anywhere as long it can be physically (and legally) visited and as long as students can get to the relevant town offices and the County Registry of Deeds.

Each report should respond to the following questions:

1. *Where is the parcel?* Give a brief written description and identify parcel on a U.S. Geological Survey (USGS) topographic map, obtainable from the Internet, a map library, or a local store. Whatever map is used, mark the approximate location of your parcel with a conspicuous symbol.

2. *What are the physical site characteristics of the parcel?* That is, determine the topography, drainage, vegetation, soils, land cover, boulders, and so forth from visual inspection and from USGS topographic maps, soils maps, or other sources.

3. *What is the current visible use of the parcel, if any?*

4. *What is the size and shape of the parcel?* Draw a map of the parcel from a site visit. Assessor's maps in the town or city tax assessor's office may be useful to determine the shape and size.

5. *Who owns the land?* This information is determined from the town or city or county assessor's maps and tax records. Don't ask anyone living on or near the property.

6. *What is the latest assessed value? and, What tax was paid on the parcel last year (from tax assessor's records)?* These figures are public information that anyone can access. Just be courteous in asking for help from office staff.

7. *What is the current zoning for the parcel?* This information is obtained from the zoning maps in the municipal or county building inspector's office or the relevant planning department, if there is one. These offices should be near the assessor's office.

8. *What is the approximate market value of the parcel?* Obtain an estimate from a local real estate agent if one is available, or give your own best guess and reasons for it.

9. *What is the legal description of the parcel?* This description is obtained from the county registry of deeds located at

or near the county courthouse. For a small fee, this office will make a copy of the latest deed to the current owner, which should contain a legal description. Attach that to your report. (There is no need to retype the legal description onto your word processor.)

10. *What utilities are available at the site?* Use visual inspection or municipal engineer's records to obtain this information.

11. *Is the property within a floodplain or wetland?* Examine the National Flood Insurance Map available from the town planner's office, local banks, or some real estate agents. Check the wetland status with conservation commissions.

12. *Is there any other relevant information?* For example, are there any easements or evidence of trespass, incomplete structures, trash, or dead bodies on the property?

13. *What is the probable future use of the property?* Give your reasoning.

You are encouraged to visit the property or at least view it from a public right-of-way. Do not trespass on the site if it is posted or if there are other indications that the owner would object (such as being confronted by a guard dog!).

Sometimes it is discovered that a parcel that appears to be private is actually publicly owned. If so, try to find another parcel to research because land in public or institutional ownership is essentially outside the private market and does not provide a very meaningful subject for this assignment.

land is sometimes subdivided for commercial or industrial parks. Buildings may be constructed by the subdivider (who then serves as developer) prior to sale of the improved lots to the ultimate buyer. Alternatively, land may be subdivided for sale as a vacant lot with the buyer responsible for constructing a suitable building. In either event, the proposed subdivision plat must be submitted for approval to the local planning authorities in accordance with state law. The subdivider must conform to local subdivision regulations concerning street layout, width, and paving, utility placement, and storm drainage. Once the plan is approved, it is filed with the county registry of deeds, like other legal documents affecting land ownership.

As individual lots within the approved subdivision are sold, they may be simply described by lot number, as shown on the approved subdivision plat, as recorded on a certain date in a certain book and page at the county registry of deeds. The plat on file provides exact survey dimensions of each lot. There is no need for a lengthy metes and bounds or FLS legal description in the deed for each lot (although the lot boundaries must be precisely described in the original plat). (See further discussion of subdivision regulation in Chapter 9.)

Recording of Legal Interests

Precise legal descriptions are necessary, but not sufficient, to ensure that land may be efficiently bought, sold, and utilized. Equally important is a public record of land ownership and all claims against each parcel of land. Public knowledge of the precise legal status of title to real property is vital. With vast sums of money at stake, the buyer and the mortgage lender must be able to ascertain whether they are receiving *clear title* from the seller. Defects that cloud the title include potential claims under wills of former owners, tax and creditor liens, easements, unexpired options, and other irregularities. Once such defects are identified, the seller is required to eliminate them or adjust the sale price to gain the buyer's consent to accept them.

Such claims are discovered through a *title search*. All deeds, probated wills, subdivision plans, liens, options, and other documents affecting title to real property must be filed with the registry of deeds for the county in which the land is located. Claims based on nonrecorded documents are usually not enforceable, but the buyer is presumed to have notice of all claims on record under the principle of *caveat emptor* (buyer beware).

All recorded documents are listed under the name of the owner then in possession of the premises. Past claims may be located by tracing the chain of title backward in time starting with the current owner to see what has been recorded under each owner's name concerning the property in question. The seller is expected to provide an *abstract of title* that is checked by an attorney for the buyer and the mortgage lender. Many states also require a borrower to purchase a title insurance policy to protect the lender against undiscovered claims.

Conclusion

This chapter briefly summarizes the institution of real property in the United States, including the rights and duties of the property owner and the purpose and forms of legal descriptions for specifying property boundaries. Such a background is necessary in a book concerned primarily with public land use control for two reasons. First, the common law of real property is itself a system of land use control. The long-established rights and duties of ownership, the procedures for acquiring and alienating land, and the recording of interests in real property using exact legal descriptions are all components of a de facto system for putting land to use. Before public land use controls were introduced in the late nineteenth century, private property rights were generally the "only game in town." The abuses fostered by that system in terms of overcrowding, unsanitary conditions, and a variety of harmful externalities on neighboring areas led to the assertion of public powers to constrain the excesses of the private land use system. Public controls, however, remain reactive, negative, and supplementary; the private property owner and investor still retains most of the initiative in land use conversion.

Second, understanding of the legal nature of land is as important to those involved in land planning, acquisition, and management as it is for a doctor to understand the working of the human body. Land is more frequently understood in terms of its physical parameters: geology, geomorphology, hydrology, climate, and vegetation. Overlaying the physical terrain, though, is a "legal stratigraphy" of diverse interests in land. Public land use control programs must cope with the latter as with the former. Although detailed knowledge of ownership of land is not requisite for "broad-brush" zoning, the administration of land use controls at the level of individual parcels and developments requires recognition and under-standing of the nuts and bolts of property ownership. This chapter therefore serves as a foundation for the discussion of governmental authority to influence the pri-vate use of land, which is considered in later chapters.

References

Bromley, D. W. 1998. Rousseau's Revenge: the Demise of the Freehold Estate. In *Who Owns America: Social Conflict over Property Rights*, ed. H. M. Jacobs, 19–28. Madison: University of Wisconsin Press.

Burby, R., ed. 1998. *Cooperating with Nature: Confronting Natural Hazards with Land Use Planning for Sustainable Communities*. Washington, DC: Joseph Henry/National Acad-emy Press.

Daily, G. C., ed., 2000. *Nature's Services: Societal Dependence on Natural Ecosystems*. Wash-ington, DC: Island Press.

McPhee, J. 1989. *The Control of Nature*. New York: Farrar, Straus and Giroux.

Palm, R. 1986. Coming Home. *Annals of the American Association of Geographers* 76 (4): 469–79.

Pattison, W. 1970. *Beginnings of the American Rectangular Land Survey System: 1784–1800*. Columbus: Ohio Historical Society.

Prosser, W. L. 1971. *Handbook of the Law of Torts*. 4th ed. St. Paul, MN: West.

U.S. Geological Survey. 1976. *Boundaries of the United States and the Several States*. Profes-sional Paper no. 909. Washington, DC: U.S. Government Printing Office.

CHAPTER 8 *The Tapestry of*
Local Governments

The American system is one of complete decentralization, the primary and vital
ideal of which is, that local affairs shall be managed by local authorities.
—THOMAS COOLEY, 1868 (AS QUOTED IN TEAFORD 1979, 5)

With power over land use fragmented among the hundreds of counties and
municipalities at the edge of most [metropolitan] regions, there was no way
to limit or direct the destructive force of large-scale speculation fueled by
government subsidies.
—ROBERT FISHMAN, 2000, 113

The modern political geography of urban America evolved from the medieval
municipal corporations in England as discussed in Chapter 3. That institutional
model, as adapted to a variety of geographical and cultural settings, became the
basic building block of the American local political landscape. The medieval
municipal corporation was described as a "legal entity that could own land, make
and enforce local laws, sue or be sued, and exist indefinitely until terminated by
process of law." The same characteristics, with a few embellishments, apply as well
to contemporary municipal governments. This chapter examines the geographical and legal nature of these ubiquitous but often disregarded participants in the
shaping of the American metropolitan landscape.

Geographic Origins and Diffusion

236

The evolution of municipal institutions in the United States, although based in
part on precedents transplanted from England and the Continent, was strongly

influenced by the physical and cultural circumstances of colonial settlement. Thus differences among the colonies in terms of factors such as geomorphology, climate, religion, and economic organization yielded contrasting forms of local governments. Although the original reasons for these variations have long since disappeared, historical differences in form, function, and terminology survive to the present time.

The New England Town

The New England town was the earliest form of local government to appear in the American colonies. It has been justly celebrated as "not only the most original but also the most democratic and, perhaps for that reason, . . . [it has displayed] remarkable power of survival" (Wager 1950, 46). Despite its origin as a refuge for religious dissidents, colonial New England was noted for its intolerance of individualism, as portrayed in Arthur Miller's play *The Crucible*. Paradoxically, however, the New England town was to approach the ideal of participatory democracy as closely as any governmental institution devised in the United States, as acclaimed by the French political philosopher Alexis de Tocqueville in his famous 1832 treatise, *Democracy in America*. The persistence of the town meeting tradition may be witnessed all over New England in late March when thousands of citizens brave the elements to fill drafty town halls. The titles, procedures, customs, and even some of the participants seem right out of the eighteenth century!

Circumstances of early settlement that shaped the evolution of the early New England town included (1) a strong religious basis, (2) a sense of independence and defiance of higher authority (other than God), (3) a harsh climate, (4) an intractable terrain requiring cooperative effort for productive utilization, and (5) fear of attack by native Americans or the French. These factors jointly influenced the establishment of small, compact settlements often widely separated from one another. "The Puritan concept of community presupposed a clustering of people, a physical grouping that would enhance interaction and social cohesion" (Meinig 1986, 104).

These early settlements were closely knit through ties of family, religion, and common purpose in converting the surrounding land to pasture and cropland. Dwellings were clustered in villages, close to the meetinghouse, which served both civil and ecclesiastical purposes. Today, in many old New England towns the "first church" and town hall stand side by side. Each town regarded itself as a self-governing institution, beholden to neither the colonial assembly nor the Crown. In some cases, these claims were supported by formal grants or charters; in others, they were simply uncontested. In either case, towns generally went their own ways.

From earliest settlement, the New England town served not only as a unit of political, religious, and social organization, but was instrumental in the organization of early patterns of colonial land allocation and use. The historian Samuel Eliot Morrison (1965, 70) describes the allocation of land and water resources within the typical town as follows:

> A committee was appointed to satisfy Indian claimants, to settle on a village site, and lay out lots. Home lots and the meeting house, which served both as church and town hall, were laid out around a village green, with a surrounding belt of planting lots for growing crops. Salt meadows on the coast, or river meads in the interior, valuable for the wild grass which could be cut and stored for winter forage, were laid out in long strips and usually cultivated in common. The rest of the township for many years remained the property of the community, where anyone could cut firewood and timber, or pasture cattle.

The pattern of land usage varied considerably from one town to another. Milford, Connecticut, allocated several dispersed parcels of irregular size, shape, and quality to each founding family. Connecticut River valley towns such as Springfield, Massachusetts, allotted long, narrow strips extending perpendicular to the river. The quantity of land allotted to each family was not necessarily equal; differences in position and wealth were recognized (and the more prominent citizens presumably served on the town council) (Meinig 1986, 104). Yet there appears to have been an effort, as in the feudal manor of England, to allocate to each household a sufficient share of the available resources to sustain itself.

Over time, the original pattern of land allocation was drastically transformed as family holdings were split by conveyance or inheritance or augmented by purchase, either from the town's own reserve lands or from other households. Some early proprietors, such as William Pyncheon who founded Springfield, Massachusetts, amassed sizable personal holdings through direct grants from the colonial assembly. After the early wave of towns established as ecclesiastic communities, most New England towns in the eighteenth century were founded by individual proprietors or speculators who laid out roads, lots, and sites for churches and schools and then sold farm units to the public, often quite profitably.

Early New England settlements maintained strict control of their population growth. As an early form of "growth management," towns limited the right of outsiders to settle within their corporate limits. Unwanted residents were forced to leave the community. When land became scarce, new towns split off from older ones. According to Morrison (1965, 70), "When members of a village community felt crowded for space, they petitioned the colonial assembly for a new township, the ideal size being six square miles." Many New England towns were spawned through splitting large territories into smaller ones, and thus the closely linked institutions of church and town could replicate themselves in each new settlement. Once it reached a sufficient size to support a minister and the other local needs, a town achieved governmental status upon incorporation by the colonial (or, later, state) legislature. From then on, towns theoretically served as governments of, by, and for their inhabitants.

Southern Counties

The Tidewater region of coastal Maryland and Virginia fostered an entirely different system of local government administration based on another English transplant: the county. According to the perceptive Tocqueville (1832/1969, 81):

> We have seen that in Massachusetts the township is the mainspring of public adminis-tration. It is the center of men's interests and of their affections. But this ceases to be so as one travels down to those states in which good education is not universally spread and where, as a result, there are fewer potential administrators and less assurance that the township will be wisely governed. Hence, the farther one goes from New England, the more the county tends to take the place of the township in communal life. The county becomes the great administrative center and the intermediary between the gov-ernment and the plain citizen.

Many of the factors that contributed to the prevalence of the town in New England were absent farther south. The climate was mild. Soils were level, easily worked, and relatively free of glacial rocks, which figure so prominently in the landscape and character of New England. The lengthy shoreline of Chesapeake Bay, deeply incised by navigable estuaries, afforded convenient maritime routes connecting the region's hinterland with England and other overseas destinations. The native populations of the area were relatively friendly, obviating the need for compact, protective communities.

Moreover, the motivation for settlement of the Tidewater region was economic rather than religious. The function of the town as a religious community did not spread to the South. And economically, towns were unnecessary as cultivation of the tobacco staple was conducted on plantations, widely separated, and largely self-sufficient. In the words of Thomas Jefferson (1782/1944, 227), a geographer by instinct:

> We have no townships. Our country being much intersected with navigable waters, and trade brought generally to our doors, instead of our being obliged to go in quest of it, has probably been one of the causes why we have no towns of any consequence. Williamsburg, which till the year 1780 was the seat of our government, never contained above 1,800 inhabitants; and Norfolk, the most populous town we ever had, contained but 6,000.

The southern county, like its English antecedent, encompassed a fairly large territory of mostly rural land, farms or plantations, and scattered settlements. A centrally located site was designated the *county seat* where were located the county courthouse, jail, and sheriff (all English imports). Maryland and Virginia both adopted laws around 1680 to establish new port and market settlements. Only one such town, however, survived: Norfolk, Virginia. In Jefferson's pithy words, "The laws have said there shall be towns; but nature has said there shall not, and they remain unworthy of enumeration" (1782/1944, 227).

The *county* thus characterized the plantation South as the *town* characterized New England. Evolving from distinct geographic and cultural conditions, each would become embedded in the political and social sense of place of its respective region. (New England also was organized into counties, but they have gradually withered away in importance as towns and cities have been the dominant instruments of local government there.)

The Prairie Synthesis

In the late eighteenth and early nineteenth centuries, the New England town and the southern county would meet in the settlement of the "Northwest Territories" beyond the Ohio River. The clash and eventual merger of the two traditions was most dramatic in Illinois, whose earliest settlers migrated from the southern portions of the Atlantic seaboard via the Ohio River. Illinois's first census in 1818 reported that 75 percent of its population was from Kentucky, Tennessee, Virginia, and Maryland (Billington 1970, 91). The county thus arrived first in Illinois and Indiana.

In 1825, the Erie Canal opened, extending across New York State "from Albany to Buffalo" (as the song goes). The canal drew pioneers from New England and New York State to the northern portions of Ohio, Indiana, and Illinois: "Now the Great Lakes, not the Ohio River, formed the pathway toward the setting sun.... In 1834, 80,000 people followed this route westward" (Billington 1970, 92).

The northeasterners brought their towns with them, which quickly spread across the northern plains in modified form as the midwestern township or "civil township." In Illinois, this institution was soon adopted within most but not all the preexisting counties. Thus the New England and southern traditions of local government found common ground in Illinois and its neighboring states.

The midwestern township resembled its ancestor, the New England town, in name only. By the time of the opening of the Erie Canal in 1825, the concept of the "pure" New England town had already been modified—some might say debased—in New York, New Jersey, and Pennsylvania (Porter 1922, 3). The township lost its roots in the town meeting as it moved westward and became merely a county administrative subdivision. Civil townships were eventually established in sixteen states outside New England: New York, New Jersey, Pennsylvania, Ohio, Indiana, Michigan, Wisconsin, and Iowa, and in portions of Illinois, Missouri, Kansas, Nebraska, Minnesota, North Dakota, South Dakota, and Washington State (Wager 1950, 35). These divisions are essentially relics of pioneer sentiment that sought to transplant the form, if not the substance, of town government to the prairie sod and beyond.

Civil or governmental townships must not be confused with "congressional" or "survey" townships established under the Federal Land Survey (FLS) described in Chapter 7. The FLS township is usually a rectangle 6 miles square. It is numbered rather than named and has no corporate governmental status as such. To confuse the issue further, "civil townships" or other governmental units in states covered by the FLS sometimes were based on "survey township" boundaries. For example, several Illinois civil townships coincide with survey townships and are thus 36 square miles in size.

The county has fared better than has the town outside its region of origin. From the Southeast, counties diffused eventually to all fifty states, in one form or another ranging from modern metropolitan governments to the rural counties of American folklore. Of the latter, the following nostalgic description was written in 1950:

Across the face of America are county seats, and at the heart of each a courthouse in a courthouse square. These courthouse squares have a peculiar American flavor; they suggest spaciousness and leisure, there are benches where old men gather to reminisce and almost invariably a monument to honor the county's military heroes. The courthouse, if old, has a certain museum quality; it is cold and austere with a slightly musty smell. The newer ones are brighter and have more of the air of office buildings. But nearly everywhere there is an atmosphere of secretiveness in county offices, a certain reluctance to reveal with frankness the details of public business. Politics is played with more finesse than in more robust days, but the professional spirit has not yet been fully adopted. On the other hand, there is a friendliness and warmth—a certain "down to earth" quality about county government that is as American as pumpkin pie. (Wager 1950, 4–5)

Cities and Metropolitan Areas

Towns and counties, as seen, originated in the agrarian societies of New England and the plantation South. Urban communities accounted for only about 5 percent of the national population in 1790. This figure would change rapidly with national independence and the Industrial Revolution. U.S. cities as "centers of assembly, processing, exchange, and distribution" have collectively evolved in response to changes in technology and communication (Borchert 1991, 219). Each major city, however, has also developed its distinct landscape, traditions, and character, reflecting the diverse influences of demographics, culture, physical site, politics, economy, and law. Three examples, Boston, Chicago, and Los Angeles, are illustrative.

The town of Boston grew from 18,320 inhabitants in 1790 to 43,298 in 1820 (Whitehill 1959, 73–74). This rapid expansion was accompanied by urban problems such as fires, water shortages, overcrowding of land, disposal of human and animal wastes, street paving, lighting, and crime. In 1822, Boston adopted a city charter, which replaced the town meeting with a mayor and city council, setting the legal stage for its transformation into a modern urban municipality.

Boston's charter clothed it with the formal attire of urban government but left many questions unresolved, such as how large it should be. Like its counterparts elsewhere:

> Boston desired more land for residential and economic development. There was also an interest in increasing the city's size, reflecting not only America's passion for bigness but also Boston's need to present a prestigious statistical position to national and international commercial interests. Furthermore, Boston felt that if it were a large political unit, it would have greater political influence in the state legislature and in Congress. (Wakstein 1972, 287)

The results of this quest for bigness in terms of annexation and boundary changes are depicted in Figure 8-1. Two towns, Brookline and Chelsea, were early defectors from Boston. Boston, however, gained South Boston in 1804 and a number of other towns later in the century. The external water supply developed by Boston in the 1840s, described in Chapter 4, was the primary reason for adjoining towns to unite with Boston (Teaford 1979, 54–55). Between 1867 and 1874, the towns of Roxbury, Dorchester, Charlestown, and West Roxbury voted to join Boston. These

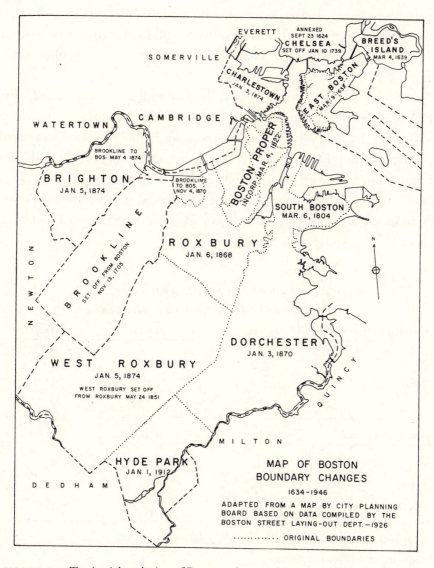

FIGURE 8-1 Territorial evolution of Boston, 1634–1946. *(Source: Wakstein 1972.)*

additions increased the population of Boston by 116 percent and its territory by 441 percent (Wakstein 1972, 280). These towns were first developed as "streetcar suburbs" (Warner 1978), but for lack of water they sought to be added to Boston.

After the addition of Hyde Park in 1912, however, Boston's territorial expansion stopped. The establishment of "metropolitan districts" for the provision of water, sewage collection, and parks in the late nineteenth century gave the suburbs access to water without the need to yield their independence to Boston. Suburban residents could thereafter enjoy the jobs and amenities of the city while living in self-governing towns. Today, Boston accounts for only about 10 percent of the population and 3 percent of the land area of its consolidated metropolitan statistical area (CMSA) (Table 8-1). (See Chapter 6 for a discussion of metropolitan statistical units.)

Chicago was originally incorporated in 1833 with a territory of only three-eighths of a square mile on the southwest shore of Lake Michigan (Mayer and Wade 1969, 14). Like Boston, Chicago experienced rapid territorial and population growth during the second half of the nineteenth century driven by the grain and timber industries of the upper Midwest (Cronon 1991). Before 1870, the city expanded to about 26 square miles through acts of the state legislature. Between 1889 and 1893 several entire townships and villages were added to Chicago (Teaford 1979, 44–45) (Figure 8-2).

TABLE 8-1 2000 POPULATION AND LAND AREA: BOSTON, CHICAGO, AND LOS ANGELES

POPULATION (1000S)	BOSTON	CHICAGO	LOS ANGELES
Central city	589	2,896	3,695
CMSA[a]	5,819	9,157	16,373
% central city	10.1%	31.6%	22.5%

LAND AREA (SQ. MI.)	BOSTON	CHICAGO	LOS ANGELES
Central city	46	222.6	463.7
MSA[b]	1,769	3,720	4,069
% central city	3%	6%	11%

SOURCE: *Statistical Abstract of the U.S.—1991* and *2003 New York Times Almanac.*

[a] As defined for the 2000 U.S. Census.

[b] As defined for the 1980 U.S. Census (covers only part of 2000 CMSAs for which land areas are not available).

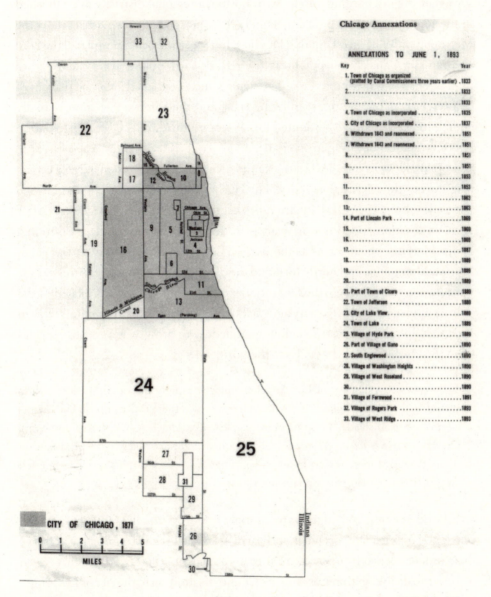

FIGURE 8-2 Territorial expansion of Chicago, 1833–1893. *(Source: Mayer and Wade 1969.)*

A growing problem for Chicago and its suburbs in the late nineteenth century was the contamination of Lake Michigan as a drinking water source by the raw sewage being discharging into it. As in Boston, a regional district was established in the 1890s to solve the problem, namely the Chicago Sanitary District (now the Metropolitan Water Reclamation District). In 1899, the district completed the Ship and Sanitary Canal to convey Chicago's wastes towards inland river systems rather than discharging them into Lake Michigan. Chicago reached about 90 percent of its present area of 222 square miles by 1900, and thereafter annexation virtually ended. In 2000, Chicago accounted for about one-third of its CMSA population but only 6 percent of its metropolitan land area (see Table 8-1).

Los Angeles provides a western example of municipal accretion, largely occurring during the twentieth century. The city was originally incorporated in 1850 with a legal territory of 25 square miles centered on the Spanish "plaza." After 1900, annexation added vast new areas to the city extending southward to San Pedro Harbor, which serves as the port of Los Angeles, westward to the Santa Monica Mountains, and northward into the San Fernando Valley (Figure 8-3). As with Boston and Chicago, the territorial expansion of Los Angeles related to the politics of water supply. The city annexed the agricultural San Fernando Valley in 1905 to help finance construction of an aqueduct to bring water to Los Angeles from the Owens Valley, 250 miles to the north:

> If the assessed valuation of Los Angeles could be rapidly increased, its debt ceiling would be that much higher. And what better way was there to accomplish this than to *add to the city?* Instead of bringing more people to Los Angeles—which was happening anyway—*the city would go to them....* Then it would have a new tax base, a natural underground storage reservoir, and a legitimate use of its surplus water in one fell swoop. (Reisner 1986, 77; emphasis in the original)

Like other cities, Los Angeles's territorial growth eventually stopped as all adjacent land became incorporated in suburban municipalities determined to preserve their independence from the central city. As of 1976, there were seventy-seven incorporated cities within Los Angeles County in addition to the city of Los Angeles. Conversely, the city itself contained twenty postal community names, such as Hollywood and San Pedro, that once were independent communities (Nelson and Clark 1976, 21, 28).

The city of Los Angeles now sprawls across approximately 465 square miles, more than twice the size of Chicago and ten times the size of Boston. Despite this impressive size, Los Angeles occupies only 11 percent of the land area of its

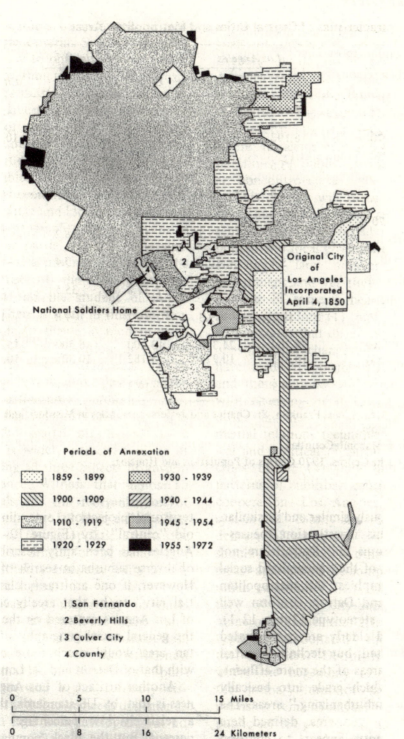

National Soldiers Home

Original City
of
Los Angeles
Incorporated
April 4, 1850

Periods of Annexation

▦ 1859 - 1899		▦ 1930 - 1939	
▨ 1900 - 1909		▨ 1940 - 1944	
▦ 1910 - 1919		▦ 1945 - 1954	
▦ 1920 - 1929		■ 1955 - 1972	

1 San Fernando
2 Beverly Hills
3 Culver City
4 County

0   5   10   15 Miles

0   8   16   24 Kilometers

FIGURE 8-3
Territorial expansion of
Los Angeles, 1850–1972.
*(Source: Reynolds 1976,
Fig. 12-1, p. 468.)*

metropolitan area and houses about one-fifth of its metropolitan population. Los Angeles resembles most other U.S. cities in occupying an odd-shaped fragment of the total urban region of which it is the heart. (In 2002, local voters rejected public referenda to split off the San Fernando Valley and Hollywood as two new cities independent of Los Angeles.)

Central cities and their suburbs have been chronically polarized in terms of economic, social, and political stressors (see Chapters 5 and 6). The formation of the metropolitan regions in the late nineteenth and early twentieth centuries was a race between new suburban incorporations on the one hand and the enlargement of existing cities on the other (Teaford 1979). The former process involved the splintering of urban regions into hundreds of municipal governments, many of them absurdly small. The latter process attempted to unite small fragments into larger urban communities. As seen, the enlargement of central cities through annexation of territory thrived briefly in various cities only to subside as incorporated suburbs opted to remain separate from both the core city and from one another. Municipal fragmentation has since prevailed as the determinant of the political geography of most metropolitan areas in the United States, although small-scale annexation to existing municipalities continues in many regions. In 1990, 48.5 million people, almost one-third of all U.S. urban residents, were scattered among 18,219 municipal units of fewer than 25,000 inhabitants (see Table 1-4).

A major factor behind the proliferation of incorporated places in the United States was the adoption of very permissive incorporation laws by many states beginning in the early 1800s (Teaford 1979, 6–7). This permissiveness was consistent with American traditions of self-government and home rule. It further facilitated the establishment of new "cities" in remote mining areas, ports along the inland river system, and elsewhere that the path of pioneer settlement led (Reps 1965). As practiced in burgeoning metropolitan areas, however, permissive incorporation has fostered a spirit of rivalry, and even hostility, that has obstructed efforts to promote regional solutions to shared problems. (See Chapter 6 for a discussion of the types of suburbs, including edge cities, that uneasily share the metropolitan landscape today.)

Local Government Jurisdiction and Powers

No matter how fragmented the political geography of metropolitan America, each unit of government possesses certain legal authority bestowed under state law. The balance of this chapter turns to the legal powers and roles of the various types of units of "local governments," which include *municipalities* (incorporated cities, towns, villages, or equivalent units); *counties*; and *special districts* and *regional authorities*.

Municipalities

AREAS OF JURISDICTION

Aside from New England, where local political boundaries seldom change, most states still experience new municipal incorporations and annexation of land to existing towns and cities. Although state laws on these matters differ, the following principles have generally governed the spatial evolution of local political units:

1. Municipalities are *mutually exclusive* in their territories, as are counties. No location can be simultaneously within more than one general-purpose municipality or county (although tracts of land under one ownership may straddle political boundaries). Municipalities may only expand with the *annexation* of adjoining unincorporated land. (In southern New England, all land is divided among towns and cities; no land is unincorporated.)

2. Annexed land must normally be *contiguous*, or physically connected to the annexing municipality (sometimes achieved through the artful use of narrow strips of incorporated land to connect one part of a municipality with another).

3. Annexations must usually be *mutually agreeable* to the annexing municipality and the annexee property owner or developer.

4. Many states permit *preannexation agreements* between owners of land and the annexing municipality regarding public services, zoning, and other issues relating to prospective development of a site.

Some municipal boundaries follow obvious physical features such as rivers, lakes, or tidal coastlines, which may shift over time. Streams that serve as political boundaries are thus bordered by different jurisdictions on each side, leading to conflicts over the management of floodplains and waterfronts. Some boundaries follow highways, railroads, or other cultural features, and some are straight line segments established in a land survey. Many boundaries, however, seem to be entirely arbitrary zigs, zags, and jogs whose explanation is obscure. The aggregate result in most metropolitan areas is a political geography of byzantine complexity (Figure 8-4).

LEGAL AUTHORITY

No matter how arbitrary and bizarre, the location of municipal boundaries affects many aspects of the human landscape of urban areas because, for better or worse, they define where the legal authority of a municipal government applies. Large or small, the powers of cities and towns (e.g., planning, zoning, taxing) are largely confined to their corporate jurisdictions.

The fundamental legal powers of municipal corporations have changed little since medieval England: (1) to sue and be sued as *legal persons*; (2) to enter into contracts (e.g., to hire staff, purchase goods, or build a new school); (3) to acquire, hold, and dispose of real property (land and buildings); (4) to adopt local laws; and (5) to possess a corporate seal to authenticate municipal documents. To these five must be added the modern necessities: (6) to borrow and to tax.

Recitation of these broad powers, however, does not suggest the potential scope of their application. For what purposes may municipalities enter into contracts, buy land, make ordinances, or impose taxes? How much autonomy and immunity from state review may local governments claim? Historically, local governments have been treated as the "sacred cows" of the U.S. political system:

> In 1868, the eminent legal authority Thomas Cooley observed that "the American legal system is one of complete decentralization, the primary and vital ideal of which is, that local affairs shall be managed by local authorities." During the following four decades Americans seemed dedicated to realizing the ideal as Cooley had stated it. Local self-determination was the rallying cry of Americans, and this meant that each fragment of the metropolis would enjoy the right to govern itself and to decide its destiny. *Local government was a sacred element of the American civil religion*, and the nation's lawmakers were devout in their adherence to the faith. (Teaford 1979, 5–6; emphasis added)

As with other religions, however, the hopes of the faithful were sometimes badly served. In the early twentieth century, U.S. cities were dominated by bosses and political machines that turned the ancient municipal prerogatives to personal gain. Abuses were (and still are) rampant with respect to municipal contracts, zoning changes, and patronage in public employment. Municipal corruption prompted progressive reformers of the 1920s to call for tighter control by states over their wayward municipal "children" (assuming that states were less corrupt than cities).

Contrary to the myth of local autonomy, municipalities are not sovereign entities. They are incorporated under state law and thereafter are controlled by the state in many respects, such as selection of officials, contracts, bonded indebtedness,

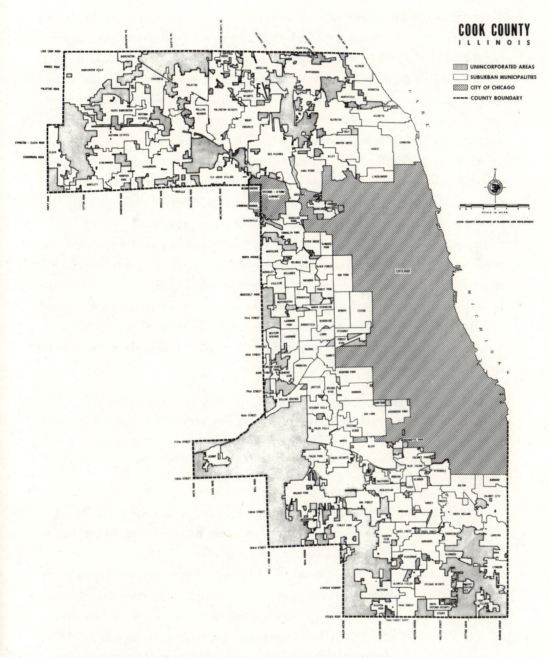

FIGURE 8-4 Municipal geography of Cook County, Illinois, including city of Chicago (shaded area).

taxation, and land use control. The history of municipal government in the United States has been a continuing struggle between states and local governments regarding the relative degree of control imposed by the former on the latter (Clark 1985).

One outgrowth of this struggle was the *home rule movement* under which certain states, beginning with Missouri in 1875, adopted state constitutional amendments expanding the scope of municipal autonomy. Under this doctrine, a community could perform functions if it was not forbidden by the state legislature or otherwise in conflict with constitution or statute. The home rule movement reached only about fifteen states, however, and has been characterized as "an uncertain privilege, for it depends entirely upon the whim of the legislature and may at any time be repealed or modified" (Zink 1939, 121).

Regardless of home rule status, questions arise frequently as to the validity of a municipal action in light of state delegation of authority. Clearly, latitude is needed to go beyond the literal provisions of state law, or municipal governments would be stifled in responding to local needs and circumstances. The fundamental question therefore is, How may a municipality ascertain the limits of its available powers? The classic response to this question is *Dillon's Rule*, first expressed in 1911 at the height of the municipal reform movement:

> A municipal corporation possesses and can exercise the following powers and no others. First, those granted in *express* words; second, those necessary or fairly *implied* in or incident to the powers expressly granted; third, those *essential* to the accomplishment of the declared objects and purposes of the corporation—not simply convenient but indispensable. (Sands and Libonati 1982, sec. 13.04; emphasis added)

Dillon's Rule is a long-settled principle that is recited by courts in resolving challenges to municipal innovation. It is an elastic test, however, and affords much judicial discretion in applying it to actual controversies.

As stated earlier, municipalities are usually limited in the exercise of their allotted powers to their corporate limits. Some states, though, authorize *extraterritorial* powers to develop public water supplies, because many communities do not have adequate water sources within their incorporated areas. Extraterritorial land also may be acquired in some states for nature refuges, parks, sewage treatment plants, and airports. Municipal services are often sold extraterritorially; Chicago, for example, supplies water from its Lake Michigan treatment works to suburban communities (at higher rates than its own residents pay).

Counties

A total of 3,041 counties virtually blanket the nation's land area. Each state is divided into counties or equivalent units (e.g., parishes in Louisiana). A few cities are independent of any county, notably Baltimore, St. Louis, and some forty cities in Virginia. Denver, Colorado, is a combined city/county unit of government. There are also several examples of metropolitan governments involving complete or partial merger of city and county functions, such as Miami–Dade County, Florida; Indianapolis–Marion County, Indiana; and Nashville–Davidson County, Tennessee.

Many counties display a split personality. For some purposes, they are agents of the *state*, as in the management of the county courthouse, prison, roads, and welfare programs. In another sense, they serve as units of *local* government for unincorporated areas (i.e., rural areas not within a municipality). In such areas, counties may exercise powers equivalent to municipalities, including land use planning and zoning. Counties differ from state to state in their functions and powers. Connecticut, Rhode Island, and Massachusetts have abolished counties as governmental units. In Maryland and Virginia, by contrast, counties serve as the basic units of local government, except in independent cities like Baltimore. Elsewhere in the nation, counties generally provide local government services such as police and fire protection, parks, and local road repairs in rural areas and unincorporated settlements.

Some metropolitan counties are major regional governments, such as Cook County, Illinois (containing Chicago), and Nassau and Suffolk Counties on Long Island, New York. Los Angeles County, for instance, with about 8 million people, has a public works budget of tens of millions of dollars. Municipalities within the county, including the city of Los Angeles and some seventy-six suburban jurisdictions, retain their local zoning prerogatives. The county or its surrogate special districts, however, influence land use within municipalities indirectly through the location, timing, and capacity of regional facilities such as flood control, storm water drainage, sewage treatment, and water supply.

Special Districts

Special districts are a very numerous and diverse potpourri of governmental units established for many purposes. Special districts (other than school districts) numbered 28,588 in 1982, an increase of 2,626 or nearly 10 percent in just five years (U.S.

Bureau of the Census, 1986, Table 470). Functions performed by individual special districts range from aviation to zoo administration. In some metropolitan areas, special districts provide such critical services as mass transportation, water supply, sewage treatment, solid waste disposal, parks and recreation, and air and water pollution control. Most districts, however, are created to serve only a single function. Districts serving different purposes may overlay one another, as well as general-purpose units of government, but districts of the same type are mutually exclusive in their service areas.

Special districts almost never engage in land use planning and zoning, which remain municipal and county prerogatives. Some, however, especially those operating at a regional scale, clearly influence land usage through the spatial distribution of their services and facilities. The location and capacity of sewer and water lines, for instance, is a crucial factor in land development patterns.

Many special districts operate as "phantom governments" unknown to the people served by them (Bollens 1957, 30). At the other extreme, some special districts or authorities are highly visible and powerful units of regional government with thousands of employees, extensive revenue sources, and bonded indebtedness in the billions of dollars. Examples include the Metropolitan Water District of southern California, the Cook County Forest Preserve District in Illinois, the Port Authority of New York and New Jersey, and the Massachusetts Water Resources Authority. Regional entities of this scale are major providers of water, sewage treatment, transportation, parks, and other vital services in many metropolitan areas.

Ideally, special districts bring professionalism and freedom from political influence to the management of urban problems. In some cases, though, they can be highly political and controversial. New York's Robert Moses, whose biography was aptly entitled *The Power Broker* (Caro 1974), was the archetype technocrat in the tradition of Georges Haussmann who redesigned Paris in the nineteenth century. (See Chapter 4.) Never elected to any office, Moses assembled a network of state and regional authorities that reshaped the face of New York City, Long Island, and other portions of New York State. The centerpiece and "cash cow" for his construction program in New York was the Triborough Bridge and Tunnel Authority. Besides the Triborough and many other bridges and tunnels, he built parkways and parks, including the immensely popular Jones Beach on the south shore of Long Island. Later he built highways, housing projects, the United Nations complex, and the 1964 World's Fair, overcoming opponents with cunning and occasional cruelty. The memory of Robert Moses still rankles those he overwhelmed legally or politically to push his projects through, but many of those projects have proven indispensable. The question that inevitable arises is, Did the ends he achieved justify the means he used?

Revenue and Debt

Revenue is a perpetual issue for local governments, states, and the federal government. For municipalities and counties, revenue may be obtained from a limited number of sources, which they constantly seek to augment.

The fundamental revenue source for most municipalities and counties is the *ad valorem property tax*. This annual tax is imposed on privately owned, taxable real property. It is based on a specified percentage of the *assessed value* of each parcel, including land and buildings. The percentage of tax levied (*tax rate*) is uniform throughout a taxing jurisdiction, although tax rates often differ substantially from one governmental unit to another.

Tax rates are usually expressed in terms of "mills per dollar of assessed value" or "dollars per $1,000 of assessed value." The ad valorem tax levy is not applied to *tax-exempt property*, which includes publicly owned land and buildings as well as property owned by charitable, religious, educational, or other exempt organizations as defined by state law. Also, allowable increases in property tax rates over the previous year may be constrained by tax limitation referenda in some states such as California and Massachusetts and by potential political hostility to tax increases everywhere.

Subject to these constraints, computation of the municipal or county tax rate and individual tax payment (*tax levy*) is simple in concept. First, the governmental unit determines its budgetary needs for the next fiscal year. It deducts revenue from nontax sources such as federal and state transfer payments to determine the net amount that must be obtained from property taxes. It then divides the needed revenue figure by the total taxable assessed property value within the jurisdiction to yield the tax rate. Thus if a small town needs $750,000 from property taxes and has $50 million total assessed property valuation, the computation is as follows:

1. Tax rate = needed revenue divided by total assessed value (AV), or $750,000/$50,000,000 = 1.5% (or $15 per $1,000 of AV).

2. Applying the tax rate to a parcel of real property assessed at $80,000, the tax levy paid by the owner is $15 × 80 = $1,200.

Certain kinds of local public improvements—for instance, the repaving of sidewalks or replacement of local sewers—may benefit particular property owners more than the public at large. Such improvements may be financed through a *special assessment* instead of through the general property tax. A special assessment is a tax imposed on property benefited by a local public improvement. It may be one lump sum or payable over several years.

Large-scale public projects such as new bridges, police and fire stations, public garages, schools, libraries, and parks require a sizable outlay of funds at one time. The normal mechanism to assemble such funds is the *general obligation bond*. These bonds, issued by a governmental unit, are repaid out of the property tax revenue and other available sources of revenue over time. If that proves insufficient, such bonds are backed by the *full faith and credit* of the borrowing government unit, which must repay the bondholders out of future taxes.

Bonds are sold to investors through national and international bond markets. The rate of interest payable over the term of the bond is a function of the creditworthiness of the issuing governmental unit as well as the term of the bond and the general economic climate. Some states impose constitutional limits to the amount of bonded indebtedness that a municipality or county may incur in relation to its total assessed value. Such limits, however, do not usually apply to special districts. Thus states such as Illinois with strict debt ceilings are awash in special districts created to circumvent debt limits on general-purpose local governments.

Certain public facilities such as swimming pools, golf courses, and solid waste disposal facilities, however, are expected to pay for themselves over time through fees paid by users. Such facilities may be funded through *revenue bonds*, which are exempt from ceilings on general obligation bonds. Revenue bonds are repaid from fees generated by the facility in question and are not backed by the issuer's general tax receipts, if any.

Fees for permits and services make up a growing source of local government revenue. In Massachusetts, for instance, when a referendum limited property tax increases in many communities, fees for sewer, water, sanitary landfill, and other services were raised to offset revenue shortfalls.

Finally, *intergovernmental transfers* are a significant proportion of revenue to municipalities, counties, and some special districts. During the 1970s and 1980s, the federal government consolidated many of its individual grant programs to local governments under programs of *revenue sharing* and *community development block grants*. State governments also transfer large sums of money (mostly from sales and income taxes) to local governments. Such allocations are usually earmarked for specific purposes such as schools, welfare, health services, housing, and conservation areas.

Beyond these traditional revenue sources, some states allow municipal governments to tax personal and corporate income and even to impose a local sales tax. Many central cities like New York seek state approval to tax suburban commuters. Taxes on hotel rooms, meals, liquor, cigarettes, and casino gambling yield additional revenue in some cities. Today, thousands of local governments and school districts across the nation face cutbacks in both federal and state assistance, as well as local property tax receipts, due to economic distress.

Conclusion

Once the proud legal expression of the autonomous medieval city, the municipal corporation in the United States is now an ironic metaphor for governmental inadequacy in the face of external economic, political, and environmental forces. It is a victim of its own success, having been replicated in such vast numbers that each individual municipality retains only a fragmentary role in the management of the overall metropolitan area.

The specific roles of local government with respect to land use control is the subject of the next chapter. The last word here on the chaotic geography of metropolitan America may be granted to political scientist Robert Wood (1961, 1):

> On the eastern seaboard of the United States, where the state of New York wedges itself between New Jersey and Connecticut, explorers of political affairs can observe one of the great unnatural wonders of the world: this is a governmental arrangement perhaps more complicated than any other that mankind has yet contrived or allowed to happen. A vigorous metropolitan area, the economic capital of the nation, governs itself by means of 1,467 distinct political entities (at latest count), each having its own power to raise and spend the public treasure, and each operating in a jurisdiction determined more by chance than by design. The whole 22-county area that we know as the New York Metropolitan Region provides beds for about 15 million people and gainful employment for about 7 million of them. Its growth, which is rapid, takes place almost entirely in its outer, less crowded parts, and this means that the Region is becoming more alike in the density of its population and jobs, more alike in community problems. But the responsibility to maintain law and order, educate the young, dig the sewers, and plan the future environment remains gloriously or ridiculously fragmented.

References

Billington, R. A. 1970. The Frontier in Illinois History. In *An Illinois Reader*, ed. Clyde C. Walton. Dekalb: Northern Illinois University Press.

Bollens, J. C. 1957. *Special District Governments in the United States*. Berkeley: University of California Press.

Borchert, J. R. 1991. Futures of American Cities. In *Our Changing Cities*, ed. J. F. Hart, 218–250. Baltimore: Johns Hopkins University Press.

Caro, R. 1974. *The Power Broker*. New York: Knopf.

Clark, G. 1985. *Judges and the Cities*. Chicago: University of Chicago Press.

Cronon, William. 1991. *Nature's Metropolis: Chicago and the Great West*. New York: W. W. Norton.

Fishman, R. 2000. The Death and Life of American Regional Planning In *Reflections on Regionalism*, ed. B. Katz, 107–26. Washington, DC: Brookings Institution Press.

Jefferson, T. 1782/1944. Notes on Virginia. In *The Life and Selected Writings of Thomas Jefferson*, ed. A. Koch and W. Peder, 187–292. New York: Random House Modern Library.

Mayer, H. M., and R. C. Wade. 1969. *Chicago: Growth of a Metropolis*. Chicago: University of Chicago Press.

Meinig, D. W. 1986. *The Shaping of America*. Vol. 1, *Atlantic America, 1492–1800*. New Haven, CT: Yale University Press.

Morrison, S. E. 1965. *The Oxford History of the American People*. New York: Oxford University Press.

Nelson, H. J., and W. A. V. Clark. 1976. *Los Angeles: The Metropolitan Experience*. Cambridge, MA: Ballinger.

Porter, K. H. 1922. *County and Township Government in the U.S.* New York: MacMillan.

Reisner, M. 1986. *Cadillac Desert: The American West and Its Disappearing Water*. New York: Penguin.

Reps, J. W. 1965. *The Making of Urban America: A History of City Planning*. Princeton, NJ: Princeton University Press.

Reynolds, D. R. 1976. Progress toward Achieving Efficient and Responsive Spatial-Political Systems in Urban America. In *Urban Policymaking and Metropolitan Dynamics*, ed. J. S. Adams, 463–538. Cambridge, MA: Ballinger.

Sands, C. D., and M. E. Libonati. 1982. *Local Government Law*. Chicago: Callahan.

Teaford, J. C. 1979. *City and Suburb: The Political Fragmentation of Metropolitan America 1850–1970*. Baltimore: Johns Hopkins University Press.

Tocqueville, A. de. 1832/1969. *Democracy in America*, ed. J. P. Mayer, trans. G. Lawrence. Garden City, NY: Doubleday Anchor.

U.S. Bureau of the Census. 1986. *City and County Data Book*. Washington, DC: U.S. Government Printing Office.

Wager, P. W. 1950. *County Government across the Nation*. Chapel Hill: University of North Carolina Press.

Wakstein, A. M. 1972. Boston's Search for a Metropolitan Solution. *Journal of the American Institute of Planners*, Sept., 285–95.

Warner, S. B., Jr. 1978. *Streetcar Suburbs: The Process of Growth in Boston, 1870–1900*. Cambridge, MA: Harvard University Press.

Whitehill, W. M. 1959. *Boston: A Topographic History*. Cambridge, MA: Harvard University Press.

Wood, R. 1961. *1400 Governments*. Cambridge, MA: Harvard University Press.

Zink, H. 1939. *Government of Cities in the United States*. New York: Macmillan.

CHAPTER 9 *Local Zoning and Growth Management*

The lack of any substantial relationship between the legal machinery and a clear concept of city planning is the firmest impression left by the origin and later course of land use control in America.

—JOHN DELAFONS, 1969, 24

In America, sprawl is the law of the land. Of the many laws that prescribe or induce sprawl, municipal zoning laws are the most direct, pervasive, and important.

—HENRY R. RICHMOND, 2000, 10

Three strands of society's response to urban overcrowding in the nineteenth century discussed in Chapter 4 are public health *regulation*, urban *redevelopment*, and population *relocation* to planned communities. Each of these approaches fostered corresponding lines of action on a much larger scale in response to urban and metropolitan growth during the twentieth century. The three nineteenth-century strategies respectively yielded programs and policies throughout the twentieth century concerned with (1) land use and environmental regulations; (2) urban redevelopment and revitalization; and (3) suburbanization, as encouraged by federal home ownership incentives and the Interstate Highway System. Specifically, the advent of zoning in 1916 may be viewed as a further enlargement of the public regulation approach that originated in the British Public Health Act of 1848, the New York Metropolitan Health Act of 1866, and their counterparts elsewhere.

Efforts to promote city planning and zoning in the early twentieth century in fact drew inspiration from a number of utopian and progressive initiatives of the period 1880–1910. As discussed in Chapters 4 and 5, these efforts notably included

(1) the *city beautiful movement*, (2) the *garden city movement*, (3) public legislation regulating nuisances and building heights under the *police power*, (4) the advent and proliferation of the *skyscraper* and related technology, and (5) the various social reform proposals associated with the *progressive movement*. Collectively, these five initiatives laid a foundation for public receptivity to limited governmental intervention in the private land market, as reflected in the rapid spread of zoning and its eventual approval by the U.S. Supreme Court.

Local municipal governments since the 1920s have been the primary instruments of public oversight of private land use and building practices, and the most commonly used legal instrument available to local governments in performing that role is land use zoning. Although it originated in Germany in the late nineteenth century, zoning is a quintessentially American institution with the blend of idealism and greed that implies. It is also a twentieth-century phenomenon, especially associated with the years 1916–1926, starting with adoption of the nation's first comprehensive zoning law in New York City and ending with U.S. Supreme Court approval of the fast-spreading zoning movement. That 1926 decision in the landmark case of *Village of Euclid v. Ambler Realty Co.* (272 U.S. 365) lent the nickname "Euclidean zoning" to the institution that has dominated local land use control at the municipal and county levels across the United States. (The *Euclid* case is fully discussed in Chapter 10.)

In the words of the planning lawyer Richard F. Babcock (1966, 3): "Zoning reached puberty in company with the Stutz Bearcat and the speakeasy. F. Scott Fitzgerald and the Lindy Hop were products of the same generation." In a more statistical vein, it might be noteworthy that the arrival of zoning coincided roughly with the 1920 U.S. Census, which reported that urban Americans outnumbered rural inhabitants for the first time.

Zoning is not the only land use regulatory measure available to local governments. They also possess important powers to regulate land subdivision; to enforce building code requirements; to regulate the use of floodplains, wetlands, or seismic risk areas; to designate historical districts; to control signs' and to perform a variety of other functions under state enabling acts and sometimes under home rule authority. Also, like other levels of government, local governments may acquire property for public purposes, either through negotiated sale or through eminent domain (condemnation). They may also utilize tax incentives and other devices to encouraged desired land use patterns (Figure 9-1).

Land use zoning, however, is the most widespread local land use control tool in use in every major U.S. city (except a longtime holdout, Houston, Texas) as well as many thousand smaller communities and counties. It is the broadest of land use control techniques, applying to virtually any private use of land and many public uses within zoned jurisdictions. It has certainly been the most contentious of land use institutions, generating passionate advocacy during the 1920s and 1930s, equally vehement denunciation and proposals for reform during the 1960s and 1970s, and weary resignation since the 1980s. In the 1990s, an aroused property rights movement dogged the efforts of planners and zoning officials to restrain the excesses of a rampant building boom. Yet zoning nevertheless remains a mainstay of local governments in shaping their evolving patterns of development, for better or worse.

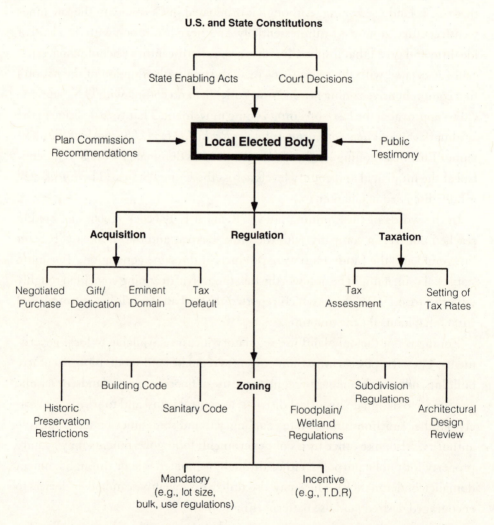

FIGURE 9-1 Diagram of land use control measures typically available to municipal or county governments.

Euclidean Zoning

Conventional land use zoning, known as *Euclidean zoning*, involves use of the public regulatory power (also called the *police power*) to specify how private land may be developed and used. Like highway traffic regulations, zoning theoretically protects the public safety and welfare from unreasonable private actions, and thus no compensation is paid to property owners affected by zoning. In cases in which zoning severely limits certain uses of private property, the affected owner may seek an administrative zoning variance or, in extreme cases, challenge the *constitutionality* of the zoning in a lawsuit against the regulating authority (usually the local government). Upon review, courts must determine whether the challenged use of zoning is constitutional, as considered in Chapter 10.

Unconventional "non-Euclidean" zoning includes various approaches to guide land use more flexibly and creatively than conventional zoning allows. Because land use regulation is largely a creature of state and local law, not a federal function, there is scope for states and local governments to experiment with alternative approaches within the overall constraints of the U.S. Constitution. Also, zoning is but one of an array of techniques and approaches available to local governments and counties to influence land use within their jurisdictions, as discussed later in this chapter. (See also Figure 9-1.)

Euclidean zoning nevertheless has proven durable as a land use control institution, perhaps because it is familiar: "The devil known is better than the devil unknown." Although it has been modified somewhat in most states over the years, in basic procedures and terminology it has remained remarkably unchanged from its 1916–1926 origins. The following summarizes the elements of that fundamental institution that still operates in thousands of localities and counties today.

Authority to Adopt Zoning

Authority to plan and zone land use is delegated to municipalities and counties by state legislatures through state zoning acts. Communities do not have to adopt zoning, but if they do so (and most have), they must follow the requirements of the state law. These requirements are largely procedural rather than substantive—they address *how* zoning must be adopted and administered, with little attention to *what* local zoning regulations may require. Limitations on substantive content have been applied primarily by courts rather than by state legislatures.

While state zoning acts differ somewhat due to amendments over the years, most originated from a common source: the Standard Zoning Enabling Act (SZEA). That model act was developed in 1926 by an Advisory Committee on Zoning established within the U.S. Department of Commerce by then Secretary of Commerce Herbert Hoover. The SZEA was furnished to all state legislatures and municipalities and was widely adopted in place of earlier acts that had been haphazardly developed during the previous decade (Bassett 1936, 28–29). A parallel State Planning Enabling Act was similarly developed in 1927.

The public regulatory power must serve to protect the *public health, safety, and welfare* as articulated in the SZEA and most state enabling acts:

> Such regulations shall be made in accordance with a comprehensive plan and designed to lessen congestion in the streets; to secure safety from fire, panic, and other dangers; to promote health and the general welfare; to provide adequate light and air; to prevent the overcrowding of land; to avoid undue concentration of population; to facilitate the adequate provision of transportation, water, sewerage, schools, parks, and other public requirements. Such regulations shall be made with reasonable consideration, among other things, to the character of the district and its peculiar suitability for particular uses, and with a view to conserving the value of buildings and encouraging the most appropriate use of land throughout such municipality. (Bassett 1936, 51–52)

This statement reflects the public concerns that underlay the advent of zoning in its early years, namely street congestion, building density, fire, loss of open space, and public services. Much of the statement is rhetorical: zoning cannot ipso facto "facilitate the adequate provision of transportation, water, sewerage, schools, and parks." It is arguable that public spending and locational decisions regarding these services influence the way land may be zoned rather than vice versa.

Two local institutions of U.S. zoning practice that originated in the model acts are the *planning board* (or plan commission) and the *zoning board of appeals*. The former assimilates the opinions of planning staff, hired consultants, and community opinion to formulate recommendations to the local elected body on zoning matters. The latter is a quasi-judicial panel that is authorized to grant exceptions from the strict rules of the zoning ordinance to individual property owners. Both of these boards consist of lay citizens elected or appointed from the local community.

What Zoning Regulates

Euclidean zoning regulates (1) the use of private land, (2) the density of structural development per unit of land, and (3) the dimensions or "bulk" of buildings. Initially, each of these variables was addressed by a separate set of districts: the Euclid ordinance involved use, height, and area zones. This method proved to be cumbersome, and zoning practice soon resorted to the division of a community into a single system of zones designated by use, with bulk and lot-size requirements specified accordingly.

The principal classes of land use for zoning purposes are *residential*, *commercial*, and *industrial*. These classes are normally divided into subclasses such as single-family residence, one- or two-family residence, rural residence, neighborhood business, and highway business. Each type of zone involves specific rules on use, building size, and lot size.

Land use regulations specify for each class of zone which activities are (1) permitted "as of right," (2) prohibited, or (3) permitted conditionally if a special permit is obtained. Originally, zoning was *cumulative* in its structure, resembling a pyramidal hierarchy of land use districts. At the apex of the pyramid was the exclusive single-family residence zone from which all other uses were banned. Next was the multiple-family zone, which allowed either single- or multiple-family dwellings. Commercial zones allowed both businesses and residential uses. Industrial zones were essentially unrestricted, except perhaps for designated nuisance-type activities. Thus zoning soon emerged as a tool to protect residential areas from business, but not vice versa (Toll 1969).

Cumulative zoning has been replaced in most communities by *noncumulative zoning* in which each class and subclass of zone is mutually exclusive as to use. Thus homes cannot be built in commercial districts, just as businesses are barred from residential zones. Noncumulative zoning requires equal attention to all parts of the community, not just its prime residential areas. This requirement imposes a much more complex burden on the planning commission, its staff, and consultants to try to envision the most appropriate use of each section of land in the community. The result has been a proliferation of classes of zones, each with its specific rules regarding use, bulk, and area. The town of Amherst, Massachusetts, for instance, with a population of 27,000, has nineteen classes of land use districts.

Population density in residential areas is regulated through establishment of minimum lot sizes for dwellings or groups of dwellings. Lots for single-family homes typically range from 12,000 to 80,000 square feet (about 0.25 to 2 acres). Lot size roughly correlates with size and cost of the home, with less expensive dwellings usually built on land zoned for smaller-sized lots. Builders used to prefer smaller lots, which allow more homes per total project area and reduce the per-unit costs for streets and utilities. The 1990s witnessed a glut of "McMansions"—

oversized homes on large lots—sometimes replacing smaller homes on the same lot ("tear-downs").

Density in commercial or office districts is regulated by establishing *floor area ratios* (FARs). An FAR specifies the maximum enclosed floor area within a structure as a multiple of the site area. Thus an FAR of 10 allows a ten-story structure to cover an entire building site or a twenty-story building on half the site. Allowable FARs are sometimes increased in central city locations when a developer provides amenities such as a public plaza or greenspace, off-street parking, or mixture of uses (Kayden 2000).

Beyond the traditional trio of use, density, and bulk regulations, zoning has encompassed other land planning concerns. Modern zoning ordinances typically address minimum off-street parking requirements in multifamily and nonresidential areas; rules regarding billboards and other forms of outdoor advertising signs; extraction of sand, gravel, and other minerals; secondary or accessory uses such as professional offices within homes and "mother-in-law" apartments; and special overlay districts for shorelines, floodplains, and wetlands. An overlay district imposes additional regulations beyond the basic Euclidean requirements for the applicable zone. Alternatively, special restrictions for sensitive lands such as wetlands may be expressed in a separate ordinance apart from the local zoning law.

The Role of Planning

It is axiomatic that land use zoning is subordinate to planning (Babcock 1966, 120). This doctrine dates back to the pioneers of zoning and the 1909 City Planning Conference and was presented to the U.S. Supreme Court in the 1926 *Euclid* case as the basis for the constitutionality of zoning.

> Zoning is based upon a thorough and comprehensive study of developments of modern American cities, with full consideration of economic factors of municipal growth, as well as the social factors.... The zone plan is one consistent whole, with parts adjusted to each other, carefully worked out on the basis of actual facts and tendencies, including actual economic factors, so as to secure development of all the territory within the city in such a way as to promote the public health, safety, convenience, order, and general welfare. (Brief of Alfred Bettman in *Village of Euclid v. Ambler Realty Co.*, reprinted in Comey 1946, 174)

State zoning laws based on a model act developed by Bettmann in the 1920s usually provide that zoning must be "in accordance with a comprehensive plan." After four decades of national experience with zoning, however, planning lawyer Charles Haar (1955, 1157) wrote, "For the most part, however, zoning has preceded planning in the communities which now provide for the latter activity, and indeed, nearly one-half the cities with comprehensive zoning ordinances have not adopted master plans at all." Haar found that the statutory (and constitutional) requirement that zoning be "in accordance with a comprehensive plan" often is construed to mean that zoning be "logically related to something broader than and beyond itself" (ibid., 1167). The meaning of *comprehensive plan* therefore differs from one court and jurisdiction to another:

> The analysis of the "comprehensive plan" requirement in terms of itself is a common judicial phenomenon. The reasoning seems to be that a comprehensive ordinance, one which blankets the entire area and is internally consistent, is automatically "in accordance with a comprehensive plan." The plan is the ordinance and the ordinance the plan. (Haar 1955, 1167)

In the face of such critics such as Haar, planning gradually evolved from obtuse technical documents to more open and issue-oriented "process" documents, well sprinkled with lofty goal statements and, more recently, prolific use of computer-generated graphics based on geographic information systems (GIS) technology. It is, however, difficult to discern any clear improvement in the use of zoning in response to these changes in planning. Except where jolted in new directions by court orders or new state and federal legislation, the piecemeal practice of zoning in thousands of cities, towns, and counties has chugged along as before.

Zoning Map and Text

The essence of zoning is that it "zones" the community into areas with different land use rules. Drawing boundaries between different kinds of land use zones is thus legally significant, equivalent to the written content of regulations. A zoning ordinance therefore consists of two legally adopted elements: the *zoning map* and the *zoning text*. The former defines *where* specific regulations apply, and the latter defines *what* those regulations consist of.

Zoning is an exercise in rational line drawing and is therefore inherently contentious. Where streets serve as boundaries, property on opposite sides of the street is assigned to different zones with perhaps very different economic implications (e.g., shopping versus residential). Also, boundaries may split larger parcels of land into two or more zones.

The zoning classification of a parcel of land may be determined from the local zoning map. Next, the zoning text is consulted to determine the exact rules applying to that class of zone. The Table of Use Regulations specifies what uses are allowed *as of right* or allowed by *special permit*. The Table of Dimensional Regulations specifies the lot size, maximum height, minimum setbacks, floor area ratio, and other bulk restrictions applicable to allowed uses in that zone. Other sections of the zoning text deal with such matters as parking, signage, wetlands and floodplains, and historic districts.

Nonconforming Uses

Zoning is largely prospective: it applies to proposed new development or redevelopment. Uses of land or buildings already existing when zoning is adopted or amended for their vicinity may continue as *legal nonconforming uses*. (In zoning jargon, they are "grandfathered.") According to an early zoning treatise: "Buildings erected according to law, even if out of place, should be allowed to stand indefinitely.... Zoning seeks to stabilize and protect and not to destroy" (Bassett 1936, 105).

Nonconforming uses under conventional Euclidean zoning, however, are tolerated grudgingly, to be phased out if and when possible, rather like unwelcome family relatives living in one's home. State zoning laws limit nonconforming uses in various ways. They may not be enlarged physically or converted to a new use as a matter of right unless it brings them into conformity with zoning. It is therefore difficult to change the use of nonconforming commercial space—say, a drugstore to a dry cleaner—even though there may be a natural market for the latter. This situation frustrates entrepreneurship and may cause a marginal use to continue in a building that is increasingly dilapidated for lack of maintenance. Another limitation is that nonconforming uses that are discontinued may be deemed to be abandoned after a given period of time, usually two years, and may not thereafter be revived. Nonconforming structures that are destroyed by fire, flood, or other calamity may be rebuilt only in conformity with zoning (including floodplain zoning where applicable). Efforts to phase out nonconforming uses through *amortization* (loss of legal protection after a specified period of years) have been widely attempted (Delafons 1969, 63–64), but without notable success except for the elimination of billboards in certain states and communities.

Where possible, rezoning of a community should avoid putting existing structures into nonconforming status. Older neighborhoods where uses and building types are mixed, as in most historic New England towns, violate the precepts of textbook Euclidean zoning, but they often possess special character lacking in the boringly homogeneous developments built since zoning arrived in the 1920s. Indeed, many older communities try to draft zoning rules that encourage rather than prohibit mixed uses and building styles in their downtowns or historic neighborhoods. In the 1990s, the New Urbanism movement began to promote design of new communities with the ambience of older ones, including mixed uses, small building lots, sidewalks, and front porches (Calthorpe 1993; Porter 1997).

Zoning Flexibility

Zoning theoretically predetermines the use of all vacant private land in the community according to a comprehensive plan. This quixotic venture of course continually encounters the windmills of reality. One of the claims made on behalf of zoning from its inception was that it would provide stability and predictability for the benefit of property owners and investors. Although it has done that to some extent, there is a contradictory trend in the evolution of zoning toward greater flexibility to cope with the unexpected and the unfair. From its earliest days, zoning involved two means of addressing those concerns: *amendments* and *variances*. Later these two were joined by *special permits* as well as *floating zones, cluster zoning, planned unit developments* (PUDs), and *transfer of development rights* (TDRs), among other devices.

Amendments are formal changes to the zoning ordinance that are adopted, like the original ordinance, by the local elected body in response to advice of the planning board and public testimony. Amendments may alter the text of the zoning ordinance, the zoning map, or both. A map amendment involves a change of boundaries and possibly the redesignation of certain areas to a different class of zone. If a new zone class is created through a text amendment, it is usual (but not absolutely necessary) to rezone some land on the map to that class. If no land is immediately rezoned for that purpose, the new class is said to be a *floating zone*, which may come down to earth in a later map amendment. Floating zones may be used to implement *planned unit developments* (Dawson 1982, 41–42).

Amendments of either the zoning text or map are intended to remedy area-wide needs or problems and should normally involve multiple parcels of land. Amendments that benefit only one property owner are subject to challenge (usually by neighbors) as unconstitutional *spot zoning*. Rezoning of a single parcel, however, may be upheld if it appears to be pursuant to sound planning. A landmark

Connecticut Supreme Court decision on this point sustained a zoning change of a single parcel from residential to business, making the following distinction: "Action by a zoning authority which gives to a single lot or small area privileges which are not extended to other land in the vicinity is in general against sound public policy and obnoxious to the law. It can be justified only when it is done in furtherance of a general plan properly adopted for and designed to serve the best interests of the community as a whole" (*Bartram v. Zoning Commission of Bridgeport,* 68 A.2d 308, 1949, at 310).

By contrast, *variances* always involve a single parcel. A variance is an administrative exception granted by the zoning board of appeals to relieve a "hardship" to property owners who cannot make reasonable use of their land if the applicable zoning rules are strictly enforced. The burden of proof is on the property owner to demonstrate such hardship. The variance is essentially a constitutional safety valve to remedy cases in which zoning unreasonably restricts the use of a single parcel. Because variances invite favoritism, courts view them sternly as compared with amendments:

> The strict letter of the ordinance may be departed from only where there are practical difficulties or unnecessary hardships in the way of carrying it out; and in such manner that the spirit of the ordinance may be observed, the public health, safety and general welfare secured and substantial justice done. No other considerations should enter into the decision. (*Devereaux Foundation Inc. Zoning Case,* 41 A.2d 744, 1945, at 745)

In Massachusetts, variances are limited to circumstances involving "soil conditions, shape, or topography of such land or structures and especially affecting such land or structures but not affecting generally the zoning district in which it is located" (Mass. Gen. Laws Anno., Ch. 40A, sec. 10). That state allows towns and cities to reject *use variances* as they are more prone to abuse than *dimensional variances*, which merely adjust the rules to accommodate odd shaped lots. Either type of variance may be denied if the alleged hardship is viewed as *self-created*, that is, foreseeable by the buyer of property.

Special permits entered zoning practice after World War II to provide municipalities with greater discretion in dealing with development proposals than amendments or variances could afford (Babcock 1966, 7). The special permit (also known as conditional use permit or special exception) is essentially a "maybe." Rather than list a particular use as either allowed or prohibited in specific zones (e.g., a branch bank or convenience store in a residential zone), it is listed "SP" in the Table of Use Regulations. This designation means that the use may be permitted in that zone by a special permit from the board of appeals pursuant to a public hearing. Unlike variances, special permits do not require the applicant to prove a "hardship" but only to show that the proposed location is reasonable.

Zoning is enforced through *building permits* issued by the local building inspector for construction or major repairs that comply with zoning and building code requirements. Building codes are usually statewide laws that regulate the quality of construction, including electrical, plumbing, and other technical standards. If a zoning problem exists, an amendment, variance, or special permit must be obtained to remedy the problem before a building permit can be issued.

Cluster zoning and *planned unit developments* are products of public concern about urban sprawl and loss of open space that emerged in the 1960s. Both techniques involve a relaxation of minimum lot-size requirements in exchange for the preservation of a portion of the project site as natural or recreational open space. A PUD also involves the possibility of mixed land uses and house types. In effect, it substitutes a set of special rules negotiated between the municipality and the developer in place of the existing conventional zoning rules. The goal is to achieve a higher quality of development with diversity of uses and retention of open land. Although a number of excellent PUDs have been constructed, the technique is applicable primarily to large developments. Small-scale developers cannot afford the front-end legal and design costs of a PUD and opt instead to follow the path of least resistance under the prevailing zoning rules.

Transfer of development rights was widely touted by planners during the 1970s as a means of achieving better regulation of growth while avoiding the problem of compensating the owner of land desired for preservation (Costonis 1974; Woodbury 1975). TDR involves severing the development rights from a *preservation site* to be retained in its existing condition (natural, agricultural, historic) and transferring them to a *receiving site* where higher than normal density is acceptable. The seller of the development right would record a permanent restriction on the future development, subdivision, or alteration (in the case of historic preservation) of the site. The buyer of the right would then be issued a density bonus usable at the receiving site. The owner of the preserved site retains existing use rights while receiving compensation for the developmental value forgone. The public ensures the preservation of the site without paying for it, and the buyer of the development right gains legal approval for a more profitable project (Figure 9-2).

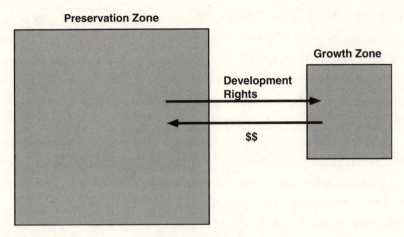

FIGURE 9-2 Diagram of transfer of development rights (TDR).

The U.S. Supreme Court upheld the TDR concept in *Penn Central Transportation Co. v. City of New York*, 98 S. Ct. 2646, 1978. The case involved a proposal by the Penn Central Railroad to build a 55-story office tower above its Grand Central Terminal in midtown Manhattan. This proposal was rejected under the city's historic preservation landmark law, which provided that development rights not usable on the station site could be transferred to nearby properties under the same ownership. Penn Central owned eight structures in the vicinity, but, instead of exercising the TDR option, it challenged the landmarks law as an unconstitutional *taking* of private property without compensation. (See Chapter 10 for a discussion of the takings issue.) The Court held that historic preservation is a valid public purpose and that the option to transfer development rights was a reasonable means to protect such landmarks:

> To the extent appellants have been denied the right to build above the terminal, it is not literally accurate to say that they have been denied all use of even those pre-existing air rights. Their ability to use these rights has not been abrogated; they are made transferable to at least eight parcels in the vicinity of the terminal, one or two of which have been found suitable for the construction of new office buildings.... While these rights may well not have constituted "just compensation" if a "taking" had occurred, the rights nevertheless undoubtedly mitigate whatever financial burdens the law has imposed on appellants and, for that reason, are to be taken into account in considering the impact of regulation. (98 S. Ct., at 2666)

Perhaps the nation's most successful TDR program has occurred in Montgomery County, Maryland, outside Washington, D.C., which has protected over

38,000 acres of farmland through some 5,000 development rights transfers to more urban parts of the county, involving a total payment of $60 million to owners of preserved land (Daniels 1999, Table 10.3). Faced with intense development pressure on the one-third of its land area that remained in agriculture, the county in 1980 established an "agricultural reserve" of some 91,000 acres. It *downzoned* this area from one dwelling per 5 acres to one per 25 acres. Landowners were allowed to sell one development right for each 5 acres to developers in the other two-thirds of the county. (In Maryland, counties exercise planning and zoning powers throughout their territories.) To ensure a ready market for development rights, the county established a publicly funded TDR "bank." Its function was to buy and sell rights when private demand languished and thus maintain the confidence of agricultural owners (Tustian 1984, Chap. 11).

Critiques of Zoning

For most of the twentieth century, government controls over private land use provoked controversy. Zoning and other land use regulations affect the use and value of property belonging to millions of households and businesses in thousands of communities. They are administered at the grassroots level by tens of thousands of volunteer board members, many of who have little professional knowledge of planning or law but have deep roots in their communities. Land use regulations therefore often reflect personal instincts or loyalties rather than abstract planning theory. Zoning in particular remains defiantly localistic and parochial, despite decades of efforts by regional planning advocates to broaden its geographic focus. In 1964, planning historian John Reps called for a "Requiem for Zoning":

> Zoning is seriously ill and its physicians—the planners—are mainly to blame. We have unnecessarily prolonged the existence of a land-use control device conceived in another era when the true and frightening complexity of urban life was barely appreciated. We have, through heroic efforts and with massive doses of legislative remedies, managed to preserve what was once a lusty infant not only past the retirement age but well into senility. What is called for is legal euthanasia, a respectful requiem, and a search for a new legislative substitute sturdy enough to survive in the modern urban world. (Quoted in Listokin 1974, 29)

At about the same time, planning lawyer Richard F. Babcock (1966, 154) deplored the process of zoning administration as practiced by local governments across the nation:

The running, ugly sore of zoning is the total failure of this system of law to develop a code of administrative ethics. Stripped of all planning jargon, zoning administration is exposed as a process under which multitudes of isolated social and political units engage in highly emotional altercations over the use of land, most of which are settled by crude tribal adaptations of medieval trial by fire, and a few of which are concluded by confessed ad hoc injunctions of bewildered courts.

Zoning has long been criticized by social progressives for giving local governments the legal ability to exclude certain kinds of development (e.g., rental apartments and inexpensive homes) and, by implication, certain classes of people who require such facilities (e.g., lower-income households, ethnic minorities, and non-traditional families). Besides such *exclusionary zoning*, the practice of *fiscal zoning* to promote the local tax base at the expense of larger regional needs is widespread. The misuse of zoning for exclusionary and fiscal purposes is further discussed in Chapter 10.

To a certain degree, the widespread dissatisfaction with the performance of zoning is misplaced. Zoning was designed for the development process and political geography of an earlier, simpler era. Its focus on the local municipality is both too small and too large to correspond with the actual scales of contemporary urbanization that occurs, on the one hand, at a metropolitan or regional scale and, on the other hand, at the scale of tiny parcels and subdivisions. Furthermore, the attempt through zoning to predesignate future land uses, densities, and development patterns is often premature and may provoke legal and political challenges. The role of the courts in resolving conflicts over zoning and other land use measures and policies is considered in Chapter 10.

Subdivision Regulation

As discussed previously, Euclidean zoning regulates the use of land, density (minimum lot size), and bulk of structures allowed to be built in a community. For development that involves the "subdivision" of larger tracts of land into smaller lots to be sold for home sites, another level of local review comes into play: *subdivision regulation*. To be marketable or buildable, individual lots created through subdivision must be part of a plan that is legally approved by the municipality or county (Figure 9-3). This practice allows local authorities and the interested public to scrutinize the detailed plan for a proposed subdivision to ensure that, in addition to satisfying all zoning provisions, it will also meet technical requirements for the layout and construction of streets, drainage, utilities, and other internal needs, as set forth in local subdivision regulations. The rationale is to protect future lot and home buyers, as well as mortgage lenders, from shoddy development practices and to protect the community from the costs of repairing substandard streets. (Typically, except in gated subdivisions which restrict public access to internal streets and common spaces, streets in a subdivision are transferred to the local government for maintenance.) Sometimes developers construct homes themselves on approved subdivision lots; other times, lots are sold to buyers who construct their own homes. Subdivision review also applies to condominium developments, but not to rental projects where the ownership is not divided.

Subdivision approval requires developers to commit to providing specified streets and other infrastructure over the course of project construction. Local governments may protect themselves against default by the developer in two ways: (1) a *surety bond* for an amount of money sufficient to cover the costs of completing the necessary work if the developer fails to do so, and (2) *restrictive covenants* on each lot that must be released by the local authority before a lot may be sold. If infrastructure serving a lot or group of lots has not been constructed, the municipality will refuse to release its covenant and the developer cannot sell those parcels.

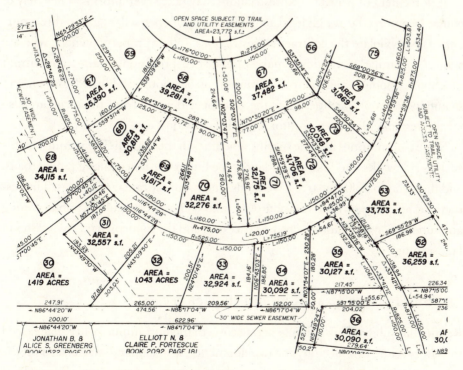

FIGURE 9-3 Excerpt from a final subdivision plan submitted to the town of Amherst, Massachusetts, 1987.

Private Deed Restrictions

Besides the *public* controls of zoning and subdivision requirements, a private sub-division is internally regulated through extensive use of *private deed restrictions* in the form of covenants and easements. As discussed in Chapter 3, these forms of pri-vate land use control originated in seventeenth-century England when aristocratic property owners sought to control the use of land in the hands of subsequent buy-ers or tenants indefinitely. Today, buyers of real estate in a subdivision must agree to comply with the private restrictions in the construction or use of the property.

Deed restrictions are useful to control many aspects of a private subdivision. Because they arise by voluntary contract between the developer and the lot pur-chaser, they can be more restrictive and "fussy" than public regulations. They may, for instance, regulate the external appearance of a dwelling, the kind of landscap-ing, or the parking of commercial vehicles in driveways. Minor alterations of a premises that would not involve zoning approval may be prohibited by deed restrictions. Condominium-type subdivisions are often especially tightly con-trolled through private restrictions.

Enforcement of private deed restrictions may take several forms. They may of course be enforced through legal action by the developer/seller against direct pur-chasers who violate the contractual restrictions. Other property owners, who are subject to similar restrictions, may enforce such provisions against recalcitrant neighbors. Homeowners or condominium associations established to own and maintain common facilities after the developer departs from the scene are also legally vested with power to enforce deed restrictions.

Some communities include specific amenities in their subdivision requirements such as sidewalks and bike paths; landscape buffers or fences along public roads; and the retention of large trees, wetlands, and natural drainage features. The aes-thetic appearance of a subdivision over time is the joint result of public zoning and subdivision regulations, deed restrictions, and the homeowners' own tastes in landscaping.

Subdivision Exactions and Impact Fees

Residential subdivisions often generate costs to the host municipality that exceed the tax revenue produced by the development. New demands are placed on the community's schools, its water and sewage treatment facilities, its police and fire departments, and its parks and recreation areas. A number of states, led by California, have authorized municipalities to require, as a condition of subdivision plan approval, that the developer *dedicate* (donate) land within the subdivision for necessary park and school sites, in addition to the usual street requirements. If the subdivision is very small or has no land suitable for school or park sites, the developer is required to pay a *fee in lieu* of dedication equal to the value of the land that would otherwise be required. These payments are *subdivision exactions* (Smith 1987).

Subdivision exactions must be set according to a local standard applicable to all new subdivisions. The critical constitutional issue, however, is how much land or fees in lieu of land the community may reasonably require. In 1971, the California Supreme Court upheld the community requirement of 2.5 acres per one thousand new residents or a fee equal to the value thereof, rejecting a developer's claim that exactions must be limited to meeting needs attributable only to the subdivision, not those of the larger community:

> We see no persuasive reason in the face of these urgent needs caused by present and anticipated future population growth on the one hand, and the disappearance of open land on the other, to hold that a statute requiring the dedication of land by a subdivider may be justified only upon the ground that the particular subdivider upon whom an exaction has been imposed will, solely by the development of his subdivision, increase the need for recreational facilities to such an extent that additional land for such facilities will be required. (*Associated Home Builders v. City of Walnut Creek*, 484 P.2d 606, 1971, at 611)

A further refinement of subdivision exactions has been to impose *impact fees* on all new development, not simply subdivisions or residential property. An impact fee is a charge levied when a building permit is issued to defray public costs for roads, sewer and water facilities, and police and fire stations related to the new project. Impact fees may be imposed on virtually any type of private construction. San Francisco, Boston, and a few other cities have imposed *linkage fees* on new commercial construction to contribute to the cost of affordable housing for the workers to be hired by the building occupants (Juergensmeyer and Blake 1984).

Local control over the subdivision of land has thus expanded since the 1920s from a concern with the layout and paving of streets to a broad range of exactions and fees for both on-site and off-site facilities and services. Traditional subdivision review was primarily a means for regulating the internal planning and habitability of the development and providing for its orderly integration into the physical framework of the community. It still serves this purpose in the majority of states and communities. Impact fees and linkage assessments, however, have augmented these public purposes to include reallocation of fiscal burdens from the existing taxpayers to newcomers. This function has little to do with the habitability of the development in question or with land planning in the community at large. If anything, it may aggravate the tendency to use zoning and other planning tools as a means of optimizing revenue and minimizing public costs. Such goals, which have characterized "fiscal zoning" for many years, are likely to conflict with the explicit purpose of local land use control: to ensure efficient, equitable, and balanced use of available land in the community.

Land Acquisition for Public Needs

The foregoing discussion has focused on local powers to plan and regulate the use of privately owned land. Yet certain land is needed for direct public use: for school sites, parks, highways, prisons, municipal offices, public waste facilities, and conservation areas. These needs cannot normally be provided through zoning or other regulations; where public use is involved, public ownership may be required. In addition, public ownership requires "just compensation" to be paid to the owner pursuant to the Fifth Amendment to the U.S. Constitution: "nor shall private property be taken for public use without just compensation." Public lands (municipal, county, regional, state, or federal) are exempt from local property taxation and usually from local zoning.

Land may be acquired for public ownership and use in several ways: (1) *negotiated purchase*, (2) *eminent domain*, (3) *gift*, (4) *dedication*, (5) *zoning incentives*, and (6) *tax default*.

Negotiated purchase is the most common way to acquire private land for public use. When authorized by legislation, a government agency may approach a private owner and offer to pay a fair price as established by independent appraisal of the property. If the offer is accepted, a deed is exchanged for payment and the land title is transferred to the public agency. No court action is required, the process is reasonably speedy, and everyone is presumably satisfied.

If it is impossible to reach agreement on a price within the limit of appraised value, the effort must either be abandoned or pursued through eminent domain, also known as *condemnation*. This term refers to the power of any government body to compel a private owner to sell at a price fixed by a court. When government pays for property it is free of the constraint of the takings issue. (Recall the Fifth Amendment: "Nor shall private property be taken for public use without just compensation.") *Just compensation* is an issue for a jury to determine, which leaves only *public use* as a constraint on the use of eminent domain. In fact, "public use" broadened greatly over the twentieth century as courts authorized eminent domain for projects to *benefit* the public rather than literal public use. For instance, the U.S. Supreme Court in *Berman v. Parker* (75 S. Ct. 98, 1954) upheld the use of eminent domain to acquire blighted property in the District of Columbia to be redeveloped privately as part of an urban renewal program. Although it is an inherent power of government, eminent domain is politically unpopular and is generally used as a last resort when negotiation fails. Sometimes, however, eminent domain is mutually agreeable as a means of efficiently clearing title to private land when the owner is willing to sell.

Gifts of land to public entities are an important source of open space and natural areas. Many national, state, and local parks originated in a philanthropic gift. Examples are portions of Acadia, Great Smoky Mountains, and Grand Teton National Parks donated to the National Park Service by the Rockefeller family and Harriman State Park along the Hudson River Palisades opposite New York City. The author's hometown of Northampton, Massachusetts, is graced with Look Park and Childs Park, both donated to the city decades ago with endowments toward their upkeep. Gifts of real property to public or nonprofit organizations are usually allowed in federal tax law as charitable contributions. Donors can deduct all or part of the current appraised value of the donated land from their taxable income.

Dedication of land refers to the transfer by developers to the local government of certain land or easements pursuant to an approved subdivision or development plan. These dedications typically include internal roads, sidewalks, bike trails, easements for utilities and drainage, and sites for playgrounds, school sites, or local parks.

Zoning incentives are used by New York and several other cities to encourage developers to set aside public spaces in the form of outdoor and indoor plazas, larger than required setbacks from streets, shopping concourses, and roof gardens accessible to the public. In exchange for such amenities, developers of high-rise commercial or residential real estate are offered zoning incentives, namely extra height and floors beyond what is otherwise permitted. Such additional rentable space has convinced New York City developers to establish some five hundred privately owned public spaces (Kayden 2000). Such sites are typically retained and maintained by the private developer subject to permanent easements of public access and use.

Finally, *tax default* is another way that land shifts from private to local public ownership involuntarily. If an owner fails to pay property taxes, the premises are subject to forfeiture and sale by the local government to pay for such unpaid taxes.

Public acquisition of land in metropolitan areas through negotiated purchase or condemnation can be very expensive. Costs per acre in the Northeast may range from a few thousand dollars for raw farmland not yet ripe for development to hundreds of thousands of dollars for sites snatched from the bulldozer in prime locations. Clearly, early action on land needed for public purposes may save much tax money. Beyond the direct costs paid to the seller, some indirect costs of public land purchase and ownership include:

- Legal and administrative costs
- Financing cost of interest on money borrowed to pay the purchase price
- Cost of taxes forgone
- Costs of improvement and maintenance
- Liability insurance (local governments)

Many private-sector organizations have participated in various ways to help acquire land for public parks at all scales. The land trust movement includes thousands of local and regional land trusts that have helped to conserve land for public open space throughout the United States. (See www.lta.org.) The Trust for Public Land (TPL) since its founding in 1972 has worked with willing landowners, local communities, and national, state, and local agencies to complete more than 2,400 land conservation projects, involving over 1.5 million acres. In 1994, the TPL launched its *Green Cities Initiative* to help create parks and protect green spaces in

---

BOX 9-1 *The Seven Measures of*
an Excellent City Park System

1. A clear expression of purpose
2. Ongoing planning and community involvement
3. Sufficient assets in land, staffing, and equipment to meet the system's goals
4. Equitable access
5. User satisfaction
6. Safety from physical hazards and crime
7. Benefits for the city beyond the boundaries of the parks

(SOURCE: Harnik 2003.)

urban areas. Peter Harnik, director of that program, has published two key appraisals, one of the status of city parks (Harnik 2000) and the other of the qualities that make a city park system successful (Harnik 2003). (See www.tpl.org.)

Growth Management and Smart Growth

The twin booms of the postwar period—babies and houses—transformed the settlement geography of the United States, as discussed in Chapters 1 and 6. Demographic change involved both absolute population growth at various scales and a massive geographic redistribution of population within and among metropolitan regions. As discussed in Chapter 6, the white middle class abandoned older central-city neighborhoods to move to new suburbs in search of better housing and schools (so-called white flight). Meanwhile, the Frost Belt or Rust Belt metropolitan areas of the Northeast and upper Midwest experienced massive outflows of population to the new jobs and retirement opportunities of the Sun Belt in the South and West. Overall, the population of metropolitan areas nearly doubled between 1960 and 2000 from 118 million to 226 million while the rest of the country ("nonmetropolitan areas") actually *declined* from 59 million to 55 million (see Figure 6-1). Inside metropolitan areas, central cities as a class gained 44 percent but this growth was very uneven, with Sun Belt cities growing rapidly and older northeastern Rust Belt cities losing much of their populations. Meanwhile, the suburbs overall grew by 138 percent and now account for slightly over half of the nation's population.

In terms of actual and percentage population change, the brunt of metropolitan growth, especially in the newly developing Sun Belt states, has fallen most heavily on smaller to medium-sized urban places. As Table 9-1 indicates, the fastest rates of growth between 1960 and 2000 were experienced in cities between 100,000 and 250,000 in population (123.6 percent); the second fastest rates were places between 50,000 and 100,000 inhabitants. (It is curious to note the rough equivalence in numbers of inhabitants in each of the size ranges in 2000.)

Smaller and newer suburban communities are frequently ill prepared for the impacts of rapid population growth such as traffic congestion, demands for new schools and other public services, loss of open space and visual amenities, and loss of "small-town atmosphere." Although most had some form of basic zoning and subdivision regulations, they generally lacked experience in dealing with "big-city" developers. Towns under 25,000 very likely had no professional planning staff and depended on their volunteer boards, occasionally assisted by an outside consultant, to cope with the onslaught. It was among these smaller but fast-growing suburban jurisdictions, especially in the Sun Belt states, that the idea of *growth management* became popular during the 1970s and 1980s, followed by *smart growth* in the 1990s.

Growth management has been around as long as Euclidean zoning, which, at least in theory, "manages" new urban growth through limits on land use, bulk, and density. Subdivision regulation also manages growth by imposing design performance standards and exactions on new subdivisions. By 1970, however, there was a growing consensus that neither zoning nor subdivision regulation could address (1) the timing or pace of growth, or (2) the ultimate character of the community when fully developed. Growth management evolved during the early 1970s in a variety of forms. Communities as diverse as Boulder, Colorado; Petaluma, California; Ramapo Township, New York; and Boca Raton, Florida, pursued their homegrown strategies with varying success.

A 1978 study of growth management experience in eighteen local or county programs by David Godschalk and colleagues disclosed a diversity of both goals and means. The former included such respectable objectives as preserving prime farmland, providing a balanced housing supply, relating new development to public services, and reducing natural hazard vulnerability. More questionable goals included minimizing tax burdens and preserving a "small-town environment." Means used by various communities included capital improvement programs,

TABLE 9-1 U.S. URBAN POPULATION SIZE AND GROWTH BY SIZE OF MUNICIPALITIES, 1960–2000 (IN MILLIONS)

SIZE	1960	1970	1980	1990	2000	1960–2000 POPULATION GAIN	1960–2000 PERCENT CHANGE
1 million +	17.5	18.9	17.5	20.0	22.9	5.4	30.8
250,000–1 million	21.9	23.5	22.7	24.3	26.2	4.3	19.6
100,000–250,000	11.4	13.9	16.6	19.1	25.5	14.1	123.6
50,000–100,000	12.5	16.2	17.6	21.2	24.9	12.4	99.2
25,000–50,000	12.7	15.7	18.4	20.0	22.6	9.9	77.9
10,000–25,000	15.1	17.6	19.8	20.3	22.6	7.5	49.6
< 10,000	24.9	26.4	28.0	28.2	28.7	3.8	15.2
Total Urban	115.9	131.9	140.3	152.9	173.4	57.5	49.6

SOURCE: *Statistical Abstract of the U.S.—2003.*

annual permit limits, dwelling unit caps, downzoning (to lower densities), site plan review, fair-share housing plans, and open-space acquisition. Most communities were relying on a combination of existing and new techniques (Godschalk et al. 1978). Many were challenged in court by developers.

Some Early Growth Management Decisions

The first major growth management case was decided in 1972 by the New York Court of Appeals (State Supreme Court) in *Golden v. Township of Ramapo*, 285 N.E.2d 291. Ramapo, a suburb of New York City, responded to a doubling of its population in the 1960s by preparing a master plan for its future growth. Unlike most other plans of this type, Ramapo's plan had teeth. It included a capital improvements program to provide the entire town with public services within eighteen years. Under a 1969 zoning amendment, all proposals for residential development (except individual homes) would be evaluated in terms of the availability of sewers, parks, firehouses, roads, and storm drainage based on a point system. If a project lacked enough points to be approved, the township issued a "rain check" in the form of a special permit to become effective in the year when services were scheduled to be provided to that site. The rain check could be sold to other parties to realize some immediate cash return, and property taxes would be reduced during the interim. Alternatively, the developer could gain points by installing services privately.

On appeal, the New York Court of Appeals acknowledged that "there is something inherently suspect in a scheme which, apart from its professed purposes, effects a restriction upon the free mobility of a people until sometime in the future when project facilities are available to meet increased demands" (285 N.E.2d, at 300). The court did recognize, however, the social and environmental ills associated with rapid growth that gave rise to the plan and in a leap of faith upheld the Ramapo plan:

> We may assume that the present amendments are the product of foresighted planning calculated to promote the welfare of the township. The Town has imposed temporary restrictions upon land use in residential areas while committing itself to a program of development. It has utilized its comprehensive plan to implement its timing controls and has coupled with restrictions provisions for low and moderate income housing on a large scale. Considered as a whole it represents both in its inception and implementation a reasonable attempt to provide for the sequential, orderly development of land. (285 N.E.2d, at 303)

The next landmark in judicial review of growth management arose in Petaluma, California, an old chicken-farming town 35 miles north of San Francisco. A surge of building activity in the early 1970s alarmed the community into conducting a major planning exercise. The resulting Petaluma plan was a complex set of documents, policies, and programs. Petaluma established a target population for itself of 55,000, well below what the trend of building permits indicated the town would soon reach. The plan imposed a limit on building permits to five hundred a year (two thousand had been issued in 1970–1971) as well as limits on annexation of unincorporated land and upon expansion of sewer and water capacity.

Upon constitutional challenge and appeal by a building trade association, the federal district court and the federal court of appeals reached opposite conclusions on the validity of the Petaluma plan (*Construction Industry Assn. of Sonoma County v. City of Petaluma,* 375 F.Supp. 574, 1974, and 522 F.2d 897, 1975, respectively). (Note that this case was filed in the federal rather than the state court system; when both federal and state constitutional grounds are involved, as here, the choice of court system is a result of negotiation between the parties.) The courts differed particularly in their *geographical* perception of the implications of the plan based on expert testimony on the regional housing market of the Bay Area. As in the 1926 *Euclid* case, the district court struck down the plan as unconstitutional, in this case due to its interference with the "right to travel" (i.e., move from one part of a region to another). The court felt that if many communities in Petaluma's position were allowed to artificially limit new development and population growth, then lower-income households further down the housing ladder would be unable to move into better homes and neighborhoods (called the *trickle-down theory* of housing markets).

The United States Court of Appeals for the Ninth Circuit saw the issue very differently. It ignored theories of urban geography and planning and even objected to the "oversized brief" submitted by the plaintiffs. In contrast to the regional perspective of the lower court, the appellate court viewed the issue strictly within the geographic compass of Petaluma. The court cited recent decisions of its own and of the U.S. Supreme Court upholding municipal zoning prerogatives where a deliberate intent to exclude was not proven. It found that the plan earmarked 8–12 percent of permits for low- and moderate-income housing (assuming that a builder turned up), which it felt obviated any exclusionary motive.

Plan or no plan, the growth of Petaluma lagged even below its allowed limit. By 1987, the city's population had reached only about 40,000. Petaluma has continued to refine its plan, however, which in 1987 received the Outstanding Planning Award of the California Chapter of the American Planning Association. The following list of chapter topics reflects its broad scope:

- ► "Community Character"
- ► "Land Use and Growth Management"
- ► "The Petaluma River"
- ► "Open Space, Conservation, and Energy"
- ► "Parks, Recreation, Schools, and Child Care"
- ► "Local Economy"
- ► "Housing"
- ► "Transportation"
- ► "Community Health and Safety"

The district court in *Petaluma* warned of a potential diffusion of growth-limitation plans to other developing communities. The voters of Livermore, California, in fact had already voted in 1972 to impose a moratorium on any further residential construction pending upgrading of school, sewer, and water services. This vote differed from Petaluma's plan in utilizing a total ban rather than an annual allotment, and it lacked the timetable for completion of services provided by Ramapo. It was legally a borderline case. The California Supreme Court in *Associated Home Builders v. City of Livermore,* 557 P.2d 473, 1975, declined to view the moratorium as inherently exclusionary, but it also avoided the simplistic approach of the court of appeals in *Petaluma* that a local town may act as a world unto itself. Instead, the *Livermore* opinion articulated a new constitutional test:

> whether the ordinance reasonably relates to the welfare of those whom it significantly affects. If the impact is limited to the city boundaries, the inquiry may be limited accordingly; if, as alleged here, the ordinance may strongly influence the supply and distribution of housing for an entire metropolitan region, judicial inquiry must consider the welfare of that region. (557 P.2d, at 487)

The court specified three steps by which a trial court might apply this test: (1) "forecast the probable effect and duration of the restriction"; (2) "identify the competing interests affected by the restriction"; and (3) determine "whether the ordinance, in light of its probable impact, represents a reasonable accommodation of the competing interests" (557 P.2d, at 488).

Livermore thus mandated the weighing of geographical evidence on regional housing, economic, and demographic trends as a basis for resolving the constitutionality of growth management plans. Like the lower court in *Petaluma*, the California Supreme Court was groping for a rationale for judging the reasonableness of such plans in terms of their real-world impacts. A fervent dissenter, Justice Mosk however, viewed the moratorium as deliberately exclusionary. Unlike the majority, which passed the buck to the trial court, Mosk applied his own geographical perception to the issue:

> Limitations on growth may be justified in resort communities, beach and lake and mountain sites, and other rural and recreational areas; such restrictions are generally designed to preserve nature's environment for the benefits of all mankind. As Thomas Jefferson wrote, the earth belongs to the living, but in usufruct.
>
> But there is a vast qualitative difference when a suburban community invokes an elitist concept to construct a mythical moat around its perimeter, not for the benefit of mankind but to exclude all but its fortunate current residents. (557 F.2d, at 493)

The complex growth management plans considered so far provoked mixed judicial reactions but were ultimately upheld. More simplistic or blatantly exclusionary measures adopted elsewhere have been emphatically rejected as unconstitutional. A 1979 Florida decision held to be arbitrary and invalid a charter amendment by the city of Boca Raton that attempted to establish an absolute limit of 40,000 dwelling units in the city (*Boca Raton v. Boca Villas Corp.*, 371 So.2d 254). In Colorado, an attempt by the city of Boulder to withhold water and sewer service from a proposed development outside its corporate limits but adjacent to areas already served was rejected in *Robinson v. City of Boulder*, 547 P.2d 228, 1976. The court held that the city had assumed the status of a public utility as sole provider of water and sewage treatment in the area and could not therefore deny service on the basis of a growth limitation plan.

Few cases involving growth management have appeared since the 1970s. In part it suggests that growth management, like subdivision regulation, has become a widely accepted practice that generates few constitutional challenges (Porter 1997). In the 1990s, however, both the rhetoric and the tactics of growth management subtly changed with the onset of *smart growth* and its cousin *new urbanism*.

Smart Growth and New Urbanism

Despite eight decades of planning and zoning and three decades of growth management, urban sprawl was seemingly out of control by the end of the twentieth

Century (Kunstler 1996; Daniels 1999; Chen 2000; Porter 2000; Gillham 2002). Urbanization of land far exceeded population growth in most metro regions, yielding lower average densities, longer hours of suburban driving, more ozone pollution, and the decline of traditional community centers (Ewing, Pendall, and Chen 2003). Metropolitan Atlanta, the fastest growing metropolitan statistical area in the United States, doubled in size during the 1990s to a north-south extent of 110 miles; its inhabitants drive 34 miles daily per capita, also a national record, and spend an average of 68 hours a year trapped in gridlock (Bullard, Johnson, and Torres 2000). These kinds of statistics, and the social and environmental costs that they represent, helped stimulate the latest wave of initiatives to tame the urban sprawl beast. Like the urban progressives of the 1920s, the conservation movement of the 1960s, and growth management in the 1970s and 1980s, smart growth advocates deplore the loss of open space; the waste of time, energy, and land resources; and the visual monotony of most recent suburban development. Unlike previous movements, however, smart growth actively seeks to enlist the development community and local government—the *bêtes noir* of past crusades—as allies rather than opponents. Henceforth, the emphasis would be not to slow or stop growth, but to guide it toward better locational and design results through partnerships of environmentalists, builders, local officials, and design professionals:

> As communities become dissatisfied with haphazard growth, they are rebelling against the conventional wisdom that continued sprawl is desirable, immutable and inevitable. Urban, suburban and rural residents have joined forces in coalitions that would once have seemed improbable. (Chen 2000, 86)

Smart growth strategies draw in part from the open-space and outdoor recreation movement of the 1960s summarized in William H. Whyte's *The Last Landscape* (1968). These strategies also deal with concerns of more recent vintage, addressing the decline of public transportation and traditional business centers, degradation of air and water resources, lack of affordable housing, and fiscal and environmental inequities borne by people of different income and race (*social justice* and *environmental justice*). One definition of smart growth is "a view that metropolitan growth patterns can and should serve the environment, the economy, and the community equally" (www.smartgrowthamerica.com, quoted in Gillham 2002, 158).

Many organizations, states, and local governments have adopted smart growth statements and policies that emphasize their particular goals. For instance, "Statement of Policy on Smart Growth" of the National Association of Home Builders

(NAHB) identifies the following principles: (1) meeting the nation's housing needs, (2) providing a wide range of housing choices, (3) preparing a comprehensive process for planning growth, (4) planning and funding infrastructure improvements, (5) using land more efficiently, and (6) revitalizing older suburban and inner-city markets (NAHB 1999). A synthesis of diverse smart growth statements yielded the following seven common elements (Gillham 2002, 158):

▸ Open-space conservation
▸ Urban growth boundaries
▸ Compact, mixed-use developments
▸ Revitalization of older downtowns and inner-ring suburbs
▸ Viable public transit
▸ Regional planning coordination
▸ Equitable sharing of fiscal resources across metropolitan regions

New urbanism, a spin-off of the smart growth movement, is an urban design paradigm promoting development that incorporates features characteristic of traditional urban communities and neighborhoods. New urbanist principles include increased density of housing, diversity of building styles, mixed-use neighborhoods, front porches, sidewalks, diminishing the use and visual impact of motor vehicles, and (one assumes) protection of mature trees and patches of habitat. The Congress for the New Urbanism (www.cnu.org) was founded in 1993 by architects Andres Duany, Peter Katz, and Peter Calthorpe to promote new urbanist principles, summarized as follows:

> Based on development patterns used prior to World War II, the New Urbanism seeks to reintegrate the components of modern life—housing, workplace, shopping, and recreation—into compact, pedestrian-friendly neighborhoods linked by transit and set in a larger regional open-space framework. (Quoted in Gillham 2002, 181)

And, in Duany's words (2000, 90):

> Whether it is street width, housing density, building placement or landscape layout, no design decision should come in isolation. This is the fundamental insight of the New Urbanists: paying careful attention to how the urban design coheres, drawing on the lessons of prewar developers.

Parallels with Ebenezer Howard's garden city movement and its U.S. counterparts come to mind. Yet although garden cities were to be built through limited-dividend investment by public-spirited progressives to help England's working classes, new urbanist model towns like Seaside and Celebration in Florida are upscale and modish alternatives to conventional subdivisions. They represent a clever, and in some respects a desirable, marketing vision. *New urbanist*, however, does not equate with *urban*. The hurly-burly of real urban neighborhoods and downtowns revered by William H. Whyte and Jane Jacobs will not be found in new urbanist communities like the Disney town of Celebration, Florida, where "the public spaces, just like the commercial buildings, will be owned and controlled by Disney [and] a long list of restrictions is written into the sales contracts for every house" (Rothchild 1995, 62). More importantly, with initial prices ranging between $120,000 and $1 million in the mid-1990s, Celebration and its counterparts scarcely address the housing or employment needs of the poor and increasingly nonwhite populations of today's cities.

References

Babcock, R. F. 1966. *The Zoning Game*. Madison: University of Wisconsin Press.

Bassett, E. M. 1936. *Zoning*. New York: Russell Sage Foundation.

Bullard, R. D., G. S. Johnson, and A. O. Torres. 2000. *Sprawl City: Race, Politics, and Planning in Atlanta*. Washington, DC: Island Press.

Calthorpe, P. 1993. *The Next American Metropolis: Ecology, Community, and the American Dream*. New York: Princeton Architectural Press.

Chen, D. 2000. The Science of Smart Growth. In *Scientific American*, Dec., 84–90.

Costonis, J. J. 1974. *Space Adrift: Saving Landmarks through the Chicago Plan*. Urbana: University of Illinois Press.

Daniels, T. 1999. *When City and Country Collide: Managing Growth in the Metropolitan Fringe*. Washington, DC: Island Press.

Dawson, A. D. 1982. *Land-Use Planning and the Law*. Hadley, MA: Author.

Delafons, J. 1969. *Land-Use Controls in the United States*. 2nd ed. Cambridge, MA: MIT Press.

Duany, A. 2000. Box. A New Theory of Urbanism. In D. Chen, The Science of Smart Growth, *Scientific American*, Dec., 90–91.

Ewing, R., R. Pendall, and D. Chen. 2003. *Measuring Sprawl and Its Impact*. Washington, DC: Smart Growth America.

Gillham, O. 2002. *The Limitless City: A Primer on the Urban Sprawl Debate*. Washington, DC: Island Press.

Godschalk, D. R., et al. 1978. *Responsible Growth Management: Cases and Materials*. Chapel Hill: University of North Carolina Center for Urban and Regional Studies.

Haar, C. M. 1955. The Master Plan: An Impermanent Constitution. *Harvard Law Review* 68:353–77.

Harnik, P. 2000. *Inside City Parks*. Washington, DC: Urban Land Institute and Trust for Public Land.

———. 2003. *The Excellent City Park System*. Washington, DC: Trust for Public Land.

Juergensmeyer, J. C., and R. M. Blake. 1984. Impact Fees: An Answer to Local Governments' Capital Funding Dilemma. In *1984 Zoning and Planning Law Handbook,* ed. J. B. Gailey. New York: Clark Boardman.

Kayden, J. 2000. *Privately Owned Public Spaces*. New York: Wiley.

Kunstler, J. H. 1996. Home from Nowhere. *Atlantic Monthly*, Sept., 43–66.

Listokin, D., ed. 1974. *Land Use Controls: Present Problems and Future Reform*. New Brunswick, NJ: Rutgers Center for Urban Policy Research.

National Association of Home Builders. 1999. NAHB's Statement of Policy on Smart Growth (March 15). Washington, DC: NAHB.

Porter, D. 1997. *Managing Growth in America's Communities*. Washington, DC: Island Press.

———. 2000. *The Practice of Sustainable Development*. Washington, DC: Urban Land Institute.

Richmond, H. R. 2000. Metropolitan Land-Use Reform: The Promise and Challenge of Majority Consensus. In *Reflections on Regionalism*, ed. B. Katz, 9–42. Washington, DC: Brookings Institution Press.

Rothchild, J. 1995. A Mouse in the House: Disney Wants to Sell Americans the Ultimate Fantasy: A Utopian Community. *Time*, Dec. 4, 62–63.

Smith, R. M. 1987. From Subdivision Improvement Requirements to Community Benefit Assessments and Linkage Payments: A Brief History of Land Development Exactions. *Law and Contemporary Problems* 50 (1): 5–30.

Toll, S. 1969. *Zoned American*. New York: Grossman.

Tustian, R. E. 1984. TDR, in Practice: A Case Study for Agricultural Preservation in Montgomery County, Maryland. In *1984 Zoning and Planning Law Handbook*, ed. J. B. Gailey. New York: Clark Boardman.

Whyte, William H. 1968. *The Last Landscape*. Garden City, NY: Doubleday. (Republished 2002 by University of Pennsylvania Press.)

Woodbury, S. R. 1975. Transfer of Development Rights: A New Tool for Planners. *Journal of American Institute of Planners* 38 (1): 3–14.

CHAPTER 10 *Land Use and*
the Courts

Every man holds his property subject to the general right of the community
to regulate its use to whatever degree the public welfare may require it.
— *THEODORE ROOSEVELT, SPEECH AT OSAWATOMIE, AUGUST 31, 1910*

The general rule at least is, that while property may be regulated to a certain
extent, if regulation goes too far, it will be recognized as a taking.
— *OLIVER WENDELL HOLMES IN PENNSYLVANIA COAL CO. V. MAHON, 1922*

As these quotations indicate, great minds differ over the appropriate balance
between the *public interest* on one side and *private property rights* on the other.
The success of zoning and other public regulations of land use in balancing these
competing interests rests in the hands of the courts that must rule in individual
challenges whether a particular measure is "constitutional." Although the U.S.
Supreme Court in its 1926 *Euclid* decision (discussed later) upheld the basic validity of zoning, it left to future state and federal courts the task of resolving whether
the application of zoning "in tedious and minute detail" to particular properties
may be "found to be clearly arbitrary and unreasonable" (47 S. Ct., at 124). That
task has yielded thousands of cases leading to hundreds of reported decisions by
higher courts reviewing those "tedious and minute details" from a constitutional
perspective. And as land use law has evolved beyond Euclidean zoning to embrace
such topics as environmental regulations, floodplains, wetlands, historic preservation, and metropolitan housing needs, the courts have been called upon to consider
the validity of these measures as well. In the process, some judges have displayed
a genuine interest in understanding the science and the geography that underlie
virtually all land use legal issues.

The Basic Constitutional Provisions

The framers of the U.S. Constitution in 1787 could scarcely have foreseen that the United States would eventually be a "Nation of Cities" (Warner 1966). Reflecting the writings of English political theorists such as John Locke and William Blackstone, though, they were acutely concerned with the protection of private property ownership against unreasonable governmental action. It was recognized that government should provide for the *general welfare*, as expressed in both the Preamble and in Article I, Section 8. Such recognition implies the existence of what has become known as the *police power* (Freund 1904) or *regulatory power,* namely the role of government in protecting the general public from private acts considered to be unreasonable by society. The police power covers a vast spectrum of private activities from operation of motor vehicles, to engaging in hazardous or illegal enterprises, to uses of land that impose harmful externalities on others. The last function continually encounters resistance from affected property owners who claim that their private ownership rights are impaired or destroyed by public regulations.

Private property rights as such were not directly mentioned in the original Constitution but were addressed by the Fifth Amendment in the Bill of Rights, added in 1791:

> No person shall be ... deprived of life, liberty, or property, without *due process* of law; nor shall private property be *taken for public use* without just compensation. (Emphasis added)

This concern was addressed again in the Fourteenth Amendment, added in 1868, with reference to states and, by implication, local governments:

> No State shall ... deprive any person of life, liberty, or property, without *due process* of law; nor deny to any person within its jurisdiction the *equal protection* of the laws. (Emphasis added)

These pithy phrases thus express the concepts of *due process*, *equal protection*, and *takings*. Each concept, as applied by courts in thousands of case decisions, defines to some degree the balance between public and private interests in land use.

The due process (Fifth and Fourteenth Amendments) and equal protection (Fourteenth Amendment) clauses each represents major branches of constitutional law beyond the scope of this discussion. Due process has evolved with two broad and distinct meanings: procedural and substantive. *Procedural due process* "centers not so much on what is done but on how it has been done, stressing general fairness in governmental procedures" (Dawson 1982, 26). As applied to land use regulation, this concept requires compliance with procedural requirements established in the applicable statutes concerning notice to all concerned, public hearings, and deadlines for public action. Violation of such procedural requirements is a ground for invalidation of the action, upon challenge by an affected party.

Substantive due process, by contrast, is more concerned with the purpose of government regulation and its impact on specific property owners. In weighing the purpose of challenged regulations, courts generally apply a two-fold test. First, do the regulatory objectives serve to protect the "public health, safety, and welfare," or, as put by the Supreme Court in *Agins v. Tiburon* (106 S. Ct. 2138, 1980), Does it "substantially advance legitimate state interests"? Second, does the regulation reasonably promote the achievement of that interest? For instance, a regulation that requires all homes in a community to be painted the same color would probably flunk the first test, because there is no public interest to be served by such a requirement (except possibly in a historic district). A regulation that limits building height to two stories as a means of alleviating traffic congestion might be held invalid under the second test, because traffic volume is not necessarily related to building heights.

Courts, however, seldom invalidate public regulations under substantive due process unless "fundamental constitutional rights" such as racial discrimination are involved. It is normally presumed by courts that the action of a state or local legislative body is valid *unless* the plaintiff proves that the action is "arbitrary, capricious, or unreasonable" (Hamann 1986, 9–10). Nine times out of ten, courts will uphold a challenged land use regulation: "If the validity of the legislative classification for zoning purposes be fairly debatable, the legislative judgment must be allowed to control" (*Village of Euclid v. Ambler Realty Co.*, 272 U.S. 365, 1926, at 375).

The challenging property owner thus bears a heavy burden of proof to overturn the presumed validity of a public regulation. The measure must be proven to be "arbitrary and capricious" and not merely "fairly debatable." (As discussed later, however, the Supreme Court has lightened this burden on the challenging property in cases in which it appears that a regulation has effectively destroyed all value of the property, as in the *Lucas* case, or allows public access to the private property without compensation, as in *Nollan* and *Dolan*.)

The equal protection clause poses the issue of equity or fairness of treatment of citizens. The Constitution is not construed to forbid all discrimination among property owners, because that would prohibit any form of land use zoning. It does require, however, that rules be uniform within zoning districts and that the boundaries between districts be drawn objectively. Equal protection requires that "similarly situated property owners must be treated similarly." The determination of similarity or dissimilarity for zoning purposes must be based on objective planning criteria so as not to be deemed arbitrary or capricious.

Reasonableness

In actual litigation, the various constitutional grounds tend to become blurred. The plaintiff typically alleges that all possible constitutional guarantees have been violated, as in the following laundry list:

> [The challenged zoning regulations] ... work an undue hardship as to use, destroy the greater part of its value, are discriminatory as a denial of the equal protection of the law, and amount to a taking of private property without just compensation contrary to due process and, as such, are invalid and void. (*Vernon Park Realty Inc. v. City of Mount Vernon*, 121 N.E.2d 517, 1954, at 519)

Such a shotgun approach invites a nonanalytical, all-purpose response by the courts. Rather than examining each allegation in detail, the court applies a single litmus test: Does the measure seem "reasonable" in light of prevailing social norms? The court in *Mount Vernon* simplified the plaintiff's allegations as follows: "While the common council has the unquestioned right to enact zoning laws respecting the use of property ... it may not be exerted *arbitrarily* or *unreasonably*" (121 N.E.2d, at 522; emphasis added).

Reasonableness is thus often used as a surrogate for *constitutionality*. Although it may beg the question, reasonableness has provided a convenient rubric for courts to resolve zoning challenges, namely is the measure "reasonable" with respect to both its public *purpose* and its *impact* on affected private parties? The inquiry takes the following form: Is the ordinance reasonably related to a valid purpose of the police power and does it reserve for the owner some reasonable way to use the property (although not necessarily the most profitable one)? In *Mount Vernon*, the city had zoned the plaintiff's property, which adjoined the railroad station, for a residence or a parking lot. The owner, who wanted to build a commercial structure, convinced the court that parking lots should be provided through public purchase of land, not zoning: "The owner ... has met the burden of proof ... that the property ... has no possibilities for [reasonable use as zoned]." The court accordingly held the zoning as applied to the plaintiff's property to be "so unreasonable and arbitrary as to constitute an invasion of property rights, contrary to constitutional due process and, as such, [is] invalid, illegal, and void" (121 N.E.2d, at 521).

Even though the plaintiff bears the burden of proving that a zoning measure is unreasonable and arbitrary, courts normally expect the municipality to present some valid planning reasons for its action. The court will not usually second-guess the wisdom of a land use plan, but a total absence of planning strongly suggests arbitrary and capricious use of the regulatory power. In short, the reasonableness (read constitutionality) of a land use regulation depends on its basis in planning. In recent decades, though, challenges to zoning have less often involved the planning rationale for a land use measure as compared with its economic impact on individual property owners. Enter the takings issue.

The Takings Issue

The most enduring constitutional question confronting zoning and other governmental regulations of property is the *takings issue*, namely to what extent can regulations reduce the value of private property without compensation to the owner? The takings issue arises from the final clause of the Fifth Amendment to the U.S. Constitution (and its counterparts in most state constitutions): "nor shall private property be taken for public use without just compensation." When private property is in fact "taken for a public use" such as for streets, parks, or schools, the public authority clearly must compensate the private owner. (Measures that compel the sale of private property to a government are an exercise of *eminent domain*, also known as *condemnation*, and are discussed in Chapter 9.)

Where land is regulated but not purchased, however, the public neither seeks legal ownership of the property nor pays any compensation to the owner. Instead, the use of property by private owners is restricted to protect the *public health, safety, and welfare*. Zoning thus encounters a paradox. On the one hand, one of its long-standing purposes, dating back to New York's Fifth Avenue merchants, is to protect and enhance property values, a somewhat strained but long-accepted interpretation of the "general welfare." On the other hand, zoning necessarily reduces some property values by limiting the range of choice and manner in which the property may be developed and used. Should such reduction in the value of some property for the benefit of others be compensable? In other words, is such a reduction in value equivalent to a *taking* for public benefit within the scope of the Fifth

Amendment? (For the best recent and comprehensive analysis of takings issue law, see Meltz, Merriam, and Frank 1999.)

As discussed in Chapter 5, public laws to abate nuisances such as noxious economic activities in residential areas were common in the early twentieth century. Because those laws did not involve compensation to the affected landowner, it was assumed that no land use regulation would be viewed as a "taking of private property for public use" within the scope of the Fifth Amendment. In 1922, however, the U.S. Supreme Court in *Pennsylvania Coal Co. v. Mahon* (260 U.S. 393) undermined this assumption, once and for all. *Mahon* involved a Pennsylvania statute that limited the right of coal producers to mine underneath inhabited areas if collapse of the surface might result. The plaintiff coal company, which had purchased the mineral rights to all the coal under the defendant's land, claimed that the statute "took" its property right in the coal without compensation. Mahon invoked the Pennsylvania statute to prevent his house from being threatened with collapse, although a preceding owner had sold the underlying mineral rights to the coal company. The Supreme Court, in a landmark opinion by Justice Oliver Wendell Holmes, agreed with the coal company. Holmes conceded that some reduction in property values due to necessary public regulations is acceptable:

> Government hardly could go on if, to some extent, values incident to property could not be diminished without paying for every such change in the general law. As long recognized, some values are enjoyed under an implied limitation, and must yield to the police power. (260 U.S., at 413)

Holmes, however, went on to drop the following bombshell that has been cited by thousands of irate property owners ever since:

> The general rule at least is, that while property may be regulated to a certain extent, if regulation goes too far, it will be recognized as a taking. (260 U.S., at 415)

Just how far is "too far" is the essence of the takings issue that has been debated in case after case ever since.

Disagreeing with Holmes, Justice Louis Brandeis in dissent urged that the challenged regulations were intended to protect life and property from the hazard of surface collapse, and as such no compensation was required. Although Holmes viewed the issue as a "case of a *single private house*" (260 U.S., at 413; emphasis added), Brandeis took a broader geographical perspective, regarded land subsidence as a matter of *public safety* affecting a much broader public:

Restriction imposed to protect the public health, safety, or morals from dangers threatened is not a taking. The restriction here in question is merely the prohibition of a noxious use. The property so restricted remains in the possession of its owner. The state does not appropriate it or make any use of it. The state merely prevents the owner from making a use which interferes with paramount rights of the public. (260 U.S., at 417)

The contrasting perspectives of Holmes and Brandeis define, respectively, the "conservative" position on the one hand and the "progressive" or "liberal" position on the other concerning the role of law in defining the balance between private property and the public interest. The former position views the role of law as affirming rather than diminishing private property values. The latter views law as an instrument for the protection of the public welfare to which property ownership is subordinate. (See also the Theodore Roosevelt quotation at beginning of this chapter in contrast to Holmes's words.) These views also reflect differing *geographical* perceptions as to the relevant spatial context to be considered in weighing public regulations: the specific property whose use is being regulated or the wider area affected by possible harmful externalities from the use of that land.

In the view of some liberal planning lawyers, the Holmes opinion in *Mahon* "rewrote the Constitution" and interpreted the Fifth Amendment to imply that the difference between regulation and taking is a "difference of *degree not kind*" (Bosselman, Callies, and Banta 1973, 134; their emphasis). Holmes's formulation, however, has withstood the test of time, challenging courts ever since to determine whether a regulation "goes too far." (As discussed later, the Supreme Court in the 1987 *Keystone* case upheld a state law similar to the one rejected in *Mahon*, yet the majority chose to distinguish rather than overrule the hallowed Holmes opinion.)

Four years after *Mahon*, the constitutionality of land use zoning was presented to the U.S. Supreme Court. By the mid-1920s, zoning had spread like dandelion seeds across the United States and development interests sought a test case to cast a constitutional death blow to zoning everywhere. The case that ultimately became the landmark decision in U.S. land use law involved the zoning ordinance of Euclid, Ohio, a newly developing suburb of Cleveland. The circumstances involved in *Village of Euclid v. Ambler Realty Co.* (272 U.S. 365, 1926) prompted an English commentator to write that "a severer test for zoning could hardly have been devised. The merits of the case were certainly dubious and the damage to private property values was impressive" (Delafons 1969, 26).

The site in question consisted of 68 acres of vacant land bordered by rail lines on the north and a major avenue on the south. It was divided by Euclid's zoning ordinance into two principal zones with a buffer strip between them. The northern portion was zoned for industry and virtually anything else. The owner, however, objected to having the southern part of the tract zoned for residence and provided evidence that the value of the latter would be $10,000 per acre for industry but only $3,500 for residential use.

The federal District Court for Northern Ohio (the trial court) emphatically held Euclid's zoning ordinance to violate the equal protection and due process clauses in its tendency to stratify the population by socioeconomic status:

> The plain truth is that the true object of the ordinance in question is to place all the property in an undeveloped area of 16 square miles in a strait-jacket. The purpose to be accomplished is really to regulate the mode of living of persons who may hereafter inhabit it. In the last analysis, the result to be accomplished is to classify the population and segregate them according to their income or situation in life. (*Ambler Realty Co. v. Village of Euclid*, 297 F. 307, 1924, at 315)

If this opinion had been upheld by the U.S. Supreme Court, the face of metropolitan America might look rather different today. It was reversed, however.

The full story of the dramatic rescue of zoning before the Supreme Court is recounted by Seymour Toll in *Zoned American* (1969). After a full hearing, it appeared that the defendant Village of Euclid would lose and an unusual rehearing was requested and granted. To bolster the municipal position in the rehearing, Alfred Bettman, a Cincinnati planning lawyer, was retained by the National Conference on City Planning and other prozoning interests to submit a brief as *amicus curiae* ("friend of the court"). Bettman's brief, one of the seminal documents in the history of zoning, sidestepped the facts of the *Euclid* case in favor of broadly addressing the theory and constitutionality of zoning, including the issue of compensation.

Bettman argued that reduction of value per se cannot be the test of constitutionality because that "begs the question." Any police power measure involves actual and perhaps severe economic impact to affected property owners. If the purpose is appropriate and necessary, Bettman maintained, loss of value is constitutionally tolerable. He compared it with the familiar governmental function of abating public nuisances, arguing that modern urban development was producing unprecedented congestion and inefficiency and urged that promoting orderly patterns of land use pursuant to a master plan is a proper use of the regulatory power. In effect, he urged in Holmes's terms that zoning did not go "too far" and did not amount to a compensable taking. (The brief is reprinted in its entirety in Comey 1946, 157–93.)

In a 6–3 decision (both Holmes and Brandeis voted with the majority), the Court upheld zoning. Its opinion reflected the tutorial on city growth provided in Bettman's brief and oral argument:

> Building zone laws are of modern origin. They began in this country about twenty-five years ago. Until recent years, urban life was comparatively simple; but with the great increase and concentration of population, problems have developed, ... which require ... additional restrictions in respect of the use and occupation of private lands in urban communities. Regulations, the wisdom, necessity and validity of which as applied to existing conditions, are so apparent that they are now uniformly sustained, under the complex conditions of our day. And the law of nuisances ... may be consulted, not for the purpose of controlling, but for the helpful aid of its analogies in the process of ascertaining the scope of the [police] power. Thus the question whether the power exists to forbid the erection of a building of a particular kind or for a particular use, ... is to be determined, not by an abstract consideration of the building or other thing considered apart, but by considering it in connection with the circumstances and the locality.... *A nuisance may be merely the right thing in the wrong place—like a pig in the parlor instead of the barnyard.* (272 U.S., at 370; emphasis added)

The *theory* of land use zoning was thus held to be constitutional, but the Supreme Court left open the possibility that individual *applications* of zoning might be rejected if a property owner proved that a restriction was arbitrary or unreasonable as applied to his or her property. Although most cases of individual hardship have been remedied through the variance procedure, landowner challenges to local regulations based on the taking issue have persisted to the present time. For the next six decades, the Supreme Court left the resolution of these issues largely to the state courts.

In 1987, the U.S. Supreme Court revisited the takings issue in three important decisions. In *Keystone Bituminous Coal Assn. v. DeBenedictis* (107 S. Ct. 1232), in a vote of 5–4, the Court upheld a Pennsylvania state law resembling the one invalidated in the 1922 *Mahon* decision. The *Keystone* majority distinguished the earlier decision (rather than directly overruling it) in upholding a new Pennsylvania Subsidence Act. Significantly, the decision explicitly acknowledged a change in judicial perception and cultural values since 1922: "The Subsidence Act is a prime example that 'circumstances may so change in time ... as to clothe with such a [public] interest what at other times ... would be a matter of purely private concern' " (107 S. Ct., at 1243). Thus the public interest argument of Brandeis's *Mahon* dissent would be embraced by the Court after sixty-five years, but without impugning the Holy Writ of Holmes's balancing test, which remains alive and well in the twenty-first century.

With a switch of one vote (Justice Byron White), the *Keystone* majority became a minority in the other two 1987 property rights cases. *First English Evangelical Lutheran Church v. County of Los Angeles* (107 S. Ct. 2378) involved a county moratorium on rebuilding a camp for children with handicaps in a canyon after a flash flood swept through the area. A pro-property 5–4 majority sustained a theory of "inverse condemnation," which allows an owner to recover monetary damages for loss of value during the time a restriction is in effect, if the restriction is subsequently held to be invalid. Upon remand to the California Supreme Court to decide whether the county flood hazard moratorium was valid under state law, that court vigorously decided in the affirmative:

> The zoning regulation ... involves the highest of public interests—the prevention of death and injury. Its enactment was prompted by the loss of life in an earlier flood. And its avowed purpose is to prevent the loss of lives in future floods. (*First English Evangelical Lutheran Church v. County of Los Angeles,* 258 Cal. Rptr. 930, at 904, 1989)

The California court seemed to be saying, "Take that, U.S. Supreme Court!"

The third 1987 case, *Nollan v. California Coastal Commission* (107 S. Ct. 3141), involved a restriction on a rebuilding permit for an oceanfront home that required the owners to allow the public an easement to walk along the dry sand (private) portion of the beach in front of their home. This restriction was consistent with similar ones placed on other shorefront homes by the commission to promote public access along beaches. The commission also argued that the easement was needed to offset the loss of "visual access" to the ocean caused by enlargement of the plaintiff's home. With the same 5–4 alignment as *First English*, the majority opinion by Justice Antonin Scalia held that the access easement lacked an "essential nexus" or relevance to the goal of maintaining visibility of the ocean from public streets:

> The Commission may well be right that [the public interest will be served by a continuous strip of publicly accessible beach along the coast] but that does not establish that the Nollans (and other coastal residents) alone can be compelled to contribute to its realization. Rather, California is free to advance its "comprehensive program," if it wishes, by using its power of eminent domain for this "public purpose" ... but if it wants an easement across the Nollans' property, it must pay for it. (107 S. Ct., at 3150)

The case thus reflected a longstanding doctrine that the police power may properly be used to prevent public harm but not to confer public benefits without compensation, as earlier analyzed by Joseph Sax (1964, 49–50). But in dissent, Justice Harry Blackmun argued that the majority hold "a narrow conception of rationality . . . [that] has long been discredited as a judicial arrogation of legislative authority" (107 S. Ct., at 3160).

Two subsequent Supreme Court opinions have further buttressed the takings issue as a barrier to certain public land use regulations. The first of these cases, *Lucas v. South Carolina Coastal Council* (112 S. Ct. 2886, 1992), involved a challenge by the owner of two lots on the oceanfront of South Carolina against the denial of building permits by the defendant. The defendant was guided by the 1988 South Carolina Beachfront Management Act, adopted after Lucas acquired his lots, that prohibited new building seaward of an erosion setback baseline. Due to recent fluctuations of the shoreline, the baseline ran entirely landward of Lucas's lots. Although homes had been built on adjoining lots before the law went into effect, the Coastal Council denied approval for any construction on the Lucas lots. Lucas did not challenge the validity of the Beachfront Management Act per se, but claimed that its application to his lots destroyed all of their value (Platt 1992, 1999, 145–51).

The trial court agreed and ordered the state to pay Lucas $1.2 million as compensation. The South Carolina Supreme Court (404 S.E.2d 895, 1991) in a 3–2 vote reversed the trial court, holding the permit denial to be a valid application of the police power consistent with the U.S. Supreme Court's *Keystone* opinion. The U.S. Supreme Court accepted Lucas's appeal from the state decision; the resulting national attention attracted numerous *amicus curiae* briefs by interested parties on both sides of the issue. According to an editorial in the *Boston Globe* (March 5, 1992, 12):

> The case has far-reaching implications for the enforcement of regulations concerning everything from billboards to wetlands, as well as the coastline. Environmentalists fear that if the court decides in Lucas's favor, virtually every environmental restriction placed on the use of property will be considered a taking, thus making environmental protection too expensive.

The High Court reversed the state ruling in a 6–3 decision, holding that where a regulation "denies all economically beneficial or productive use of land" (112 S. Ct., at 2893), it is a "categorical taking" equivalent to a physical invasion of the property by governmental action. Scalia writing for the majority argued that the need to compensate for "total takings" could not be avoided by merely reciting harms that the regulation would prevent. Yet in an awkward distinction, he wrote that compensation would, however, not be required for total takings where a regulation merely reflected a state's "background principles of nuisance and property law" (112 S. Ct., at 2901) (apparently meaning that if Lucas could have been prevented from building on his lots under state nuisance doctrines, he could *not* claim compensation).

Blackmun in dissent wrote, "Today the Court launches a missile to kill a mouse." Citing *Keystone* among other cases, Blackmun argued:

> These cases rest on the principle that the State has full power to prohibit an owner's use of property if it is harmful to the public. Since no individual has a right to use his property so as to create a nuisance or otherwise harm others, the State has not "taken" anything of value when it asserts its power to enjoin the nuisance-like activity.... It would make no sense under this theory to suggest that an owner has a constitutionally protected right to harm others, if only he makes the proper showing of economic loss. (112 S. Ct., at 2912)

It is Holmes versus Brandeis all over again. Both Scalia for the majority and Blackmun in dissent agree that government can restrain private owners from causing external harm in their use of land. They differ as to what constitutes "harm" and who should make that determination, the legislature or the courts. Moreover, they differ as to whether the state has a higher obligation to compensate if the case involves a "total taking" rather than a partial loss of value. The case was remanded to the state court, which found that no such common-law nuisance was involved and agreed that it was a temporary taking for the time that the restriction remained in effect. South Carolina ended up paying Lucas and then selling the properties, with building permits, no less. The lots are now developed (Figure 10-1).

The political impact of *Lucas* far outweighed its legal significance. Pro- and anti-regulation factions vied with each other to interpret the decision favorably to their positions. For example, one property rights advocate has paraphrased the decision as follows: "the U.S. Supreme Court said [in *Lucas*] that it will require close scrutiny of land use regulations that devalue private property" (Stoddard 1995, 30). An environmental writer, on the other hand, views *Lucas* as "a decision full of sound and fury signifying nothing" (Sugameli 1993).

On June 24, 1994, the Supreme Court decided another property rights case, *Dolan v. City of Tigard*, 114 S. Ct. 2309. Like *Nollan*, this case involved disputed conditions imposed on the plaintiff in exchange for a permit to enlarge an existing business premises. The conditions were that the owner dedicate to the city a portion of her property in the one-hundred-year floodplain, plus an additional strip to be part

FIGURE 10-1 The site of the *Lucas v. South Carolina Coastal Council* case. The state's defeat in the U.S. Supreme Court eventually led to the construction of the house on the right on one of the Lucas lots. The beach scarp indicates that the inlet is shifting toward the houses again. *(Photo by author.)*

of a public bikeway system. Elaborating on its *Nollan* ruling, the U.S. Supreme Court reversed the Oregon Supreme Court in another 5–4 decision and held these conditions to be invalid as "takings."

The majority opinion in *Dolan* by Chief Justice William Rehnquist required the defendant city to demonstrate "rough proportionality" between the burden upon the property owner and the benefit to the public: "No precise mathematical calculation is required, but the city must make some sort of individualized determination that the required dedication is related both in nature and extent to the impact of the proposed development" (114 S. Ct., at 2329–20). The majority believed that this test was not met by the city and the mandatory dedication of the bikeway, at least, was invalid.

As with *Lucas*, the political importance of the decision far transcended its narrow legal significance. As Justice John Paul Stevens dryly observed in dissent: "The mountain of briefs that the case has generated ... makes it obvious that the pecuniary value of [the owner's] victory is far less important than the rule of law that this case has been used to establish. It is unquestionably an important case" (114 S. Ct., at 2322). Stevens argued that the "rough proportionality" test places the burden of proof on the city, reversing the longstanding presumption of validity extended by courts to the regulatory actions of local governments. "Rough proportionality," he stated, also is difficult to satisfy in the real world, and professional judgments of planners should be given the benefit of the doubt:

> In our changing world one thing is certain: uncertainty will characterize predictions about the impact of new urban developments on the risks of floods, earthquakes, traffic congestion, or environmental harms. When there is doubt concerning the magnitude of those impacts, the public interest in averting them must outweigh the private interest of the commercial entrepreneur. (114 S. Ct., at 2329)

With a shift of one justice, this view could have been that of the majority and thus the "law of the land." The June 25, 1994, *New York Times* reported the decision with the headline "High Court Limits the Public Power on Private Land ... Opinion by Rehnquist Curbs Environmental and Other Land-Use Measures." This apocalyptic view, shared by some other media and the property rights movement, however, was exaggerated. Rehnquist's majority opinion, but for its outcome, is rife with favorable commentary on city planning, floodplain management, greenways, bike paths, and other elements of planning.

As with *Lucas*, the importance of the *Dolan* case may not lie so much in its narrow legal significance but in what it is thought to represent, namely a broadening of property owner rights in relation to public land use regulations. This perception, whether or not strictly justified by the decisions themselves, may become a self-fulfilling expectation if political bodies, administrative agencies, and lower courts are persuaded that the pendulum is swinging in the direction of private rather than public interests.

In 2002, the Supreme Court reverted to a more pragmatic, less ideological, approach to the takings issue in *Tahoe-Sierra Preservation Council v. Tahoe Regional Planning Agency,* 2002 LW 654431 (U.S.). The case involved a moratorium imposed by the defendant regional planning agency on development along the shores of Lake Tahoe. The plaintiff property owner association (cloaked in the mantle of a "preservation council") charged that the moratorium was equivalent to a "taking" due to the delay it caused in their development plans. In a 6–3 decision, the High Court upheld the moratorium as not inflicting a taking. Stephens, writing for the majority, stated, "A rule that required compensation for every delay in the use of property would render routine government processes prohibitive expensive or encourage hasty decision-making." In an editorial, the *New York Times* (2002) wrote:

> The Supreme Court acted wisely this week to preserve the ability of state localities to institute land use and zoning regulations to control growth and protect the environment. In doing so, the court dealt a major setback to the conservative-led property rights movement, ending its string of recent Supreme Court victories elevating the rights of individual property owners over valid planning and community needs.

Floodplain and Wetland Regulation

For decades, Euclidean zoning took little notice of physical variation in the land. Just as the rectangular townships of the Federal Land Survey marched relentlessly across prairie, desert, and mountain, the geometry of suburbia imposed by zoning until the 1970s ignored natural impediments to building. Those limitations included areas at risk from natural hazards such as seismic faults, unstable slopes, coastal and riverine floodplains, and wetlands. Such disregard of natural hazards in land use planning allowed much postwar urban development to be located "in harm's way" and resulting losses have been costly (Mileti 1999). Geographer Gilbert F. White and his associates (1964, 1975) found that flood control projects often led to increased flood losses by encouraging encroachment in the "protected" floodplain, which may then be inundated by a flood exceeding the project's design capacity. Such disclosures prompted a reversal of public policies that had long tolerated encroachment on floodplains in reliance on structural flood control projects (Platt 1999).

Similarly, millions of acres of coastal and inland wetlands were filled, drained, paved, and built over for urban development and agriculture between the Civil War and the 1960s out of ignorance of the ecological benefits and functions they provide. The perception of wetlands as "wastelands" was finally challenged by scientist writers such as John and Mildred Teal (1969), leading to adoption of federal, state, and local laws to protect wetlands.

Thus public perception and policies regarding both natural hazards and natural habitats began to be changed by the political decision process in response to scientific research findings and increasing awareness of the socioeconomic and environmental costs of ignoring Mother Nature, exactly as postulated in the three-circle model of land-society interaction presented in Figure 2-8!

Physical Characteristics

As summarized in Chapter 1, *floodplains* are natural overflow areas adjoining surface waters, including streams, rivers, lakes, estuaries, bays, and the open ocean (Figure 10-2). Riverine floodplains are formed where a watercourse over time has weathered away bordering uplands and deposited sediment on the resulting level surface adjoining its normal channel. The floodplain is narrow or nonexistent in steep, less erodible terrain and broader in more erodible lowlands. The latter are characterized by deposits of fertile alluvial soils ideal for agriculture. In regions such as Appalachia, however, floodplains may be the only level land available for urban development and communications linkages such as highways, railroads, power lines, and airports. Agriculture is reasonably compatible with occasional flooding, especially that which occurs in the early spring in northern climes, the "spring freshet." Yet urban development, unless suitably designed or fortified by protective measures, is inherently at risk in times of flood.

Floodplains are not uniformly risk-prone. Levels of hazard are distinguished in terms of estimated frequency of inundation for specific elevations of land within the overall floodplain. Thus low ground close to the river may be flooded nearly every year, whereas slightly higher ground farther from the channel may be

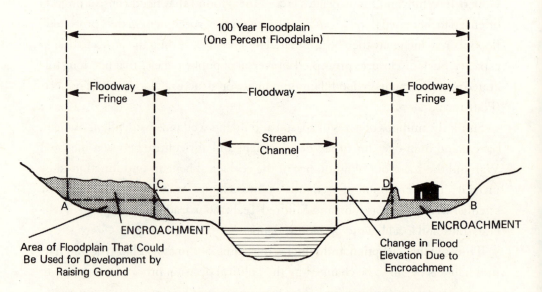

FIGURE 10-2 Cross section of riverine floodplain. Line A-B is the width of natural floodplain; line C-D is the width of floodplain after fill and construction of flood levees. *(Source: U.S. Army Corps of Engineers.)*

FIGURE 10-3 Aerial view of freshwater wetlands in the Connecticut River Valley. *(Photo by author.)*

flooded on the average only every fifty to one hundred years. (The close-in areas of course are flooded more deeply during those events.) The *one-hundred-year flood-plain*, which has a probability of 1 percent of being flooded in any given year, is the geographic area regulated in most public floodplain management programs in the United States (Figure 10-3).

Wetlands are natural depressions where the groundwater table is normally at or just below the land surface. The wetness of wetlands and their special biological characteristics provide nutrients to support a rich diversity of flora and fauna (Figure 10-3). The ecology of wetlands varies according to their location, soil chemistry, hydrology, elevation, and size (Figure 10-4). Coastal wetlands include salt marshes, mudflats, and other estuarine wetlands subject to tidal influence and some degree of salinity. Inland or freshwater wetlands are of many types, including cattail swamps, riparian habitat along stream banks, isolated bogs, prairie pot-holes, and bottomland hardwood forests of the lower Mississippi Valley (Kusler 1983; Tiner 1984). Wetlands of all types are estimated to cover slightly more than 3 percent of the continental U.S. land area, or about 70 million acres (U.S. Council on Environmental Quality 1981).

Depending on their location and ecological type, wetlands provide a number of benefits in their natural state

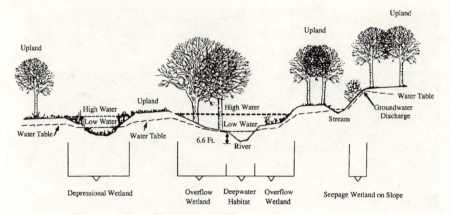

FIGURE 10-4 Cross section of various types of freshwater wetlands.
(Source: U.S. Fish and Wildlife Service.)

as food producers, spawning sites, and sanctuaries for many forms of fish and bird life. They produce timber, peat moss, and crops such as wild rice and cranberries. They serve as storage areas for storm and flood waters, reduce erosion, provide for groundwater retention, and at times purify polluted waters.

Educating the Courts

Public efforts to regulate floodplains and wetlands were rare before 1960, as were judicial decisions reviewing them. Courts were initially baffled by the seeming confusion of purposes involved in early floodplain and wetlands laws. In 1966, the New Jersey Supreme Court held a local floodplain management ordinance to be invalid because it appeared to the court to be more a wetlands protection measure than a flood reduction measure (*Morris County Land Improvement Co. v. Parsippany-Troy Hills Twp.*, 192 A.2d 232, 1963). The site was actually *both* a wetland and a natural flood storage basin in the headwaters of the Passaic River with much urban land in the floodplain downstream. The court misunderstood all this information, and this decision has been cited by owners of floodplain and wetland property ever since in challenging public regulation of their land. The judge who wrote the *Morris County* opinion apologized in a later floodplain decision, attributing his revised perception to *"vital ecological and environmental considerations of recent cognizance"* (*A.M.G. Associates v. Springfield Township*, 319 A.2d 705, at 711; emphasis added). The willingness of at least this judge to learn from physical and social science (provided by legal counsel, one hopes) was thus acknowledged.

For a decade, *Morris County* cast its shadow over floodplain and wetland regulations, and several states followed it. In 1972, however, landmark decisions in Massachusetts and Wisconsin went in exactly the opposite direction, namely to hold such regulations valid and constitutional. These decisions laid a foundation for the subsequent approval of such measures in nearly every jurisdiction that has considered them.

The Massachusetts case, *Turnpike Realty Co. v. Town of Dedham*, 284 N.E.2d 891 (1972), involved a proposal to fill a wetland site bordering the Charles River in Dedham, a suburb of Boston. The area lay along Route 1, which was lined with commercial development partly built on earlier wetland fill (Figure 10-5). The town of Dedham, however, had amended its zoning in 1963 to establish a flood-plain district that prohibited the plaintiff's site from being filled.

Dedham was more careful than the New Jersey township in *Morris County* to specify the purposes of the regulations, which included (1) groundwater protection, (2) protection of public health and safety against floods, (3) avoidance of community costs due to unwise construction in wetlands and floodplains, and (4) conservation of "natural conditions, wildlife, and open spaces for the education, recreation and general welfare of the public" (284 N.E.2d, at 894). Of course, the last point raised the specter of "public benefit" that had tainted the *Morris County* ordinance. The Massachusetts court, however, accepted the first three purposes as valid. It ruled that the fourth goal would not justify the measure on its own, but was not fatal since "the by-law is fully supported by other valid considerations of public welfare" (284 N.E.2d, at 894). Citing a law review article by a Chicago colleague of Gilbert White's (Dunham 1959), the court declared that "The general necessity of flood plain zoning to reduce the damage to life and property caused by flooding is unquestionable" (284 N.E.2d, at 899).

The *Turnpike Realty* decision, however, left dangling the question of whether a wetland regulation *per se* could be upheld in the absence of flood risk. That issue was faced in a Wisconsin case, *Just v. Marinette County*, 201 N.W.2d 761, 1972, involving construction on the shore of a glacial lake in central Wisconsin. The owners filled the site to build a summer cottage despite a Marinette County shoreland zoning ordinance and state law that required a permit to be obtained for filling of wetlands within 300 feet of navigable waters. After being held in violation in an enforcement action by the county, the plaintiffs appealed their case to the Wisconsin Supreme Court, which denied their claim and upheld the county ordinance and state shoreland zoning law.

The *Just* decision rested not on flood hazards but on water quality. Wisconsin is a public trust jurisdiction in which the state "owns" navigable waters and

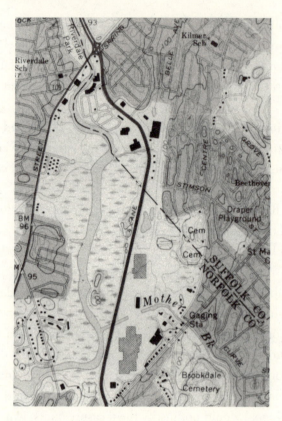

FIGURE 10-5
Site of the *Turnpike Realty*
case located between the
Charles River (left center)
and U.S. Route 1 (heavy
dark line).

land beneath them in trust for the people. The court viewed the purpose of the
shoreland zoning ordinance as protecting "navigable waters and the public rights
therein from the degradation and deterioration which result from uncontrolled
use and development of shorelands" (201 N.W.2d, at 765).

The court might have upheld the measure on narrow technical grounds. In the
spirit of Aldo Leopold, author of *Sand County Almanac* (1949/1966) and Wisconsin's environmental guru, it chose, however, to view the issue as "a conflict between
the public interest in stopping the despoliation of natural resources, which our citizens until recently have taken as inevitable and for granted, and an owner's
asserted right to use his property as he wishes" (201 N.W.2d, at 767). Shifting into
high gear, the court declared:

> It seems to us that filling a swamp not otherwise commercially usable is not in and of
> itself an existing use, which is prevented, but rather is the preparation for some future
> use which is not indigenous to a swamp. ...
>
> The shoreland zoning ordinance preserves nature, the environment, and natural
> resources as they were created and to which the people have a present right. The ordi-

nance does not create or improve the public condition but only preserves nature from the despoilage [*sic*] and harm resulting from the unrestricted activities of humans. (201 N.W.2d, at 770–71)

This environmental "Magna Carta" went beyond the call of duty or demands of this modest case. To other courts around the country, it was probably seen as beyond the Constitution as well. *Just*, though, remains "the law" in Wisconsin, and its rhetorical flourishes continue to thrill students and practitioners of natural resource management.

The trilogy of cases discussed in this section delimits the range of possible judicial response to floodplain and wetland regulations. *Morris County* reflected the cautious preenvironmental approach. *Turnpike Realty* broke new ground through careful judicial craftsmanship, and *Just* was a glimpse of utopia! All three decisions are still cited in cases challenging local floodplain and wetland regulations.

By the early 1990s, such measures were generally accepted in most of the United States (Platt 1999, Chap. 5). As a 1991 Illinois case indicates, state courts sometimes uphold very severe limits on development in floodplains where the hazard is well documented. After flooding struck the Chicago metropolitan area in 1986 and 1987, a governor's flood control task force was established to study the causes and recommend legal changes. Pursuant to this report, the Illinois legislature passed a state floodplain management law that *prohibited all new residential construction* in the one-hundred-year floodway in the Chicago metropolitan area. Upon challenge of a denial of a building permit under this law, the Illinois Supreme Court declared that

> the General Assembly has the authority to prohibit all new residential construction in the 100-year floodway. It is reasonable for the General Assembly to rely on the extensive research contained in the Governor's flood control task force report which documented the demographic and land use changes which have contributed to the increased flooding in the 100-year floodway [and the need for] prohibition of all new residential construction in the floodway. It is also reasonable for the General Assembly to rely on the scientific study [on] the importance of maintaining existing natural storage areas in the watershed to reduce flood damage. (*Beverly Bank v. Illinois Department of Transportation*, 579 N.E.2d 815, Ill. 1991, at 822)

Thus the cycle of (1) disaster, (2) study and recommendations, and (3) adoption of new laws regarding land use leading to (4) safer development practices was complete. The ability to learn from disaster and take steps to avoid its repetition that began with the Act for Rebuilding London of 1667 (see Chapter 3) thus continues today.

Regulating Aesthetics

Courts have long struggled with the limits of achieving aesthetic objectives without compensation to the property owner. The concept of aesthetics as "beauty" is virtually impossible to define in terms of legislative criteria sufficient to provide objective guidance to zoning officials. In the words of one court:

> [A] primary objective to aesthetic zoning is founded upon its subjective nature, for what may be attractive to one may be an abomination to another.... Therefore many courts have long been unwilling to act as super art critics by ruling on the reasonableness of ordinances which are essentially based on subjective aesthetic considerations, and they have held all such ordinances invalid. (*Naegele Outdoor Advertising Co. v. Village of Minnetonka*, 162 N.W.2d 206, 1962, at 212)

The early period of zoning was marked by a paradox concerning aesthetics. On the one hand, the basic elements of Euclidean zoning—segregation of uses, minimum lot size, setbacks, and so forth—embody the aesthetic of the early-twentieth-century garden suburb: single-family detached homes with spacious landscaped front yards set back evenly from the street with nonresidential activities banished from the area. Yet early zoning advocates steadfastly denied that zoning was intended to serve aesthetic purposes. In his *Euclid* brief, Bettman distinguished civic *orderliness* from *aesthetics*: "Promoting what might be called orderliness in the layout of cities is not the satisfaction of taste or aesthetic desires, but rather the promotion of those beneficial effects upon health and morals which come from living in orderly and decent surroundings (quoted in Comey 1946, 172).

The 1926 Standard Zoning Enabling Act made no reference to aesthetics in its section on purposes. The justification for zoning has subsequently been expressed in terms of "public health, safety, and welfare" as reflected in reduction of population congestion, efficient arrangement of land uses, and avoidance of fire, flood and other public perils.

Aesthetics, though, has crept into local land use regulations in various ways such as the long debate over roadside *billboards*. Originally, courts struggled to find a public health (i.e., nonaesthetic) basis to uphold antibillboard laws. For example, a 1919 Illinois decision found that

> nuisances were permitted to exist in the rear of surface billboards, and physicians testified that deposits found behind billboards breed disease germs which may be car-

ried and scattered in the dust by the wind and by flies and other insects. It was shown that dissolute and immoral practices were carried on under the cover and shield furnished by these billboards. (*Thomas Cusack Co. v. City of Chicago*, 108 N.E. 340, at 344)

This strained decision may be contrasted in rationale with a 1975 opinion of the Massachusetts Supreme Judicial Court that upheld a total ban on off-premises billboards in the town of Brookline, stating:

We live in a changing world where the law must respond to the demands of a modern society. [*Euclid* quote omitted.] What was deemed unreasonable in the past may now be reasonable due to changing community values. Among these changes is the growing notion that towns and cities can and should be aesthetically pleasing; that a visually satisfying environment tends to contribute to the well-being of its inhabitants. (*John Donnelly and Sons, Inc. v. Outdoor Advertising Board*, 339 N.E.2d 709, at 717)

Billboard regulations are authorized in all fifty states and are widely in effect. Restraints and even total bans of billboards have been upheld in many states. There appears to be widespread consensus that billboards and other types of outdoor advertising are per se unattractive, distracting, and exploitive of the captive audience of highway users. As a class of aesthetic nuisance, billboards have been categorically disfavored though by no means eliminated in many states.

Several issues, however, arise when local governments begin to regulate billboards and other signs. Considerations include the size and characteristics of the sign, whether it is on-site or off-site (i.e., advertises the business on whose premises the sign is located), lighted or unlighted, freestanding or supported by a building, commercial or noncommercial. Signs may occasionally assume the status of landmarks, such as the "Citgo" sign that looms over the left field wall at Boston's Fenway Park. Other signs may be obstructions to traffic, pornographic, excessively distracting, or otherwise nuisancelike. Thus communities do not usually prohibit all signs. Discrimination among different types of signs, however, may generate constitutional difficulty.

In 1981, the U.S. Supreme Court addressed the problem of potential conflict between sign regulation and the First Amendment protection of freedom of speech. The Court endorsed the general principle that signs may be regulated in the public interest, but it invalidated an ordinance that banned noncommercial advertising throughout the city while allowing on-site commercial signs, viewing that as impermissible discrimination against noncommercial (for example, political) signs (*Metromedia Inc. v. City of San Diego*, 101 S. Ct. 2882).

Beyond billboard laws, a major landmark in the recognition of aesthetics in planning law was the 1954 U.S. Supreme Court decision in *Berman v. Parker* (75 S. Ct. 98). The opinion by Justice William O. Douglas, an ardent conservationist, declared:

> The concept of the public welfare is broad and inclusive. . . . The values it represents are spiritual as well as physical, aesthetic as well as monetary. It is within the power of the legislature to determine that the community should be beautiful as well as healthy, spacious as well as clean, well-balanced as well as carefully patrolled. . . . If those who govern the District of Columbia decide that the Nation's Capital should be beautiful as well as sanitary, there is nothing in the Fifth Amendment that stands in the way. (75 S. Ct., at 102–3)

Strictly speaking, this statement did not apply to zoning. *Berman*, which arose from a challenge to the constitutionality of the federal urban renewal program, involved the eminent domain power, not the police power or zoning. The plaintiff's store was being condemned and razed by the District of Columbia as part of a widespread program to eliminate "blighted areas" to make way for modern and expensive new homes and businesses. (The project was located in the Southwest quadrant of Washington, D.C., where the Department of Housing and Urban Development now sits on land cleared by urban renewal.) When government pays for land, much broader latitude exists as to public purpose than when the land is restricted under the police power. Nevertheless, Douglas's statement has been widely quoted in zoning cases involving aesthetics, including the 1975 *Donnelly* case cited earlier. Douglas in fact quoted the statement himself in a zoning case that upheld community limitations on the occupancy of dwelling units by more than two unrelated adults (*Village of Belle Terre v. Borass*, 94 S. Ct. 1536, 1974).

The Douglas dictum, however, should not be taken too literally. A zoning measure that forbids building on scenic land in the interest of maintaining a "beautiful community" would almost certainly be held invalid. The taking clause of the Fifth Amendment certainly "stands in the way," notwithstanding Douglas's sweeping disclaimer.

Historic and Architectural Controls

Historic preservation districts are another instance of aesthetic zoning that has received widespread but often qualified judicial support. The concept of the historic district originated with the designation of the Vieux Carré District in New

Orleans through an amendment to the Louisiana Constitution in 1921. Other early districts were established in Charleston, South Carolina; San Antonio, Texas; and Nantucket, Massachusetts. The distinctive architecture and renowned atmosphere of these prototype districts facilitated judicial approval of regulations to control construction, demolition, and renovation. For instance, in 1941, the Louisiana Supreme Court upheld the Vieux Carré ordinance in *City of New Orleans v. Pergament* (5 S.2d 129, at 135) with the following rationale:

> There is nothing arbitrary or discriminating in forbidding the proprietor of a modern building, as well as the proprietor of one of the ancient landmarks, in the Vieux Carré to display an unusually large sign upon his premises. The purpose of the ordinance is not only to preserve the old buildings themselves, but to preserve the antiquity of the whole French and Spanish quarter, *tout ensemble,* so to speak, by defending this relic against iconoclasm or vandalism. Preventing or prohibiting eyesores in such a locality is within the police power.

Historic district regulations typically go beyond traditional zoning controls in requiring approval from a local review board for any alteration or demolition. Even an affirmative duty to maintain the exterior appearance of the premises may be imposed (*Maher v. City of New Orleans*, 37 F. Supp. 653). The effect of these types of regulations to particular property owners, however, may be harsh. Many historic districts are less homogeneous or distinctive than the Vieux Carré. Issues arise concerning the status of nonhistoric structures within a designated district, accessory structures (e.g., solar panels and satellite dishes), mixture of architectural styles, approval of new construction within a district, the need for owner consent, eleventh-hour designations to obstruct a redevelopment plan, and the status of religious property in a district (Duerksen 1985, 1503). As with other zoning, objective standards must be provided by the local or state legislative body to guide the local review body in its permitting process.

The U.S. Supreme Court upheld New York's designation of Grand Central Station as an architectural landmark in *Penn Central Transportation Co. v. City of New York* (98 S. Ct. 2646, 1978). The Court broadly endorsed the principle of landmark preservation: "States and cities may enact land-use restrictions or controls to enhance the quality of life by preserving the character and desirable aesthetic features of a city" (98 S. Ct., at 266). The Court noted that Grand Central Station provided some economic return to the owner, albeit not optimal, and that the ordinance permitted the owner to transfer the unusable development rights to other parcels of real estate in the vicinity. (See Chapter 9.) Nationally, thousands of local

FIGURE 10-6 Jackson Square, part of the French Quarter historic district in New Orleans. *(Photo by author.)*

historic preservation laws are in effect today. According to the April 9, 1995, *New York Times,* New York City had designated 1,021 individual structures and sixty-six historic districts by then.

Nonhistoric architectural controls pose a more difficult problem. How can a community regulate the appearance of new structures in relation to an existing potpourri of styles? Many communities have established architectural review boards to certify that a new structure will be compatible with the surrounding area. The problem is to define "compatibility" or "suitability" of a design in the absence of a clear-cut historic or otherwise homogeneous style. Response to this problem is approached in two ways, namely by attempting to write objective standards to guide the architectural board and by designating certain types of experts to be represented on the board. The Ohio Court of Appeals relied on the presence of both these safeguards in *Reid v. Architectural Review Board of City of Cleveland Heights* (192 N.E.2d 74, 1963). It upheld the board's disapproval of a modernistic "flat-roofed complex of twenty modules" in a "well-regulated and carefully groomed community." Some communities have even sought to regulate against "excessive similarity" of building styles.

Aesthetic regulation is not necessarily an unmixed blessing. According to John Costonis (1982, 367): "Aesthetics has been transformed from an idea into an ideology that is being employed by preservationists, environmentalists, and developers alike to rationalize pursuits that are at best tenuously related to visual beauty." The notion of aesthetics, Costonis notes, is inherently vague and expansive. Judicial approval of the objectives of aesthetic regulations in the context of signs and historic preservation should not necessarily be extended to any public action nominally taken in the spirit of "aesthetic protection."

Metropolitan Needs and Exclusionary Zoning

Local land use regulation, especially zoning, is criticized not only by property owners but also by regional planners, social justice advocates, and environmentalists, who argue that zoning promotes local rather than regional needs and forecloses housing and employment opportunities to lower-income and nonwhite populations. Localism obstructs the development of a broad-based regional housing supply, interferes with the location of certain facilities of regional importance, and encourages urban sprawl by promoting single-family homes and redundant commercial development. The major types of zoning abuses decried by these critics are the following:

- ► *Exclusionary zoning*: the use of zoning to deter construction of homes, apartments, or mobile home parks for low- and moderate-income families or members of racial or other minorities
- ► *Fiscal zoning*: the use of zoning to minimize local property taxes by encouraging revenue generating activities such as shopping centers and industrial parks while discouraging revenue demanding uses such as lower-cost homes for families with children (regardless of race)
- ► *NIMBY*ism ("not in my backyard"): the use of zoning and other legal means to resist the location of unwanted uses, facilities, or activities within the municipality (e.g., regional incinerators or toxic waste disposal sites, prisons, mental health facilities, oil refineries, halfway houses, drug clinics)

Localism in zoning is not necessarily a bad idea. The local government is most familiar with the circumstances of particular land use decisions and has a valid interest in protecting the public health, safety, and welfare of its inhabitants. It is arguably the best-qualified level of government to plan and regulate the use of private land within its borders. But as exercised by countless local governments, many of them minuscule in territory and population, localism in zoning can and does obstruct broader regional or national objectives.

The essence of the issue is *which public* is implied in constitutional protection of the "general welfare": just the local public, or the larger publics of the region, state, nation, or globe (Clark 1985)? Richard F. Babcock (1966) was one of the first to criticize the conventional wisdom that zoning is necessarily constitutional if it is "in accordance with" a local comprehensive or master plan:

> The municipal plan may be just as arbitrary and irresponsible as the municipal zoning ordinance if that plan reflects no more than the municipality's arbitrary desires. If the plan ignores the responsibility of the municipality to its municipal neighbors and to landowners and taxpayers who happen to reside outside the municipal boundaries, and if that irresponsibility results in added burdens to other public agencies and to outsiders ... then a zoning ordinance bottomed on such a plan should be as vulnerable to attack as a zoning ordinance based on no municipal plan. (Babcock 1966, 123)

The "Metropolitan Factor"

The possibility of conflict between municipal and larger regional objectives in zoning policy was recognized as early as the *Euclid* decision. By the 1920s, suburbanization and metropolitan growth had been in progress for decades; Euclid, Ohio, itself was a suburb of Cleveland. Bettman's brief somewhat disingenuously extolled zoning as a tool for bringing order to the "modern American city" while ignoring that a "city" such as Euclid was only a fragment of its metropolitan region. The Supreme Court's opinion, however, included a portentous comment on this issue: "It is not meant ... to exclude the possibility of cases where the *general public interest would so far outweigh the interest of the municipality that the municipality would not be allowed to stand in the way* (272 U.S., at 390; emphasis added).

Bettman himself addressed the "metropolitan factor" in 1927 just after the *Euclid* decision: "Insofar as the fact of the location of a municipality within a metropolitan urban area has a bearing upon these factors of development trends, land values, and appropriateness of use, such fact has a relation to the social validity and, consequently, in the last analysis, to the constitutional validity of the zone plan" (quoted in Comey 1946, 55). The 1928 Standard City Planning Enabling Act that Bettman helped write included in the coverage of a municipal master plan: "any areas outside of its boundaries which, in the planning commission's judgment, bear relation to the planning of such municipality." In addition, the purpose of such plan was stated to be "the harmonious development of the municipality *and its environs*" (quoted in Beuscher, Wright, and Gitelman 1976, 272–73; emphasis added).

Many state planning acts today permit municipalities to exercise limited planning and regulatory control over unincorporated land within a specified distance (e.g., 2 miles outside their corporate boundaries). This practice, however, merely reflects the expectation that such land will eventually be annexed to that municipality. It is scarcely a mandate to consider external implications of local zoning policies, particularly to other municipalities and their inhabitants. In Massachusetts, where there is no unincorporated land, municipal planning boards are encouraged to consider the area around them (although zoning only applies within the unit of government adopting it):

> In the preparation of [a master] plan the commission shall make careful and comprehensive surveys and studies of *present conditions and future growth of the municipality and with due regard to its relations to neighboring territory*. (MGLA Chap. 41, Sec. 81; emphasis added)

Surprisingly few cases addressed the regional context of zoning before the 1960s. Two early landmark decisions involved the obscure New Jersey borough of Cresskill. *Duffcon Concrete Products, Inc. v. Borough of Cresskill*, 64 A.2d 347, 1949, upheld Cresskill's ban on industry in light of available sites in nearby jurisdictions. The court's opinion included what has been called "probably the best judicial statement on regional planning" (Haar 1963, 204):

> What may be the most appropriate use of any particular property depends not only on all the conditions, physical, economic and social, prevailing within the municipality and its needs, present and reasonably prospective, but also on the nature of the entire region in which the municipality is located and the use to which the land in that region has been or may be put most advantageously. (64 A.2d, at 349–50)

The principle was restated in *Borough of Cresskill v. Borough of Dumont*, 104 A.2d 441, 1954, in which three neighboring boroughs challenged Dumont's rezoning for a small shopping center a parcel that coincidentally abutted the boundaries of all three plaintiff jurisdictions. In response to Dumont's assertion that "the responsibility of a municipality for zoning halts at the municipal boundary lines," the court stated:

> Such a view might prevail where there are large undeveloped areas at the borders of two contiguous towns, but it cannot be tolerated where, as here, the area is built up and one cannot tell when one is passing from one borough to another. Knickerbocker Road

and Massachusetts Avenue are not Chinese Walls separating Dumont from the adjoining boroughs. At the very least Dumont owes a duty to hear any residents and taxpayers of adjoining municipalities who may be adversely affected by proposed zoning changes.... To do less would be to make a fetish out of invisible municipal boundary lines and a mockery of the principles of zoning. (104 A.2d, at 445–46)

Both Cresskill cases, however, were exclusionary, rather than inclusionary. One holds that a municipality may, and the other that it must, *exclude* land uses that conflict with the interests of adjoining areas. That was step one toward recognition of a metropolitan dimension to zoning. Step two, beginning in New Jersey and Pennsylvania in the 1960s, would assert that a municipality must also zone to *include* those land uses necessary to meet regional deficiencies.

Opening the Suburbs

The exclusion of apartments from single-family neighborhoods was approved by the U.S. Supreme Court in a widely cited dictum in *Euclid* that stated that

> the development of detached house sections is greatly retarded by the coming of apartment houses ... [and] *very often the apartment house is a mere parasite*, constructed in order to take advantage of the open spaces and attractive surroundings. Moreover, the coming of one apartment house is followed by others, ... until, finally, the residential character of the neighborhood and its desirability as a place of detached residences are utterly destroyed. Under these circumstances, apartment houses, which in a different environment would be ... highly desirable, come very near to being nuisances. (272 U.S., at 394–95; emphasis added)

If "municipality" is substituted for "neighborhood," this ruling would appear to legitimize zoning that excludes apartments and other multifamily housing from entire communities. This issue probably did not occur to the Court, nor did the plaintiff in *Euclid* seek to build apartments. The Court was merely airing its views on the bulky, nonsetback apartment buildings that were invading single-family neighborhoods in the 1920s (Williams 1975, Vol. 6, Plates 6 and 7).

As discussed in Chapter 6, the federal government beginning in the 1930s actually practiced segregation in the location, design, and occupancy of new homes built under national housing programs. Kenneth T. Jackson in *Crabgrass Frontier* (1985, Chap. 11) attributes the origins of socioeconomic "redlining" of neighborhoods and communities to the appraisal practices of the Home Owners Loan Corporation (HOLC) established by Congress in 1933. HOLC's mission was to provide federal mortgage assistance at low interest rates to forestall owner default on home loans during the Depression. Surveys of residential neighborhoods by the HOLC codified prevailing real estate assumptions regarding the effects of race, religion, and wealth on residential property values. Detailed "residential security maps" prepared by the HOLC for many cities and suburbs throughout the nation influenced the lending practices of financial institutions and thus became self-fulfilling prophecies. Both the Federal Housing Administration (FHA) and the Veterans Administration (VA) incorporated the HOLC's racist and economic assumptions regarding neighborhood quality and housing type into their home loan guarantee programs. The postwar middle-class, single-family suburb for whites only was the result (Jackson 1985, 206–9).

Municipal exclusion of apartments was to remain virtually unchallenged until the Pennsylvania Supreme Court addressed the issue in 1970. In *Appeal of Girsh*, 263 A.2d 395, a developer seeking to construct two luxury apartment buildings sued the township, which zoned none of its land area for apartments. In holding for the plaintiff, the court quoted extensively from its own prior decision that invalidated a 4-acre minimum lot requirement in *National Land and Investment Co. v. Easttown Twp. Board of Adjustment*, 215 A.2d 597, 1965, at 397:

> Zoning is a tool in the hands of governmental bodies which enables them to more effectively meet the demands of evolving and growing communities. It must not and cannot be used by those officials as an instrument by which they may shirk their responsibilities. Zoning is a means by which a governmental body can plan for the future.... *Zoning provisions may not be used ... to avoid the increased responsibilities and economic burdens which time and natural growth invariably bring*. (Emphasis added)

Girsh, *National Land*, and another 1970 Pennsylvania decision, *Appeal of Kit-Mar Builders* (269 A.2d 765, invalidating a 2- to 3-acre minimum lot size), reflected a recognition by the Pennsylvania court that the geographical functions and morphology of suburbs were changing. No longer simply bedrooms for central-city executives, suburbs were increasingly attracting new jobs, thereby creating a demand for a wider range of housing opportunities. According to these cases, suburbs that welcome new commercial investment may not use zoning to avoid the burden of accommodating new residents and building types. The concept of a "fair share" of regional housing needs was thereby introduced into Pennsylvania zoning law. A portentous footnote to the *Girsh* opinion stated:

As long as we allow zoning to be done community by community, it is intolerable to allow one municipality (or many municipalities) to close its doors at the expense of surrounding communities and the central city. (263 A.2d, at 399)

Girsh fired a warning shot across the bow of exclusionary-minded communities in Pennsylvania, and although not directly applicable to other states it bolstered similar challenges elsewhere through its constitutional rationale. *Girsh*, though, was vague as to what a municipality must do to avoid exclusionary challenges, and it did not involve lower-cost housing. Indeed, the luxury apartments proposed by Girsh were perhaps more akin to the "parasitic" apartments invading single-family districts of the *Euclid* era than to subsidized housing of the late 1960s. Also, the Pennsylvania cases including *Girsh* did not specify which geographic types of communities were "denying the future": developing suburbs, central cities with remaining vacant land, rural townships? How was each of these types to be judged as to the adequacy of its zoning?

The onerous task of applying a *Girsh*-type rationale to the specific circumstances of regional housing markets was assumed by the New Jersey Supreme Court in its unanimous 1975 decision in *Southern Burlington County NAACP v. Township of Mount Laurel*, 336 A.2d 713 ("*Mount Laurel I*"). As early as 1962, Justice Hall, who wrote this opinion, had signaled the judicial revolution to come in a famous dissent in *Vickers v. Township Committee of Gloucester Township*, 181 A.2d 129. In objection to the majority's upholding of a total ban on mobile homes by a large rural township, Hall had declared:

The import of the holding gives almost boundless freedom to developing municipalities to erect exclusionary walls on their boundaries, according to local whim or selfish desire, and to use the zoning power for aims beyond its legitimate purposes. (181 A.2d, at 140)

The conversion of his viewpoint from dissent in *Vickers* to majority opinion in *Mount Laurel* was influenced by research at Rutgers University (Williams and Norman 1974) that documented the practice of exclusionary zoning in four northeastern New Jersey counties. Of 474,000 acres of vacant buildable land in those counties, 99.5 percent was zoned for single-family use and no land was available for mobile homes. Minimum lots of 1 acre or more were required for 77 percent of suitable land. Only 0.5 percent of the four counties was zoned for multifamily dwellings. Although Mount Laurel is not within the counties included in that study, the Williams and Norman findings clearly influenced the court's perception in the case that arose there.

Mount Laurel, New Jersey, is a flat, sprawling, 22-square-mile township of mixed-developed and agricultural land uses within commuting distance of Camden and Philadelphia. Between 1960 and 1970, its population more than doubled to 11,221. Most of the vacant land remaining at the time of the lawsuit was zoned for industry. In the court's opinion:

> The record thoroughly substantiates the findings of the trial court that over the years Mount Laurel "has acted affirmatively to control development and to attract a selective type of growth" and that "through its zoning ordinances has exhibited economic discrimination in that the poor have been deprived of adequate housing, and has used federal, state, county, and local finances and resources solely for the betterment of middle- and upper-income persons."
>
> There cannot be the slightest doubt that the reason for this course of conduct has been to keep down local taxes on *property* ... and that the policy was carried out without regard for non-fiscal considerations with respect to *people*, either within or without its boundaries. (336 A.2d, at 723; Justice Hall's emphasis)

The opinion explicitly raises for perhaps the first time the constitutional issue as to "whose general welfare must be served or not violated in the field of land-use regulation" (336 A.2d, at 726). The court answered its own question by declaring that the constitutionality of zoning requires that in the case of "developing municipalities":

> Every such municipality must, by its land-use regulations, presumptively make realistically possible *an appropriate variety and choice of housing* ..." at least to the extent of the municipality's fair share of the present and prospective regional need therefor. (336 A.2d, at 724; emphasis added)

Thus it was no longer constitutional in New Jersey for communities in the "developing" category to use zoning to serve only their own parochial objectives. They were now required to accommodate a *fair share* of the regional demand for lower-cost housing. The court ordered Mount Laurel and other developing municipalities to revise their zoning accordingly.

The constitutional reverberations of *Mount Laurel* thundered across the land. Although a state court decision, it was widely regarded as a national precedent. An appeal to the U.S. Supreme Court was dismissed for "want of jurisdiction" (98 S. Ct. 18, 1976) because the Hall opinion was deliberately based on state, not federal, constitutional grounds (although both involve the same principles), thus avoiding possible reversal by the U.S. Supreme Court.

In New Jersey, the case provoked a deluge of lawsuits against other municipalities on *Mount Laurel* grounds (Babcock and Siemon 1985, Chap. 11). The Hall opinion had not provided detailed guidance as to the meaning of key concepts such as "region," "developing municipality," and "fair share." Nor was it clear whether a municipality must do more than merely rezone land for lower-cost housing and wait to see if a developer comes along. In a lengthy 1977 opinion in *Oakwood at Madison v. Twp. of Madison*, 371 A.2d 1192, the New Jersey Supreme Court advised trial courts to examine the substance of challenged zoning ordinances and to look for bona fide efforts to meet *Mount Laurel* obligations. It declined to specify a particular numerical approach:

> We do not regard it as mandatory for developing municipalities whose ordinances are challenged as exclusionary to devise specific formulae for estimating their precise fair share of the lower income housing needs of a specifically demarcated region.... Firstly, numerical housing goals are not realistically translatable into specific substantive changes in a zoning ordinance.... Secondly, the breadth of approach by the experts to the factors of the appropriate region and to the criteria for allocation of regional housing goals to municipal "sub-regions" is so great and the pertinent economic and sociological [and geographical] considerations so diverse as to preclude judicial dictation or acceptance of any one solution as authoritative. (371 A.2d, at 1200)

The court, however, could not long avoid the task of bringing order to the legal and planning chaos resulting from *Mount Laurel I*. In 1983, it responded in a 270-page unanimous decision in *Southern Burlington County NAACP v. Township of Mount Laurel*, 456 A.2d 390 ("*Mount Laurel II*"). It began by stating that the court was "more firmly committed to the original *Mount Laurel* doctrine than ever" but recognized a "need to put some steel into that doctrine." In a level of detail more characteristic of a legislature or the federal courts, the New Jersey court articulated a series of policies and standards for the resolution of the myriad *Mount Laurel* cases then clogging the state's lower courts. Among these rules were the following:

1. Every municipality must provide lower-cost housing opportunities for its resident poor.

2. The concept of "developing municipality" was replaced by "growth areas" designated in the State Development Guide Plan.

3. Municipalities must demonstrate that they are providing specific numbers of lower-cost housing units to meet their fair share of immediate and prospective regional needs. "Numberless" determinations based on provision for "some" lower-cost units will be insufficient.

4. A special panel of judges was to be designated to hear *Mount Laurel* cases.

5. Municipalities must do more than merely rezone land for lower-cost housing. Affirmative action such as subsidies, tax incentives, density bonuses, and mandatory set-asides of lower-cost units in new developments may be required.

The ball then passed from the judiciary to the legislative branch. The New Jersey legislature enacted a state Fair Housing Act (*N.J. Laws* 1985, Chap. 222) that codified the *Mount Laurel II* approach with some modification. The act established a Council on Affordable Housing that is empowered to determine housing regions and calculate regional housing needs and municipal fair-share allocations. The act also provides a mediation and review process to resolve *Mount Laurel* litigation, a procedure for "substantive certification" of municipal zoning ordinances, authority for "regional contribution agreements" among municipalities, amendment of the state zoning law to require a housing element, and a program of financial assistance to help municipalities meet their fair-share allocations (Rose 1987, 448–49). In another mammoth opinion, *Hills Development Co. v. Somerset County*, 510 A.2d 621, 1986 ("*Mount Laurel III*"), the New Jersey Supreme Court held the Fair Housing Act to be constitutional despite objections that it diluted the impact of the court's earlier decision.

The last word on the New Jersey approach to the problem of exclusionary zoning has certainly not been uttered. It will require many years and certainly more litigation before the results of this judicial/legislative revolution may be fairly evaluated. It is clear, however, that the *Mount Laurel* experience is consistent with the model set forth in Chapter 2 that legal innovation in land use control arises from the changing perception of those in authority that the existing legal rules are yielding undesirable consequences. *Mount Laurel* demonstrated the power of empirical research of a strongly geographical flavor to influence public decision making. The case also exemplified the role of states, and the courts within states, as catalysts for legal innovation that may subsequently spread to other jurisdictions.

The Inner City and The Courts: *Berman*, *Gautreaux*, Desperation

While housing activists labored to open the suburbs to affordable housing, existing stocks of older housing in the central cities continued to decline. Beginning in the 1930s and continuing in the 1950s and 1960s, efforts to save or replace urban housing followed two general approaches: urban renewal and public housing. Both approaches were to be challenged as ineffective and counterproductive.

As discussed in Chapter 5, the Urban Renewal Program under the Housing Acts of 1949 and 1954 provided federal funds to local cities to plan, acquire, clear, and redevelop designated areas of "urban blight." Nationally, the program cleared thousands of acres of inner-city tenements and displaced tens of thousands of low-income households and small businesses. Aside from areas rebuilt with public facilities such as schools and parks, most urban renewal land was sold at a subsidized price to private redevelopers to be reused according to the urban renewal plan. This practice resulted in the construction of new office buildings, hotels, shopping malls, and medium- to high-cost dwelling units in place of the former tenements. Some sites were never redeveloped, leaving pockets of litter-strewn vacant land in many inner-city neighborhoods to the present time.

Urban renewal was initially challenged judicially as an unconstitutional use of public eminent domain power to purchase private property and then sell it to another private party for redevelopment. The U.S. Supreme Court in *Berman v. Parker* (75 S. Ct. 98, 1954) held the concept of urban renewal to be a valid use of government power to promote the public welfare: "It is within the power of the legislature to determine that the community should be beautiful as well as healthy, spacious as well as clean, well-balanced as well as carefully patrolled" (75 S. Ct. 98, at 102). (See Chapter 9.) This ruling essentially settled the constitutionality of urban renewal; subsequent challenges were expressed largely through literature rather than litigation, most notably in critiques of urban renewal by William H. Whyte (1957), Jane Jacobs (1961), Herbert Gans (1962), Charles Abrams (1965), and Oscar Newman (1972). After a number of changes in policy, urban renewal gradually withered away as a federal program in the 1970s and 1980s, leaving inner cities pockmarked with vacant lots cleared but never redeveloped. (Among many substitute approaches was the Reagan administration concept of *enterprise zones*, designated areas of central cities where private investment would be encouraged through public incentives and relaxation of certain land use control and environmental regulations.)

Unlike urban renewal, which relied on private redevelopment of "blighted" property, public housing involves direct government construction, ownership, and management of housing for the very poor. Federal assistance to local public housing programs began with the Public Works Emergency Housing Corporation in 1933 (Feiss 1985, 176). In 1938, Congress established a slum clearance program for replacement of tenements with publicly owned housing projects. By 1970, this program, as modified in various later housing acts, had resulted in the construction of about 870,000 units of low-rent public housing. If fully occupied, these units could accommodate about three million people or 1.5 percent of the nation's population, compared with twenty-five million people (13 percent of the population) who were below the federally established poverty level in 1970 (Downs 1973, 48).

Although "shamefully small in relation to the nation's housing needs" (Fried 1971, 73), the actual picture was even worse. Many public housing units were uninhabitable by the mid-1960s due to inappropriate design, isolated location, occupancy policies, and lack of upkeep. Most were in large high-rise projects that lacked convenient access to jobs, decent schools, social services, and physical security for their inhabitants. Rife with crime and drug problems, much of the public housing built with federal assistance has been abandoned and razed or entirely remodeled (Figure 10-7).

Aside from poor design, a fundamental objection of civil rights advocates in the

FIGURE 10-7 Chicago public housing project, ca. 1970, the type of low-income minority ghetto that *Gautreaux* sought to abolish. *(Photo by author.)*

1960s to federal public housing policy was that local housing authorities generally located new projects (except elderly housing) in black ghetto areas, thus reinforcing patterns of racial segregation as most occupants of the projects were nonwhite. Of 19,011 units built by the Chicago Housing Authority (CHA) since 1950, all but 300 were in black neighborhoods. In 1966, this practice of racism in the location of public housing was challenged by the National Association for the Advancement of Colored People (NAACP) as a violation of the due process and equal protection clauses of the Fourteenth Amendment, as well as the Civil Rights Act of 1964, in suits against the CHA and the U.S. Department of Housing and Urban Development (HUD). Thus began one of the nation's longest and ultimately fruitless attempts to enlist the court system in the struggle for social justice in America's cities. The legal battle of *Gautreaux v. CHA* and its spin-offs would yield more than twenty federal court decisions over sixteen years, including one by the U.S. Supreme Court. In the end, *Gautreaux* would be characterized by two legal writers sympathetic to its goals as "Chicago's Tragedy" (Babcock and Siemon 1985, Chap. 9).

The tragedy lay in the collision of an activist and reform-minded federal district court justice (Richard Austin) with the entrenched political geography of racial and economic segregation prevalent in Chicago and elsewhere in the 1960s and 1970s (which substantially remains the case today). The effort seemed promising at first: Austin upheld the NAACP claim that the CHA and HUD were each violating the Fourteenth Amendment and the Civil Rights Act (*Gautreaux v. Chicago Housing Authority* 296 F. Supp. 907, 1969, and 304 F. Supp. 736, 1969). The court ordered the CHA to prepare a plan to construct seven hundred units of public housing in white areas of Chicago and thereafter at least four units of public housing in white neighborhoods for every additional unit built in black neighborhoods. The order, as written by the plaintiff's attorney, also placed limits on building height, density, and number of units at any site to avoid further high-rise "projects." Two years later, Austin's frustration at the city's defiance of the order was colorfully expressed:

> There have been occasions in the past when chief executives have stood at the schoolhouse and statehouse doors with their faces livid and with wattles flapping have defied the federal government to enforce its laws and decrees. It is an anomaly that the "law and order" chief executive of this City [Mayor Richard J. Daley] should challenge and defy federal law. (332 F.Supp 366, at 368)

The crux of the issue turned on the geographic scope of the proposed remedial plan. The court's order initially applied only to the city of Chicago, rallying

Chicago's white neighborhoods under the banner of "Neighbors Opposing the Chicago Housing Authority," or NO-CHA, to file their own lawsuit to prevent enforcement of the order. Daley denounced the policy of limiting new public housing to the city alone: "The city ... has voluntarily assumed a responsibility to provide housing for poor, low and moderate income families ... with 38,000 units of public housing now in our city [as compared with] fewer than 2,500 units in the Chicago metropolitan area outside the city" (quoted in Babcock and Siemon 1985, 165). Ironically agreeing with Daley for once, the plaintiffs petitioned the court to expand its order to include white suburbs. This proposal was rejected in 1973 by Austin, who sought to keep pressure on the city (363 F. Supp. 690), but his decision was reversed by the U.S. Court of Appeals for the Seventh Circuit (503 F.2d 930). Upon further appeal by the plaintiffs to the U.S. Supreme Court, the metropolitan-scale plan was upheld by the High Court, which declared, "The relevant geographic area for purposes of the respondents' housing options is the Chicago housing market, not the Chicago city limits" (*Hills v. Gautreaux*, 96 S. Ct. 1538, 1976, at 1542).

Even the Supreme Court of the United States failed to break down the barriers of local politics and racism in metropolitan Chicago. Despite further judicial efforts to produce action, the construction of public housing in Chicago essentially ended; by the mid-1970s, there were 10,000 families on the CHA waiting list. At this point, the *black community began to attack the plan* as denying them needed housing (Babcock and Siemon 1985, 172; emphasis added)! Some units were eventually constructed in white neighborhoods, but continued spreading out of the nonwhite population in Chicago gradually blurred the distinction, and public housing for poor families largely ceased to be built anywhere. Nor has Chicago become less segregated: in 1999, 80 percent of all African Americans in the city lived in only 20 of its 77 community areas. Two-thirds of Chicago's suburban African Americans resided in just 18 of 260 suburban municipalities (Commercial Club of Chicago 1999, 17).

Nationally, the entire concept of public housing, other than for the elderly, has been discredited, in part due to the well-intended but "tragic" *Gautreaux* case. The preferred approach since the 1970s has been "Section 8 federal housing vouchers" (derived from Section 8 of the Housing Act of 1937 as amended by the Housing and Community Development Act of 1974) issued to eligible households by HUD through state housing agencies. These vouchers allow recipients to rent housing within specified rental levels, with the tenants paying 30 percent of their income and the federal government paying the rest.

Affordable housing of any type, however, is a vanishing dream for millions of

Americans. Rising prices, demolition and gentrification, and suburban zoning barriers to rental developments have all worsened the housing shortage for lower-income households. In the late 1990s, about 15 million households were poor enough to qualify for federal housing assistance, but only 4.5 million of them received it. Of those, about one-third lived in public housing projects and two-thirds rented from private landlords with government housing assistance (Section 8 vouchers or other assistance). Some 5 million households not receiving assistance were spending more than half of their income on rent (Wright 2002, 289; DeParle 1996, 52). As of 2003, a federal freeze on new Section 8 vouchers has been imposed. In Massachusetts alone, 33,000 families—many of whom are stuck in temporary shelters, motel rooms at state expense, or are homeless—are waiting to receive them.

References

Abrams, C. 1965. *The City Is the Frontier*. New York: Harper and Row.

Babcock, R. F. 1966. *The Zoning Game*. Madison: University of Wisconsin Press.

Babcock, R. F., and C. L. Siemon. 1985. *Gautreaux*: Chicago's Tragedy. In *The Zoning Game Revisited*, ed. R. F. Babcock and C. L. Siemon, 159–182. Boston: Oelgeschlager, Gunn, and Hain.

Beuscher, J. H., R. R. Wright, and M. Gitelman. 1976. *Land Use: Cases and Materials*. St. Paul, MN: West.

Bosselman, F. P., D. Callies, and J. Banta. 1973. *The Taking Issue*. Washington, DC: U.S. Government Printing Office.

Boston Globe. 1992. Editorial: Private Rights, Public Benefit. March 5.

Clark, G. 1985. *Judges and the Cities*. Chicago: University of Chicago Press.

Comey, A. C., ed. 1946. *City and Regional Planning Papers of Alfred Bettman*. Cambridge, MA: Harvard University Press.

Commercial Club of Chicago. 1999. *Executive Summary: Chicago Metropolis 2020*. Chicago: Commercial Club.

Costonis, J. J. 1982. Law and Aesthetic: A Critique and a Reformulation of the Dilemmas. *Michigan Law Review* 80: 361–461.

Dawson, A. 1982. *Land-Use Planning and the Law*. Hadley, MA: Author.

Delafons, J. 1969. *Land-Use Controls in the United States*. 2nd ed. Cambridge, MA: MIT Press.

DeParle, J. 1996. Slamming the Door. *New York Times Magazine*, Oct. 20, 52–57.

Downs, A. 1973. *Opening Up the Suburbs: An Urban Strategy for America*. New Haven, CT: Yale University Press.

Dunham, A. 1959. Flood Control via the Police Power. *University of Pennsylvania Law Review* 107: 1098–1132.

Duerksen, C. J. 1985. Administering Historic Drafting and Ordinances. In *1985 Zoning and Planning Handbook,* ed. J. B. Gailen. New York: Clark Boardman.

Feiss, C. 1985. The Foundations of Federal Planning Assistance. *Journal of the American Planning Association* 51 (2): 175–84.

Fried, J. P. 1971. *Housing Crisis U.S.A.* New York: Praeger.

Freund, E. 1904. *The Police Power: Public Policy and Constitutional Law.* Chicago: Callaghan.

Gans, H. 1962. *The Urban Villagers.* New York: Free Press of Glencoe.

Haar, C. M. 1963. The Social Control of Urban Space. In *Cities and Space: The Future Use of Urban Land,* ed. L. Wingo Jr. Baltimore: Johns Hopkins University Press.

Hamann, R. G. 1986. *Constitutional Issues in Local Coastal Resource Protection.* Report no. 85. Gainesville: Florida Sea Grant College.

Jacobs, J. 1961. *The Death and Life of Great American Cities.* New York: Random House.

Jackson, K. T. 1985. *Crabgrass Frontier: The Suburbanization of the United States.* New York: Oxford University Press.

Kusler, J. A. 1983. *Our National Wetland Heritage: A Protection Guidebook.* Washington, DC: Environmental Law Institute.

Leopold, A. 1949/1966. *A Sand County Almanac.* New York: Oxford University Press.

Meltz, R., D. H. Merriam, and R. M. Frank. 1999. *The Takings Issue: Constitutional Limits on Land Use Control and Environmental Regulation.* Washington, DC: Island Press.

Mileti, D. S., ed. 1999. *Disasters by Design: A Reassessment of Natural Hazards in the U.S.* Washington, DC: Joseph Henry Press.

Newman, O. 1972. *Defensible Space: Crime Prevention through Urban Design.* New York: Macmillan.

Platt, R. H. 1992. An Eroding Base. *Environmental Forum* 9 (6): 10–15.

———. 1999. *Disasters and Democracy: The Politics of Extreme Natural Events.* Washington, DC: Island Press.

Rose, J. 1987. New Jersey Enacts a Fair Housing Law. In *1987 Zoning and Planning Law,* ed. N. J. Gordon. New York: Clark Boardman.

Sax, J. L. 1964. Takings and the Police Power. *Yale Law Journal* 74 (1): 36–76.

Stoddard, G. 1995. Coastal Policy Implications of Right to Rebuild Questions. *Shore and Beach,* Jan., 25–35.

Sugameli, G. P. 1993. Taking Issues in Light of *Lucas v. South Carolina Coastal Council*: A Decision Full of Sound and Fury Signifying Nothing. *Virginia Environmental Law Review* 12 (3): 439–504.

Teal, J., and M. Teal. 1969. *Life and Death of the Salt Marsh.* New York: Ballantine.

Tiner, R. W., Jr. 1984. *Wetlands of the United States: Current Status and Recent Trends.* Washington, DC: U.S. Government Printing Office.

Toll, S. 1969. *Zoned American.* New York: Grossman.

————. 1981. *Environmental Trends.* Washington, DC: U.S. Government Printing Office.

Warner, S. B. 1966. *Planning for a Nation of Cities.* Cambridge, MA: MIT Press.

White, G. F. 1964. *Choice of Adjustment to Floods.* Research Paper no. 93. Chicago: University of Chicago Department of Geography.

————. 1975. *Flood Hazard in the United States: A Research Assessment.* Boulder: University of Colorado Institute of Behavioral Studies.

Whyte, W. H. 1957. Are Cities Un-American? In *The Exploding Metropolis*, ed. Editors of *Fortune.* New York: Doubleday Anchor.

Williams, N., Jr. 1975. *American Planning Use: Land Use and the Police Power.* Chicago: Callaghan.

Williams, N., Jr., and T. Norman. 1974. Exclusionary Land Use Controls: The Case of North-Eastern New Jersey. In *Land Use Controls: Present Problems and Future Reform*, ed. D. Listokin. New Brunswick, NJ: Rutgers University Center for Urban Policy Research.

Wright, J. W., ed. 2002. *New York Times Almanac — 2003.* New York: Penguin.

PART IV

Beyond Localism: The Search for Broader Land Use Policies

CHAPTER 11 *Land Programs:*

Regional, State, Federal

> *In wildness is the preservation of the world.*
> —HENRY DAVID THOREAU, 1862/1937, 672
>
> *Drawing a line between the workshop and the temple was,*
> *and still is today, the most sensitive assignment for*
> *conservation planners.*
> —STEWART L. UDALL, 1963, 132

As discussed in earlier chapters, *privatism* and *localism* are the twin sacred cows of land use and development in the United States. Local oversight of the private market, however, has yielded often undesirable and occasionally disastrous results, including wasteful land use patterns, urban sprawl, degradation of air and water, loss of biodiversity, traffic congestion, decline of older cities and neighborhoods, lack of affordable housing, and natural disaster losses. This chapter reviews some strategies and roles of government at the regional, state, and federal levels that help offset some of the harmful results of a predominantly local land use control system. These strategies include intergovernmental programs for public parks and open space, regional and state land programs, and federal lands management for multiple uses.

Parks and other protected open lands provide many benefits to metropolitan America, including outdoor recreation, visual amenity, ecological habitat, water supply, flood mitigation, specialty farm products, and protection of historic and cultural landscapes. By far the largest public landholder is the federal government, but much land is also held for various purposes by states, counties, local governments, and special districts. Public lands are sometimes conveyed or leased for private uses, but this practice is limited in certain states like Massachusetts, Illinois, and Wisconsin that adhere to the *public trust doctrine*, a legal tradition derived from England under which certain lands and water resources are held "in trust for the people" (Archer et al. 1994).

Accomplishing regional open-space plans is not simple. Each tract or cluster of tracts requires an individual funding strategy, often involving more than one unit or level of government. "Horizontal" agreements are needed between neighboring governments that share jurisdiction over a specific resource area. "Vertical" coordination is essential among local, regional, state, and federal levels regarding the sharing of costs of acquisition and management. The private land market does not stand still, waiting for government to assemble funds. To rescue key parcels of open land from the bulldozer, intervention by a private conservation organization or land trust may be needed. Today, thousands of regional and local land trusts, often backed by endowments or bank lines of credit, help to save open land that they either hold indefinitely or resell to a public land agency. (For further information, see the Land Trust Alliance's Web site, www.lta.org.)

Regionalism and Partnerships

Regional Plans

Given the fragmented political geography of U.S. metropolitan areas, intergovernmental cooperation is needed to acquire and manage land and provide facilities that lie within or serve multiple political units. And increasingly, nongovernmental organizations (NGOs) at the national or regional level play critical roles in the planning and acquisition of urban open spaces. Regional plans that include open-space elements may be prepared by a state planning office, a regional planning agency, a council of governments, or civic or environmental NGOs. The landmark *1909 Plan of Chicago* by Daniel Burnham ("Make no little plans") and Edward Bennett was sponsored by the Commercial Club of Chicago. Among other elements, the *Plan of Chicago* proposed a network of regional forest preserves protecting stream corridors and wooded lands, which has largely been accomplished by the Forest Preserve District of Cook County and its counterparts in neighboring counties (Figure 11-1). The Commercial Club today is coordinating a new study called *Chicago Metropolis 2020* (www.chicagometropolis2020.org).

Another showcase of privately sponsored regional planning is the Regional Plan Association (RPA), which serves the tri-state New York metropolitan region. A

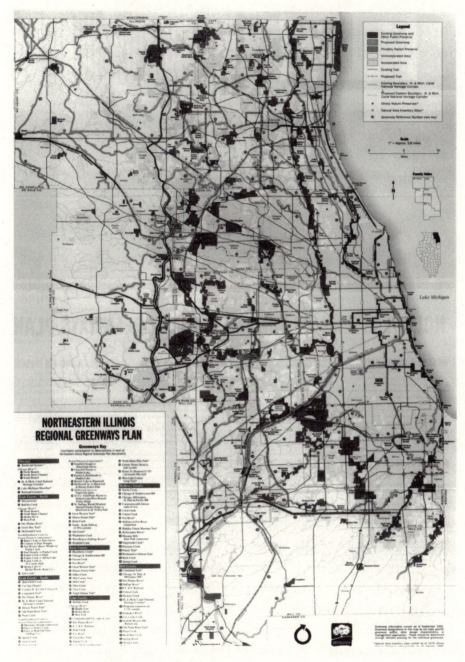

FIGURE 11-1 Northeastern Illinois Regional Greenways Plan, 1995.
(Source: Northeastern Illinois Planning Commission.)

product of progressive business and civic leadership, RPA has published three major regional plans for the New York area in 1929, 1968, and 1996. Each has addressed a broad range of regional issues, including transportation, economic development, education, health, and public parks and greenspaces. Its latest plan, *A Region at Risk* (Yaro and Hiss 1996), proposes a twenty-five-year, $75 billion program to invest in infrastructure, the environment, education, and cities (Yaro 2000, 62). A central element of *A Region at Risk* is the *Regional Greensward Plan*, which envisions a vast network of existing and proposed open spaces extending from the Litchfield Hills in northwestern Connecticut to the Pinelands in southern New Jersey (www.rpa.org).

Elsewhere, new regional plans are appearing in places not usually associated with public support for planning and environmental protection. Riverside County, California, directly east of Los Angeles, gained 375,000 people during the 1990s, a decadal growth rate of 32 percent, one of the fastest in the United States. The Riverside–San Bernardino primary metropolitan statistical area gained over 666,000 people or 25.7 percent during the same period and was ranked first in the nation in urban sprawl by a recent study by Smart Growth America (Ewing, Pendall, and Chen 2003). Riverside County is a semiarid region of scrub-sage and high desert where water is scarce and the variety of endangered species is remarkable (Thomas 2003). It is also a region of ethnic and cultural diversity: during the 1990s, the non-Hispanic white population of the region changed from 85 percent to 51 percent as Hispanic families moved into the county in search of affordable housing. In the face of ill-coordinated development of housing and infrastructure, public and private stakeholders led by former county commissioner Tom Mullins spent four years preparing the *Riverside County Integrated Plan* (RCIP) (www.rcip.org). The RCIP addresses the full spectrum of development issues facing the county, including housing, employment, transportation, education, water resources, environmental protection, and endangered species' habitat protection. Like most regional plans, it is advisory; its impact on the county's future growth and evolution remains to be seen.

Some important regional plans are based on *urban watersheds* that overlap multiple cities, counties, and sometimes states. Houston's principal drainage system is Buffalo Bayou, a muddy and flood-prone stream that meanders past wealthy and poor neighborhoods before flowing through downtown Houston and an industrial corridor to its mouth at the Houston Ship Channel. Houston's early settlement and growth were closely tied to Buffalo Bayou. Beginning in the 1950s, portions of the bayou were channelized and two upstream dams and reservoirs were constructed to control rising levels of downstream flood damage. Efforts by the Bayou Preservation Association beginning in the 1970s helped persuade the county flood control district and the Army Corps of Engineers to cease further structural flood control projects in favor of floodplain land acquisition and the use of vegetation and landscape techniques ("bioengineering") to stabilize stream banks. In 2002, the *Master Plan for Buffalo Bayou and Beyond* was released jointly by the Buffalo Bayou Partnership, the city of Houston, Harris County, and the Harris County Flood Control District (available at www.bayoupreservation.org). The goals of the master plan for Buffalo Bayou include the following:

- ▸ Create and develop new areas for parkland
- ▸ Define key sites for future urban development near the bayou
- ▸ Reduce potential for flooding
- ▸ Build a network of trails
- ▸ Reclaim former industrial sites and remediate damaged areas (*brownfields*)
- ▸ Develop landscaping along the bayou

Although most regional plans apply to multiple jurisdictions, there are cases where a "regional plan" applies to a specific subarea of one city. A significant case in point is the *Calumet Area Land Use Plan* developed by the city of Chicago for the redevelopment of a vast area surrounding Lake Calumet on the city's far south side (Figure 11-2). The Lake Calumet region in its presettlement state has been described as "flat, grassy, and wet. It varied from stretches of relatively dry prairies on slight ridges, to sedge meadows and marshes in low swales, to the open water of the lakes and seasonal ponds" (Riddell 2001, 1). Lake Calumet itself was a shallow water body of several thousand acres connected to Lake Michigan by a meandering creek. In the mid-nineteenth century, the Calumet area was crisscrossed by railroads connecting Chicago to the South and East. That was followed by dredging and channelizing Lake Calumet and its associated streams to accommodate deep-draft lake vessels. With rail, navigation, and, later, highway access immediately at hand, the region became the heavy industrial zone for Chicago by the mid-twentieth century with grain elevators and steel, automobile assembly, oil, chemical, and building material plants lining the ever-shrinking lake and the waterways connected to it. Calumet Lake was gradually reduced in size by filling for industrial sites and later by solid waste landfills.

In the 1990s, global restructuring forced many Calumet industrial operations to close, leaving a wasteland of abandoned plants and industrial brownfields lying amid some 3,000 acres of surviving wetlands. The area is surrounded by distressed

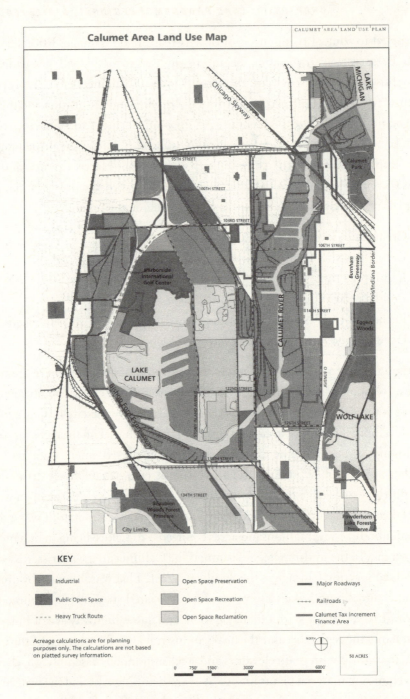

Calumet Area Land Use Map

KEY

- Industrial
- Public Open Space
- Heavy Truck Route
- Open Space Preservation
- Open Space Recreation
- Open Space Reclamation
- Major Roadways
- Railroads
- Calumet Tax Increment Finance Area

Acreage calculations are for planning purposes only. The calculations are not based on platted survey information.

0   750'   1500'   3000'   6000'

50 ACRES

FIGURE 11-2 Calumet Area Land Use Map, 2003. *(Source: City of Chicago Department of Planning and Development.)*

working-class neighborhoods of varied socioeconomic character. Proposals to reclaim the region for a world's fair site and alternatively for an airport were shelved, and by the end of the 1990s, the Calumet area faced an uncertain future. In 1999, the city launched a new comprehensive planning initiative for the Calumet area with support from the city and its mayor, Richard M. Daley, and a $200,000 sustainable development challenge grant from the federal Environmental Protection Agency (Riddell 2001, 11). Like the master plan for Buffalo Bayou, the Calumet plan is intended to promote both economic redevelopment and environmental protection. Specifically, its goals are as follows:

▸ To improve quality of life in the Calumet area and surrounding communities
▸ To retain and enhance existing businesses and industries within the Calumet area
▸ To attract new industrial and business development, and create new job opportunities
▸ To protect and enhance wetland and natural areas within the Calumet area and improve habitat for rare and endangered species

To advance the redevelopment objectives of the plan, a *tax increment financing* (TIF) district covering 12,000 acres was established by the city council in 2000. The purpose of the TIF district is to allow the city to issue revenue bonds to pay for infrastructure improvements and loans to developers. The bonds would be repayable through expected increases from property tax receipts as the area redevelops. The open-space elements of the plan involve certain sites already in public ownership and others to be protected through public or private acquisition. Already, existing wetland preserves are being used by local schools for environmental education under a program coordinated by Chicago Wilderness, a network of environmental programs headed by three pillars of conservation in Chicago: the Field Museum of Natural History, the Brookfield Zoo, and The Nature Conservancy.

Regional Services and Tax Sharing

Not every outgrowth of regionalism takes the form of regional plans. Certain states and metropolitan areas have pioneered a variety of programs under which various functions are transferred from local governments to a regional entity created by state law. Regional special districts and authorities are widely used to construct and operate large-scale public services such as water supply and sewage treatment, public transportation, airports, flood control and drainage, and regional parks and conservation lands. As one example among many, the water supply and sewage systems serving Boston, Massachusetts, were transferred to regional districts in the 1890s to permit nearby suburbs to benefit from these services without having to be annexed to Boston. In 1919, the metropolitan water, sewer, and parks districts were combined into the Metropolitan District Commission, a state agency. In 1985, the water and sewage treatment services were transferred to the new Massachusetts Water Resources Authority (MWRA), whose immediate charge was to build a new sewage treatment plant to relieve pollution of Boston Harbor. Today, the MWRA provides water and sewage treatment to some fifty Boston-area cities and towns with a total population of about 2.5 million. (See Chapter 12 for further discussion of the MWRA's watershed management program.)

BOX 11-1 *The Chicago Wilderness Network
(www.chicagowilderness.org)*

The Chicago Wilderness (CW) network was established in the mid-1990s to promote regional biodiversity and environmental education. CW is an open-access, public-private consortium of regional stakeholders concerned with the protection, restoration, and management of habitat sites as well as research and education on biodiversity. Although CW does not take positions per se on biodiversity issues, its value lies in facilitating collaborative efforts to analyze issues and formulate recommendations for public policy by subgroups of member organizations organized as task forces.

CW currently includes about 160 member governmental agencies, nongovernmental organizations, educational institutions, and business corporations.

Its geographic reach loosely includes the six Illinois counties of the Chicago Metropolitan Statistical Area, Kenosha County in Wisconsin, and Lake and Porter counties in Indiana. Office space and staff resources are provided by three Chicago area organizations: the Field Museum of Natural History, the Brookfield Zoo, and The Nature Conservancy Chicago Chapter. Startup funding was provided by grants from the U.S. Environmental Protection Agency, the U.S. Forest Service, and the U.S. Fish and Wildlife Service for research on biodiversity.

Chicago Wilderness, also known as the Chicago Region Biodiversity Council, is "governed" by three leadership entities established under its Policies and Procedures: (1) an executive council comprising

Elsewhere, a variety of "flavors" of regional service authorities and programs have evolved in many metropolitan areas. The Twin Cities Metropolitan Council serving Minneapolis, St. Paul, and the seven-county region surrounding them was established in the mid-1970s to assume management of regional sewage collection and treatment, regional parks, highways, public transit, and airports. Under the Metropolitan Land Planning Act of 1975, the council was charged with assisting local governments in its region in the preparation of local land use plans with functional elements parallel with its regional plans. In 1974, the Fiscal Disparities Act launched the nation's first experiment with sharing of property tax revenue between "have" and "have-not" local governments. The law allocates 40 percent of the growth in property tax revenues from commercial industrial development to a metropolitan tax base pool. The funds in the pool are redistributed among communities based on their commercial tax capacity. Thus communities attracting new industrial parks and shopping malls are obliged to share a portion of

the above three organizations plus addition members that provide resources to CW, (2) a steering committee that includes representation of specified sectors and classes of governments and private interest groups, and (3) a coordinating group established by the steering committee that holds monthly meetings open to all CW members. The coordinating group (1) implements steering committee decisions, (2) oversees the CW work plan, (3) sets agendas for meetings, and (4) represents CW at professional meetings.

CW is not incorporated and does not have tax-exempt status so that it does not compete with its member organizations for funding. The work of CW is carried out through meetings of members, mission-specific task forces, a proposals committee, and a nominating committee. The CW corporate council includes participating business firms. CW supports ecological restoration activities through a network of citizen volunteers.

In its first few years, CW has become a respected voice for "ecological citizenship" in the Chicago region. In addition to its Web site, it has published the *Atlas of Biodiversity of the Chicago Region*, which describes the major ecosystems and selected species with text and graphics directed to the general public. CW coordinates environmental education programs for inner-city and suburban school systems and is helping protect and restore habitat sites in the Chicago region. It conducts research on biodiversity through various task forces and subgroups. It participates in regional planning initiatives such as the Chicago Regional Transportation Plan and the Green Infrastructure Regional Mapping Project, and it provides speakers for conferences in the region and around the country.

their tax revenue gains with the central cities and less fortunate suburbs (Orfield 1997).

In the Atlanta region, sprawl and associated traffic congestion and air pollution increased dramatically during the 1990s. Most development and job creation occurred in the northern suburbs, whereas other communities and the city itself experienced the environmental burdens of sprawl without the financial benefits (Bullard, Johnson, and Torres 2000). In 1999, newly elected Governor Roy Barnes persuaded the legislature to create the Georgia Regional Transportation Authority (GRTA). According to Bullard and colleagues:

> The GRTA board has the authority to coordinate projects in the metro region; fund and operate a new mass transit system and coordinate existing systems; withhold state funding to counties to motivate participation in regional transportation; veto regional development and transportation projects; provide loans or construction agreements to industries that contribute to lowering air emissions; and identify nonregional air pollution sources impacting the region and offer assistance or bring them under authority auspices. (Ibid., 20)

Greenways

As long ago as Frederick Law Olmsted's 1880s "Emerald Necklace" plan for the Boston parks system, urban designers have proposed systems of linked open spaces that today are referred to as "greenways." Greenways are corridors of largely natural open land or connected systems of open spaces and parks that provide environmental, recreational, flood reduction, and other benefits. *National Geographic* has identified "four E's" served by greenways: (1) environment, (2) ecology, (3) education, and (4) exercise (Grove 1990). To these four, landscape architect Annaliese Bischoff (1995) adds (5) "expression," referring to the role of greenways as corridors of art, communication, and other forms of cultural expression.

Hundreds of greenways have been established or are under development throughout metropolitan America (Little 1990). Most are oriented to linear physical features such as stream valleys, shorelines, ridgelines, or abandoned rail rights-of-way. Greenways typically cross political boundaries and thus require extensive intergovernmental coordination. Case studies by the National Park Service (1991) examined experience with organizing metropolitan greenway projects in Massachusetts, Colorado, California, Florida, Oklahoma, and Georgia. The national Rails to Trails Conservancy (www.railtrails.org) has overseen the creation of several thousand miles of improved trails for cycling and pedestrian use throughout the United States.

State Lands and Planning Programs

States are the sovereign units of the United States. The federal government gained its existence and authority through the delegation of certain powers by the original thirteen states in the Constitution of 1787. Also, municipalities and special districts are creatures of the states, exercising powers expressly or implicitly delegated to them by state law. Having divested some of their powers upward to the federal level and others downward to municipalities, what functions do states retain to exercise on their own?

It is difficult to generalize about state land use programs because they differ widely. Although similar in their legal status and potential capabilities, states have evolved differently in their land use policies and efforts, as articulated in their respective constitutions, legislation, administrative regulations, executive orders, and court decisions. It is a strength of the federalist system of the United States that states are free, within the bounds of the U.S. Constitution, to develop their individual approaches to land use problems according to their respective physical and fiscal resources, politics, and perceived needs. For example, certain "high-amenity" states such as Hawaii, Oregon, Vermont, Maine, and Florida during the 1960s and 1970s launched ambitious state land use management programs, while more "resource-dominated" states such as Texas, Ohio, West Virginia, and Colorado did not (DeGrove 1984).

Certain fundamental roles of state government may be identified which are performed with differing levels of zeal and effectiveness in the fifty states (parallel with equivalent functions of the federal government, discussed later):

- Land ownership and management
- Funding of state and local public infrastructure, including highways, water and sewer systems, state colleges, and emergency management facilities
- Regulation of certain private land and water activities such as encroachment on wetlands and waterways, waste facility siting and design, and in some states any large-scale development
- Planning and technical assistance
- Taxation

States often serve as agents for or partners with the federal government. Many federal programs, such as the Land and Water Conservation Fund and the Coastal Zone Management Program, rely on state initiative to promulgate national policies and goals and to utilize federal funds. States may also, however, act autonomously to influence the use of land and patterns of metropolitan development within their jurisdictions. Or they may sit back and let the federal and local levels of government exercise their respective powers with little state input.

State Parks

Before 1970, practically the only land-management function of most states was the operation of state parks and recreation areas. One of the earliest and largest state facilities was the Adirondack State Forest Preserve established in New York State in 1885 (Nash 1982, 119). During the 1930s, many state parks were added, expanded, and improved with federal assistance. Much of the infrastructure of older state parks—including roads, trails, restrooms, and recreation fields—dates back to the Civilian Conservation Corps and other public works programs of that era.

Assisted by the federal Land and Water Conservation Fund and state-level bond issues, many states have substantially enlarged and improved their park systems in recent decades. In 2001, the fifty state park systems collectively managed about 13 million acres, up from 10 million in 1980. Although state parks have about one-sixth of the total acreage of the National Park System (13 million acres state versus 79 million federal), they have over twice as many visitor "user-days" per year as the national park system (701 million state versus 279 million federal). State parks tend to be smaller, more widely distributed, and more accessible to metropolitan populations than national parks.

Many states have incorporated new kinds of facilities and administrative concepts into their open-space preservation programs, including historic sites, scenic and wild rivers, trail corridors, and greenways along metropolitan streams. Massachusetts has pioneered the concept of the "heritage park" to combine the functions of urban renewal, cultural preservation, and recreation in several old mill cities such as Lowell, Holyoke, and North Adams. In 1971, New York established an Adirondack State Park Agency to plan and control land use for the 6-million-acre Adirondack Park region surrounding the actual state-owned forest reserve. Conservation easements have been used in some places to protect parks from visual encroachment. A number of states have also asserted ownership rights over the beds of rivers, lakes, and coastal waters under the *public trust doctrine* (Archer et al. 1994).

Sometimes, states have served as the cornerstone of cooperative intergovernmental approaches to land preservation. Thorn Creek Woods in the south suburbs of Chicago was saved from development in the early 1970s through public purchase by the state of Illinois, the Will County Forest Preserve District, two incorporated villages, and a new state university. None of these public entities could geographically or fiscally preserve the entire woods on its own. The entire joint acquisition was facilitated by federal grants under the Department of Housing and Urban Development's Open Space and New Communities programs, amounting to 70 percent of the total costs. Thorn Creek Woods State Park is today managed by the state under cooperative agreements with the other landholding entities.

State Land Use Planning

Between 1965 and the 1980s, many states adopted new laws to assert stronger state-level review and permitting of new development, a function traditionally left to local governments. This surge of state activism was documented and encouraged by two key studies by land use lawyers: *The Quiet Revolution in State Land Use Planning* (Bosselman and Callies 1971) and *The Use of Land* (Reilly 1973). According to the former report:

> This country is in the midst of a revolution in the way we regulate the use of our land. It is a peaceful revolution, conducted entirely within the law. It is a quiet revolution, and its supporters include both conservatives and liberals. It is a disorganized revolution, with no central cadre of leaders, but it is a revolution nonetheless.
>
> The "ancien regime" being overthrown is the feudal system under which the entire pattern of land development has been controlled by thousands of individual local governments, each seeking to maximize its tax base and minimize its social problems, and caring less what happens to all the others.
>
> The tools of the revolution are new laws taking a wide variety of forms but each sharing a common theme—the need to provide some degree of state or regional participation in the major decisions that affect the use of our increasingly limited supply of land. (Bosselman and Callies 1971, 1)

One product of the "quiet revolution" movement, in parallel with the original planning and zoning movement in the 1920s, was the development of a new Model Land Development Code by the American Law Institute (1975) to guide states in updating their land use laws. Its most controversial element was article 7, which proposed state review and possible override of local zoning decisions concerning (1) areas of particular concern, (2) large-scale developments, and (3) developments of regional benefit. In the first two categories, the role of the state was likely to be more protective (less permissive) than local government. The third category raised the possibility of state veto of local zoning that prohibited a locally unwanted but regionally needed facility (e.g., a power plant, prison, incinerator, or wastewater treatment facility). The code was not entirely adopted anywhere. A few states (e.g., Vermont, Maine, Oregon, and Florida) adopted state land planning laws based in spirit on article 7. It served also as the inspiration for the state management requirements of the federal Coastal Zone Management Act of 1972, discussed in Chapter 12.

The momentum of the quiet revolution diminished in the late 1970s as development pressures abated due to high interest rates and as energy issues dominated public attention. The state programs that it inspired, however, remained in place and in several instances were expanded (Popper 1988).

The relative scarcity of comprehensive state planning laws has fostered the view among proponents of centralization that the quiet revolution fizzled out prematurely. The Reagan administration, however, believed that land use was overregulated and advocated regulation-free "enterprise zones" to assist private investment. Although the 1990s were not kind to proponents of land use planning at any level of government, many states, particularly on the East and West Coasts, continued to "quietly" refine their land use programs under the rubric of growth management, now termed *smart growth,* as discussed in Chapter 9 (Figure 11-3).

> Growth management in the 1980s and 1990s has emerged as a powerful concept that can reorder relations among states, regions, localities, and private interests in important ways. State growth management systems such as those long in place in Oregon and Florida and new systems in Washington and Maryland have introduced important new concepts and given fresh meaning to traditional planning principles such as consistency, concurrency, and compact urban form. (DeGrove 1997, 246)

Special Area State Programs

The 1971 *Quiet Revolution* report studied several state programs focused on specific geographic areas, for example:

- San Francisco Bay Conservation and Development Commission (California)
- Adirondack State Park Agency (New York)
- Twin Cities Metropolitan Council (Minnesota)
- Tahoe Regional Planning Agency (California and Nevada)
- Hackensack Meadowland Development Commission (New Jersey)

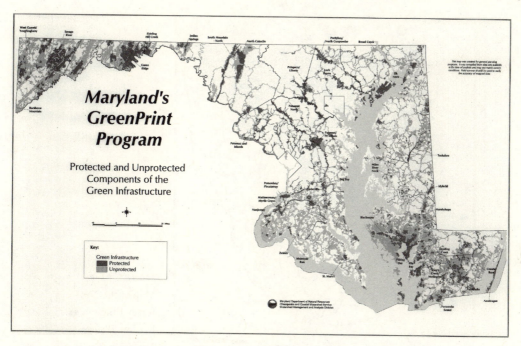

FIGURE 11-3 Map of Maryland's GreenPrint Program.
(Source: Gillham 2002, Fig. 14.7.)

Each of these programs is alive and apparently well in the early 2000s. Except for the Twin Cities Metro Council, which does not regulate land use, each has survived political and legal challenges to its land-management functions. They each have influenced to some degree the pattern of development in their respective regions.

The New Jersey Pinelands Commission, which appeared in the late 1970s, provides another example of a state program, initiated with some federal nudging, that is achieving a remarkable degree of control over the use of sensitive lands. The Pinelands or "Pine Barrens" covers about 1 million acres of sandy, wooded terrain in southern New Jersey, of which about two-thirds is privately owned (Figure 11-4). The region is underlain by a vast aquifer estimated to hold some 17 trillion gallons of freshwater. Cranberry and blueberry cultivation are prominent agricultural activities in portions of the region. The Pinelands was vividly portrayed in John McPhee's *The Pine Barrens* (1968), which helped stimulate public support for conserving its natural and cultural heritage. It is an excellent example of what has been termed a *bioregion*, namely a geographic area with a definable identity or "sense of place" based on its distinctive blend of physical, ecological, and human characteristics (Foster 2002).

FIGURE 11-4
Map of the New
Jersey Pinelands
Region. *(Source:*
New Jersey Pinelands
Commission.)

New Jersey Pinelands

Lying between Philadelphia and the coast, the Pinelands attracted growing interest from real estate developers beginning in the 1970s. With jurisdiction over the region divided among seven counties and fifty-five towns and villages, efforts to protect its natural resources at the local level would have been fruitless. Instead, preservationists, armed with McPhee's book and great persistence, achieved a unique three-fold designation of the Pinelands region as (1) a national reserve, (2) an international biosphere reserve, and, most important, (3) a special state planning region administered by the New Jersey Pinelands Commission.

At the request of New Jersey legislators, Congress designated some 1.1 million acres of the Pinelands as the first "national reserve" (in Section 502 of the National Parks and Recreation Act of 1978). It authorized $26 million for land acquisition and planning by the state and localities if the state established a special planning commission for the area. In response, New Jersey's Governor Brendon Byrne by executive order established the state-level Pinelands Commission and banned new development in the region until a comprehensive plan and land use regulations were prepared. These powers were confirmed in the New Jersey Pinelands Act of

1979 despite some local opposition (Babcock and Siemon 1985, Chap. 8). (The state law applied to an area of 933,000 acres, slightly smaller than the national reserve.)

The Pinelands Comprehensive Management Plan, developed under the 1979 state law, designated a central *preservation area* of 368,000 acres and a surrounding *protection area* of 565,000 acres. The plan further divided the Pinelands into nine land use zones based on the physical and human characteristics of each area. The preservation area, also known as the "heart of the pines," is described by the commission as follows:

> Here are the unique forests of pygmy pines and oaks known as the East and West Plains. The ruins of long-deserted towns and factories poke through the underbrush amidst a maze of twisting, barely passable sand roads. The solemn gloom of cedar swamps gives way to the flowery brilliance of inland marshes and bogs. (Pinelands Commission 1989, 4)

Within this core area, no new residential development was permitted, with the exception that "Pineys"—long-term inhabitants of the area—may construct a new home under certain conditions. The remainder of the Pinelands—the "protection area"—was divided into (1) forest areas, (2) agricultural protection areas, (3) regional growth areas, and (4) rural development areas. Additional areas are designated as Pinelands towns and villages and for military purposes.

To avoid takings issue challenges, the plan provided for *transfer of development rights* from the inner restricted areas to peripheral locations where growth is allowed. It was estimated that as many as 24,000 units of housing could be built in the growth areas through transfers of credits from restricted areas of the Pinelands, in addition to 86,000 units otherwise permitted to be built in the growth areas. Table 11-1 lists some other landscapes and bioregions whose protection has been stimulated by writers, artists, and poets.

Special-Issue State Programs

In addition to *special-area* programs, most states have developed *special-issue* land use management programs. These programs include laws concerning farmland preservation, critical environmental areas, coastal zone management, energy conservation, septic systems, wetland and floodplains, housing, large-scale facilities, and waste management. Such issue-focused laws apply statewide in tandem with local planning and zoning decisions, which may occasionally be overruled.

Some state land use laws consider a broad range of "special issues" in reviewing proposals for new development For instance, under Vermont's Act 250, certain types of development are scrutinized by state planning agencies with respect to water supply, soil erosion, highway congestion, schools, governmental services, aesthetics, and historic preservation, among other matters (Healy and Rosenberg 1979, 45). Florida's State and Regional Planning Act of 1984 established a statewide planning framework keyed to a legislatively adopted state comprehensive plan. The plan is "a relatively concise statement of goals and policies for 25 major state issues ranging from problems of the elderly to protection of property rights to transportation issues" (DeGrove and Stroud 1987, 7).

Far more numerous are state laws that address land use issues selectively rather than comprehensively. All fifty states have statutes of this nature, which are most readily found and compared in the Bureau of National Affairs *Environmental Law Reporter*. Many such laws have been adopted in response to or in imitation of federal legislation, as, for instance, state environmental impact laws modeled on the National Environmental Policy Act. Others have been passed in response to a severe state problem or at the insistence of a strong governor, as with Maryland's

TABLE 11-1 *THE ARTS AND LANDSCAPE PROTECTION*

ARTISTS, POETS, WRITERS	LANDSCAPE	APPROXIMATE DATE
William Wordsworth	English Lake District	Early nineteenth century
William Cullen Bryant, Andrew Jackson Downing	Central Park (New York City), Prospect Park (Brooklyn)	1840s–1880s
Nathaniel Hawthorne, Ralph Waldo Emerson, William Cullen Bryant	Berkshires (western Massachusetts)	Nineteenth–twentieth centuries
"The Hudson River School" (Thomas Cole, Frederic Church, Albert Bierstadt, etc.)	Adirondack Forest Reserve, Catskills, Yosemite, etc.	1860s–1890s
Henry David Thoreau, Henry Beston, Edward Hopper	Cape Cod National Seashore	1850s–1960s
Carl Sandburg, Jens Jensen, various Chicago artists	Indiana Dunes National Lakeshore	1920s–1960s
Marjorie Stoneham Douglas	Everglades National Park	1940s–1980s
Wallace Stegner	Dinosaur National Monument	1960s
John McPhee	New Jersey Pine Barrens	1960s–1970s
Pete Seeger	Hudson River ·	1960s–present

SOURCE: Compiled by Charles E. Little and Rutherford H. Platt, Placitas, New Mexico, October 2002.

statewide Smart Growth and Neighborhood Conservation Act of 1997, which was promoted by former Governor Parris Glendening. Many state special-issue programs such as agricultural land protection, coastal zone and floodplain management, floodplain, and surface water and groundwater quality have been stimulated by federal laws on these topics, as discussed in Chapter 12.

The Federal Lands: Policies in Conflict

The federal government of the United States owns outright about 730 million acres, or about one-third of the nation's total land and water area (Figure 11-5). This vast expanse, about the size of India, is unevenly distributed spatially. Alaska alone accounts for about 313 million acres; the balance is predominantly located in the lightly settled mountain and arid regions of the western states. Several states are substantially owned by the federal government: Alaska (96 percent), Nevada (86 percent), Utah (66 percent), Idaho (63 percent), and Oregon (52 percent). Federal ownership east of the Rocky Mountains is much sparser, although most land west of the Appalachians was at one time federally owned. The rest of this

Percent of Land in Federal Ownership, 1997

Percent

■ 95 or more
11.9% of change
2.3% of watersheds

50 to 95
52.7% of change
13.9% of watersheds

5 to 50
32.6% of change
27.9% of watersheds

Less than 5
2.8% of change
55.9% of watersheds

No data

Approximately 402 million acres or 21% of the total land area is Federally owned (excluding Alaska).

FIGURE 11-5 Map of federal lands of the United States. *(Source: Gillham 2002, Fig. 5.3.)*

chapter is devoted to a somewhat expansive discussion of the federal lands; although this coverage departs from the urban/metropolitan focus of the book overall, it is a rich chapter of U.S. history not to be omitted. Table 11-2 lists some of the major laws and events punctuating the history of federal land policies.

Origins of the Public Domain

The vast majority of federal lands, past and present, belong to what is known as the *public domain*. Historically, these lands came into federal ownership through transfers by states, purchases from foreign nations, and in one case by assimilation of an independent republic, namely Texas. At the end of the American Revolution, several of the new Atlantic seaboard states initially included territories reaching as far west as the Mississippi River. In settlement of war debts, seven states between 1784 and 1786 ceded their claims to lands beyond the Appalachians to the national government. Thus began the public domain and nation's founders faced a literal embarrassment of (land) riches: "It seems paradoxical ... that a Congress too poor to own and maintain a capital, too weak to protect itself from the insults of a band of ragged mutineers, should yet be concerned with the disposal of a vast domain of over 220,000 [actually 370,000] square miles of the richest of virgin soil (Treat 1962, 7).

As if this were not enough, President Thomas Jefferson's Louisiana Purchase from France in 1803 added another 831,000 square miles, extending the nation's western limit to the western boundary of the Mississippi-Missouri drainage system (the Continental Divide). This addition doubled the territory of the nation and tripled the public domain (Clawson 1983, 17). Later territorial cessions and pur-

TABLE 11-2 DISPOSITION OF THE PUBLIC DOMAIN

Total Public Domain (1781–1867)	1,837 million acres
Minus: Grants to states	328 million acres
Grants to railroads	94 million acres
Grants to homesteaders	287 million acres
Other grants	435 million acres
Total dispositions (1803–1975)	1,144 million acres
Remaining public domain (1975)	693 million acres

SOURCE: Bureau of Land Management, 1975, Tables 2 and 3.

chases further expanded the public domain, which peaked in 1867 with the acquisition of Alaska. At one time or another, 1,800 million acres (2.8 million square miles) have belonged to the public domain, of which 730 million acres remain today. The disposal of nearly 1,100 million acres clearly was the dominant feature of federal land management until the late nineteenth century (see Figure 11-5).

Disposal

The disposal of vast tracts of unsettled public land was substantially influenced by the Land Ordinance of 1785, the most important act of the short-lived Confederation. This law established the rectangular Federal Land Survey as a means of organizing the management, disposition, and use of the public domain. From its "point of beginning" where the Ohio River crosses the western boundary of Pennsylvania, the federal survey grid was extended across the nation's hinterland during the nineteenth century, eventually including all the continental United States except for the original thirteen states as well as West Virginia, Kentucky, Tennessee, Texas, and parts of Ohio. (See Figure 7-6 and discussion in Chapter 7.)

Disposition of the public domain began with transfers of land to promote settlement in the "Northwest Territories" (Ohio, Indiana, Illinois, Michigan, Wisconsin, and Minnesota). From the outset, however, the disposal of federal domain lands was fraught with conflict between competing policies that respectively favored free or very low-cost land grants to attract settlers to the frontier (the view of Thomas Jefferson) and transfer for significant payment to promote federal revenue (Alexander Hamilton). An additional complication was the prevalence of illegal squatters who entered and settled federal land without any legal title. Technically lawbreakers, these pioneers epitomized the westward movement. During the early decades of the nineteenth century, support increased among northern and "western" states to grant such settlers a *right of preemption*. that is, the right to purchase before the land was sold to speculators, leading to the Preemption Act of 1841 (Hibbard 1965).

By far the largest transfers of federal land occurred in wholesale congressional land grants to subsidize the building of national roads, canals, and railroads totaling 125 million acres and grants to states, and land grant schools totaling 328 million acres (Table 11-3). The railroad grants conveyed land in a checkerboard of square-mile sections along a proposed new right-of-way, with "white squares" donated to railroads and "red squares" retained by the government. Both were expected to gain value for future sale to settlers attracted by the availability of

TABLE 11-3 *HOLDINGS OF MAJOR FEDERAL LAND MANAGEMENT AGENCIES, 1984*

AGENCY	HOLDINGS
Department of the Interior	
Bureau of Land Management	398 million acres
National Park Service	75 million acres
Fish and Wildlife Service	43 million acres
Department of Agriculture	
U.S. Forest Service	188 million acres
Other	41 million acres
Total federal land ownership	745 million acres[a]

SOURCE: Clawson 1983, Table 2-2.

[a] This total includes public domain lands shown in Table 11-1 as well as other federal lands subsequently acquired.

the railroad (rather like today's use of *tax increment financing,* where a public improvement is funded out of the future stream of revenue it generates). The railroad companies, however, engaged in shady real estate promotion such as inveigling European settlers unused to arid lands with the canard that "Rainfall follows the Plow" (Raban 1996, Chap. 2).

Another barrier to orderly disposal of federal lands was the issue of slavery. Southern states feared that settlers from the Northeast would inhabit the western territories and outvote the South in Congress. Secession of the South from the Union led to passage of the Homestead Act of 1862, granting title to 160 acres (one quarter-section) of federal land to anyone settling on it for a period of five years. During the decade 1870–1880, some 140,000 claims were filed involving 16 million acres of land (Hibbard 1965, 396). Altogether, nearly 300 million acres have been conveyed under the Homestead Act. The results, however, were often tragic: an area of 160 acres was simply insufficient to support a family in the arid West without access to irrigation; rainfall did not follow the plow. Homesteaders either had to obtain additional land or starve. No one has described the plight of the two million homesteaders better than Wallace Stegner (1953/1982, 220–21):

> Suppose a pioneer tried. Suppose he did (most couldn't) get together enough money to bring his family out to Dakota or Nebraska, or Kansas or Colorado. Suppose he did (most couldn't) get a loan big enough to let him build the dwelling demanded by the [Homestead] law, buy a team and a sodbuster plow…. Suppose he and his family

endured the sun and glare on their treeless prairie, and were not demolished by the cyclones that swept across the plains like great scythes. Suppose they found fuel in a fuelless country ... and sat out the blizzards and the loneliness of their tundra-like home. Suppose they resisted cabin fever, and their family affection withstood the hard fare and the isolation, and suppose they emerged into spring again. It would be like emerging from a cave. Spring would enchant them with crocus and primrose and prairies green as meadows. It might also break their hearts and spirits if it browned into summer drouth.

Reaction and Reappraisal

At the peak of the disposal binge during the last third of the nineteenth century, a new conflict regarding the public domain was emerging between *disposal* and *retention* of federal lands. Before the Civil War, there was consensus at least that federal land should be conveyed, not retained. By the 1860s, however, the effects of profligate squandering of the nation's natural resources were becoming inescapable. The lumber industry moved rapidly westward from Maine to Minnesota, and on to the Pacific Northwest, stripping forests and leaving a wasteland that in turn caused soil erosion, which clogged streams and lakes. In the Rocky Mountains and California, mining fever drew thousands of fortune seekers from the East. Mining also ravaged the natural environment and left behind a swath of abandoned "boomtowns," denuded hillslopes, and polluted streams. The pursuit of oil and gas in the late nineteenth century caused equivalent devastation to many areas in the Southwest. In the words of Stewart Udall (1963, 66), "It was the intoxicating profusion of the American continent which induced a state of mind that made waste and plunder inevitable."

In 1864, George Perkins Marsh published his seminal treatise, *Man and Nature or Physical Geography as Modified by Human Action*. A learned and well-traveled lawyer and sometime diplomat from Vermont, Marsh assembled an incredible body of empirical evidence from European and U.S. history of the effects of deforestation, soil erosion, loss of biological diversity, and alteration of rivers and estuaries (Lowenthal 1965, 2000):

> Few books have had more impact on the way men view and use land. Appearing at the peak of American confidence in the inexhaustibility of resources, it was the first book to controvert the myth of superabundance and to spell out the need for reform.... *Man and Nature* was indeed "the fountainhead of the conservation movement." (Lowenthal 1965, ix)

He related his findings with a moralistic tone that anticipated the rhetoric of the environmental movement a century later:

Man has too long forgotten that the earth was given to him for usufruct alone, not for consumption, still less for profligate waste.... Man everywhere is a disturbing agent. Wherever he plants his food, the harmonies of nature are turned to discords. The proportions and accommodations which insured the stability of existing arrangements are overthrown. Indigenous vegetable and animal species are extirpated, and supplanted by others of foreign origin, ... Of all organic beings, man alone is to be regarded as essentially a destructive power ... [against which] nature ... is wholly impotent. (Marsh 1864/1965, 36)

Marsh's plea joined a growing outcry against the despoliation of the nation's natural resources. It served as scientific counterpoint to the romantic laments for a vanishing America expressed in the great Hudson River School paintings of Thomas Cole, Frederick Church, and Albert Bierstadt; the bird paintings of John James Audubon; the poetry of William Cullen Bryant, Emily Dickinson, and Henry Wadsworth Longfellow; the essays of Henry David Thoreau and Ralph Waldo Emerson, and the novels of Nathanial Hawthorne and James Fenimore Cooper (Nash 1982; Stewart 1995) (see Table 11-1).

In the 1880s, John Muir, the wilderness mystic of the Sierra Nevada, began to fan the flames of public indignation. From his base in San Francisco, he divided his time between treks into the mountains (where he allegedly relished climbing tall trees during thunderstorms) and courting the eastern establishment through essays, poems, and lectures (Fox 1981). In 1891, he founded the Sierra Club, and his influence peaked in the Hetch Hetchy dispute two decades later.

A very different voice from the West was that of Major John Wesley Powell, one-armed geologist, geographer, ethnologist, and exemplar of scientist in service to government. Powell gained fame for his explorations of the Grand Canyon of the Colorado River in 1869 and 1871. These trips were followed by survey expeditions through the Colorado Plateau and the arid regions of the Columbia, Rio Grande, and Missouri river basins. His 1878 *Report on the Lands of the Arid Region* and subsequent reports of the U.S. Geological Survey (USGS) (of which he was the second director) documented the unworkability of existing national policy toward disposition of the public domain in arid areas (Stegner 1953/1982). Powell advocated the need to organize human use of western land in relation to its physical limitations, especially water. He urged that allocation of public land be based not on political determinations in Washington but rather on scientific appraisal of the physical resources of the area in question. The USGS topographic mapping system was initiated under his direction.

Powell's advocacy of large-scale dams and irrigation projects, which served as a blueprint for the future work of the Bureau of Reclamation and the Army Corps of Engineers in the West, earned him the contempt of some environmental writers today (e.g., Reisner 1986). His criticism of prevailing national policies, however, lent authority to arguments against heedless disposal of the public domain. Furthermore, his insistence on a scientific basis for government decisions regarding land anticipated the modern practice of environmental impact assessment.

The diverse voices of Marsh, Muir, Powell, and others helped forge a new national policy favoring *retention*, first reflected in the establishment of Yellowstone National Park by Congress in 1872. With spectacular scenery, lakes, water falls, wilderness, hot springs, and geysers, this 2-million-acre preserve carved out of the public domain remains one of the world's foremost national parks (Nash 1982, 108). Yellowstone was followed in the 1890s with designation of huge tracts of federal land as "forest reserves," marking the advent of the national forests that today amount to 187 million acres. In 1903, President Theodore Roosevelt designated Pelican Island in Florida as a "national refuge," the first unit of the National Wildlife Refuge System, that today includes more than 90 million acres in more than 400 refuges. The National Park Service, established in 1916, now manages about 79 million acres (including 30 million acres in Alaska).

Wilderness *versus* Wise Use

The shift from disposal to retention as the dominant policy on federal lands provoked yet another debate, namely between the wilderness ethic of John Muir on the one hand and the philosophy of *wise use* advocated by Gifford Pinchot, the first director of the U.S. Forest Service, on the other. The conflict crystallized over the pristine Hetch Hetchy Valley within the newly created Yosemite National Park. A proposal was made to dam the valley for a water supply reservoir to serve San Francisco after the disastrous earthquake and fire in 1906 revealed the inadequacy of that city's local water supply. Pinchot, a Yale-educated forester and Theodore Roosevelt's chief conservation advisor, supported the project (Miller 2001). John Muir passionately opposed it: "Dam Hetch Hetchy! As well dam for water-tanks the people's cathedrals and churches, for no holier temple has ever been consecrated by the heart of man" (quoted in Nash 1982, 168).

The conflict, which raged from San Francisco to Washington, D.C., highlighted the dilemma in the management of retained public lands between preservation in their natural state *versus* beneficial human use. Muir's position, being absolute, was simpler in concept: wilderness is wilderness—it cannot be tampered with. Pinchot, like John Wesley Powell, represented the progressive position, namely that natural resources should be managed rationally to promote the public welfare. President Theodore Roosevelt was caught in the middle between his trust in Pinchot and his admiration for Muir (Nash 1982, 162–64). Ultimately, the decision to dam the "cathedral" was made by President Woodrow Wilson in 1913. In the words of Roderick Nash, "The preservationists had lost the fight for the valley, but they had gained much ground in the larger war for the existence of wilderness" (ibid., 180).

Fifty years after Hetch Hetchy, the Sierra Club and the Wilderness Society successfully blocked construction of a Bureau of Reclamation dam in Echo Park inside Dinosaur National Park (Gottlieb 1993, 41). In the 1960s, the bureau constructed the Glen Canyon Dam on the middle reach of the Colorado despite similar opposition. This project, which impounded the 186-mile-long Lake Powell, was one of the last major dams to be constructed in the United States, for both economic and environmental reasons. A subsequent proposal by the Bureau of Reclamation to dam a portion of Grand Canyon was handily defeated by outraged environmentalists in 1966 (Reisner 1986, Chap. 8). In 1964, Congress adopted the Wilderness Act under which about 9 million acres of federal lands were designated as wilderness with limitations on mining, water development, recreation, and livestock grazing (Gottlieb 1993, 43).

"Multiple Use"

Not every tract of public land is a Hetch Hetchy or a Grand Canyon. Hundreds of millions of federal acres consist of undistinguished forests, grasslands, desert, tundra, and wetlands (Table 11-4.) Although most of this land is "wild" in the sense of minimal human presence, even the most ardent preservationist has not called for the nonuse of *all* federal land, and there is widespread consensus that public lands in general should be managed to achieve multiple uses. The Taylor Grazing Act of 1934 marked the end of the "open range" by establishing grazing districts to replace the chaos of unlimited grazing of private livestock on federal grasslands. Minerals, timber, water, recreation, and other valuable resources of the federal lands were also brought under various forms of federal oversight and management beginning in the 1930s.

1784–1785	Cession of "Northwest Territories" to national government
1785	Land Ordinance—beginning of Federal Land Survey
1787	Northwest Ordinance—organization of territorial governments
1803	Louisiana Purchase—doubled size of the United States
1823–1868	Road and canal land grants
1841	General Improvement Act—land grants to ten states
1849–1850	Swampland Acts—further grants to certain states
1850–1872	Land grants to railroads
1862	Homestead Act—free land grants to settlers
1872	Yellowstone Park established—first national park
1878	Powell Report on the arid lands
1879	U.S. Geological Survey established
1891	Forest Reserve Act—beginning of National Forest System
1902	Newlands Act—Bureau of Reclamation established
1905	U.S. Forest Service established
1908–1913	Hetch Hetchy controversy—first "environmental" battle
1911	Weeks Act—to purchase private land for national forests
1916	National Park Service established
1920	Mineral Leasing Act
1933–1940	New Deal Programs (e.g., TVA, SCS, CCC)
1934	Taylor Grazing Act—closing of the "open range"
1953	Submerged Lands Act
1960	Multiple Use and Sustained Yield Act—U.S. Forest Service
1961	Cape Cod National Seashore Act—first national seashore
1964	Land and Water Conservation Fund Act
	Wilderness Act
	Classification and Multiple Use Act—BLM
1968	National Wild and Scenic Rivers Act
	National Trails Act
1970	National Environmental Policy Act
	Public Land Law Review Commission Report
1976	Federal Land Policy and Management Act

The central concept guiding public lands management since 1960 has been *multiple use*. This concept was declared national policy in two congressional acts, one concerning the Forest Service (USFS) in 1960 and the other, the Bureau of Land Management (BLM) in 1964. Together these agencies account for nearly 600 million of the 730 million acres of total federal land. Both acts were replaced by the Federal Lands Policy and Management Act of 1976, which further broadened federal land planning objectives. Thus instead of listening only to its timber company constituents (who lease timber rights), the USFS is required to incorporate watershed management, wildlife habitat protection, and recreation into its management plans for each national forest. Similarly, the BLM must weigh those needs alongside its traditional grazing, mining, and timber interests (Cutter, Renwick, and Renwick 1985, 176–77). As Clawson (1983, 137) suggests, however: "The meaning [of multiple use] implied by those acts and in today's popular usage expresses a desire for a kind of management that is defined in the minds of the users rather than in specific instructions to the agencies. Almost everyone supports the general idea; it is its translation into practice that produces controversies."

Public participation is fundamental to planning procedures by federal land agencies. Draft plans are published and available for public comment, which is often negative. Public hearings are required at each step in the development of plans. Environmental impact statements under the National Environmental Policy Act of 1969 are required for major plans and policy initiatives, and they generate another layer of public involvement and contention. Finally, lawsuits by public-interest organizations or special user groups frequently challenge and delay the implementation of proposed actions on federal lands. Frustration of states and private interests with federal resource policies prompted the "Sagebrush Rebellion" of the 1980s, when western states demanded more control over federal lands and resources within their territories. Native American rights in portions of the public domain also led to conflicts with other stakeholders.

Some of the most bitter disputes on federal lands policies have involved national parks. The National Park System (NPS) is best known for its "crown jewels," the great western parks of Yosemite, Yellowstone, Rocky Mountain, Grand Canyon, Zion, Bryce Canyon, Grand Teton, Glacier, and Olympic. In the East, Acadia in Maine attracts 4.5 million visitors a year and Shenandoah, 2 million. Since the 1960s these traditional scenic marvels have been supplemented by a variety of new kinds of NPS units. Beginning with Cape Cod National Seashore in 1961, there are now ten national seashores (nine on the Atlantic and Gulf and one, Point Reyes, on the Pacific) and four national lakeshores on the Great Lakes. Seventeen "national recreation areas" have been established in or near urban areas, including Gateway in New York City, Golden Gate in San Francisco, and Santa Monica in Los Angeles. The Park Service also operates many smaller facilities including historic sites and battlefields, national monuments (including the venerable Muir Woods north of San Francisco), and miscellaneous units such as an industrial museum park at Lowell, Massachusetts.

This assortment of national park units, both traditional and nontraditional, has provoked many conflicts over NPS management policies. Some place-specific and generic issues have involved:

- Water supply for the Everglades
- Off-road vehicles at Cape Cod and elsewhere
- Mining in Death Valley
- Moving the Cape Hatteras Lighthouse
- Clear-cutting timber adjacent to national parks
- Controlling forest fires in Yellowstone and elsewhere
- Airplane flights through the Grand Canyon
- Nude bathing
- Quotas for wilderness backpacking
- Traffic and parking
- Private concessions
- Land use planning in "gateway communities"
- Wildlife management
- Erosion control on beaches
- Rights of inholders and enclave communities
- Sewage and solid waste

In charting its course through these and other minefields, the NPS has little guidance from Congress. The 1916 National Park Service Organic Act generally ordered the NPS: "to *conserve* the scenery and the natural and historic objects and the wildlife therein and to provide for the *enjoyment* of the same in such manner and by such means as will leave them unimpaired for the enjoyment of future generations" (16 U.S.C. Sec. 1; emphasis added). This mandate poses the eternal dilemma for the NPS as to how it may both "preserve" the resources entrusted to it while promoting "public enjoyment" of them. Further guidance is provided in authorizing legislation for particular parks, as well as generic federal laws such as the National Environmental Policy Act (discussed in Chapter 12).

Much of the controversy swirling around the NPS involves long-standing issues pertaining to the internal management of parks: recreation, traffic, wildlife, primitive areas, off-road vehicles, and so forth. Such issues relate to the essence of the parks, their very raison d'être—scenery, water, biodiversity, quiet, and solitude. Protection of these qualities arouses passionate advocacy even from people far from the scene (a tradition dating back at least to Hetch Hetchy). Users of parks, however, have been equally outspoken on behalf of more facilities for the public, more concessions, parking, campgrounds, and opportunities for specialized pastimes. Visitorship to the National Park System quadrupled from 79 million in 1960 to 332 million in 1984 (then dropping slightly to 279 million in 2001) (Wright 2002). Increasing mobility of middle-class Americans has facilitated access to and pressure on the "crown jewels." Meanwhile, the newer urban-oriented facilities have attracted visitation far disproportionate to the relatively small acreage they represent. New recreation preferences such as snowmobiles, jet skis, high-tech rafting, and hang gliding create demands for special-use areas or privileges within parks. Growing cultural and ethnic diversity of users creates additional needs (e.g., bilingual signs). Users with handicaps and elderly users require specially designed trails and other facilities.

A separate cluster of management issues stems from the intermingling of public and private ownership in many facilities. In the great western parks, private inholdings and adjacent land uses consist largely of agricultural or timber holdings. There are few local governments to deal with except for gateway communities like Estes Park at the entrance to Rocky Mountain National Park in Colorado.

A different political geography applies to NPS facilities in more metropolitan locations, such as the national seashores and lakeshores. Those sites were not carved out of the public domain like the western parks but instead have been acquired from private owners. Typically, the authorized areas of these parks are much larger than the land actually acquired to date, and the result is a hodgepodge of NPS land interspersed with private holdings and tracts owned by other units of government. This mosaic of public and private ownership and multiple local jurisdictions is challenging to NPS managers. In coastal areas, high property values and scarcity of access to the shore arouse passions. The NPS is a mixed blessing to pre-existing communities such as those affected by the Cape Cod, Fire Island, and Cape Hatteras national seashores. Federal acquisition preserves key areas from development, such as the "Sunken Forest" on Fire Island, a renowned ecological preserve. The NPS mission to facilitate public usage, however, brings traffic, crowds, pollution, and ethnic diversity to previously aloof summer enclaves.

Under such circumstances, the NPS is thrust reluctantly into the local and regional planning process. At Cape Cod and Fire Island, Congress authorized the NPS to intervene in local development decisions within the authorized park boundaries. Elsewhere, theNPS exercises at least the same rights as any other landowner to testify in zoning proceedings and otherwise make its views known. Subdivisions, condominiums, shopping centers, and amusement parks, which are often attracted to the vicinity of national parks, may detract from the quality of the park environment. Adverse impacts include visual blight, traffic congestion, water quality degradation, littering, and reduction of natural wildlife habitat.

The overriding question for NPS management is, What is the purpose of the national parks? Should they cater to the desires of the user public (however those terms may be defined), or should they provide a "park experience" that uplifts and refreshes those who choose to experience it (Conservation Foundation 1985, Chap. 7)? Environmental lawyer Joseph Sax, drawing on Thoreau and Olmsted, strongly advocates the latter:

> Engagement with nature provides an opportunity for detachment from the submissiveness, conformity, and mass behavior that dog us in our daily lives; it offers a chance to express distinctiveness and to explore our deeper longings....
>
> From this perspective, what distinguishes a national park idea from a merely generalized interest in nature may be the special role that the nature park plays as an institution within a developed and industrialized society, in contrast to those traditions in which nature is offered as an alternative to society. (Sax 1980, 42)

References

American Law Institute. 1975. *A Model Land Development Code*. Philadelphia: American Law Institute.

Archer, J. H., D. L. Connors, K. Lawrence, and S. Columbia. 1994. *The Public Trust Doctrine and the Management of America's Coasts*. Amherst: University of Massachusetts Press.

Babcock, R. F., and C. L. Siemon. 1985. *The Zoning Game Revisited*. Boston: Oelgeschlager, Gunn, and Hain.

Bischoff, A. 1995. Greenways as Vehicles for Expression. *Landscape and Urban Planning*.

Bosselman, F., and D. Callies. 1971. *The Quiet Revolution in Land Use Control*. Washington, DC: U.S. Government Printing Office.

Bullard, R. D., G. S. Johnson, and A. O. Torres. 2000. *Sprawl City: Race, Politics, and Planning in Atlanta*. Washington, DC: Island Press.

Bureau of Land Management. 1975. *Public Land Statistics*. Washington, DC: U.S. Government Printing Office.

Clawson, M. 1983. *The Federal Lands Revisited*. Baltimore: Johns Hopkins University Press.

Conservation Foundation. 1985. *National Parks for a New Generation*. Washington, DC: Author.

Cutter, S. L., H. L. Renwick, and W. H. Renwick. 1985. *Exploitation, Conservation, Preservation: A Geographic Perspective on Natural Resource Use*. Totowa, NJ: Rowman and Allanheld.

DeGrove, J. M. 1984. *Land Growth and Politics*. Chicago: American Planning Association Planners Press.

———. 1997. Why States Should Manage Growth. In *Managing Growth in America's Communities*, ed. D. R. Porter. Washington, DC: Island Press.

DeGrove, J. M., and N. E. Stroud. 1987. State Land Planning and Regulation: Innovative Roles in the 1980s and Beyond. *Land Use Law*, March, 3–8.

Ewing, R., R. Pendall, and D. Chen. 2003. *Measuring Sprawl and Its Impact*. Washington, DC: Smart Growth America.

Foster, C. H. W. 2002. Reviving Environmental Regionalism. *Land Lines* (Newsletter of the Lincoln Institute for Land Use Policy), Oct. 7–10.

Fox, S. 1981. *John Muir and His Legacy*. Boston: Little, Brown.

Gottlieb, R. 1993. *Forcing the Spring: The Transformation of the American Environmental Movement*. Washington, DC: Island Press.

Grove, N. 1990. Greenways: Paths to the Future. *National Geographic*, June, 277–94.

Healy, R. G., and J. S. Rosenberg. 1979. *Land Use and the States*. 2nd ed. Baltimore: Johns Hopkins University Press for Resources for the Future.

Hibbard, B. H. 1965. *A History of the Public Land Policies*. Madison: University of Wisconsin Press.

Little, C. E. 1990. *Greenways for America*. Baltimore: Johns Hopkins University Press.

Lowenthal, D., ed. 1864/1965. *Man and Nature Or, Physical Geography as Modified by Human Action*. Cambridge, MA: Belknap Press.

———. 2000. *George Perkins Marsh: Prophet of Conservation*. Seattle: University of Washington Press.

Marsh, G. P. 1864/1965. *Man and Nature Or, Physical Geography as Modified by Human Action*, ed. D. Lowenthal. Cambridge, MA: Belknap Press.

McPhee, J. 1968. *The Pine Barrens*. New York: Farrar, Straus and Giroux.

Miller, C. 2001. *Gifford Pinchot and the Making of Modern Environmentalism*. Washington, DC: Island Press.

Nash, R. N. 1982. *Wilderness and the American Mind*. 3rd ed. New Haven, CT: Yale University Press.

National Park Service. 1991. *A Casebook on Managing Rivers for Multiple Uses*. Washington, DC: Author.

Orfield, M. 1997. *Metropolitics: A Regional Agenda for Community and Stability*. Washington, DC: Brookings Institution Press and Lincoln Institute of Land Policy.

Pinelands Commission. 1989. A Brief History of the New Jersey Pinelands and the Pinelands Comprehensive Development Plan. Mimeo.

Popper, F. J. 1988. Understanding American Land Use Regulation Since 1970. *Journal of the American Planning Association* 54 (3): 291–301.

Powell, J. W. 1878. *Report on the Lands of the Arid Region of the United States*. 45th Cong., 2d Sess. H. Doc. 73. (Reprinted 1978 by Harvard University Press.)

Raban, J. 1996. *Bad Land: An American Romance*. New York: Vintage.

Reilly, W. K., ed. 1973. *The Use of Land: A Citizen's Guide to Urban Growth*. New York: Thomas Y. Crowell.

Reisner, M. 1986. *Cadillac Desert: The American West and Its Disappearing Water*. New York: Penguin.

Riddell, J. 2001. *Calumet Area Land Use Plan*. Chicago: Chicago Department of Planning and Development.

Sax, J. L. 1980. *Mountains without Handrails: Reflections on the National Parks*. Ann Arbor: University of Michigan Press.

Stegner, W. 1953/1982. *Beyond the Hundredth Meridian: John Wesley Powell and the Second Opening of the West*. Lincoln: University of Nebraska Press.

Stewart, F. 1995. *A Natural History of Nature Writing*. Washington, DC: Island Press.

Thomas, C. W. 2003. *Bureaucratic Landscapes: Interagency Cooperation and the Preservation of Biodiversity*. Cambridge, MA: MIT Press.

Thoreau, H. D. 1862/1937. Walking. In *The Works of Thoreau*, ed. H. S. Canby. Boston: Houghton Mifflin.

Treat, J. P. 1962. Origin of the National Land System under the Confederation. In *The Public Lands*, ed. V. Carstenson. Madison: University of Wisconsin Press.

Udall, S. L. 1963. *The Quiet Crisis*. New York: Avon Books.

Wright, J. W., ed. 2002. *New York Times Almanac—2003*. New York: Penquin.

Yaro, R. 2000. Growing and Governing Smart: A Case Study of the New York Region. In *Reflections on Regionalism*, ed. B. Katz, 43–77. Washington, DC: Brookings Institution Press.

Yaro, R., and T. Hiss. 1996 *A Region at Risk: The Third Regional Plan*. Washington, DC: Island Press.

CHAPTER 12 *Congress and*
the Metropolitan
Environment

A thing is right when it tends to preserve the integrity, stability, and beauty
of the biotic community. It is wrong when it tends otherwise.
— *ALDO LEOPOLD*, SAND COUNTY ALMANAC, 1949/1966, 12

The city, suburbs, and the countryside must be viewed as a single, evolving system
within nature, as must every individual park and building within that larger
whole.... Nature in the city must be cultivated, like a garden, rather than ignored
and subdued.
— *ANNE WHISTON SPIRN*, THE GRANITE GARDEN, 1984

It is the continuing policy of the federal government, in cooperation with state
and local governments ... to foster and promote the general welfare, to create
and maintain conditions under which man and nature can exist in productive
harmony, and fulfill the social, economic, and other requirements of
present and future generations of Americans.
— *NATIONAL ENVIRONMENTAL POLICY ACT*, 1970, SEC. 101(A)

Twice during the twentieth century, demographic thresholds signaled major innovations in land use planning and management in the United States. In 1920, the
federal census first reported that *urban* residents outnumbered *rural* population.
In 1960, the *suburbs* were reported to be more populous than *central cities* for the
first time. In both cases, the shift in the demographic center of balance—from rural
to urban in 1920 and from city to suburb in 1960—closely coincided with a radical

change in the structure of public authority over land use. In the 1920s, the proliferation of Euclidean zoning ordinances across the country marked a new era of
municipal intervention in the private land market. In the 1960s, the federal government, in collaboration with the states, began to reassert the powers with which
it had experimented during the New Deal and to play an increasingly significant,
albeit indirect, role in shaping the contemporary American metropolitan region.

Two factors may be cited to account for the importance of the 1960 demographic
threshold. First, suburban growth involved a proliferation of increasingly fragmented local governments (as discussed in Chapters 6 and 8). Although these clung
tenaciously to their land use prerogatives, it was gradually recognized that local
units are inadequate—spatially, fiscally, and philosophically—to address metropolitan, state, and national needs. Second, spatial redistribution of population was
accompanied by a shift in political power in state legislatures and in Congress. This
shift was facilitated by the 1963 Supreme Court decision in *Baker v. Carr* (369 U.S.
186), which declared that electoral districts must be redrawn to reflect demographic shifts to ensure the principle of "one man, one vote." Thus suburbanites
began to outvote as well as outnumber central-city inhabitants in the 1960s. This
increasing political dominance of the suburbs continues today; the 2000 U.S. Census reported that a majority of all Americans now live in suburbs.

In theory, public power over private land use is vested in the sovereign states, not
the federal government. In addition, the states, as discussed in earlier chapters,
have long delegated most of their authority to local municipalities and counties.
The mighty federal government of the United States is essentially powerless to
interfere in a local zoning determination. States for their part have the legal power
but often lack the political will to influence local actions, and they generally
ignored land use entirely until the 1970s.

Between the 1960s and the late 1980s, however, the relative balance of local
government versus state and federal influence over land use decisions shifted
markedly toward the latter. According to Frank Popper (1988, 291): "Two decades
ago, American land use regulation consisted almost entirely of local zoning: it no
longer does. Instead it has become increasingly centralized—that is, more likely to
originate with regional, state and federal agencies rather than with local ones."
Today the pendulum seems to have swung back once again toward localism, at
least rhetorically, but the state and federal legal reforms adopted since the early
1970s substantially remain in place (although their enforcement since the 2000
election has been uneven at best).

Precursors to the Modern Environmental Movement

Although federal land use planning is not in vogue today, it is not totally unprecedented. President Franklin D. Roosevelt's New Deal during the 1930s briefly interjected the federal government into the planning and development of the nation's natural resources on a massive scale. One of the most durable legacies of the New Deal, the Tennessee Valley Authority (TVA), was chartered by Congress in 1933 as a public corporation to focus federal resources on an impoverished and environmentally stressed region: the drainage basin of the Tennessee River. The TVA is best known for its series of main-stem dams that harnessed the river for power, navigation, recreation, and flood control. The TVA also, however, developed pioneering programs in soil erosion management, reforestation, economic development, and improvement of housing, medical care, schools, and recreation. It proved to be an internationally important experiment in governmental resource management (White 1969). Although direct federal land planning languished after the New Deal, the federal government has long been involved in water resource and river basin planning, beginning in the 1920s and 1930s, and revived with the Water Resources Planning Act of 1965 and federal water quality laws in the 1970s (Platt 1993).

Another New Deal federal land planning agency, the Soil Conservation Service (SCS), which was was created by Congress in 1935 in response to a national soil erosion crisis, fostered the establishment of soil and water conservation districts in most of the nation's counties. With SCS funding and guidance, the districts assist private landowners improve land management and development practices. This and other New Deal programs began a tradition of federal funding and technical assistance to nonfederal planning and resources management agencies. Primarily, however, they were addressed to rural rather than urban issues.

Post–World War II America was much more interested in building than in planning. (See Chapter 6.) Single-family residential subdivisions for white middle-class families proliferated with low-interest federal loans and mortgage guarantees. The Interstate Highway System, authorized by Congress in 1956, promoted development at the fringes of metropolitan areas and helped white suburban commuters leave older urban neighborhoods. For central cities, the federal urban renewal laws of 1949 and 1954 sponsored local programs to acquire, clear, and redevelop "blighted" urban land.

These federal programs and policies profoundly changed the face of metropolitan America. Although they did not technically violate the doctrine that land use is a nonfederal concern, they demonstrated the immense potential of the federal government to indirectly influence—through spending, tax incentives, and technical guidelines—the use of private land. Federal Housing Authority regulations literally specified suburban single-family homes as the approved style of housing to be constructed with its assistance (Fried 1971, 66–70). Tying strings to federal benefits was thus a means of exerting federal influence over the form of urban development in the 1950s, whether or not so recognized at the time.

Who would have predicted in the complacent 1950s the turmoil of the 1960s: the civil rights movement, the anti–Vietnam War movement, and—more genteel but ultimately powerful—the rebirth of the conservation movement, which laid the foundation for the environmental movement of the 1970s? As discussed in Chapter 6, the first exception to the prevailing euphoria about "growth" in the 1950s was the 1955 conference on *Man's Role in Changing the Face of the Earth*. The monumental proceedings volume from this symposium (Thomas 1956) was appropriately dedicated to George Perkins Marsh, whose 1864 treatise *Man and Nature* had articulated environmental concerns a full century before the modern era of environmental reform.

Beginning with *The Exploding Metropolis* essays by William H. Whyte, Jane Jacobs, and others (Editors of *Fortune* 1957), perceptions of "urban sprawl" and the loss of open space provoked a deluge of reports and publications by reputable organizations such as the Urban Land Institute (1959), the Committee for Economic Development (1960), Resources for the Future (Wingo 1963), and the Regional Plan Association (1965). Ian McHarg published his influential *Design with Nature* in 1968, and Charles E. Little (1965) and William H. Whyte (1968) surveyed various approaches to protecting urban open spaces. Meanwhile, the civil rights movement was beginning to gain national attention in its demands for better housing, schools, and economic opportunity for low-income minorities left behind by the white exodus to the sprawling suburbs.

Urban development issues, including both inner-city renewal and suburban sprawl, received sympathetic attention from the Kennedy and Johnson administrations (1961–1969). Pursuant to his "War on Poverty" and "Great Society" initiatives, President Lyndon B. Johnson in 1964 signed the Civil Rights Act. Other new acts of Congress established the Department of Housing and Urban Development in 1965, the Department of Transportation in 1966, and a cornucopia of new programs in 1968 (Table 12-1).

The "rumblings of dissent" that began with the *Man's Role* symposium in 1955 extended well beyond urban planning issues to broader ecological and environmental concerns. An important source of inspiration was the American tradition of natural history writing for the nonscientist, as pioneered by Thoreau's *Walden*, Henry Beston's *The Outermost House*, and John Burroughs (Stewart 1995). The tradition continued in the 1960s with Edwin Way Teale, Joseph Wood Krutch, Edward Abbey, and this writer's father, Rutherford Platt (Sr.) (1966).

Aldo Leopold's *A Sand County Almanac*, originally published in 1949, proposed a "land ethic" to guide human use of natural resources, namely that humans should live in harmony rather than in conflict with the biosphere of which they are a part. Republished in 1966 and again in 1989, *A Sand County Almanac* became the Holy

TABLE 12-1 MAJOR FEDERAL LAWS OF THE 1960S CONCERNING CITIES AND LAND USE

1961	Cape Cod National Seashore Act (PL 87-126)
1963	Outdoor Recreation (PL 88-29)
1964	Wilderness Act (PL 88-577)
	Civil Rights Act (PL 88-352)
1965	Appalachian Regional Development Act (PL 89-4)
	Land and Water Conservation Fund Act (PL 88-578)
	Department of Housing and Urban Development Act (PL 89-174)
	Highway Beautification Act (PL 89-285)
	Water Resources Planning Act (PL 89-80)
1966	Historic Preservation Act (PL 89-665)
	Department of Transportation Act (PL 89-670)
	Demonstrations Cities ("Model Cities") Act (PL 89-754)
1968	Civil Rights Act (PL 90-284)
	Fair Housing Act (Title VII)
	Housing and Urban Development Act (PL 90-448)
	Urban Mass Transportation (Title VII)
	New Communities Act (Title IV)
	National Flood Insurance Act (Title XIII)
	Interstate Land Sales Act (Title XIV)
	Wild and Scenic Rivers Act (PL 90-542)
	National Trails System Act (PL 90-543)

Note: Subsequent amendments to these acts are not listed. Consult *U.S. Code Annotated* for current versions.

Writ of the incipient environmentalism. Of similar stature, Rachel Carson's *Silent Spring* woke up much of the world to the hazards of DDT and other toxic chemicals in the environment:

> The most alarming of all man's assaults upon the environment is the contamination of air, rivers, and sea with dangerous and even lethal materials. This pollution is for the most part irrecoverable; the chain of evil it initiates not only in the world that must support life but in living tissues is for the most part irreversible. In this now universal contamination of the environment, chemicals are the sinister and little-recognized partners of radiation in changing the very nature of the world—the very nature of its life. (1962, 6)

Carson's powerful book marked the beginning of the politics of ecology on the national scene. Subsequent contributions included Garret Hardin's essay "The Tragedy of the Commons" (1968), Edward Abbey's *Desert Solitaire* (1968), the Teals' *Life and Death of the Salt Marsh* (1969), Barry Commoner's *The Closing Circle* (1971), and John McPhee's *The Pine Barrens* (1968) and "Encounters with the Archdruid" (1971). Coinciding with the "Age of Aquarius" and the antiwar movement, the new environmentalism attracted an unlikely alliance of "flower children," concerned scientists, journalists, public-interest lawyers, women and men in tennis shoes, and even Richard M. Nixon! Its troubadour was Pete Seeger, whose Hudson River sloop *Clearwater* became both a symbol and an organization for environmental protest. The movement's success reflected the rising influence of national environmental nongovernmental organizations such as the Sierra Club, National Wildlife Federation, Friends of the Earth, and the National Resources Defense Council (Gottlieb 1993). New journals such as *Environment, Environmental Action*, and *Environmental Management* were started. Conferences were held by the dozens, and media reporters and environmental activists avidly courted each other. Consistent with the land use and society model shown in Figure 2-8, change in public perception of the environment fostered by these scientific and cultural forces led inexorably to legal and political reforms of unprecedented magnitude in the 1970s.

The Environmental Decade of the 1970s

It may have appeared to some observers at the end of the 1960s that Congress, with a conservative Republican in the White House, was unlikely to adopt more laws on the environment. In the clear light of hindsight, however, the conservation movement of the 1960s can now be viewed as merely a prelude to the environmental revolution of the 1970s. The former was the larval stage, so to speak; the latter, the butterfly.

The "decade of environmentalism" (the 1970s) was inaugurated symbolically by the first Earth Day, April 15, 1969, and by the signing of the National Environmental Policy Act (NEPA) by President Nixon on January 1, 1970. The U.S. Environmental Protection Agency (EPA) was created by executive order that same auspicious year, along with adoption of the Clean Air Act. The cover of *Time* for February 5, 1970, acclaimed "Ecologist Barry Commoner—The Emerging Science of Survival" with the subtitle "Environment: Nixon's New Issue." (For the record, *Time* and President Nixon were both Republican!)

The federal environmental laws of the 1970s (Table 12-2) did not merely refine the conservation measures of the 1960s; they also enlarged both the range of problems addressed and the means used to solve them. In air and water pollution, the federal role shifted from a passive reliance on the states to set their own standards to direct federal regulation, accompanied by massive funding for infrastructure such as sewage treatment plants. Other new federal laws addressed such issues as pesticides, solid and hazardous wastes, floodplain management, wetlands, surface mine reclamation, safe drinking water, occupational safety, ocean dumping, oil spills, coastal management, and noise control.

The environmental reforms of the 1970s redefined the meaning of *federalism*, the relative balance of power between the federal government on the one hand and states and local governments on the other. A broadened federal role depended on an expansive interpretation of the commerce clause, which grants Congress the power to "regulate commerce ... among the several states" (U.S. Constitution, Art. I, Sec. 8). The emission of pollution by vehicles or in economic production of goods for sale in interstate commerce has been held in many court decisions to justify federal pollution regulations. Also, the movement of air and water across state lines itself gives rise to a federal interest in controlling the pollution that they convey (Dolgin and Guilbert 1974, 22–27).

Natural science-based *environmentalism* of the 1970s would substantially part company with the social science-based *urbanism* of the 1960s. As a foretaste of this shift, a major volume of natural science perspectives on *Future Environments of North America* (Darling 1965) entirely ignored cities even though they are the "future environments" of a third of Americans! While cities occupied center stage

TABLE 12-2 *SELECTED FEDERAL ENVIRONMENTAL LAWS SINCE 1970*

1970	National Environmental Policy Act (PL 90-190)
	Environmental Quality Improvement Act (PL 91-224)
	Clean Air Act Amendments (PL 91-604)
	Resources Recovery Act (PL 91-512)
	Occupational Health and Safety Act (PL 91-596)
1972	Federal Water Pollution Amendments (PL 92-500)
	Noise Control Act (PL 92-574)
	Coastal Zone Management Act (PL 92-583)
	Federal Environmental Pesticide Control Act (PL 92-516)
	Marine Protection, Research, and Sanctuaries Act (PL 92-532)
1973	Flood Disaster Protection Act (PL 93-234)
	Endangered Species Act (PL 93-205)
	Safe Drinking Water Act (PL 93-523)
1976	Resources Conservation and Recovery Act (PL 94-580)
	Federal Land Policy and Management Act (PL 94-579)
	Surface Mining Control and Reclamation Act (PL 95-87)
	Toxic Substances Control Act (PL 94-469)
1977	Soil and Water Resources Conservation Act (PL 95-102)
1980	Comprehensive Environmental Response Compensation and Liability Act (PL 96-510) ("Supervened")
1982	Coastal Barrier Resources Act (PL 97-348)
1984	Hazardous and Solid Waste Amendments (PL 98-616)
1985	Food Security Act (PL 99-198)
1986	Superfund Amendments and Reauthorization Act (PL 99-499)
1991	Intermodal Surface Transportation Efficiency Act (ISTEA) PL 102-240)
1998	Transportation Equity Act for the 21st Century (TEA-21) (PL 105-206)

Note: Amendments to most of these acts are not listed. Consult *U.S. Code Annotated* for current versions.

in President Johnson's "Great Society" and "War on Poverty," environmentalism expanded the area of concern to the entire nation with particular emphasis on rural and urban fringe areas. Although the inauguration of Richard Nixon in January 1969 would spell a rise in federal action on the environment writ large, it also marked the demise of much of the urban and community development agenda of the Kennedy and Johnson administrations. For better or worse, suburban Republicans were in the ascendancy and they worried more about clean air and water and open space than inner-city housing. (With political power shifting to Sun Belt conservatives in the 1990s, much of the bipartisan environmental agenda of the past has been shelved along with earlier urban programs.)

The National Environmental Policy Act

The National Environmental Policy Act was the keystone of federal environmental reforms of the 1970s. NEPA united both a statutory declaration of national commitment to a safer, healthier environment with a new decision-making procedure applicable to all federal agencies. It also created a new agency, the U.S. Council on Environmental Quality (CEQ), to administer the new policy and procedures established by the act.

NEPA reflected a perception that the federal government should get its own house in order before, or at least while, it sought improvement in nonfederal activities affecting the environment. Federally sponsored domestic and military construction programs of the 1950s and 1960s were accompanied by widespread land degradation, air and water pollution, habitat destruction, and aesthetic blight. Also, federal licensing and regulatory authorities were deemed to be administered in disregard of environmental consequences of proposed actions. According to the first Annual Report of the U.S. Council on Environmental Quality (1970, 191), harmful environmental impacts arise from

> a myriad of federal loans, grants, projects, and other programs enacted for specific public purposes.... The most significant federal activities include the highway, airport, and mass transit programs, the sewer and water grant programs,... the location of Federal facilities, and water resource projects.

In addition to federal spending programs, environmental neglect was charged in the administration of diverse federal licensing and regulatory activities involving, for example, pesticide usage, offshore oil and gas leasing, nuclear and fossil fuel power plant siting and design, discharges into navigable waters, and federal land management. Some notable controversies involving federal actions during the 1960s included the following:

▸ The proposal by the Bureau of Reclamation to dam portions of the Grand Canyon

▸ A proposed 39-square-mile jetport to be built just north of Everglades National Park in Florida

▸ The Cross-Florida Barge Canal initiated (but never completed) by the U.S. Army Corps of Engineers (COE)

▸ Competing proposals for a national park and a federally funded harbor in the Indiana Dunes on Lake Michigan (Platt 1972; Engel 1985)

▸ The 1969 oil spill disaster in Santa Barbara Channel

▸ Innumerable conflicts over the siting and design of interstate highways in, for example, Franconia Notch, New Hampshire; San Francisco (Bay Freeway); New Orleans; Boston; and Seattle

▸ The Rampart Dam proposal for the Yukon River in Alaska

▸ The North American Water and Power Alliance proposal to impound massive quantities of water from British Columbia for diversion to arid regions of the United States and Canada (Reisner 1986)

There were precedents for a requirement, as adopted in NEPA, that adverse effects of a proposed action be identified before a federal action is taken. The Fish and Wildlife Coordination Act of 1958 required that any proposal to impound, divert, deepen, or otherwise control or modify any stream or water body under the auspices of a federal project or permit must be reviewed by the U.S. Fish and Wildlife Service (FWS) of the Department of the Interior. The proposed Rampart Dam in Alaska was abandoned due in part to foreseeable impacts on wildlife habitat as disclosed by FWS review. Another precedent was Section 4(f) of the Department of Transportation Act of 1966, which limited the encroachment of federally funded highways on public parks and other preserved open spaces.

NEPA, like the Declaration of Independence, is short, clear, and bold. It first states the intent of Congress: "to foster and promote the general welfare, to create and maintain conditions under which man and nature can exist in productive harmony, and fulfill the social, economic, and other requirements of present and future generations of Americans" (PL 91-190, Sec. 101(a)). NEPA requires all federal agencies to prepare "detailed statements" disclosing potential environmental consequences of their proposed actions. The requirement applies to any proposed "major federal actions significantly affecting the quality of the human environment" (Sec. 103) including (1) direct federal actions such as the siting of federal facilities, (2) funding commitments for nonfederal activities, (3) federal licensing and permits, and (4) proposals for federal legislation.

Environmental Impact Statements

An *environmental impact statement* (EIS) must be prepared and circulated for public review before a federal agency makes a final decision concerning a proposed action. An EIS must consider the following:

i)   The environmental impact of the proposed action;

ii) Adverse environmental effects which cannot be avoided should the proposal be implemented;

iii) Alternatives to the proposed action;

iv) The relationships between local short-term uses of man's environment and the maintenance and enhancement of long-term productivity; and

v)   Any irreversible and irretrievable commitments of resources which would be involved in the proposed action should it be implemented. (Sec. 102(c))

Many early EISs were excessively long and detailed, and environmentalists complained that some agencies engaged in overkill to bury opposing views in prolixity. The agencies, on the other hand, responded that they were only trying to avoid being sued for producing an insufficient EIS. In 1978, the CEQ issued new regulations to refine the EIS preparation process (40 *Code of Federal Regulations* Parts 1500–1508).

NEPA does not directly prohibit proposed actions that may be environmentally damaging. Rather, it serves as a "full disclosure" document or process to enable public and private stakeholders to register their support or, more likely, opposition to a proposed federal action. Sufficient public outcry may translate into executive or legislative action to cancel or modify a project, as occurred with the Cross-Florida Barge Canal and New York City's proposed "Westway" highway project.

Along with facilitating public dialogue about a proposed project, NEPA has been often used to apply legal leverage to stop or modify a particular project. Hundreds of legal challenges based on NEPA grounds have been filed by environmental organizations and other objectors since the early 1970. Although NEPA does not prohibit unwise federal actions, it does require full disclosure of adverse implications. Therefore, lawsuits generally challenge the *sufficiency* of such disclosures in an EIS or demand that one be prepared when it has not been. Often such challenges delay a project and raise its cost, both of which may ultimately result in its cancellation or substantial modification. Out of hundreds of possible cases, the use of NEPA to delay and ultimately kill a project of dubious value was well illustrated in the prolonged lawsuit challenging a proposed port at Sears Island, Maine (Box 12-1).

As illustrated in the Sears Island case, NEPA is poorly adapted to fostering a broader regional planning perspective, and it certainly cannot force states to spend money for parks. Sometimes, though, NEPA can be useful in suspending a project long enough to allow the entire plan to be reconsidered. The Environmental Law Institute (1989, 10060) praised NEPA as "Congress's first modern environmental law [which] has set the tone for the complex superstructure of federal environmental law that was to follow." On the other hand, however, Lynton K. Caldwell (1989), who participated in the drafting of the original NEPA in the late 1960s, urges that a constitutional amendment on the environment would offer more reliable protection than the statute alone, whose application has often been swayed by politics.

Coastal Zone Management

The tidal and Great Lakes shorelines of the United States extend about 58,000 miles (National Oceanographic and Atmospheric Administration 1975). These shorelines include many different geomorphic types, of which the following are representative (National Academy of Sciences 1990):

- Crystalline bedrock (e.g., central and northern Maine)
- Eroding bluff (e.g., outer Cape Cod, Great Lakes)
- Pocket beach (e.g., southern New England, Pacific Coast)
- Strand-plain beach (e.g., Myrtle Beach, South Carolina)
- Coastal barriers (e.g., Long Island, New York, to Texas)
- Coral reef and mangrove (e.g., south Florida)
- Coastal wetland (e.g., Louisiana)

Coasts also vary as to type and intensity of human usage and modification. Coastal settlements include (1) totally urbanized industrial, port, and resort development; (2) medium-density, older summer colonies, often converted to

BOX 12-1 *The Sears Island Case*

In 1978, the state of Maine proposed to construct a small cargo port on Sears Island, an undeveloped, mostly forested island at the head of scenic Penobscot Bay within easy connection to coastal highway and rail facilities (Figure 12-1). A federal permit to "dredge and fill" in tidal wetlands was granted, federal funds were committed to the project, and a causeway to the mainland was constructed in the early 1980s. The responsible federal and state agencies prepared limited *environmental assessments* but concluded that a full-scale environmental impact statement (EIS) would not be needed.

The Sierra Club New England Chapter filed suit in 1984 on behalf of summer residents of the vicinity to block the project due to lack of an EIS. The Federal Court of Appeals in Boston (First Circuit) reversed a lower-court ruling and suspended construction pending preparation of an EIS by the sponsoring agencies. (*Sierra Club v. Marsh*, 769 F.2d 868, 1985). A draft and "final" EIS (the first of many) were prepared, and work was allowed to resume in 1987.

The Sierra Club returned to court in 1988. It sought a renewed injunction and further work on the EIS to reflect new

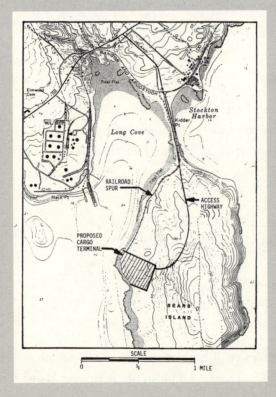

FIGURE 12-1

Map of Sears Island, Maine, and site of proposed bulk cargo terminal (never built).

findings of an EPA study that undercut the state's assumptions regarding the economic viability of the port. As approved by the courts, the EIS was now required to assess what kinds of industries might be located on Sears Island, with consequent analysis of the economic geography of the region.

Astonishingly, in 1991 the Maine Department of Transportation "discovered" some 200 acres of freshwater wetlands on Sears Island not before noticed or considered in the EIS. Legal pandemonium ensued, with the final result that the state was faced with huge costs to comply with the Clean Water Act regarding both salt water and freshwater wetland impacts, ongoing legal and consultant costs, and diminishing prospects that the port if built would attract any users. In 1997, the state canceled the port and bought the entire island from the railroad that owned it. It has lain idle ever since.

The Sears Island case generated thirteen federal court decisions (seven by the District Court and six by the Court of Appeals in Boston.) Port advocates blamed the Sierra Club and EPA (both in Boston) for using the NEPA to block development in an economically depressed area of Maine. Others, however, suggest that the 900-acre undeveloped Sears Island could better be used as a state park. (For a more detailed case study, see Platt and Kendra 1999.)

Moral of the story: Environmental impact assessment under NEPA requires competent analysis of relevant geographical factors.

year-round use and higher-density condominiums; (3) still-picturesque fishing and artist villages becoming "yuppified"; and (4) new megadevelopments like Hilton Head, South Carolina, and Amelia Island Plantation, Florida.

Public or quasi-public agencies own extensive tracts of unspoiled or less developed coastal lands. The National Park Service operates ten national seashores, four national lakeshores, and several other coastal recreation facilities. Other undeveloped shorelines are included in units of the National Wildlife Refuge System or are owned by the military. There are eighteen National Estuarine Sanctuaries in fifteen states under the administration of the National Oceanographic and Atmospheric Administration (NOAA). Some key ecological sites on the coast (e.g., the Coastal Reserve in Virginia) have been preserved by private organizations such as The Nature Conservancy and the various Audubon Societies.

Of course, not all privately owned shorelines are developed. Some areas remain undeveloped due to isolation, personal preference of the owner, or some form of development restriction. Certain undeveloped and privately owned coastal barriers were placed off-limits to flood insurance and other federal growth incentives by the Coastal Barrier Resources Act of 1982. Accessible private shore frontage, however, tends to be extremely valuable for development.

Coastal regions, broadly speaking, encompass much of the nation's population growth. Eight of the ten largest metropolitan areas are situated on tidal waters or the Great Lakes. The aggregate population of counties substantially within 50 miles of coasts grew from 94.5 million in 1960 to 138.5 million in 1994, slightly over half the nation's total population (U.S. Bureau of the Census 1995–96, Table 39).

Both within and outside metropolitan areas, coasts are "awash with disputes." They are the scene of intense competition between public and private interests, between economic and environmental values, and between diverse land and water uses: residence, business, industry, transportation, recreation, fisheries and natural habitat. The results are sometimes mutually conflicting, as in the case of the Indiana Dunes where fifty years of controversy yielded a national lakeshore wrapped around a major industrial complex, to the detriment of both (Platt 1978).

Vast areas of estuarine wetlands and related natural habitat have been lost to filling, dredging, pollution, and land subsidence (Frayer et al. 1983). Tidal freshwater wetlands and mangrove habitat also have sustained losses at the hands of developers. Coastal wetland losses endanger commercial and sport fisheries, and impair other natural functions of wetlands such as bird habitat, water purification, and protection against wave damage (Mitsch and Gosselink 1986, Chap. 16).

Another concern is the vulnerability of coastal development, especially on low-lying barrier beaches, to natural hazards including hurricanes, northeasters, erosion, landslides, erosion, and tsunamis. Often the very physical characteristics that attract humans to the shore are directly responsible for potential disaster. Pacific Coast residents seeking ocean views build on unstable slopes that collapse during heavy winter rains. Atlantic and Gulf coast barrier residents of "cities on the beach" (Figure 12-2) (Platt, Pelczarski, and Burbank 1987) may be entirely stranded at times of storm surge, unable to flee to the mainland across an impassable causeway. Cottages on the Great Lakes cling to the rim of eroding bluffs and are undermined during periods of high lake levels. The experience of the Great 1938 Hurricane in New England, several others in the 1950s and 1960s, and the catastrophic Hurricane Camille in 1969 signaled even greater losses in the future as the coasts fill up with homes. In 1989, Hurricane Hugo damaged or destroyed nearly all of several hundred shorefront homes lining the coastal barriers near Charleston, South Carolina (Platt, Beatley, and Miller 1991). The growing aware-

FIGURE 12-2 Reconstruction of expensive homes on eroding barrier beach at Isle of Palms, South Carolina, after Hurricane Hugo in 1989. The middle house is under construction. *(Photo by author.)*

ness of coastal hazards, focused by a succession of disastrous hurricanes and north-easters, has yielded a diverse array of public responses, including structural protection, beach and dune restoration, setback laws, and incentives to retreat from the water's edge (Figure 12-3) (Platt 1994).

The Federal Coastal Zone Management Act

The federal Coastal Zone Management Act of 1972 (CZMA) (PL 92-583) arose from the ashes of more than three hundred land and water management bills filed in the Ninety-first and Ninety-second Congresses (U.S. Congress 1973). The rancor surrounding various proposals for a National Land Use Policy Act apparently could not withstand the charm of the seacoast. The CZMA passed the Senate by a vote of 68–0 and the House by 376–6 and has generally enjoyed strong congressional support ever since. It applies to all states bordering the tidal waters or the Great Lakes.

Like many Congressional initiatives, the federal coastal zone management

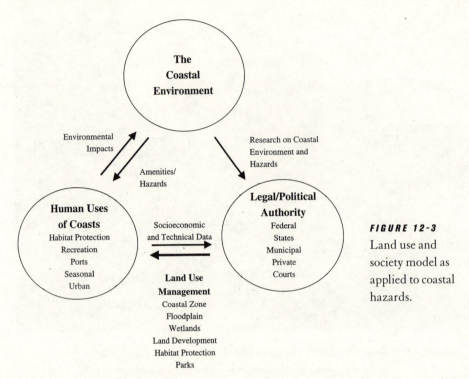

FIGURE 12-3
Land use and society model as applied to coastal hazards.

(CZM) program resulted from an expert panel, the Commission on Marine Science, Engineering, and Resources (1969), also known as the Stratton Commission. A few states—notably California, Washington, and Rhode Island—had adopted their own coastal management laws before Congress acted in 1972, providing models for what the federal act might encourage other coastal states to do.

The CZMA is an experiment in creative and dynamic federalism (Godschalk 1992). It tries to strike a balance between direct federal regulation of the coast (politically unpalatable) and simply generating endless studies that no one implements. It supports *state* planning and management programs subject to *federal* guidelines. It seeks to achieve its objectives by working with and through coastal states and territories and granting much latitude for them to develop programs consistent with their particular physical, settlement, and political characteristics. For states to receive ongoing federal funding, their plans must be approved by the CZM unit of NOAA.

The objectives of the CZM program are extremely broad. The original 1972 act specified diverse and often incompatible coastal activities to be considered, such as "industry, commerce, residential development, recreation, extraction of mineral resources and fossil fuels, transportation and navigation, waste disposal, and harvesting of fish, shellfish, and other living marine resources, wildlife." Subsequent amendments added more concerns: public access to beaches and coastal waters, natural hazard reduction, energy development, estuarine research, and protection of cultural and natural landmarks (Beatley, Brower, and Schwab 2002).

The first step in coastal zone planning was for each state to designate its *coastal zone*. The CZMA defined the coastal zone to include "coastal waters ... and the adjacent shorelands ... strongly influenced by each other and in proximity to the shorelines of the several coastal states." The offshore boundary was set by the act as the seaward limit of state sovereignty (generally 3 miles from mean high water along ocean shorelines). The inland boundary was to be designated by each state.

Within its coastal zone, each state was required to identify "permissible land and water uses" and "areas of planning concern" within which special restrictions would apply. The CZMA further required that state coastal plans include some form of control over important coastal land use decisions through "(A) State establishment of criteria and standards for local implementation; (B) Direct state land- and water-use planning and regulation; and/or (C) State administrative review ... of all coastal developments." This wording sounds suspiciously like "state zoning": states must walk a tightrope between adopting significant restrictions on the use of coastal land as specified in federal guidelines while minimizing interference with the prerogatives of local governments and private owners. (See the discussion of *Nollan v. California Coastal Commission* and *Lucas v. South Carolina Coastal Council* in Chapter 10.)

Section 307 of the CZMA requires that federal actions be "consistent with approved state management programs." State CZM plans may thus theoretically "veto" federal activities, a reversal of the normal federal-state relationship. Congress in 1990 amended Section 307 of the act to clarify that all federal agency activities, including leasing of federal offshore oil and gas resources in state coastal zones, are subject to state CZM plans (Godschalk 1992, 110).

Results of the CZM program are difficult to evaluate due to its multiplicity of objectives—environmental, economic, social—and the complexity of federal-state-local-private interaction from which measurable results emerge. Thus the preservation of coastal wetlands, for example, may result from the CZM program, but may equally be attributable to the federal wetlands program (Sec. 404 of the Clean Water Act), to state or local laws, or to private actions. Apart from individual projects, the CZM program may fairly be credited with fostering a variety of new state laws, regulations, and bond issues concerning coastal management. An important example is the adoption of coastal setback requirements for new construction in over a dozen states (Platt et al. 1992). The program is sometimes viewed as timid (as in the Sears Island dispute, where federal and state CZM officials were conspicuously silent). In balance, however, it has strengthened state skills and confidence in confronting coastal disputes and may indirectly have contributed to upgrading the management of noncoastal resources as well.

The National Flood Insurance Program

National Effects of Floods

Riverine and coastal disasters inflict an ever-rising toll of economic, social, and emotional costs on the United States. Damage data are very inexact, but one Federal Interagency Floodplain Management Task Force (FMTF) study (1992, 18) estimates that the per capita costs of floods to public and private property were almost two and a half times greater for the period 1951 to 1986 as from 1916 through 1950. (According to the Interagency Floodplain Management Review Committee (IFMRC) (1994, 15, 22), the Midwest floods of 1993 inflicted an estimated $12–$16 billion in agricultural and urban damage, including $4.2 billion in direct federal disaster assistance costs and $1.3 billion from federal insurance programs (Figure 12-4).

The federal government is chiefly concerned with hazards within the *one-hundred-year floodplain*, namely the area with a probability of at least 1 percent of being flooded in any given year. (See Chapter 10 for a discussion of the physical nature of floodplains.) This standard represents a compromise between very frequent and the most rare catastrophic events. Although it sounds fairly remote, a one-hundred-year flood has a 26 percent chance of occurring during the lifetime of a thirty-year mortgage. And only the outer edges of the one-hundred-year floodplain have a risk as low as 1 percent per year: closer to the stream channel the risk is progressively higher.

The total land area within one-hundred-year floodplains is approximately 150,000 square miles (94 million acres), or about 7 percent of the nation's land area (Federal Emergency Management Agency 1994, 3). More than 90 percent of these flood hazard areas are rural, but some 3.5 to 5.5 million acres of floodplain are urbanized (FMTF 1992, 16). Urban floodplains contain millions of homes, industrial and commercial infrastructure (i.e., highways, airports, bridges), water and sewer treatment plants, and electrical facilities. The disruptive effects of floods may extent far beyond the area actually under water when these facilities are dis-

abled. Storm drainage backup causes extensive flooding both within and outside mapped floodplains in many flat urban areas such as Chicago, Atlanta, and
Houston.

Flash floods crest within hours or even minutes after a heavy deluge, thus
endangering both lives and property. Flash floods are very destructive in narrow,
steep canyons or valleys, as in the Rocky Mountains and Appalachia. The 1976 Big
Thompson Canyon flood in Colorado was described as a "wall of water" carrying
boulders, trees, cars, building debris, and bodies (Gruntfest 1987). Flash floods also
strike small watersheds in urban areas where paving of natural land surfaces and
sewers convey runoff directly to local streams, converting them into raging and
destructive torrents.

Most flood damage and injuries stems from human encroachment on natural
floodplains. Floodplains attract development despite the risk involved because

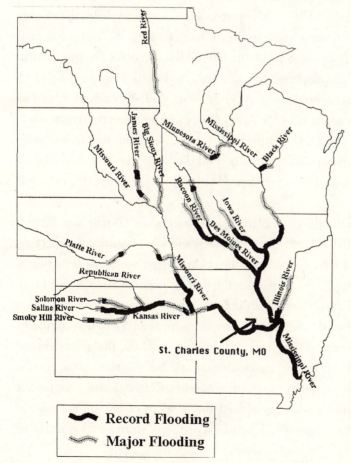

FIGURE 12-4
Areas of major flooding
during the Midwest floods
of 1993. *(Source: Interagency
Floodplain Management Review
Committee, Fig. 1-6.)*

they offer level building sites. Buildings may be built compatibly with occasional flooding, but the hazard is typically ignored by builders and investors who may fairly assume that if the site is unsafe, the government will offer protection against loss.

Structural Flood Control

From the 1930s through the 1960s, the U.S. Corps of Engineers and other federal agencies sought to control flooding through the construction of dams, reservoirs, levees, diversion channels, and coastal protection works. Such projects made economic sense only if they protected buildings from flooding. Thus structural flood control implicitly was intended to attract *more building* in "protected" floodplains. The projects themselves gave an illusion of safety to new investments in floodplains.

Flood control projects, however, are designed to provide a certain level of safety. Floods that exceed that design level can overtop a levee or overwhelm the storage capacity of a reservoir, creating havoc in the built-up floodplain. Average annual flood losses may actually be *increased* by the federal flood control program due to the failure to limit new development in areas protected against ordinary flooding but still vulnerable to catastrophic events (White 1964). A classic example occurred in Jackson, Mississippi, where the U.S. Army Corps of Engineers constructed levees and channelized the Pearl River during the 1960s. New commercial and public buildings constructed in the floodplain behind the levee were inundated by up to 14 feet of water when the river overtopped the levee in April 1979 (Figure 12-5) (Platt 1982).

Federal response to the flood problem has been episodic (Burby and French 1985, 6). Consistent with the Land Use and Society model in Figure 2-8, new laws, policies, and initiatives have tended to follow closely major floods or series of floods, as perceived by policy makers with the help of expert advice (Table 12-3).

A turning point in federal flood policy occurred in the mid-1960s when a series of disasters drove federal disaster relief costs to more than $1 billion annually. Two studies commissioned by Congress and the Bureau of the Budget examined the feasibility of a federal flood insurance program (U.S. Congress 1966a, 1966b), directed respectively by resource economist Marion Clawson and geographer Gilbert White. The latter report questioned the wisdom of relying entirely on structural flood control and proposed instead a broad set of strategies that included the following:

FIGURE 12-5 The 1979 Pearl River flood at Jackson, Mississippi. State Coliseum and industrial and commercial buildings built in area protected by Corps of Engineers flood control project were inundated. *(Photo by author.)*

▸ *Floodproofing* of existing structures or new structures that must be built in floodplains

▸ Improvement of *forecast* and *warning* systems

▸ *Land use management*, including floodplain zoning and land acquisition

▸ *Flood insurance* provided at affordable rates by the federal government but subject to community floodplain management to control further development in hazard areas

▸ *Relief and rehabilitation* following a flood disaster

The White report further urged caution in the establishment of a national flood insurance program:

A flood insurance program is a tool that should be used expertly or not at all. Correctly applied, it could promote wise use of flood plains. Incorrectly applied, it could exacerbate the whole problem of flood losses. For the Federal Government to subsidize low premium disaster insurance ... would be to invite economic waste of great magnitude. Further, insurance coverage is necessarily restricted to tangible property; no matter how

TABLE 12-3 *CHRONOLOGY OF SOME MAJOR FLOODS AND PUBLIC RESPONSE*

YEAR	FLOOD DISASTER	NEW LAW OR STUDY
1927	Lower Mississippi	Lower Mississippi Flood Control Act—1928
1936	Eastern river basins	
	Ohio-Mississippi	Flood Control Act—1936
1938	New England	Flood Control Act—1938
1944	Hurricane—Florida	Flood Control Act—1944
1954–1955	New England hurricanes	PL 84-71—structural protection
1962	Atlantic Coast	PL 87-874—structural protection
1965	Hurricane Betsy	SE Hurricane Relief Act, PL 89-339; House Doc. 465; HUD Report on Flood Insurance
1968		National Flood Insurance Act
1969	Hurricane Camille	
1972	Tropical Storm Agnes; Rapid City flash flood	
1973	Upper Mississippi	Flood Disaster Protection Act
1974		Federal Disaster Relief Act, PL 93-288
1979	Hurricane Frederic; Pearl River flood	
1980	Hurricane David	
1982		Coastal Barrier Resources Act
1988		Federal Disaster Relief Amendments
1989	Hurricane Hugo	
1993	Mississippi/Missouri	"Sharing the Challenge" Report
1996	Hurricanes Bertha and Fran	

great a subsidy might be made, it could never be sufficient to offset the tragic personal consequences which would follow enticement of the population into hazard areas. (U.S. Congress 1966b, 17)

The task force report was forwarded to Congress by President Lyndon Johnson together with Executive Order 11296 directing federal agencies to evaluate flood hazards before funding new construction or the purchase or disposal of land. Congress then adopted the National Flood Insurance Act of 1968.

The National Flood Insurance Program:
A New Approach

The National Flood Insurance Program (NFIP) has been the mainstay of federal response to floods since the early 1970s. Instead of flood control, the NFIP offers an array of nonstructural means to flood losses, including (1) floodplain mapping, (2) floodplain management, (3) flood insurance, and, to a modest extent (4) floodplain land acquisition.

The NFIP is really two programs rolled into one. First, it is a government insurance program that seeks to reallocated flood losses from taxpayer-funded disaster relief to property owner-funded flood insurance. Because the private insurance industry had ceased to provide coverage against floods, the NFIP provides government-backed insurance against flood damage to buildings and their contents.

Second, the NFIP promotes floodplain management to limit flood risk to new construction along the nation's rivers and shorelines. As noted in the White report, unless new encroachments are controlled, the NFIP could inadvertently subsidize new floodplain development. The idea of federal control over land use in floodplains, however, has always been politically unviable. Therefore, a clever backdoor approach is employed by the NFIP. It establishes minimum standards for local adoption as a condition to the availability of flood insurance within a given community. Communities are free to ignore the floodplain management guidelines and deny flood insurance to owners of property at risk within their jurisdictions.

At first, the NFIP began with a whimper. Only four communities entered the program, and only twenty policies were sold during its first year. Most communities lacked detailed maps of their flood hazard areas, and few property owners were interested in buying flood insurance.

To address the lack of maps, the NFIP has spent several billion dollars over three decades mapping the nation's floodplains at a scale suitable for local land use regulations. The maps are based on standard engineering models of stream flow and coastal flooding (HEC-2 and SLOSH are the usual models). Using available hydrologic or oceanographic data, the models estimate the elevation of the one-hundred-year flood at specific points along a stream or coast. Elevation data are then converted to estimates of the geographic extent of the floodplain, using topographic data. The typical NFIP map depicts the one-hundred-year floodplain (*base flood* in NFIP jargon) and also in some cases a *floodway*, a *coastal high hazard area* (on open ocean coasts), and a five-hundred-year floodplain. The maps also provide data on the level of risk from which insurance rates may be calculated

(Figure 12-6). Once a community is mapped, it may appeal possible errors but otherwise must adopt floodplain management restrictions or fail to be eligible for insurance under the program.

Buyer resistance was addressed in the Flood Disaster Protection Act of 1973, which closely followed Tropical Storm Agnes (see Table 12-3). This act required that anyone borrowing money from a federal or federally related source for purchase or improvement of a structure in a floodplain identified by the NFIP must purchase a flood insurance policy. Because many lending institutions are insured or regulated by federal agencies, this requirement covered a large proportion of mortgage loans involving flood-prone structures.

With these two midcourse corrections, the NFIP began to grow rapidly. By 1990, of nearly 22,000 communities in which flood hazards had been identified, 18,200 had joined the NFIP and 16,470 of those had satisfied the minimum federal standards for floodplain management (FMTF 1992.) As of 2003, more than five million policies are in effect, covering flood-prone property worth hundreds of billions of dollars.

Flood Loss Reduction Under the NFIP

The NFIP seeks to reduce flood losses to structures in two ways: (1) by charging actuarial rates for new or substantially improved structures and (2) by setting minimum standards for local regulation of development and redevelopment in floodplains. These practices are intended to be mutually supportive. Actuarial rates are insurance premiums calibrated to the assumed level of risk to which a structure is exposed; thus a greater likelihood of loss would necessitate a higher premium. Actuarial rates are charged for flood insurance on "new construction," for example, construction that began after the community entered the NFIP. Older buildings may be insured to a specified amount at a subsidized, flat rate. There is therefore a strong incentive for new structures to be located and designed so as to minimize the actuarial rate charged. Elevation of coastal structures is the most conspicuous example: the higher the ground-floor elevation, the lower the flood insurance premium. The Atlantic and Gulf shorelines are lined with post-NFIP structures standing high in the air atop substantial pilings. Such construction in part reflects the influence of actuarial rates and in part reflects the effect of local minimum-elevation requirements pursuant to NFIP floodplain management standards.

Land use and building regulations in floodplains were rare before 1970. The

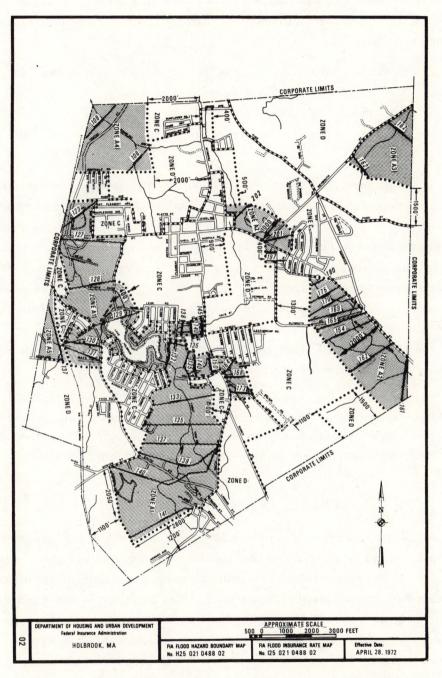

FIGURE 12-6 An early example of a Flood Insurance Rate Map for Holbrook, Massachusetts, 1972. *(Source: Federal Insurance Administration.)*

NFIP entered the turbulent waters of floodplain management cautiously. Section 1361 of the act mandates the development of federal criteria for state and local measures to do the following:

- ▸ "Guide the development of proposed construction away from locations which are threatened by flood hazards,
- ▸ "Assist in reducing damage caused by floods, and
- ▸ "Otherwise improve the long-range land management and use of flood-prone areas."

Under the nonstructural approach to floodplain management, responsibilities are fragmented among the federal, state, regional, and local levels of government. Federal flood-related efforts alone are widely diffused among many agencies and program purposes. The NFIP is the cornerstone of federal response, but many functions, such as flood prediction and warning, mapping, and emergency planning, cross program and agency boundaries. Following the original call for coordination (U.S. Congress 1966b), various blueprints for a "unified national program on floodplain management" have been prepared by the U.S. Water Resources Council (1976) and FEMA (1994) but as the National Review Committee on Floodplain Management (1989) concluded:

> There is no central direction for the Unified National Program. No agency has the charter or capability to carry it out in its entirety, and no agency has authority for assuring coordination of the numerous programs targeted on its objectives. There are serious overlaps, gaps, and conflicts among programs aimed at solving the same problem.

The Coastal Barrier Resources Act of 1982

Coastal barriers are elongated spits or islands, composed mainly of sand, which fringe much of the Atlantic and Gulf coastlines (Figure 12-7). In a natural state, they provide important habitat for marine life and birds and dramatic expanses of beach, dune, and salt marsh. When developed, they are exposed to the destructive force of hurricanes and winter storms that sometimes overwash an entire barrier. They also tend to erode readily when beach material is obstructed and in response to sea level rise.

Various federal programs were hopelessly at loggerheads, some promoting and some discouraging development on fragile coastal barriers. In 1982, Congress decided to cut through the Gordian knot. The Coastal Barrier Resources Act of 1982 declared: "Coastal barriers contain resources of extraordinary scenic, scientific, recreational, natural, historic, archeological, cultural, and economic importance, which are being irretrievably damaged and lost due to development on, among, and adjacent to such barriers." The act further stated that federal assistance was contributing to "the loss of barrier resources, threats to human life, health, and property, and the expenditure of millions of tax dollars each year"; and therefore, "A program of coordinated action by Federal, State, and local governments is critical to the more appropriate use and conservation of coastal barriers."

To effectuate such a program, the act established a Coastal Barrier Resources System (CBRS) within which certain federal benefits would be withheld. The CBRS was based on an inventory of nonpublic, nonprotected, undeveloped coastal barriers prepared by the Department of the Interior (see Figure 12-7). Included were 186 geographic units extending along 656 miles of oceanfront shoreline (about 24 percent of the total U.S. barrier coastline along the Atlantic and Gulf of Mexico) (Platt, Pelczarski, and Burbank 198). The CBRS was later expanded to include some 1.3 million acres extending along 1,200 shoreline miles.

Within the CBRS, the act prohibits most federal incentives to growth

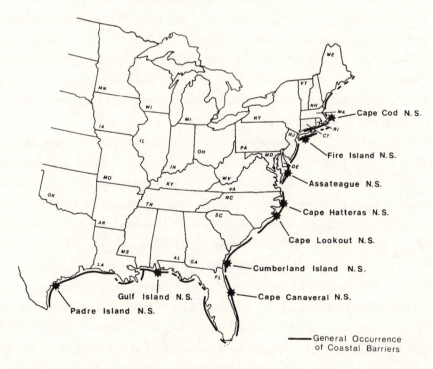

FIGURE 12-7 General locations of coastal barriers and national seashores (N.S.) on Atlantic and Gulf of Mexico shorelines. *(Source: Federal Register, 47:158, August 1982.)*

including flood insurance, road and bridge funds, sewer and water construction, and beach protection (Figures 12-8 and 12-9). Areas within the CBRS may still be developed without federal involvement if local law allows. The denial of flood insurance and other federal benefits, however, is an innovative approach to slowing growth in sensitive areas (Kuehn 1984). It is also a bold, if fairly crude, method of "orchestrating" federal policies for specified geographical circumstances.

Federal Wetlands Programs

Wetlands are an important subset of the total land and water resources of the United States. (See Chapters 1 and 10.) The term *wetlands* encompasses a variety of ecological and hydrological regimes generally characterized by (1) the presence of water, (2) predominance of saturated hydric soils, and (3) prevalence of vegetation adapted to wet conditions (*hydrophytes*). Many kinds of physical features share these broad characteristics; examples are red maple swamps and black spruce swamps in the northern states (associated with glaciation), estuarine salt marshes behind coastal barriers, bottomland hardwood forests in the lower Mississippi Valley, prairie potholes in the Great Plains, playa and riparian wetlands in the West, and wet tundra in Alaska. Depending on their physical type, size, and location, wetlands provide many natural values, including habitat for flora and fauna, natural flood detention (inland wetlands) or shoreline buffering (coastal wetlands), aquifer recharge and pollution filtration, scenic beauty, and open space (Kusler 1983; Mitsch and Gosselink 1986).

Many floodplains are also wetlands and vice versa. Despite considerable geographical overlap, federal programs concerning wetlands evolved independently from those addressing floods. Each involves a different set of statutes, agencies, goals, procedures, and terminology. The need for coordination of federal floodplain and wetland management efforts with each other and with the Coastal Zone Management Program is obvious (Kusler and Larson 1993).

Since 1937, Congress has supported the acquisition, restoration, and maintenance of wildlife areas including wetlands under the Pittman-Robertson Act (16 USCA Sec. 66a). This act authorizes grants of up to 75 percent of the cost of projects from excise taxes on firearms and ammunition. The 1950 Dingell-Johnson Act (16 USCA Sec. 777) similarly has supported wetland acquisition for fish habitat restoration. The 1958 Fish and Wildlife Coordination Act mentioned earlier required consideration of impacts on wetlands and other wildlife habitat before a federal water development project could be approved. Since 1972, federal

FIGURE 12-8 Truth in advertising. The name of the house for sale or rent is "The Edge Water." *(Photo by author.)*

FIGURE 12-9 Remains of oceanfront home elevated on pilings embedded in concrete after Hurricane Alicia in 1982 at Galveston Island. *(Photo by author.)*

oversight of wetlands has been based on Section 404 of the Clean Water Act under the joint administration of the U.S. Army Corps of Engineers and the U.S. Environmental Protection Agency.

The National Wetlands Inventory

A long-standing federal activity has been to identify the types, extent, and distribution of wetlands and to estimate their rates of change. The first conservation-oriented wetland survey was conducted during the mid-1950s by the U.S. Fish and Wildlife Service (1956). In 1974, the FWS launched the National Wetlands Inventory (NWI), a massive project to classify and map virtually all the nation's wetlands. The NWI has used various technologies from aerial photography to satellite remote sensing imagery and geographic information systems (GIS). Wetland data are superimposed on conventional topographic base maps or other base map products. As of the mid-1990s, NWI maps had been prepared for most areas of the nation at various scales. Increasing numbers of these maps are being digitized for GIS use. The maps are explicitly not intended to be used directly for wetlands regulation. Unlike NFIP flood hazard maps, they have no legal weight. (In addition, they are often difficult to decipher.)

Measuring rates of wetland loss is hampered by differing definitions from one survey to another as well as by technical inaccuracy of measurement techniques. The NWI has estimated total wetlands in the early 1980s to be about 99 million acres in the contiguous states, of which 93.7 million were inland freshwater wetlands and the rest coastal. This acreage represented a loss since the mid-1950s of approximately 14.8 million acres of freshwater wetlands and 482,000 acres of saltwater wetlands (Figure 12-10) (Frayer et al. 1983). (See Figure 10-3.)

About one-fourth of wetlands are fully protected under public ownership. Extensive areas of salt marsh are contained within National Seashores and National Wildlife Refuges. Other federal, state, and local landholdings include diverse types of wetlands. Certain wetlands are owned by private conservation organizations such as The Nature Conservancy and the National Audubon Society. The remaining wetlands are privately owned and in many areas are ripe for drainage or filling for development. There is little technical difficulty in filling or dredging wetlands, and alteration is practically irreversible. Governmental intervention in the private land market through wetland regulatory programs has sought to moderate this process.

The Section 404 Program

Section 404 of the federal Clean Water Act (33 USCA Sec. 1344) is the basis for the federal wetlands regulatory program, although the term *wetland* does not actually appear in the law. The law regulates dredge and fill in *waters of the United States*. but this term has been interpreted to include bottom and hardwood forests, mangrove swamps and prairie potholes that are dry most of the year. The program is administered jointly by an uneasy alliance between the U.S. Army Corps of Engineers and the U.S. Environmental Protection Agency. Also, the U.S. Fish and Wildlife Service of the Department of the Interior and the National Marine and Fisheries Service of the Department of Commerce are notified of 404 applications and given opportunity to offer their own recommendations regarding their respective agency interests in a particular wetland.

Section 404 was enacted in 1972 as part of extensive amendments to the federal Water Pollution Control Act, later renamed the Clean Water Act. It was intended to supplement the COE's existing authority under Section 10 of the 1899 Rivers and Harbors Act (33 USCA Sec. 403) to prohibit "unauthorized obstruction or alteration of any navigable water of the United States" in the absence of a permit from the COE. In 1968, the COE amended its Section 10 regulations to require permit reviews to consider "the effect of the proposed work on navigation, fish and wildlife, conservation, pollution, aesthetics, ecology and the general public interest." The denial of a permit to fill 11 acres of mangrove swamp was upheld by a federal court of appeals in *Zabel v. Tabb* (430 F.2d 199, 5th Cir., 1970).

When Section 404 was adopted in 1972, however, the COE interpreted its authority as extending only to traditional *navigable waters*, not including wetlands. This narrow interpretation of its jurisdiction under Section 404 was rejected in *Natural Resources Defense Council v. Callahan* (392 F. Supp. 685, 1975), which held that the phrase was intended by Congress to apply broadly to include wetland features as well as actual water bodies.

The geographic reach of the Section 404 program was eventually defined by COE regulations (33 CFR 323.2) to include the following:

- "Navigable waters" (including waters that once were navigable or that could be made navigable, and including all tidal waters)
- All interstate waters including interstate wetlands
- "All other waters ... the use, degradation or destruction of which could affect interstate or foreign commerce"

- ▸ Impoundments of waters described above
- ▸ Tributaries of waters described above
- ▸ The territorial sea
- ▸ Wetlands adjacent to the waters described above

The regulations defined the term *wetlands* to include

those areas that are inundated or saturated by surface or groundwater at a frequency and duration sufficient to support, and that under normal circumstances do support, a prevalence of vegetation typically adapted for life in saturative soil conditions. Wetlands generally include swamps, marshes, bogs, and similar areas. (33 CFR Subpart E)

The first task in wetland permitting is to determine whether a site falls within a "regulatory wetland," that is, is it within the jurisdiction of Section 404 or a state wetlands program. The COE's permit jurisdiction under 404 must be established by site visit in most cases. FWS National Wetland Inventory maps are indicative of areas that probably fall under 404 jurisdiction but are not legally conclusive. Parties subject to 404 are defined broadly to include "any individual, commercial enterprise, organization, or governmental agency" that intends to construct or fill in areas covered by Section 404. Even federal agencies other than the COE itself must obtain a permit.

Under Section 404, the Corps of Engineers district office receives permit applications, determines whether the site is in a regulatory wetland, and conducts a *public interest review* to see whether a permit is justified and what conditions should be attached. Under Section 404(b)(1), however, the COE review must conform to "environmental guidelines" issued by the EPA (40 CFR Part 230). It is unusual for one federal agency to have statutory authority over the administrative actions of another. Furthermore, the EPA has the right to review any case submitted to the COE and, if it wishes, to veto a permit that has already been issued by the latter (Platt 1987).

The EPA's guidelines articulate two key management concepts: *water dependency* and *mitigation*. Water dependency refers to activities that require access or proximity to water to fulfill their purpose, such as marinas and fishing docks. For activities that are not water dependent, it is presumed that an alternative nonwetland site is available unless the applicant proves otherwise.

Mitigation refers to actions that minimize adverse effects of fill or discharge into regulated areas. The EPA's guidelines specify a series of remedial measures to reduce the effects of the proposed project relating to the location, type of material, and restoration or creation of replacement wetlands. The last of these options has introduced a number of experiments with the rehabilitation of degraded wetlands and in a few cases attempts to create entirely new wetlands to offset the loss of areas to be dredged or filled.

Both of these concepts were applied in a landmark case involving a proposal to fill part of a swamp in southeastern Massachusetts for a regional shopping mall in the mid-1980s. The COE permitting staff concluded that the only alternative site was owned by a competing shopping center developer and therefore unavailable to the applicant. It issued a Section 404 permit for the project contingent on the creation of substitute wetland habitat on a tract 2 miles from the project site. The EPA vetoed the permit under its 404(c) authority, finding that the alternative site could have been purchased by the developer and that the proposed creation of a replacement wetland was unreliable. On appeal, the court of appeals in Boston upheld the EPA (*Bersani v. Robichaud,* 850 F.2d 36, 1988).

Some wetland conversions slip through the 404 net, either legally or illegally. Agricultural drainage of wetlands and several other activities are exempted by statute or "general permit" from 404 review. In states that have their own wetland laws, the state review may serve as a substitute for COE review in minor cases. In other cases, state and federal reviews may both be required. And in really important cases, an Environmental Impact Statement may be required prior to decision on a federal 404 permit. (See the discussion of Sears Island, Maine, in Box 12-1.)

Section 404 compliance is a cumbersome and often time-consuming process. Sometimes it duplicates state or local reviews, and it can be used as a lever for tying up unpopular projects in court. It is not an effective substitute for preserving key wetlands through acquisition. Nor is it a surrogate for advance comprehensive planning at a state or regional level (Platt 1987). It is, however, a "Rube Goldberg" attempt to impose a de facto national wetlands policy through the medium of water pollution legislation where federal jurisdiction is stronger than on dry land.

Endangered Species: Habitat Conservation Plans

The Endangered Species Act (ESA) of 1973 (16 USCA Secs. 1631–1643) is the cornerstone of federal efforts to protect endangered or threatened flora and fauna (Beatley 1994; C. W. Thomas 2003). It has been called "the nation's toughest environmental law, a measure so strict that it can stop a $100 million dam project to protect a rare fish or ban logging on millions of acres of federal land to save an owl" (*Boston Globe* 1993). The ESA has also been assailed by many critics as rigid and inflexible (Beatley 1994, 10).

BOX 12-2 *Protecting Urban Water Supplies through*
Watershed Management: New York City and Boston

New York City and Boston each developed hinterland water supply systems in the mid-nineteeth century, as recounted in Chapter 4. These systems were considerably enlarged through additional reservoirs and delivery aqueducts by the 1960s. The New York system now serves about 9 million people; MWRA serves about 2.5 million. Both cities rely on the purity of their rural hinterland sources and deliver water to user communities with minimum chlorine disinfection but without filtration.

Filtration of public water supplies is now mandated by the EPA under the federal Safe Drinking Water Act of 1974 (PL 93-253, 42 USCA Secs. 300f et seq.). EPA's 1989 surface water treatment rule now requires filtration for public surface water sources unless a water supplier demonstrates that it will "maintain a watershed control program which minimizes the potential for contamination by *giardia lamblia* cysts and viruses in the source water" (40 CFR Sec. 141.71(b)(2)). The EPA intends also to require removal of possible *cryptospiridia*, which was blamed for a serious outbreak of gastrointestinal illness in Milwaukee in 1989.

Both New York City and the Massachusetts Water Resources Authority (MWRA) serving metropolitan Boston have opted to pursue watershed management to protect their source reservoirs and thereby gain a "filtration avoidance determination" (FAD) from EPA. (In New York's case, the FAD is sought for its large reservoirs in the Catskill Mountains; the older Croton Reservoir closer to the city is subject to court order that its water be filtered.)

The watershed management strategy is complicated: large portions of the watersheds that drain into both systems' reservoirs are in private ownership. Private land uses may thus pollute the public water sources with agricultural runoff, septic wastes, and other contaminants. This situation has forced both systems to engage in complex, multipronged programs to prevent future contamination from private land uses. Moreover, rural communities in the watersheds have been wary of the efforts to influence local land use for the benefit of "big-city" water users.

In the case of New York City, an epic "memorandum of agreement" (MOA) was signed on January 21, 1997, after months of negotiation between the city, the watershed communities, EPA, the state, and certain environmental organizations. The MOA launched a massive program of watershed management and collateral payments to watershed interests in exchange for suspension of litigation against the city and the issuance by the EPA of an interim filtration waiver in effect until December 31, 2002. Under the MOA, the city is now implementing its watershed management agenda, while concurrently preparing designs for a filtration plant if deemed to be needed (the so-called dual track approach).

The major elements of the MOA are the following:

▸ Water quality and public health monitoring
▸ EPA-mandated water quality protection initiatives

  ▸ Total maximum daily load program
  ▸ Phosphorous offset pilot program
  ▸ Antidegradation policy

▸ Land acquisition and comprehensive planning
▸ Best management practices to control nonpoint source pollution

  ▸ Watershed agricultural program
  ▸ Watershed forestry program
  ▸ Stormwater pollution prevention plans

▸ Wastewater treatment

  ▸ Sewage treatment plant upgrades
  ▸ Septic system upgrades

▸ Setbacks and buffers along reservoirs and tributaries
▸ Watershed partnership programs

The MWRA on behalf of metropolitan Boston is pursuing a generally similar strategy but under a *consent decree* with the state instead of an MOA. The MWRA's approach was recently upheld by the federal court of appeals against a claim by the EPA that watershed management would not be sufficient to protect the public health in *U.S. v. Mass. Water Resources Authority*, 256 F.2d 36 (1st Cir., 2001). (For further details, see Platt, Barten, and Pfeffer 2000.)

Before the ESA, Congress had expressed interest in protecting wildlife in several earlier laws, including the Lacey Act of 1900, which restricted interstate trade and transport of specified wildlife, and the Fish and Wildlife Coordination Act of 1958, which required review of the wildlife habitat impacts of proposed federal water projects by the Fish and Wildlife Service. Endangered species laws passed in 1966 and 1969, although lacking regulatory teeth, established a list of endangered species and generally laid a framework for later federal efforts.

The intent of Congress in adopting the ESA was

to provide a means whereby the *ecosystems upon which endangered species and threatened species depend may be conserved*, to provide a program for the conservation of such . . . species and to take such steps as may be appropriate to achieve the purposes of . . . treaties and conventions. (ESA Sec. 2(b); emphasis added)

This statement implies that land use planning and regulation will be utilized to conserve *ecosystems* and thus the species that depend on them. Significantly, the act applies to privately owned land as well as public land—a source of much controversy.

Two tiers of species, *endangered* and *threatened*, are listed under procedures established by the ESA. An endangered species is one that "is in danger of extinction throughout all or a significant portion of its range" while a threatened species is one that "is likely to become an endangered species within the foreseeable future" (ESA Sec. 3). More than 950 domestic animal and plant species have been listed as endangered or threatened, and some 3,900 additional species have been classified as candidates for possible future listing. Nearly two-thirds of all mammals are either listed or are candidates, along with 14 percent of birds, 12 percent of plants, and 10 percent of fish (*New York Times* 1995). A few species, notably the American bald eagle and the American alligator, have been delisted due to the recovery of their populations. A handful of listed species are believed to have become extinct since the ESA was adopted in 1973.

The act is administered by the FWS and the National Marine Fisheries Service (NMFS) with respect to terrestrial and aquatic species, respectively. They are charged with the preparation of a *species recovery plan*, which evaluates the status of a particular species and identifies goals and actions necessary to promote its recovery. In furtherance of such plans, federal agencies are required to consult with the FWS and the NMFS to "insure that any action authorized, funded, or carried out by such agency is not likely to jeopardize the continued existence of any endangered species or threatened species or result in the destruction or adverse modification of critical habitat of such species" (ESA Sec. 7(a)(2)). The listing of a species and its habitat is a scientific determination by the responsible agencies that is often the subject of heated dispute.

The ESA prohibits anyone from "taking" any listed species. Section 3(19) broadly defines *taking* (not to be confused with the *takings issue* discussed in Chapter 10) to include actions that: "harass, harm, pursue, hunt, wound, kill, trap, capture, or collect, or attempt to engage in any such conduct." Thus activities such as land development or timber cutting that destroy habitat of listed species may lead to civil or criminal prosecution.

It is frequently charged that the ESA is used as a tool to block land uses changes or development that cannot otherwise be prevented. Completion of the Tellico Dam in Tennessee was halted temporarily after the FWS listed the tiny snail darter fish—believed to be found only in the valley about to be flooded—as endangered. In an appeal to the U.S. Supreme Court by the Tennessee Valley Authority, the ESA was upheld despite the plea that the dam was largely completed by the time the species was listed (*TVA v. Hill,* 98 S. Ct. 2279, 1978). Congress then amended the act to establish an interagency "endangered species committee" to review applications for exemptions from the act. This committee (known as the "God Committee") rejected an appeal to delist the snail darter, but the Tellico Dam was later completed under a congressional exemption.

Other controversial applications of the act have included limitations on logging of old-growth forests in the Pacific Northwest to protect the northern spotted owl; the temporary closing of public bathing beaches along the Atlantic Coast to protect nesting habitat for the piping plover; and proposed limits on development to protect the diminutive key deer in the Florida Keys and the Stephens kangaroo rat in western Riverside County, California (Feldman and Jonas 2000).

In 1982, Congress amended the ESA to permit limited *takes* of designated habitat and species pursuant to the development of a *habitat conservation plan* (HCP) for a particular area. An HCP requires a formal planning process involving all interested parties, such as landowners, developers, local governments, state and federal wildlife agencies, and environmental organizations. This process seeks to achieve an agreement among all parties that specifies (1) the impacts that will result from proposed land use changes, (2) steps to be taken to minimize and mitigate such impacts and funding to implement those steps, and (3) alternatives to the "taking" and why they were not adopted.

The preparation of HCPs for multiple species habitat protection on private land has involved enormous and time-consuming efforts. Critical to these programs has been the development of complex agreements involving many classes of stakeholders: federal, state, local, environmental, landowner, and developer (Beatley 1994; C. W. Thomas 2003). A multicounty regional HCP for the sage-scrub bioregion of inland southern California (the Natural Communities Conservation Plan) was heralded by the California Resources Agency as a "new era in wildlife conservation." This plan, however, was found by geographers Thomas Feldman and Andrew Jonas to have floundered under the weight of political and stakeholder fragmentation: "[It] reproduces rather than transforms the region's unevenly developed governance structures and suburban mode of social regulation" (Feldman and Jonas 2000, 257).

In 1995, the U.S. Supreme Court rejected by a vote of 6–3 a challenge by timber interests claiming that logging on private land should not be restricted under the ESA (*Babbitt v. Sweet Home Chapter of Communities for a Greater Oregon,* 115 S.Ct. 2407, 1995). The future of the Endangered Species Act, though, appears troubled. It is a prime target of property rights opposition, particularly in the West. It is widely accused of being overly concerned with the protection of butterflies, birds, lizards, rats, and plants at the expense of human economic activities. It is often viewed as a subterfuge for blocking land use changes where no other legal mechanism is available. And like the NEPA in the Sears Island case discussed in Box 12-1, the ESA is a poor substitute for explicit, geographically based comprehensive land use planning. As of May 2003, the FWS stopped issuing new critical habitat listings due to shortage of funding. According to the *New York Times*:

> Court cases have piled up because the law says critical habitat has to be designated at the time a species is listed as endangered—a fact environmental groups have used to force designations. Of 1,250 species on the list, about 400 have designated habitats [under HCPs]. Court cases have ... created a backlog ... through 2008. (*New York Times* 2003, A21)

Funding for Open Space

In 1958, Congress established the Outdoor Recreation Resources Review Commission (ORRRC) in response to a growing perception that postwar urbanization was creating a shortage of outdoor recreation opportunities and facilities. A final report was published by the ORRRC in 1962, and numerous working papers reflected the best professional thinking of the time on recreation, open space, and urban planning. ORRRC found that "public areas designated for outdoor recreation include one-eighth of the total land of the country" but "the problem is not one of number of acres but of effective acres—acres of land and water available to the public and usable for specific types of recreation" (ORRRC 1962, 49).

The ORRRC report discussed statistically, graphically, and in prose the existing and the anticipated status of outdoor recreation opportunities, with the notable exception of central cities. Today, the report seems remarkably dated in its nonrecognition of ethnic and racial minorities, persons with handicap, and the elderly. Its photographs portrayed white, middle-class families driving Chevrolets and picnicking in bucolic surroundings.

Few national reports, however, have had faster and more lasting results. Soon after its release, a new Bureau of Outdoor Recreation was established by Secretary of the Interior Stewart Udall and later ratified by Congress as recommended by the commission. ORRRC's proposal to establish a federal land acquisition fund was immediately endorsed by President John F. Kennedy and ultimately adopted in the federal Land and Water Conservation Fund Act of 1965 (P.L. 88-588). This act (known as LAWCON) became the primary source of federal matching grants for acquisition and improvement of open spaces by all levels of government. It is funded through earmarked revenue from federal off-shore oil and gas royalties and other sources. Congress, however, must appropriate money annually for LAWCON, and program outlays have accordingly fluctuated over the years, generally downward since the 1980s. Approximately $269 million was allocated from LAWCON to states during the three-year period 2000–2002 (www.fs.fed.us/land/staff/LWCF).

Forty percent of LAWCON outlays are used for land purchases by federal agencies (e.g., to fill in holes in national parks). The rest is distributed to the states under a congressional formula. States must prepare and maintain a Statewide Comprehensive Outdoor Recreation Plan, approved by the Department of the Interior, to qualify for its allocation. LAWCON provides half of eligible costs of acquiring or improving open space at the state or local level. The nonfederal 50 percent share is derived from state open-space bond issues, local tax-supported funds, and private gifts.

Further federal funding for bike paths, trails, greenways, and related purposes has been provided under the inelegantly named Intermodal Surface Transportation Efficiency Act of 1991 (ISTEA), as amended in 1998 by the Transportation Efficiency Act for the 21st Century (TEA-21). These acts set aside billions of dollars of federal highway funds for unconventional "transportation enhancements." The Department of Transportation funds 80 percent of the costs of bicycle and pedestrian trails, scenic easements, historic preservation, billboard removal, and other purposes. Between 1991 and 2002, ISTEA and TEA-21 allocated $3.3 billion in the following proportions (Congressional Research Service study as reported at www.istea.org):

- ▶ 55 percent for 8,105 projects for bicycle and pedestrian facilities, rails to trails, and safety and education for users of these facilities
- ▶ 24 percent for 3,203 projects for historic preservation including historic transportation buildings, transportation museums and welcome centers
- ▶ 21 percent for 3,601 projects for landscaping, beautification, and environmental mitigation

Hazardous Waste Management

The United States, like other high-technology societies, was shockingly slow to recognize the risks to life, health, and property associated with the careless use and disposal of chemical and other hazardous substances. Not until the mid-1970s, when immense actual and potential damage had already been caused, was remedial legislation adopted by Congress, and it was well into the 1980s before this legislation, as subsequently amended, began to exert some impact on the management and disposal of hazardous substances. As with so many other legal reforms discussed in this book, the necessary prerequisite was a heightened understanding, perception—and indeed fear—of the magnitude of the threat to the physical environment and human health.

For one class of hazardous chemicals, namely pesticides, Rachel Carson's *Silent Spring* (1962) sounded a clear warning. Her disclosures regarding DDT and other agricultural poisons helped ignite the environmental movement generally and reform of federal pesticide law in particular. As early as 1947, Congress had adopted the Federal Insecticide, Fungicide, and Rodenticide Act, which merely required labeling of pesticides sold in interstate commerce. This act was considerably strengthened by the federal Environmental Pesticide Control Act of 1972, which regulates the sale and application of agricultural chemicals.

The CEQ's first annual report (1970) devoted ten pages to pesticides, with a direct reference to *Silent Spring*, but mentioned no other types of hazardous substances. Where was the Carson for asbestos, mercury, PCBs, lead, vinyl chlorides, radioactive wastes, hospital wastes, and dozens of other hazardous substances? In recognition of this void in public awareness, the CEQ itself prepared a brief report on the problem entitled *Toxic Substances* (U.S. CEQ 1971). It concluded that regulatory mechanisms to protect the public health from a wide variety of chemical hazards were inadequate. Although not as charismatic as Carson's book, this report was a major impetus to the adoption in 1976 of the Toxic Substances Control Act (TSCA) (PL 94-469). Citing the CEQ report, the committee report on that law noted:

> It is estimated that there are presently 2 million recognized chemical compounds in existence with nearly 250,000 new compounds produced each year.... Approximately 1,000 new chemicals will find their way into the marketplace and subsequently into the environment through use or disposal. As the chemical industry has grown, we have become literally surrounded by a man-made chemical environment. (U.S. Code, Congressional and Administrative News, "Legislative History of PL 94-469," 4493)

The TSCA directed the EPA to test potentially hazardous substances, particularly those thought to be carcinogens. The act also requires labeling of such substances to disclose risks to the user or the public.

Resource Conservation and Recovery Act

The Resource Conservation and Recovery Act (RCRA) (PL 94-580) also was adopted in 1976. The RCRA marked a major expansion of the earlier federal solid waste legislation and the first explicit congressional action on hazardous wastes.

> The [RCRA] prescrib[ed] in 45 pages a regime for the management of solid and hazardous wastes that included many features (grants, planning, compliance orders, citizen suits, imminent hazards) borrowed from the Clean Air and Clean Water Acts. For the first time in 1976, serious regulatory measures appeared in the federal law—a qualified prohibition on the open dumping of solid or hazardous wastes, and the initiation (in a mere 7 pages in Subtitle C) of the famed "cradle to grave" regime for the control of hazardous wastes. (Rodgers 1988, 510)

The "cradle to grave" provision instituted a system of manifests or documentation to accompany designated hazardous materials through each stage of their "lifetime": manufacture, transport, use, and disposition. This system allows federal and state authorities to track the quantities and location of hazardous substances and to monitor their safe disposal. It also requires that those who generate hazardous materials certify that they are minimizing the amount and toxicity of their waste and that the method of treatment, storage, or disposal they have chosen will minimize the risk to human health and the environment. The implementation of this system, however, was to be delayed and frustrated for years by problems of definition and accountability and by the immense number of generators involved. Inevitably, considerable quantities of wastes continued to be dumped illegally down drains or wells, in fields, or on highways.

The magnitude of the problem in terms of volume of hazardous materials to be managed was vastly underestimated at first. Estimates of total amounts of such substances—defined by the U.S. EPA (1986, 5) to include ignitable, corrosive, reactive, or toxic materials—have risen from 9 million metric tons in 1973, to between 27.5 and 41.2 million metric tons in the 1976 RCRA hearings, to 150 million metric tons in 1984, to 260 million metric tons in subsequent studies (Rodgers 1988, 519). This expansion reflects in part a broadening of the definition of "hazardous substances" to include additional materials and in part the discovery that some materials are more abundant than originally recognized. In 1988, the EPA estimated that there were some three thousand facilities handling a total of 275 million metric tons of RCRA hazardous wastes (U.S. EPA 1986, 85).

The RCRA was significantly amended in 1980 and 1984. The former comprised a retrenchment with the exemption of several classes of wastes from the terms of the act. The 1984 Hazardous and Solid Waste Amendments (HSWA) (PL 98-616) was an important midcourse correction that greatly strengthened the RCRA, including a major revision and tightening of the cradle to grave regulations for tracking hazardous materials. It extended RCRA's coverage to "small generators" of hazardous wastes, adding some 100,000 firms producing between 220 and 2,200 pounds of hazardous waste monthly to the 15,000 large generators (U.S. EPA 1986, 89). It initiated regulations for leaking underground storage tanks ("LUSTs"), which were estimated to number about 400,000 out of a total of 5–6 million underground tanks for storing petroleum products or hazardous chemicals (U.S. EPA 1988, 102). And land disposal of certain hazardous wastes was totally prohibited. Rodgers (1988, 510) describes the 1984 HSWA as "passionate, confident, and demanding."

States play a key role in the administration of the RCRA. By late 1986, the EPA had certified forty state hazardous waste programs to assume day-to-day responsibility for implementing the RCRA.

Superfund

The RCRA applies prospectively to hazardous wastes from the time of their generation until their final disposition. A major gap in its coverage was the problem of wastes already discarded improperly: in pits, lagoons, injection wells, or leaking containers strewn on the ground behind chemical plants. National perception was finally directed to this issue by the tragic disclosures of the Love Canal disaster in Niagara Falls, New York. Love Canal was an artificial ditch dating back to the late nineteenth century that was used for decades as a waste dump by the Hooker Chemical Co. In 1977, signs of desperate problems began to appear in the residential neighborhood that bordered the canal. Children were born with birth defects, high rates of cancer were prevalent, and foul-smelling chemical wastes oozed through basement walls and formed puddles in yards and playgrounds. After much denial by Hooker, the city of Niagara Falls, and the county health commissioner, the crisis was finally addressed by state and federal authorities. A preliminary investigation led to the declaration of a "major disaster" by President Jimmy Carter in August 1978, the first such declaration for a technological disaster. The state, with the help of federal funds, then acquired the homes and assisted the relocation of 237 families from the vicinity. The canal was sealed off and a remedial drainage project initiated. Subsequently, it became apparent that the chemicals had spread much farther through the ground than originally estimated, and the brew of toxic chemicals was found to contain, in addition to benzene and a dozen other carcinogens, a measurable amount of the most deadly chemical ever synthesized: dioxin. The Love Canal Homeowners Association campaigned for further public assistance. Eventually, more than six hundred homes were acquired.

Media attention soon disclosed many other chemical waste horrors lurking in America's industrial backyards. Woburn, Massachusetts, was characterized as "a tangle of dumps and disease" (*Boston Globe* 1980). ("Woburn" became a synonym for corporate irresponsibility in relation to hazardous waste disposal due to Jonathon Harr's 1995 best-selling book and the film based on it: *A Civil Action.*) Times Beach, Missouri, was found to be contaminated by dioxin contained in oil used to resurface the streets. (The entire town was bought by the Federal Emergency Management Agency and its residents relocated.) Even the staid journal *Science* (Maugh 1979) described Love Canal and its counterparts as "an environmental time bomb gone off."

Seldom can a legislative enactment be attributed so directly to a traumatic jolt in public environmental perception: within months after the second round of Love Canal findings, Congress adopted the Comprehensive Environmental Response, Compensation, and Liability Act of 1980 (CERCLA) (PL 96-510), commonly known as *Superfund*. The act's purpose was: "To provide for liability, compensation, cleanup, and emergency response for hazardous substances released into the environment and the cleanup of inactive hazardous waste sites" (Sec. 2).

CERCLA authorized $1.6 billion over five years for a comprehensive program to clean up the worst abandoned or inactive waste dumps in the nation (U.S. EPA 1986, 80). The funds were to be derived from an excise tax on the sale or use of petroleum and forty-two chemicals used commercially to produce hazardous substances. States must provide at least 10 percent of cleanup costs for a site within their jurisdictions. Wherever a "responsible party" could be identified, the party would either be required to perform remedial actions themselves, or the government would do so and sue for the costs plus penalties. In 1986, Superfund was reauthorized by PL 99-499 and expanded to a potential funding level of $8.5 billion. (The Superfund law is codified at 42 USCA Secs. 9601 et seq.)

"Throwing money at the problem" was a necessary but not sufficient (or efficient) response to the threat of hazardous waste contamination. Because the problem of abandoned waste dumps had only recently been recognized, no accurate inventory of the location, size, and contents of such sites had been compiled. By definition, such sites tend to be concealed and often below ground, where wastes have been buried or injected into groundwater. Furthermore, it was often very difficult and dangerous to ascertain which of several hundred hazardous substances were present at any given site. A massive task for the EPA during the 1980s and 1990s was to identify sites and to allocate cleanup resources. By late 1989, more than 31,500 sites were identified as eligible for Superfund listing nationally. The EPA has conducted preliminary assessments on most of them. Based on evaluation of a complex array of risk factors, the "worst" sites are placed on a National Priorities List (NPL), which qualifies them for Superfund cleanup, eventually. By late 1989, more than 1,200 sites were listed on the NPL. The Office of Technology Assessment (OTA) (1989, 6) estimated that as many as 9,000 additional sites are eligible for the NPL, and the potential cost to all parties of cleaning them up could amount to $500 billion over several decades.

A permanent cleanup of a hazardous waste site is immensely difficult and costly. Obviously, risks to the cleanup workers and to the surrounding area must be minimized. Removal of wastes to another location may simply transfer the problem elsewhere, unless the receiving site is properly located and designed. Few approved hazardous waste sites were available. Other than removal to land disposal sites, management options are complex and expensive. They include destruction through thermal, biological, or chemical treatment; stabilization; engineering controls; institutional controls; and natural treatment (OTA 1989, 45). A management approach must be formulated individually for each site with the participation of all levels of government and affected private interests. Also involved in the decision process for each site are a variety of professional consultants: chemists, soil scientists, biologists, hydrologists, and, of course, lawyers.

The OTA has identified a "Superfund syndrome" that impedes progress in making the program work effectively. This condition is a state of "constant confrontation" among the interested parties, produced by the high economic costs, the scientific uncertainties, the emotionalism, and what OTA considers to be "excessive flexibility" in Superfund implementation: "Unless everyone breaks out of the Superfund syndrome, most cleanups will seem to do too little or too much. Billions will be spent. Hardly anyone will be satisfied. Hardly anyone will feel treated fairly. Hardly anyone will seem in control."

Cleaning up Superfund sites and the location of new storage, treatment, and disposal facilities inherently pose geographical as well as legal and public health issues. At the heart of the problem is the pervasive issue of externalities: each site poses potential off-site risks to the surrounding area, as in the possibility of groundwater pollution. Even where actual risks are minimized through appropriate treatment and facility design, a zone of perceived risk may extend widely beyond the area of actual risk. Such spatial distribution of actual or perceptual risks apply not only to the sites of generation, use, and disposal, but also in linear form along the routes of transport (e.g., highway, rail, barge) of hazardous substances (Ziegler, Johnson, and Brunn 1983).

Recognition of the spatial patterns of opposition (NIMBYism), whether or not limited to actual zones of risk, is essential. Ultimately, the resolution of the Superfund syndrome will depend on (1) effectively reducing the actual risks of hazardous wastes through proper management practices, and (2) allaying the fears of those who perceive themselves and their property values to be at risk, through public involvement, education, and, in appropriate cases, compensation.

Conclusion

This chapter has reviewed selected federal policies and programs relating to land use. Federal involvement land use originated in the nineteenth-century debates over competing policies for disposal versus retention and management of the public domain. (See Chapter 11.) Another longstanding federal role has been the development of water resources on major rivers for navigation, power, flood control, recreation, and, more recently, habitat protection and restoration. During the 1930s, the federal budget and bureaucracy expanded massively to administer the array of new public works programs, including both public lands and water development programs. Progressive concepts of managing natural resources to benefit the American people underlay such New Deal innovations as the Tennessee Valley Authority, the Soil Conservation Service, and the National Resources Planning Board.

The federal government grew even larger during World War II. The conservative mood of the 1950s, though, largely trimmed back the planning and resource management programs of the New Deal. City and regional planning, however, were promoted by federal funding for urban renewal and "701 plans," but Congress took little interest in the results of these activities and largely ignored the quality of the nation's environment until the mid-1960s.

Beginning with the 1955 symposium on *Man's Role in Changing the Face of the Earth* and culminating with Rachel Carson's *Silent Spring*, a growing chorus of dissent challenged the laissez-faire policies of postwar growth. In response, a

Democratic Congress and a Republican president outdid the New Deal in creating new agencies, programs, mandates, and funding commitments to restore and
protect the nation's land, air, and water resources during the early 1970s.

Thirty-plus years after the National Environmental Policy Act, many of the
bipartisan environmental initiatives described in this chapter seem to be themselves "endangered species." A vocal constituency demands that private property
rights should prevail over public goals, unless compensation is paid to the affected
owners. A government controlled by conservatives in Congress, the courts, and
the White House after the 2000 and 2002 elections is ill-disposed toward both
environmental and urban issues, from the global to the neighborhood scale. In
addition, the drain of national resources to the military and combating terrorism,
at a time of worldwide economic slump, proved a convenient alibi for under- or
zero-funding of federal programs directed to the improving cities and the environment. Yet public polls indicate that the American people still strongly support
federal intervention to protect environmental quality. How these conflicting views
of the balance of public and private welfare will be reconciled will undoubtedly be
one of the defining issues of the years ahead.

References

Abbey, E. 1968. *Desert Solitaire*. New York: Simon and Schuster.

Beatley, T. 1994. *Habitat Conservation Planning: Endangered Species and Urban Growth*.
Austin: University of Texas Press.

Beatley, T., D. J. Brower, and A. K. Schwab. 2002. *An Introduction to Coastal Zone Management*. 2nd ed. Washington, DC: Island Press.

Boston Globe. 1980. Woburn: A Tangle of Dumps and Disease. June 28, 1, 18.

————. 1993. A Tough Environmental Law May Get Tougher. Jan. 4, 1, 12.

Burby, R., and S. French. 1985. *Flood Plain Land Use Management: A National Assessment*.
Boulder, CO: Westview Press.

Caldwell, L. K. 1989. A Constitutional Amendment for the Environment. *Environment* 31
(10): 6–11, 25–28.

Carson, R. 1962. *Silent Spring*. Boston: Houghton Mifflin.

Commission on Marine Science, Engineering, and Resources. 1969. *Our Nation and the Sea*.
Washington, DC: U.S. Government Printing Office.

Committee for Economic Development. 1960. *Guiding Metropolitan Growth*. Washington,
DC: Author.

Commoner, B. 1970. *The Closing Circle*. New York: Knopf.

Darling, F. F., ed. 1965. *Future Environments of North America*. Garden City, NY: Natural
History Press.

Dolgin, E. L., and T. G. P. Guilbert. 1974. *Federal Environmental Law*. St. Paul, MN: West.

Engel, R. 1985. *Sacred Sands: The Struggle for Community in the Indiana Dunes*. Middletown, CT: Wesleyan University Press.

Environmental Law Institute. 1989. News and Analysis. *Environmental Law Reporter* 19:10060.

Federal Emergency Management Agency. 1994. *A Unified National Program for Floodplain Management—1994*. Washington, DC: Federal Emergency Management Agency.

Federal Interagency Floodplain Management Task Force (FMTF). 1992. *Floodplain Management in the United States: An Assessment Report*. Vol. 1, *Summary*. Washington, DC: Federal Insurance Administration.

Feldman, T. D., and A. E. G. Jonas. 2000. Sage Scrub Revolution? Property Rights, Political Fragmentation, and Conservation Planning under the Federal Endangered Species Act. *Annals of the Association of American Geographers* 90 (2): 256–92.

Frayer, W. E., T. J. Monahan, D. C. Bowden, and F. A. Graybill. 1983. *Status and Trends of Wetlands and Deepwater Habitats in the Conterminous United States: 1950s to 1970s*. Fort Collins: Colorado State University, Department of Forest and Wood Sciences.

Fried, J. P. 1971. *Housing Crisis U.S.A.* New York: Praeger.

Godschalk, D. R. 1992. Implementing Coastal Zone Management: 1972–1990. *Coastal Management* 20: 93–116.

Gottlieb, R. 1993. *Forcing the Spring: The Transformation of the American Environmental Movement*. Washington, DC: Island Press.

Gruntfest, E. C. 1987. *What We Have Learned since the Big Thompson Disaster*. Special Pub. no. 16. Boulder: University of Colorado, Natural Hazards Research Center.

Hardin, G. 1968. Tragedy of the Commons. *Science* 162: 1243–1248.

Harr, J. 1995. *A Civil Action*. New York: Vintage.

Interagency Floodplain Management Review Committee (IFMRC). 1994. *Sharing the Challenge: Floodplain Management into the 21st Century*. Washington, DC: U.S. Government Printing Office.

Kuehn, R. R. 1984. The Coastal Barrier Resources Act and the Expenditures Limitation Approach to Natural Resources Conservation: Wave of the Future or Island Unto Itself? *Ecology Law Quarterly* 11 (3): 583–670.

Kusler, J. A. 1983. *Our National Wetland Heritage*. Washington, DC: Environmental Law Institute.

Kusler, J. A., and L. Larson. 1993. Beyond the Ark: A New Approach to U.S. Floodplain Management. *Environment* 35 (5): 6–11, 31–34.

Leopold, A. 1949/1966. *A Sand County Almanac*. New York: Oxford University Press.

Little, C. E. 1965. *Challenge of the Land*. New York: Open Space Institute.

Marsh, G. P. 1864/1975. In *Man and Nature: Physical Geography as Modified by Human Action*, ed. D. Lowenthal. Cambridge, MA: Belknap Press.

Maugh, T. H. 1979. Toxic Waste Disposal a Growing Problem." *Science* 204 (May 25): 819–24.

McHarg, I. 1968. *Design with Nature*. Garden City, NY: Natural History Press.

McPhee, J. 1968. *The Pine Barrens*. New York: Farrar, Straus and Giroux.

————. 1971/1976. Encounters with the Archdruid. In *The John McPhee Reader*, ed. W. L. Howarth, 189–232. New York: Vintage.

Mitsch, W. J., and J. G. Gosselink. 1986. *Wetlands*. New York: Van Nostrand Reinhold.

National Academy of Sciences. 1990. *Managing Coastal Erosion*. Washington, DC: National Academy Press.

National Oceanographic and Atmospheric Administration. 1975. *The Coastline of the United States*. Washington, DC: U.S. Government Printing Office.

National Review Committee on Floodplain Management. 1989. Action Agenda For Managing the Nation's Floodplains. Mimeo, Natural Hazards Center, University of Colorado, Boulder.

New York Times. 1995. Future of Endangered Species Act in Doubt as Law is Debated. May 16, C4.

————. 2002. Editorial: The Court Reverses Direction. April 24, 24.

————. 2003. Money Gone, U.S. Suspends Designations of Habitats. March 29, A21.

Office of Technology Assessment. 1989. *Coming Clean: Superfund Problems Can Be Solved*. Washington, DC: U.S. Government Printing Office.

Outdoor Recreation Resources Review Commission (ORRRC). 1962. *Outdoor Recreation for America*. Washington, DC: U.S. Government Printing Office.

Platt, R. (Sr.). 1966. *The Great American Forest*. Englewood Cliffs, NJ: Prentice Hall.

Platt, R. H. 1972. *The Open Space Decision Process: Spatial Allocation of Costs and Benefits*. Research Paper no. 142. Chicago: University of Chicago, Department of Geography.

————. 1978. Coastal Hazards and National Policy: A Jury-Rig Approach. *Journal of the American Institute of Planners* 44 (2): 170–80.

————. 1982. The Jackson Flood of 1979: A Public Policy Disaster. *Journal of the American Planning Association* 48 (2): 219–31.

————. 1987. Coastal Wetland Management: The Advance Designation Approach. *Environment* 29 (9): 16–20, 38–43.

————. 1993. Geographers and Water Resource Policy. In *Water Resources Administration in the United States*, ed. M. Reuss, 36–54. Lansing: Michigan State University Press.

————. 1994. Evolution of Coastal Hazard Policies in the United States. *Coastal Management* 22:265–84.

Platt, R. H., P. K. Barten, and M. J. Pfeffer. 2000. A Full, Clean Glass? Managing New York City's Watersheds. *Environment* (June): 8–20.

Platt, R. H., T. Beatley, and H. C. Miller. 1991. The Folly at Folly Beach and Other Failings of U.S. Coastal Erosion Policy. *Environment* 33 (9): 6–9, 25–32.

Platt, R. H., and J. M. Kendra 1999. The Sears Island Saga: Law in Search of Geography. *Economic Geography* (Special Issue): 46–61.

Platt, R. H., S. G. Pelczarski, and B. K. R. Burbank, eds. 1987. Cities on the Beach: An

Overview. In *Cities on the Beach: Management Issues of Developed Coastal Barriers*, 3–13. Research Paper no. 224. Chicago: University of Chicago, Department of Geography.

Platt, R. H., et al. 1992. *Coastal Erosion: Has Retreat Sounded?* Program on Environment and Behavior Monograph no. 53. Boulder: University of Colorado Institute of Behavioral Science.

Popper, F. J. 1988. Understanding American Land Use Regulation Since 1970: A Revisionist Interpretation. *Journal of the American Planning Association* 54 (3): 291–301.

Regional Plan Association. 1965. *The Race for Open Space*. New York: Author.

Reisner, M. 1986. *Cadillac Desert: The American West and Its Disappearing Water*. New York: Penguin.

Rodgers, W. H., Jr. 1988. *Environmental Law*: Vol. 3, *Pesticides and Toxic Substances*. St. Paul, MN: West.

Spirn, A. W. 1984. *The Granite Garden*. Cambridge, MA: MIT Press.

Stewart. F. 1995. *A Natural History of Nature Writing*. Washington, DC: Island Press.

Teal, J., and M. Teal. 1969. *Life and Death of the Salt Marsh*. New York: Ballantine.

Thomas, C. W. 2003. *Bureaucratic Landscapes: Interagency Cooperation and the Preservation of Biodiversity*. Cambridge, MA: MIT Press.

Thomas, W. L., Jr., ed. 1956. *Man's Role in Changing the Face of the Earth*. Chicago: University of Chicago Press.

Urban Land Institute. 1959. *Securing Open Space for Urban America: Conservation Easements*. Technical Bulletin no. 36, written by W. H. Whyte. Washington, DC: ULI.

U.S. Bureau of the Census. 1994–95. *Statistical Abstract of the United States*. Austin, TX: The Reference Press.

U.S. Congress. 1966a. *Insurance and Other Programs for Financial Assistance to Flood Victims*. 89th Cong., 2d Sess. Washington, DC: U.S. Government Printing Office.

———. 1966b. *A Unified National Program for Managing Flood Losses*. 89th Cong., 2d Sess., H. Doc. 465. Washington, DC: U.S. Government Printing Office.

———. 1973. *National Land Use Policy Legislation, 93rd Congress: An Analysis of Legislative Proposals and State Laws*. Washington, DC: U.S. Government Printing Office.

U.S. Council on Environmental Quality (U.S. CEQ). 1970. *Environmental Quality*. Washington, DC: U.S. Government Printing Office.

———. 1971. *Toxic Substances*. Washington, DC: U.S. Government Printing Office.

U.S. Environmental Protection Agency (U.S. EPA). 1986. *Solving the Hazardous Waste Problem*. Washington, DC: Author.

U.S. Fish and Wildlife Service. 1956. *Wetlands of the United States*. Circular 39. Washington, DC: U.S. Government Printing Office.

U.S. Water Resources Council. 1976. *A Unified National Program for Floodplain Management*. Washington, DC: Author.

White, G. F. 1964. *Choice of Adjustment to Floods*. Research Paper no. 93. Chicago: University of Chicago, Department of Geography.

————. 1969. *Strategies of American Water Management*. Ann Arbor: University of Michigan Press.

Whyte, W. H. 1968. *The Last Landscape*. Garden City, NY: Doubleday. Republished 2002 by University of Pennsylvania Press.

Wingo, L., Jr., ed. 1963. *Cities and Space: The Future Use of Urban Land*. Baltimore: Johns Hopkins University Press.

Ziegler, D. J., J. H. Johnson Jr., and S. D. Brunn. 1983. *Technology Hazards*. Washington, DC: Association of American Geographers.

CONCLUSION *Status and Prospects*

This book has reviewed the evolution of public controls over land use in the United States from their feudal origins in England to the smart growth movement of today. As discussed in Chapter 2, the primary purpose of public involvement in the private land market is to limit or modify *negative* or harmful land use externalities—viewed as "market failures"—such as pollution, visual blight, traffic congestion, natural hazard losses, and lack of affordable housing. At the same time, public planning and land use programs seek to promote *positive* externalities through safe, efficient, and attractive land use and building practices.

In essence, this book argues that public involvement in the use of land is a "balancing act" whereby the right of owners to gain reasonable economic and personal benefit from their property must be balanced with the need to protect other individuals from harm arising therefrom. Thus the *legal* framework of rules, policies, and incentives to influence "good" land use practices is informed by the *geographical* context of the physical and socioeconomic systems in which land use operates. In other words, the effectiveness and validity of legal measures to control harmful externalities depend upon understanding of the geographical context in which such effects arise. *Law based on sound geography yields beneficial land use policy.*

The interaction of law and geography is described by the *land use and society model* introduced in Chapter 2 and referred to frequently thereafter. The process described by the model has been at work for a long time: it has been three and a half centuries since the "first modern building law"—the 1667 Act for Rebuilding London—and 150 years since the first general sanitary laws appeared in England and the United States. Nine decades have elapsed since the First National Conference on City Planning and Congestion in 1909, more than seventy-five years since the *Euclid* decision, and more than thirty years since the National Environmental Policy Act and the first Earth Day. What has all this accumulated experience of social tinkering with the private land market accomplished, and where do we stand today?

A statistical response to this question is difficult as hard data are unevenly available and subjective value judgments are unavoidable. Also, the response will depend on the geographic locale or region considered. Like the proverbial blind men describing the elephant, describing the current state of metropolitan and rural land use must depend on what is viewed and by whom, and where they stand. The contemporary U.S. landscape is a mosaic of public policy successes and failures, some of which change character depending on the function, scale, and location considered. In the spirit of "the cup is half empty/half full," some topics may be viewed either as successes or as failures.

Central Cities

Some central-city downtowns have new vitality, architectural distinction, cultural diversity, and economic viability due to a combination of public and private investment and the return of some suburbanites seeking a more urbane lifestyle and less dependence on cars (Birch 2002). Thanks to the critiques of William H. Whyte, Jane Jacobs, and others, many urban design professionals and city officials have learned that "downtowns are for people." (See Chapter 6.) Public plazas (indoor or outdoor) have become standard fixtures of new downtown construction, although their utility differs according to their design and management practices (Whyte 1988; Kayden 2000). Pedestrian malls, public gardens, lobby exhibit areas, skywalks, outdoor concerts and festivals, and public art also help to enliven downtowns. The new urbanist movement and organizations like Project for Public Spaces, Inc. (www.pps.org) are promoting more walkable and transit-based redevelopment designs for older commercial districts in cities and suburbs.

U.S. cities have become increasingly accessible to individuals with *disabilities* due to the federal Americans with Disabilities Act and its state counterparts, which require handicapped access and restrooms in new construction as well as renovation of older structures. Commercial, governmental, transportation, educational, cultural, and religious facilities are now widely usable by persons with mobility impairments.

Although some *historic buildings* have been lost to demolition (e.g., Louis Sullivan's Stock Exchange in Chicago and New York's old Penn Station), much has been accomplished since the 1960s to protect and enhance some of the nation's cultural heritage. National and state registers of historic landmarks list thousands of structures and sites of special historic or architectural importance. Beginning with the Battery District of Charleston, South Carolina, and the New Orleans French

Quarter, historic districts have been widely established under federal, state, or local laws that regulate in minute detail the exterior appearance of structures. By 1995, New York City alone had designated 1,021 individual structures and 66 historic districts.

Many historic properties have been acquired by public agencies or private non-profit foundations for permanent preservation. In older communities that have experienced economic transition, many structures such as mills, railroad depots, wharfs, and warehouses have been "adaptively reused" as retail outlets, restaurants, offices, condominiums, and new kinds of manufacturing space. This process has been fostered in part by public tax credits and other legal and financial incentives.

The renaissance of many urban downtowns, however, often does not ripple into adjacent older low-income neighborhoods. Where gentrification does occur, as in Chicago's Near North Side, Boston's Fenway, or Washington's Adams-Morgan neighborhood, affordable living units are converted to shops, street-level coffee bars are topped with condominiums on upper floors, and the former tenants are forced to seek affordable housing elsewhere. Close to most central-city downtowns are "no man's land" districts of vacant lots, abandoned cars, and derelict buildings. The urban renewal programs of the 1950s and 1960s in many places left a patchwork of now-dilapidated or razed housing projects, cleared land, and boarded-up tenements (see Figure 10-7). Although these former neighborhoods are still served by streets, water, sewerage, schools, and parks—legacies from a more prosperous past—the condition of inner-city public facilities, particularly schools, is generally abysmal (Kaplan 1998, Chap. 4; Suarez 1999). Meanwhile, those services are being replicated on the expanding urban fringe at great cost, in part paid from taxes on the central cities from which the middle class has fled (Orfield 1997).

Nearly seven decades of public housing programs has yielded only about 1 million family units and 375,000 elderly units nationally, in comparison with 31.1 million people in 6.7 million households who were classified as below the federal poverty level in the 2000 U.S. Census. Despite, or maybe because of, the quixotic *Gautreaux* case (discussed in Chapter 10) to desegregate public housing, most units are still in predominantly low-income, minority neighborhoods. "Section 8 housing vouchers," the other option for low-income households, are in short supply and do not address the rising demand for and shrinking supply of affordable housing units. As a result, homelessness has become endemic in most U.S. cities.

Suburbia

Over half of Americans now live in metropolitan communities outside central cities, i.e., "suburbs" (see Figure 6-1). Many suburban communities have little in common: some are old, some new; some rich, some poor; some lily-white, some ethnically diverse; some large, some tiny (see Chapter 8). Older "inner-ring" suburbs often share the plight of central cities: obsolescence of housing stock and public infrastructures, loss of employment, declining tax revenues, and rising proportions of elderly, foreign-born, and other special needs populations. Newer suburban development is frequently "gated" and marketed to well-off and frequently childless households (Blakely and Snyder 1997). While golf courses loom large, community playgrounds, sidewalks, and street-side retail shops are forgotten amenities of a more sociable urban past. Federal tax policies, especially deductions for property taxes and mortgage interest, still favor construction of ownership units over rental development. New homes in many suburbs are increasingly large and ostentatious ("McMansions") and affordable only by the affluent.

According to the "trickle down theory" of housing markets, as embraced by the federal district court in the *Petaluma* decision (see Chapter 9), the proliferation of these high-end new communities should be opening up new housing opportunities in older, less opulent neighborhoods to upwardly mobile middle-class households, including nonwhite families and nontraditional households. That in fact is the case in some housing markets like metropolitan Washington, D.C., and Los Angeles (Frey and Berube 2002). Yet the "trickle down" of some formerly white middle class bedroom suburbs, like Park Forest, Illinois—the home of William Whyte's 1950s "Organization Man"—has been accompanied by decline of tax revenue, public services, and housing values. Both public and private investment has favored new communities over older ones. Land consumption per capita has grown far more rapidly than population at the urban fringe, with consequent declining average density and great cost per capita to provide public services (Orfield 1997; Rusk 1999; Fulton et al. 2001).

New outlying regional centers and "edge cities" are challenging the dominance of the older central business districts in many metropolitan areas (Garreau 1989) Houston's Galleria, Atlanta's Perimeter Mall and Cumberland/Galleria Mall, and South Coast Plaza in Orange County, California, are prototypes of twenty-first-century urbanization. These complexes, situated at strategic crossings of metropolitan highways and other transportation nodes, contain opulent retail shops, millions of square feet of office space, major hotels, restaurants, and convention facilities, all interconnected by climate-controlled pedestrian concourses, but lacking a sense of community past, present, or future.

Although internally planned for the comfort and convenience of their occupants (not always successfully), such developments inflict various negative externalities on surrounding areas such as traffic congestion, air pollution, energy waste, visual discord, and loss of preexisting neighborhoods or open space. Such developments create large numbers of low-wage service jobs but do not provide affordable housing, schools, parks, community health facilities, and other necessities of working-class communities. In short, the people who work in these "pods" usually must commute long distances, often by very inadequate public transportation from the inner city or lower-cost suburbs (Leinberger and Lockwood 1986). In the process, the central city loses not only jobs but corporate taxes as well, while still housing and educating the families of the reverse commuters.

Traffic congestion has become a chronic externality from lower-density, private vehicle-dependent land use patterns. As discussed in Chapter 6, the U.S. population grew by 40 percent between 1970 and 2000 while the number of registered vehicles doubled. *Private vehicles have thus proliferated more than twice as fast as the population*, and the average vehicle has grown larger, heavier, and less fuel-efficient. For political reasons, so-called light trucks and SUVs that make up more than half of new vehicles sold today are not subject to as strict emission standards as conventional automobiles under the Clean Air Act.

In addition to the time wasted in gridlock and the ever-present risk of accidents from overcrowded traffic arteries, vehicle-generated air pollutants disproportionately affect lower-income neighborhoods through which highways have been built (Weisman 1989). A higher than average childhood asthma rate in such neighborhoods than elsewhere manifests *environmental injustice*: inhabitants of low-income communities are isolated from employment opportunities in the suburbs yet suffer the effects of air pollution from the vehicles of more fortunate people able to commute to distant jobs (Bullard, Johnson, and Torres 2000).

Waste Management

Smoldering garbage dumps, commonplace before the 1970s, have largely been abolished by solid waste management laws, although their toxic contents may continue to pose a threat to groundwater. "Sanitary landfills" replaced dumps as the approved method of land disposal of solid waste. Landfills in turn are being replaced by energy recovery incinerators, materials recycling programs, composting, and other approaches. Hundreds of former landfills have been closed, capped, and planted with grass, left as pungent smelling landmarks to the nation's prodigious production of waste. With new landfills becoming politically and environmentally unacceptable in metropolitan areas, and with ocean dumping long banned, many cities like New York are trucking their solid wastes to distant rural disposal sites at great expense and hazard to the populations of the destination areas.

Toxic and hazardous waste disposal sites (*brownfields*) pose an array of unsolved problems. In 1988, the Environmental Protection Agency estimated that there were some 3,000 facilities handling a total of 275 million metric tons of wastes classified as hazardous under the Resource Conservation and Recovery Act. The 1984 Hazardous and solid waste amendments tightened the "cradle to grave" regulations for tracking hazardous materials and initiated regulations for leaking underground storage tanks ("LUSTs"), which were estimated to number about 400,000 out of a total of 5–6 million underground tanks. (See Chapter 12.)

Cleanup of existing hazardous and toxic wastes has been under way since passage of the 1980 Superfund law, as amended, and its state counterparts. As of 2003, there are 729 Superfund clean-up projects currently in progress at 450 sites across the nation. Overall, since 1980, nearly 44,700 sites have been investigated; of those, 33,000 sites have been removed from the Superfund list and made available for potential economic reuse (www.epa.gov/superfund). In many cases, however, the original hazardous waste generator has disappeared and the entire cost falls on federal and state governments. Cleanup programs have often been mired in economic, technical, and legal controversy.

Natural and Hazardous Areas

Since 1960, many *natural sites and open spaces* have been protected through public measures. Over the three-year period 2000–2002, the federal Land and Water Conservation Fund (LWCF) allocated more than $250 million as matching grants to states and local governments for the purchase and improvement of open land. The acreage in the National Park System, excluding Alaska, has increased by 40 percent since 1960, reflecting the establishment of fourteen new national seashores and lakeshores, several national recreation areas, and a number of specialized urban sites such as a jazz historic site in New Orleans and an industrial history site in Lowell, Massachusetts.

The National Forests and National Wildlife Refuge systems have been augmented by new land purchases funded by the LWCF. Several million acres of federal land have been classified as "wilderness" areas under the 1964 Wilderness Act. By the mid-1990s it was reported that "the acreage of America held in preservation has risen steadily during this century and now amounts to more than two times the area of California" (Easterbrook 1995, 40).

Private nonprofit organizations, ranging from The Nature Conservancy and Trust for Public Land at the national level to thousands of local land trusts, have bought or accepted gifts of thousands of acres of natural land. Land philanthropy by private owners has been encouraged by federal income tax deductions for the value of such gifts. *Greenways* have been established along hundreds of metropolitan streams, for example, in the Bay Area of California; Boulder, Colorado; Portland, Oregon; Seattle, Atlanta; San Antonio; Denver; and St. Louis. The greenway approach to resource management combines several public objectives: water quality improvement, protection of riparian and fish habitat, public recreation, flood hazard reduction, and visual separation of urban districts. Means used to effectuate greenways include public acquisition, regulation, and financial incentives (Little 1995).

Federal and state coastal zone and wetlands programs have sought to improve public access and protect natural resources in coastal areas, although high property values (subsidized by federal tax policies and flood insurance) continue to encourage development and upsizing of coastal structures. The rate of wetland loss nationally has apparently been slowed but not stopped by the federal Section 404 program and state programs. Most remaining coastal salt marshes have been protected under various regulatory programs and, in some cases, by acquisition. (See Chapters 1, 10, and 12.)

Habitat for threatened and endangered species has been unevenly protected under federal and state law, as discussed in Chapter 12. Some efforts to protect critical habitat such as old-growth forests in Oregon and desert biomes in southern California have generated nationally publicized conflicts, pitting economic interests against ecological values. Elsewhere, endangered species regulation has imposed marginal restrictions on public recreation resources (e.g., piping plover habitat on East Coast beaches). Efforts to develop multispecies *habitat conservation plans* have generated protracted negotiations and occasional litigation in areas of prospective new development such as Riverside County, California (Thomas 2003).

Metropolitan America has achieved a measure of safety against some types of natural hazards while becoming more vulnerable to other types. Urban conflagration, the scourge of wood-built cities from the colonial period until the San Francisco earthquake in 1906, is a much reduced threat today, thanks to planning and building regulations, more reliable water supplies, and modern firefighting technology. Fire hazards on the "urban-wildland fringe" in the West, however, have become more serious with the popularity of homes in wooded settings and the pervasive drought of recent years (see www.nfpa.org).

Loss of life in coastal and riverine floods and hurricanes decreased markedly over the twentieth century due to improved forecasting, warning, and evacuation systems. Urban property and economic losses due to floods, however, has continued to increase due to the expansion of public and private investment in flood hazard areas. State and local policies, guided by the National Flood Insurance Program, seek to regulate the location, elevation, and use of new or rebuilt structures (www.floods.org). In the aftermath of the Midwest floods of 1993, the Federal Emergency Management Agency and affected states acquired and demolished more than 10,000 low-cost floodplain structures to enable their owners to move to higher ground (www.fema.gov). The National Flood Insurance Program has not prevented new coastal development, but it has caused new and rebuilt structures to be elevated above estimated one-hundred-year storm levels (although erosion may eventually leave them stranded in the surf) (Platt 1999). Investment in "homeland security" since the terrorist attacks of September 11, 2001, may gradually strengthen state and local capacity to cope with various kinds of disasters. A closely related concern is the reliability in either natural or human-caused disasters of both public and privately owned *lifelines*, such as transportation facilities, electrical power, water and sewage service, hospitals, and other key facilities. Even without a disaster, much public infrastructure today is unreliable due to aging and deferred maintenance, a situation that will be worsened by the present fiscal situation.

Zoning and Smart Growth

In 1969, the English planning lawyer John Delafons observed that zoning had long outlived its usefulness and probably causes more problems than it resolves. This judgment is probably even more valid today: zoning legitimates the petty actions of local municipalities, the smallest and most geographically irrational unit of U.S. political geography. Like the premature reports of Mark Twain's death, however, declarations of zoning's imminent demise have been greatly exaggerated. Zoning thrives, tenacious as a bittersweet vine and about as useful in many cases. The attempt to reform or overthrow zoning that occurred in the 1970s through the Model Land Development Code succeeded chiefly in bringing states into the land use control process in certain locations and on certain issues.

Meanwhile many local governments, despairing of zoning but unable to rid themselves of it, have resorted to a number of supplementary strategies under the broad rubric of *growth management*, as now subsumed into the *smart growth* movement. As considered in Chapter 9, devices such as transfer of development rights and impact fees attempt to "privatize" the provision of public needs through incentives or exactions directed at developers. The jury is still out as to how effective the nonzoning techniques developed since the early 1970s and 1980s have been and what their external impacts beyond the implementing municipality will be. The "rough proportionality test" set forth in *Dolan v. City of Tigard*—balancing of benefit to the public with burden to the property owner (as discussed in Chapter 10)—will likely be a major factor in how such measures fare in the near future.

The primary need for land use planning in the United States is to get back to basics: protecting the public health, safety, and welfare. In the nineteenth century, light, air, water, sanitation, and structural soundness were the goals of urban reformers who produced the modern city planning movement. Today, building and sanitary codes are virtually ubiquitous, although enforced unevenly. Although structures are less likely to collapse or burn to the ground and most are provided with ventilation, water, and some form of sewage disposal, the overall habitability of metropolitan areas is deteriorating. Cities and their metropolitan regions are increasingly dysfunctional in light of social, economic, and environmental limits. New perceptions, policies, doctrines, and institutions are needed to address the interrelated problems of housing, transportation, water supply, waste management, loss of biodiversity, energy waste, and vulnerability to disaster (Ruckelshaus 1989; National Research Council 1999). *In short, the land use and society model needs to move into high gear!*

In a sense, we stand where Chadwick stood in the 1830s, confronting a cesspool of public neglect which threatens to engulf the national society. Chadwick, Olmsted, Haussmann, Pullman, Howard, Riis, Marsh, Burnham, Bettmann, and their allies recognized the evils and dangers associated with urban conditions of their times (Chapters 4 and 8). Each in diverse ways helped initiate or promote new forms of public response to those conditions as recounted in Chapters 4 through 6. Similarly, environmental seers such as Marsh, Powell, Muir, Pinchot, Leopold,

Carson, Hardin, Commoner (Chapters 11 and 12) helped define the conditions that gave rise to the conservation and environmental reforms of the 1960s through the 1980s, and continue unevenly today. *Now for the next act.*

Toward More Ecological Cities

As of 2003, the nation's social and urban problems were worsening as a result of economic decline, budget cutbacks, fear of terrorism, and hostility toward environmental and urban programs on the part of "Sun Belt/suburban conservatives." Even in highly urban states like California and Massachusetts, catastrophic budget shortfalls are threatening the staffing and funding of many initiatives (e.g., the Massachusetts Watershed Initiative).

There are, however, rays of hope in various sectors. One is the smart growth movement, which promotes sensible reinvestment in older urban communities (*infill*) while advocating more compact development, mixed land uses, walkable neighborhoods, and public transit (see www.smartgrowthamerica.com). (Unfortunately, Maryland's smart growth program championed by former Governor Parris Glendening was derailed by his successor in 2002.) Another ray of hope is that record low-interest rates are assisting many households of all ethnicities to purchase their first homes or move into better housing. (Of course, prices may rise in tight housing markets and thus offset the benefit of lower mortgage rates.)

In contrast to smart growth, which is largely concerned with the quality of the *built* environment, many cities are quietly beginning to rediscover their *unbuilt* environments. Public and private initiatives to promote "urban regreening," which are widespread in European cities (Beatley 2000), are cropping up, so to speak, in cities and metro areas across the United States. The Ecological Cities Project (www.ecologicalcities.org), based at the University of Massachusetts, Amherst, has begun to inventory and document some of these loosely connected activities, such as the following:

- ▸ Rehabilitation of older parks and open spaces
- ▸ Protection and restoration of urban wetlands and other sensitive habitat
- ▸ Development of greenways and rail trails
- ▸ Urban gardening and farm markets
- ▸ Green design of buildings, including green roofs and green schools
- ▸ Brownfield remediation and reuse
- ▸ Urban environmental education sites and programs

- ▸ Urban watershed management to protect water supplies and other purposes
- ▸ Riverine and coastal floodplain management to reduce flood damage
- ▸ Environmental justice programs

Such efforts are conducted at various scales from the neighborhood, to the city, to the metropolitan region. They are typically led by nongovernmental organizations (NGOs) such as block and community groups, watershed associations, regional planning bodies, and local chapters of national environmental organizations, including Trust for Public Land, the Sierra Club, and the National Audubon Society. The NGOs provide vision, persistence, and volunteers to work in the field. Public-sector agencies at all levels play supporting roles, providing funds, staff resources, technical know-how, and (where applicable) regulatory muscle. Researchers in universities, public agencies, and NGOs help define the scientific and social goals and means.

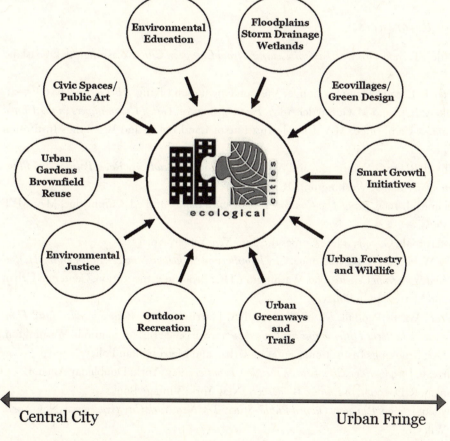

FIGURE C-1 Ecological cities: a shared vision.

Urban regreening initiatives are necessarily scattered, uneven, and underfunded. They depend on spontaneous and often voluntary local leadership. They are pragmatic and often creative in stitching together existing program resources, available funding, and donations of money, time, and office space. Most involve public-private partnerships, some of which are small, local alliances to save a particular site or pursue a single goal such as environmental education or urban gardening. Others have evolved into influential regional networks such as Chicago Wilderness (www.chicagowilderness.org), which currently involves more than 160 public and private partners in nine counties and three states of the greater Chicago region. (See Box 11-1; Figure C-1.) (A counterpart agency is now under consideration in the New York region.)

Large or small, such initiatives to promote greener urban communities share a common theme: metropolitan America is here to stay, most of us live in it, and we need to make our nest as comfortable, sustainable, and equitable as possible.

References

Beatley, T. 2000. *Green Urbanism: Learning from European Cities*. Washington, DC: Island Press.

Birch, E. L. 2002. Having a Longer View on Downtown Living. *APA Journal* 68 (1): 5–21.

Blakely, E. J., and M. G. Snyder. 1997. *Fortress America: Gated Communities in the United States*. Cambridge, MA: Lincoln Institute of Land Policy and Brookings Institution Press.

Bullard, R. D., G. S. Johnson, and A. O. Torres. 2000. *Sprawl City:Race, Politics, and Planning in Atlanta*. Washington, DC: Island Press.

Delafons, J. 1969. *Land-Use Controls in the United States*. 2nd ed. Cambridge, MA: MIT Press.

Easterbrook, G. 1995. Here Comes the Sun. *New Yorker*, April 10.

Frey, W. H., and A. Berube. 2002. *City Families and Suburban Singles: An Emerging Household Story from Census 2000*. Washington, DC: Brookings Institution, Center on Urban and Metropolitan Policy.

Fulton, W., R. Pendall, M. Nguyen, and A. Harrison. 2001. *Who Sprawls Most? How Growth Patterns Differ across the United States*. Survey Series Monograph. Washington, DC: Brookings Institution, Center on Urban and Metropolitan Policy.

Garreau, J. 1989. *Edge City: Life on the New Frontier*. New York: Doubleday Anchor.

Kaplan, R. D. 1998. *An Empire Wilderness*. New York: Vintage Books.

Kayden, J. 2000. *Privately Owned Public Space: The New York City Experience*. New York: Wiley.

Leinberger, C. B., and C. Lockwood. 1986. How Business Is Reshaping America. *Atlantic Monthly* 258 (4): 43–52.

Little, C. E. 1995. *Greenways for America*. Baltimore: Johns Hopkins University Press.

National Research Council. 1999. *Our Common Journey: A Transition Toward Sustainability*. Washington, DC: National Academy Press.

Orfield, M. 1997. *Metropolitics: A Regional Agenda for Community and Stability*. Washington, DC: Brookings Institution Press.

Platt, R. H. 1999. *Disasters and Democracy: The Politics of Extreme Natural Events*. Washington, DC: Island Press.

Ruckelshaus, E. D. 1989. Toward a Sustainable World. *Scientific American* 261 (3): 166–74.

Rusk, D. 1999. *Inside Game, Outside Game*. Washington, DC: Brookings Institution Press.

Suarez, R. 1999. *The Old Neighborhood*. New York: Free Press.

Thomas, C W. 2003. *Bureaucratic Landscapes: Interagency Cooperation and the Preservation of Biodiversity*. Cambridge, MA: MIT Press.

Weisman, A. 1989. L.A. Fights for Breath. *New York Times Magazine*, July 30, 15ff.

Whyte, W. H. 1988. *City: Rediscovering the Center*. New York: Doubleday.

ACKNOWLEDGMENTS

I want to express profound appreciation to editor and good friend Kathleen Lafferty of Roaring Mountain Editorial Services for her incredibly capable and cheerful assistance in every stage of preparing this book for publication. I also thank Laurin Sievert, graduate student *extraordinaire*, for her calm and upbeat ability to solve technical challenges (sometimes backed up by her most helpful husband, Jim) as well as her effectiveness in obtaining information, preparing graphics, and keeping the Ecological Cities Project on track administratively. I am also grateful to the many students in my seminars who have helped educate me as much as I may have taught them.

At Island Press, I want to thank my editor Heather Boyer, who encouraged me to undertake this complete revision of the 1996 edition of *Land Use and Society* and who also oversaw my 1999 Island Press book, *Disasters and Democracy: The Politics of Extreme Natural Events*. Cecilia González, senior production editor, has once again ably guided me through the rapids and shoals of the book publication process.

Finally, I want to thank many friends and colleagues around the United States whose cutting-edge work in policy formulation, implementation, and research has influenced my own perception of cities as places to be nurtured rather than abandoned. They include but are certainly not limited to Jerry Adelmann, Tim Beatley, Edward Blakely, Lester Brown, Armando Carbonell, Chris DeSousa, Carol Fialkowski, Charles Little, Peter Harnik, Mike Houck, Jerold Kayden, Jon Kusler, Larry Larson, Andrew Light, Charlie Lord, Colleen Murphy-Dunning, Mary Pelletier, Bill Solecki, Gilbert White, Rae Zimmerman, and the late William H. Whyte.

ABOUT THE AUTHOR

RUTHERFORD H. PLATT is a professor of geography and planning law in the Department of Geosciences and the Center for Public Policy and Administration at the University of Massachusetts, Amherst. He earned a B.A. in political science from Yale University and both a J.D. (law) and Ph.D. (geography) from the University of Chicago. He served as staff attorney at the Chicago Open Lands Project before assuming a faculty position at the University of Massachusetts in 1972. He specializes in public policy concerning urban land and water resources. In addition to the 1996 Island Press edition of this book, he is the author of *Disasters and Democracy: The Politics of Extreme Natural Events* (Island Press, 1999) and lead editor of *The Ecological City: Preserving and Restoring Urban Biodiversity* (University of Massachusetts Press, 1994), among dozens of other publications. He directs the Ecological Cities Project, a national program of research and outreach based at the University of Massachusetts, Amherst. He has served on many national and regional panels, including the National Research Council (NRC) Water Science and Technology Board and several of its committees. He chaired the NRC Natural Disasters Roundtable from 1999 to 2002. In 2002, he was designated a Lifetime National Associate of the National Academies. He is a member of the Cosmos Club in Washington, D.C. He resides with his wife, Barbara Kirchner, and their cat, Tigger, in Northampton, Massachusetts.

SOME COMMON ACRONYMS

BLM	Bureau of Land Management
CEQ	Council on Environmental Quality
CERCLA	Comprehensive Environmental Response, Compensation, and Liability Act
CFCs	chlorofluorocarbons
COE	Corps of Engineers
CZMA	Coastal Zone Management Act
EIS	environmental impact statement
EPA	Environmental Protection Agency
ESA	Endangered Species Act
FHA	Federal Housing Administration
FWS	Fish and Wildlife Service
GIS	geographic information systems
GPS	global positioning systems
HCP	Habitat Conservation Plan
HUD	Housing and Urban Development
IFMRC	Interagency Floodplain Management Review Committee
LAWCON	Land and Water Conservation Fund Act
MSA	metropolitan statistical area
NAACP	National Association for the Advancement of Colored People
NAHB	National Association of Home Builders
NEPA	National Environmental Policy Act
NFIP	National Flood Insurance Program
NGOs	nongovernmental organizations
NMFS	National Marine Fisheries Service
NOAA	National Oceanographic and Atmospheric Administration
NPL	National Priorities List
NPS	National Park System
NWI	National Wetlands Inventory
SCS	Soil Conservation Service
TDR	transfer of development rights
TEA-21	Transportation Efficiency Act for the 21st Century

TIF	tax increment financing
TSCA	Toxic Substances Control Act
TVA	Tennessee Valley Authority
USCA	*U.S. Code Annotated*
USDA	U.S. Department of Agriculture
USFS	U.S. Forest Service
USGS	U.S. Geological Survey

LIST OF CASES

INDEX